PACIFIC
AIR

Also by David Sears

Such Men As These:
The Story of the Navy Pilots Who Flew the Deadly Skies over Korea

The Last Epic Naval Battle:
Voices from Leyte Gulf

At War with the Wind:
The Epic Struggle with Japan's World War II Suicide Bombers

PACIFIC
AIR

How Fearless Flyboys,
Peerless Aircraft,
and Fast Flattops
Conquered a Vast
Ocean's Wartime Skies

David Sears

DA CAPO PRESS
A Member of the Perseus Books Group

Designed by David Janik
Set in 11 point Berkeley by the Perseus Books Group

Cataloging-in-Publication data for this book is available from the Library of Congress.
ISBN 978-0-306-81948-3 (hardcover)
ISBN 978-0-306-82078-6 (paperback)
ISBN 978-0-306-81979-7 (e-book)

First Da Capo Press hardcover edition 2011
Paperback edition first published in 2012
Published by Da Capo Press
A Member of the Perseus Books Group
www.dacapopress.com

Da Capo Press books are available at special discounts for bulk purchases in the U.S. by corporations, institutions, and other organizations. For more information, please contact the Special Markets Department at the Perseus Books Group, 2300 Chestnut Street, Suite 200, Philadelphia, PA 19103, or call (800) 810-4145, ext. 5000, or e-mail special.markets@perseusbooks.com.

10 9 8 7 6 5 4 3

To Alex Vraciu, a magnificent fighter pilot…
an even better man

CONTENTS

   Illustrations follow page 180

An aircraft carrier is a noble thing. It lacks almost everything that seems to denote nobility, yet deep nobility is there. A carrier has no poise. It has no grace. It is top-heavy and lopsided. It has the lines of a cow. It doesn't cut through the water like a cruiser, knifing romantically along…It just plows…Yet a carrier is a ferocious thing, and out of its heritage of action has grown its nobility. I believe that every Navy in the world has as its No. 1 priority the destruction of enemy carriers. That's a precarious honor, but it's a proud one.

Ernie Pyle, 1945

Hawaiian Islands,
World War II

Nihau

Kauai

Schofield
Barracks

Wheeler
Army Airfield

Kaneohe Bay

Barbers Point
Naval Air Station

Oahu

Ewa Airfield

Diamond
Head

Pearl Harbor,
Ford Island,
Hickam Field

Molokai

Puunene Naval Air Station

Maui

Lanai

Kahoolawe

Hawaii

0   miles   80

RLP

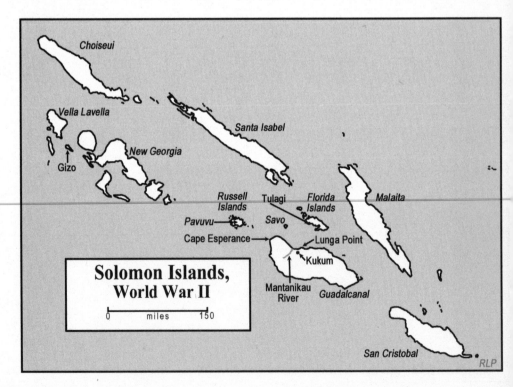

Solomon Islands,
World War II

Choiseui

Vella Lavella

Santa Isabel

New Georgia

Gizo

*Russell
Islands*

Tulagi

*Florida
Islands*

Malaita

Pavuvu

Savo

Cape Esperance

Lunga Point

Kukum

Mantanikau
River

Guadalcanal

San Cristobal

0   miles   150

RLP

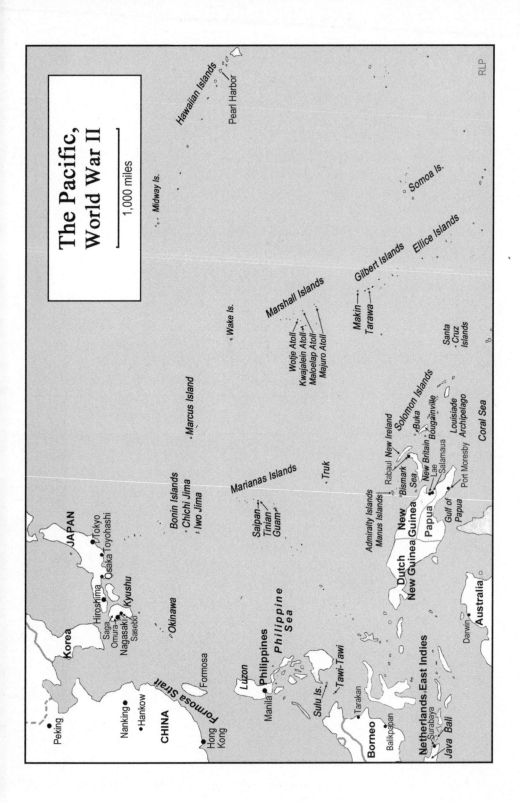

The Pacific, World War II

1,000 miles

Hawaiian Islands
Pearl Harbor

Midway Is.

Somoa Is.

Gilbert Islands
Ellice Islands

Marshall Islands
Makin
Tarawa

Wake Is.

Wojje Atoll
Kwajalein Atoll
Maloelap Atoll
Majuro Atoll

Marcus Island

Santa Cruz Islands

Solomon Islands
Buka
Bougainville
Louisiade Archipelago
Coral Sea

Bonin Islands
Chichi Jima
Iwo Jima

Marianas Islands
Truk

Rabaul New Ireland
New Britain
Bismarck Sea
Lae
Salamaua
Port Moresby

JAPAN
Tokyo
Osaka Toyohashi
Hiroshima
Saga
Omura
Nagasaki
Sasebo
Kyushu

Saipan
Tinian
Guam

Admiralty Islands
Manus Islands
New Guinea
Papua
Gulf of Papua

Korea

Okinawa

Dutch New Guinea

Philippine Sea

Peking

Nanking
Hankow

CHINA

Formosa Strait

Formosa

Hong Kong

Luzon
Philippines
Manila

Tawi-Tawi

Sulu Is.
Tarakan

Borneo
Balikpapan

Netherlands East Indies
Surabaya
Java Bali

Darwin

Australia

RLP

PART ONE

STATE OF WAR

1

THE EMBATTLED FARMERS

DECEMBER 7, 1941, BETHPAGE, LONG ISLAND

The jewel in the crown of this festive Sunday at Grumman Aircraft Engineering was the weather: unseasonably warm (for a late autumn tipping into winter and the Christmas holidays) with brilliant sunshine. While the shops, assembly areas, hangars and offices of the company's immense new facility—double the floor space of its four-year-old sister plant—were closed for the day, they pulsed with crowds, excited chatter and the occasional blare of PA announcements, as spouses (mostly wives but more than a few husbands) and children mingled with plant workers. Though not all were here, there were nearly seven thousand Grumman employees now—up from two thousand at the beginning of the year—and most had been hired in anticipation of today.

There had been just 362 people on the Grumman payroll when Plant Number 1 opened its doors in April 1937, a population small enough to enable an en masse relocation from a rented facility fronting the Hempstead Turnpike in nearby Farmingdale to a company-built plant—also twice the size of its predecessor.

However, the current migration approached biblical proportions: reason enough to mark the move's successful conclusion. While Plant Number 2's personnel, whether old-timers or fledglings, had arrived with their work cut out for them—a backlog of six million dollars in military airplane orders at the start of the decade had ballooned by a factor of ten—the mood for this Sunday was relaxed and celebratory. After company official Leon A. "Jake" Swirbul's welcoming speech (a rousing, shirt-sleeved, stem-winder from everybody's favorite co-founder), there would be band music, refreshments and the much-anticipated unveiling (for in-house eyes only) of the firm's latest aerial marvel. The party was buzzing with pride and self-congratulation.

———

Comparatively speaking, the employment surge for Plant 2's opening had gone smoothly as well as quickly. Despite the country's muscular climb from a nearly decade-long economic depression, there remained enough labor market slack when it came to hiring experienced shop and administrative personnel.

To be sure, things were more difficult when it came to landing good aeronautical engineers. The Long Island aviation industry, which had boomed after Charles Lindbergh's epic 1927 solo cross-Atlantic flight (his launch point had been Roosevelt Field, a dozen or so miles to the west), had as abruptly wilted in the Great Crash and the ensuing hard times. Now at last reviving, the industry—including Long Island neighbors such as Republic, Chance Vought and Pratt and Whitney—had reabsorbed nearly all the specialized talent that had weathered those bad years. Grumman had little choice but to adapt to this labor shortage; its solution was to hire good engineers of nearly any cast (chemical, electrical, mechanical or civil) and then give them crash courses in statics, aerodynamics and aircraft power plants.

Despite this success, Grumman brass understood that such concessions to talent scarcity would not be nearly enough should war hit. Grumman's production pipeline was one more unmistakable sign that America would almost certainly be drawn onto Europe's and Asia's battlegrounds and when that happened Grumman aircraft designs would no longer be competing just for a profitable share of military contracts. Instead, those aircraft would be vital instruments of securing the country's survival. Then, too, with American men going to war, all bets would be off when it came to home front labor supply.

Already the previous summer, these worrisome contingencies fully in mind, Swirbul, the firm's production head, had taken a bomber-ferry to England. Britain's Royal Air Force (RAF) had by then demonstrated its gritty resilience by checking the predations of Germany's Luftwaffe and souring Adolf Hitler's plans for a cross-Channel invasion. Of particular interest (given Grumman's naval aviation niche and its latest government contract), the Naval Air Branch, the RAF's sister service using bi-planes launched from the aircraft carrier HMS *Ark*

Royal, staged a crippling mid-Atlantic aerial torpedo strike against Germany's doomed *über*-battleship *Bismarck.*

During his overseas foray, Swirbul got to see the RAF in action, but he also toured England's war plants, returning impressed with its efforts to disperse wartime production when and wherever possible. The Brits' logic had been twofold: avoid a concentration of bombing targets under the German aerial blitz; and make maximum use of all available labor and production capacity.

While neither Grumman nor its defense industry neighbors were particularly concerned about threats of aerial bombing, production dispersal had other merits. If done imaginatively and coordinated well, it could provide ready-made factory space for smaller, self-contained production units. Just as important, as a builder of gas-gulping war aircraft, Grumman knew only too well that a domestic fuel crisis loomed. Dispersal would allow the company to tap into pockets of neighborhood workers who otherwise might be out of reach when fuel-rationed transportation kicked in. Even as the grand opening of its newest and largest facility approached, company officials were scouring Long Island county buildings, lots and potato fields in search of potential work sites. In the years ahead, having staked out scores of parcels of Long Island agricultural land, Grumman executives took to calling themselves the Embattled Farmers.

———

Assistant Treasurer Clint Towl,[1] one of the Grumman executives engaged in this hop-scotching expansion, was also today's de facto party planner. The thirty-five-year-old Towl had joined the firm at its startup in 1929. An outsider then, he was a two-year Cornell University engineering undergrad until illness prompted him to return home to Long Island. Using family connections, Towl then worked briefly on Wall Street as a brokerage runner and trainee—long enough to learn that he had greater interest in building things than in crunching numbers. The first rumblings of an approaching stock market upheaval gave Towl his exit from Wall Street while the start of Grumman Aircraft Engineering—he was the boyhood friend of Edmund Poor, the fledgling company's finance guy and one of the five original founders—gave him his foothold in aviation manufacturing. Actually more toehold than foothold: Towl had put in some of his family's money (making him a founder as well when the firm was

---

[1] Pronounced "Toll"

first capitalized) in exchange for a low-paying job, "whatever it turned out to be."

What it turned out to be first was sweeping and shoveling out the company's very first Long Island plant, a rented rectangular cinder block structure in Baldwin, on Long Island's southern shore twenty miles east of New York. The building had once housed an airplane manufacturer and then been transformed into a combination garage and showroom for an auto dealership. When Towl—already doubling as a Grumman investor—first visited the site in December 1930 he was appalled. The facility's supposed "showroom" fronted south on a dirt road call Railroad Avenue; on the other side were the tracks of the Long Island Railroad and, beyond, the clattering traffic of the Sunrise Highway. The real eyesores, however, waited inside: The windows were broken, as were the skylights atop its trussed roof, and a thick carpet of leaves had drifted in from the line of oaks across the road. Even as he rolled up his sleeves, Towl wondered, "What have I put my money into?"

———

In Towl's case, site cleanup—an all-hands affair—gave way to financial and administrative support for company treasurer Ed Poor. Poor, a cautious, self-effacing young man from a prosperous New York family, had been the bookkeeper and treasurer for the Loening Aircraft Engineering Corporation, a 1917 New York City start-up that designed early Army and Navy fighter aircraft in a mid-Manhattan loft space.

Looking to adapt to the postwar market and the first prospects for civilian aviation, founder Grover Loening (a path-breaking aeronautical engineer who had once worked for Orville Wright) moved his firm to a three-story plant fronting the East River at Thirty-First Street. There, it branched into designing and building water-borne aircraft, both for the military and (in the form of well-appointed, multi-passenger "air yachts") for Roaring Twenties tycoons. Diversification and expansion were necessary moves, but they also meant an unremitting struggle for financing, until Lucky Lindy's pioneering flight and the federal government's adoption of air transport and construction regulations, coupled with the late twenties' stock boom, finally attracted the lusting gaze of venture capitalists.

True to his engineering nature, Grover Loening was a realist about the sudden, seemingly limitless infusion of capital. In late 1928, he cashed out, selling his company for a reported three million dollars to New York investment bankers, who in turn peddled it to Keystone Aircraft Company, then producing a twin-engine bomber for the Army. With Grover Loening out of the picture (he and a brother-partner left with a non-compete agreement) and facing the prospect of relocating to Bristol, Pennsylvania, a handful of key Loening Aircraft employees hashed out their options.

One was Jake Swirbul, then thirty-two, the stocky, balding, moon-faced, New York–born son of a first-generation Latvian father and Swiss mother who, after his own two years at Cornell, joined the Marine Corps in World War I. In the postwar years Swirbul worked in the shops of several other start-up aircraft manufacturers and served as a civilian inspector for the Army Air Corps before joining Loening as its shop and production supervisor.

It was the gregarious, straightforward, hands-on Swirbul who most likely broached the possibility of starting "our own company" to three others with whom he shared Loening's day-to-day management. One was William T. Schwendler, a design whiz who had joined Loening in 1924 after graduating from New York University, where his was the first NYU engineering school class to be offered a major in aeronautics. Aside from a pre-graduation summer at Chance Vought, Schwendler had worked nowhere except Loening.

When it came to the temperaments and tensions of the military aircraft business, the two men were polar opposites: the younger, introspective Schwendler a design engineer versed in the latest aviation technologies whose passion was conceiving planes that could outfly anything in the air; the older, pragmatic Swirbul a production engineer who lived to turn out more planes than a rival. Bill Schwendler's instincts leaned toward interrupting production in the interests of a better design, while Jake Swirbul's pressed toward keeping it moving at all costs.

Despite their vastly different dispositions, the two men got along well; they even shared a Loening office where, during the uncertain lull between the Keystone deal announcement and the firm's uprooting to Philadelphia, Jake Swirbul most likely convinced Bill Schwendler that striking out on their own, even in the face of looming economic uncertainty, was the best path.

If Swirbul needed Schwendler and Schwendler needed Swirbul, they both needed a third man, Loening's plant manager (and Schwendler's immediate boss), Leroy Randle Grumman. In a real sense, Roy Grumman was the essential ingredient—someone whose background, skills and personality would not only bridge the ostensible divide between Swirbul and Schwendler, but would also give the new firm an indispensable advantage when it came to winning over its most promising customer.

––––––––

Grumman possessed remarkable, though seemingly contradictory qualities. Though as much an aeronautical visionary as Bill Schwendler, he was, if anything, more logic-driven and, if possible, more diffident. While Roy Grumman's Scotch-Irish ancestry, solid build, blue eyes and fair, red-blond hair had earned him the nickname "Red Mike" among Loening Aircraft Engineering's population of second-generation Italian, German and Polish artisans, his reserve (one reason why Jake Swirbul, rather than Roy Grumman, was making today's welcoming speech) soon enough prompted people to address him—nearly without exception—as "Mr. Grumman."

If in some ways Roy Grumman could "Out-Schwendler" Bill Schwendler, he could also, when it came to matters of business economy, pragmatism and steely resolve, match the production beast that was Jake Swirbul. Grumman's reserve was of a piece with his ability to cut to the heart of a design or production problem and drive it forward with a minimum of second-thought chatter or corporate circumlocution.

Grumman would, in his time, puzzle over—and solve—one of the impending war's most vexing and consequential air combat dilemmas by means of a gum eraser and two paper clips. He would also, as fortune and markets demanded, throw his considerable talents into producing airplanes, truck trailers, camping canoes and lunar modules. However, as far as the immediate fortunes of the yet unformed, unnamed break-off were concerned, his singular worth lay in an emblematic credential: Roy Grumman had earned his Wings of Gold.

––––––––

To be precise, Roy Grumman was Naval Aviator No. 1216, a distinction he earned after completing advanced flight training in Pensacola, Florida in September 1918, during the closing months of the Great War. After not only attending Cornell University—as had Swirbul before him and Schwendler after—but also (in 1916) graduating as a mechanical engineer, Grumman began his career in New York Telephone's engineering department, though he left his post to enlist in the Navy when America entered the war. On the strength of his educational background, Grumman joined a military branch more reputed for arcane maritime traditions than technical know-how as a second-class petty officer machinist. But his flight wings—and his officer commission—came more aptly as the result of his quiet reserve and persistence.

Sent by the Navy to a Columbia University-taught course in sub-chaser engines, Grumman applied for flight training only to be disqualified, supposedly because of flat feet. Grumman didn't argue about the disqualification (though he apparently could have), but when the Navy next sent him to Boston's MIT for what was purported to be an aircraft inspection class, he instead found himself part of a ground school class for prospective naval aviation flight candidates. Grumman simply kept his mouth shut about the mistake, subsequently progressing (apparently with no further scrutiny of his arches) to NAS Miami for primary flight training and from there to advanced training, graduation and commissioning at Pensacola.

Grumman was initially posted to a bombing squadron as a flight instructor but, with the Great War winding down, the Navy soon returned him to MIT, this time for an aeronautical program open to engineering graduates with flight training. Next, equipped with both an advanced aeronautical degree and a lieutenant's rank, Grumman received orders to report to the Navy Aircraft Factory in Philadelphia, serving as a combination test pilot, production supervisor and industry liaison for a run of two-seater fighter aircraft. The Loening designs were being built both in the Naval Aircraft Factory and in Loening's own plant and, by October 1920, Grover Loening had convinced the twenty-five-year-old naval officer to become Loening Aircraft's plant manager.

In doing so, Roy Grumman was leaving a niche industry segment—naval aviation—that seemed to have a diminished postwar horizon and a career (a way of life, really) where he had not shown particular promise. As Raymond P. Applegate, a Pensacola instructor (reminiscing years later) recalled, Grumman "was very, very reticent." While most trainees, after learning to fly, "became tougher than hell," Grumman somehow didn't.

———

Raymond Applegate's other flight students would have ample cause to show they were tougher than hell: Even as Roy Grumman resigned his commission, the Navy was in the midst of converting (and renaming) collier *Jupiter* (AC-3) to *Langley* (CV-1). America's first single-purpose "flattop" would be the prototype of new opportunities—and new risks—for its still-meager cadre of naval aviators.

For his part, if Roy Grumman didn't demonstrate sufficient swagger to Raymond Applegate back in 1918, he would evidence it in his own way—and his own time—as his run as Loening's plant manager wound down. When Jake Swirbul confided his start-up idea, Grumman at first asked time to consider but also revealed that he had already spoken to the Loening brothers. Although contractually prevented from actively participating, the Loening brothers favored the idea and were even willing to invest.

Then, a few days later, after confirming that he was in, Grumman promptly set in motion the steps to make it happen.

————

The first step was to enlist Ed Poor, Loening's bookkeeper and assistant treasurer. Poor would be the firm's conservative, rational, one-step-at-a-time money guy—a facts-and-figures soulmate for Roy Grumman. But Poor (his surname notwithstanding) also came from a prosperous New York family that could invest in the enterprise. His participation—and his family's money—was the catalyst for a pivotal decision. The four-man cohort (five, when Clint Towl and his investment were dealt in) would be their own masters. Even assuming some silent partner backing from the Loenings, the new aviation firm would be able to chart its own path.

On this bright, unseasonable December 1941 day, now a decade and more since the company's formation, Grumman, Swirbul, Schwendler, Poor and Towl had every reason for mutual backslapping. It was the absence of second-guessing by distant corporate masters or the impatient clamoring stockholding mobs that had facilitated the success Grumman Aircraft bathed in today.

————

The first sign of something amiss came when Clint Towl was called to the phone by the man running the facility's PA system. The man had just heard over the radio that Pearl Harbor had been attacked by the Japanese.

Already envisioning the day's reverie churning into mass hysteria, Towl at once admonished the PA man to say nothing. He then instructed a group of guards and maintenance personnel to quietly curtail the flow of refreshments. As expected, this soon had the crowd shuffling towards the exits—and what they imagined was the balance of their Sunday's leisure.

With crowd ushered out, Grumman security men began to shut and secure the gates, making the facility suddenly off limits (for the day and the duration) to the public. Meanwhile a group of executives and supervisors fanned out for a check of the offices and shop floors. As these earnest vigilantes patrolled the far reaches of the Bethpage facility, intent on rooting out any would-be saboteurs, their immediate concern was vouchsafing the secrets of Grumman's latest product—a big, gleaming, new monster of a torpedo bomber aircraft dubbed the TBF[2].

Meanwhile, both the vigilantes and Grumman's founders could only wonder just how their F4F Wildcat, the younger, small fighter-aircraft cousin of the TBF, might be faring. After all, the Wildcat could now be in the very thick of its first combat action on behalf of its home country—and on behalf of Grumman's bread-and-butter client, the United States Navy.

---

[2] See chapter notes for a detailed explanation of World War II U.S. Navy aircraft designations. See the Glossary for information on the naming conventions for this and other American and Japanese aircraft.

2

MY GOD! WHAT'S HAPPENED?

DECEMBER 7, 1941, SOUTHEAST OF THE HAWAIIAN ISLANDS

After losing contact with their flock of strike aircraft in the twilight skies southeast of Oahu, the six barrel-chested F4F Wildcat fighter escorts eventually turned northwest toward carrier *Enterprise* (CV-6).

At 9:50 a.m. that same Sunday, the escorts' flight leader, Fighting Six's Lieutenant (junior grade) Francis Frederick Hebel, had flown "Big E's" first wartime combat air patrol (CAP). The novelty of flying CAP with explicit orders to shoot—instructions they'd received when they'd flown out to *Enterprise* from Naval Air Stations (NAS) Pearl Harbor a little more than a week before—had only recently worn off. As it was, they were still getting accustomed to the different way their aircraft handled with the added weight of eighteen hundred rounds of ammunition belted into their Browning .50 caliber wing guns.

While "Fritz" Hebel's CAP aircraft guarded the morning skies above Vice Admiral William F. Halsey's Task Force (TF) 8 as it marked time awaiting further orders, radio circuits had buzzed with conflicting reports of damage and casualties ashore and wild speculation about the location of the Japanese task force that had inflicted them. At 10:20 a.m., fifteen Dauntless SBD[1] dive bombers were poised for launch based on a sighting of two enemy carriers thirty miles south of Barbers Point, only to be held when the report, like so many others, proved mistaken.

Then, in mid-afternoon, one of *Enterprise's* own aerial scouts, chasing down a position report on a Japanese carrier sent by a radio direction finding unit ashore, sighted a carrier and a cruiser being attacked by a fighter just sixty miles from Pearl Harbor. Convinced by this visual from one of his own pilots, Halsey quickly dispatched a strike. It was this flight of

---

1. The S stands for Scout, the B for Bomber and the D for Douglas Aircraft.

eighteen VT-6 Devastators and six VB-6 Dauntlesses t̸
Wildcats had shepherded.

———

Hebel, at twenty-nine the oldest of the six Wildcat pi⌐
squadron in March 1941 and, having originally earned his Nav̸
wings in 1937, was among VF-6's most seasoned men. He had enlisted in
the Navy a year before, part of the inaugural class of naval aviation cadets,
a recruiting and training pool that had produced, over several years in
the midst of the Great Depression, a burgeoning corps of fledgling aviators who had since become veterans.

Next senior in the flight, though only by dint of his 1938 U.S. Naval
Academy (USNA) graduation (Hebel's 1939 commissioning in the regular navy was backdated coincident with the receipt of his wings), was
twenty-five-year-old Lieutenant (junior grade) Eric Allen, Jr. However,
Allen, a strong swimmer and talented choral tenor at the Academy, was
this day the escort formation's "Ass-End Charlie." Its least experienced
member, Allen had just earned his wings in early 1941 (as had five other
Academy graduates assigned to the squadron).

Sandwiched between Hebel and Allen in the Wildcats' right echelon
formation (as they were, more or less, also bracketed by age, rank, career
track and flying experience), flew four other VF-6 pilots. Ensigns James
G. Daniels III and Gayle L. Hermann, both twenty-six and both with regular Navy commissions, were also among the first aviation cadet graduates. Ensigns David R. Flynn (next oldest to Hebel, having just turned
twenty-seven that same day) and Herbert H. Menges (at twenty-four,
youngest of the six) had each joined the Navy in 1939 and earned their
wings the next year.

All six pilots shared, in common with the squadron's roughly 140 officers and enlisted personnel, VF-6's command chain, traditions and organi-
zational esprit. Fighting Squadron Six had originally been formed in 1935
as Fighting Squadron One, assigned to serve aboard what was in effect "carrier one": the pioneering but doughty USS *Langley* (CV-1). The confusion
of an interim designation (as Fighting Eight) and a temporary ship reas-
signment (to *Lexington* [CV-2]) were finally resolved when the Navy decided to reduce confusion by aligning squadron numbers with carrier hull
numbers. Fighting Six, whose "Shooting Stars" squadron insignia depicted

———

2. See chapter notes for a detailed explanation of U.S. Navy air squadron letter and number designations.

.ed comet streaking across a star-emblazoned deep blue quadrant of the global heavens, joined CV-6, the U.S. Navy's newest and biggest flattop.

Not surprisingly, bonds were tighter within VF-6's nineteen-man aviator cadre. The men berthed, ate, socialized, trained, briefed, complained and, most of all, flew together. Fighting Six had been among the first Pacific Fleet fighting squadrons to convert from biplanes to monoplanes, having taken delivery of eighteen F4F-3A Wildcats in May 1941. Marvels of their time, the Grumman aircraft were equipped with robust supercharged 1200-hp Pratt and Whitney engines that delivered a top flight speed of 317 miles per hour, well over fifty miles-per-hour faster than VF-6's biplane trade-ins. In speed, maneuverability and firepower they were the U.S. Navy's hottest aircraft—although, it soon became apparent, not the world's.

Organizing these eighteen aircraft (the squadron roster carried a pilot "spare") into three divisions of six aircraft—one division led by VF-6's thirty-nine-year-old commanding officer (CO) Lieutenant Commander Clarence Wade McClusky, the other two by the squadron's executive officer (XO) Frank T. Corbin, thirty-four, and flight officer James S. Gray Jr., twenty-seven—the flyers had worked intensely to ready the F4Fs for combat. They were—and knew they were—among the best-trained fighter pilots in theirs or any country's air force.

Of particular note, the Shooting Stars veterans had perfected the still-esoteric art of aerial deflection gunnery, the skill of leading a target approached from any angle—not just ahead or astern—so that the paths of bullets and opponent converged. (Gray, a USNA graduate and gunnery specialist, had even written a manual on aerial gunnery for fighter pilots.) It was high-speed deflection gunnery that enabled them, at least in theory and with target sleeve practice, to make repeated, complex and evasive gunnery runs on any aerial prey.

But on this chaotic and now darkening day, fate stalked three of the men—theirs was a blood bond deeper than even shared traditions or camaraderie. The possibility of it went unacknowledged—perhaps even unimagined—by Fritz Hebel, Eric Allen, Jim Daniels, Gayle Hermann, Dave Flynn, or Herb Menges as they scoured ocean and sky on what was, after all, Fighting Six's first combat foray. Hereafter, fate's call would be implicit in thousands of wartime sorties. In the next months stretching into years, it would snuff the lives (to enemy fire, captivity or torture; to aircraft malfunctions, collisions or crashes; to darkness, fog, squalls or typhoons;

to drowning, exposure, starvation, dehydration, hypoxia, hypothermia or vertigo; to hesitation or overconfidence; to uncounted instances of the unknowable) of a third of the men who ventured from aircraft carrier decks over a hostile, pitiless and seemingly boundless Pacific Ocean.

————

Though eager for revenge and loaded for bear, the Air Group's strike force never found its quarry. It turned out the *Enterprise* Scouting Six pilot had actually been searching on the reciprocal—the exact opposite—bearing of the target's actual position. (The Japanese carriers, the devastation wrought by their strike aircraft finished, were by now well to the northwest, retreating into the same cold front that had masked their approach.) The "enemy formation" the Scouting Six pilot had seen was actually a flight of Army Air Force (AAF) light bombers whose pilots were on their own wild goose chase. Now, to boot, the high altitude Wildcat component had even lost touch with its charges in the nighttime murk. Fritz Hebel finally decided there was little to do but grope their way home.

To compensate for the darkness as he navigated the hundred or so aerial miles back to *Enterprise*, Hebel had to rely on his Zed Baker, a quirky radio homing receiver. He did so expertly (another sign of VF-6's exquisite training); at 7:50 p.m., his six fighters were over the task force and ready to land. Surprised to find some of his strike planes already returned and wary of recovering them after dark, Halsey instead redirected them to land ashore at Oahu.

Hebel's Wildcats dutifully banked to the northeast, even though the pilots doubtless understood they were bound for a blacked out destination where ship and shore battery gun crews wouldn't hesitate to shoot. TF 8 personnel, well aware of these risks, took the precaution of breaking radio silence to warn Oahu installations of inbound friendlies. In response, Navy aviation duty officers hurriedly made the rounds of Pearl Harbor's smoldering docks and facilities to warn that Big E's fighter aircraft were en route and would land. For his part, *Enterprise*'s air group CO, Commander Howard L. "Brigham" Young, who had already flown ashore that morning with an advance contingent of eighteen VB-6 and VS-6 Dauntlesses (five of which had been shot down or crash landed after stumbling into the maelstrom) stationed himself in the Ford Island control tower. Using the tower's low power transmitter, Young repeatedly tried—to no avail—to raise both Hebel and *Enterprise*.

————

Ahead of him in the darkness, Fritz Hebel eventually spotted an island dotted with fires. Assuming it to be Kauai, where sugar cane fields were often burned before harvest, Hebel led his flight farther east over Molokai before realizing that what he'd seen instead were Oahu's ships and shore installations still ablaze from the daylight attacks.

Still heedless of Young's warning transmissions, the Wildcats reversed course, bound for Oahu's Makapuu Point; from there the fighters followed the firelit coast south and west over Diamond Head and Waikiki toward Pearl Harbor and its Naval Air Station. With thick smoke temporarily obscuring Ford Island's runway lights, Hebel briefly detoured his flight towards Hickam Field, only to turn back when the smoke lifted. It was 8:45 p.m. when Fritz Hebel nervously radioed Ford Island's tower for landing instructions.

Hearing Hebel's request, the tower controller handed the microphone to Brig Young. "Come on over the field and break up for landing," Young told them. He also instructed them to turn on their running lights—more proof to those below that the aircraft were friendly. In response, Hebel and his flight immediately descended to one thousand feet and simultaneously turned on their red and green wing lights and lowered their wheels. Opening their cockpits prior to landing, they could smell the stench of burned oil, paint, fabric, wood and flesh that suffused the harbor air. It was thick and sulfurous enough to be mistaken for Diamond Head's volcanic spew rather than the work of man.

Wheels and landing struts dangling from fuselage bellies, slowing, but still loosely organized in a right echelon formation, the six Wildcats circled Ford Island counterclockwise as if lining for a carrier landing. In doing so, the planes swept low in sight of edgy sailors on the battered ships in Drydock Channel, the Navy Yard's berths and along Battleship Row.

———

Aboard many of the ships, word had been passed that these were U.S. Navy aircraft inbound from *Enterprise*. Aboard cruiser *New Orleans* (CL-32), still tied dockside in East Loch, Marine Sergeant Joseph Fleck got the word. So did Ensign Leon Grabowski, then manning a 1.1-inch gun station on battleship *Maryland* (BB-46), who realized the information countered a shipboard rumor that the Japanese had sunk *Enterprise* at sea.

Aboard Cruiser Force flagship *Honolulu* (CL-48) in the Navy Yard's Berth 21, Seaman Clair E. Boggs and his shipmates also had instructions to hold their fire. Boggs had been watching the planes ever since they first came in above Diamond Head. Despite seeing the running lights,

Boggs clung to the suspicion that the intruders might be "Japs coming in for another sneak attack."

Personnel ashore, among them Navy air crewman Maury Meister (whose flying boat had arrived that afternoon from distant Midway Atoll), watching from a Ford Island hangar, saw the planes circle the fully lit runway and break formation as they readied to land. Another, a yeoman named Harry Rorman, thought (upon reflection years later) that things might have turned out differently if they had approached from directly south instead of circling.

As Hebel's lead plane peeled off and settled towards the runway, wary gunners aboard battleship *Pennsylvania* (BB-38) (which, though raked by Japanese aerial strafing, was still intact and cradled in Dry Dock One's massive caisson) opened fire. A strand of red tracers reached for the Wildcats. When Hebel instinctively aborted his landing and the planes behind him scattered, it was enough to convince other jumpy gunners to join in. "There was about a five second hesitation," *Honolulu's* Clair Boggs recalled, "and then everything in the harbor opened up."

Aboard battleship *California* (BB-44), whose thick steel decks had been penetrated by Japanese bombs, salvage officer Lieutenant Louis E. Kelley saw *Maryland's* forward antiaircraft guns open up. Flashes of yellow from these bigger shipboard guns joined the red winks of smaller caliber guns. Black puffs from fused projectiles were interspersed among the converging arcs of machine gun tracers. (To the southeast and out of the direct line of fire, Hickam Field even reported being bombed.) Anything within reach, anything that could shoot, now turned on the innocent Wildcats. In the words of Ford Island's commanding officer Captain James H. Shoemaker, "all hell broke loose."

"My God," Fritz Hebel screamed to the tower as he banked his Wildcat north through heavy gunfire, intent on reaching distant Wheeler Field. "What's happened?"

———

Pre-war preparations of VF-6's new Wildcats had not yet included installation of cockpit armor plate, bulletproof wind screens or self-sealing fuel tanks, defensive features that the air war over Europe was already showing vastly increased the odds for pilot survival in combat. But, in the minds of carrier fighter pilots, the idea of adding a hundred-plus pounds of pilot armor (in effect, the weight of a second pilot) to the seven thousand gross weight pounds of an aircraft built for speed and maneuverability seemed a mixed blessing.

Likewise, self-sealing fuel tanks, rubber bladders installed in place of aluminum tanks, were also controversial. The bladder tanks doubtless prevented in-flight explosions, but they added still more weight. More importantly, the thick, vulcanized bladders reduced fuel capacity and made fuel gauge readings unreliable. Today, though, for Fritz Hebel's unexpectedly embattled planes and pilots, either of the innovations might have saved a life.

Pilot armor might, for example, have made the difference for Hebel's wingman, Herb Menges. Instead, bullets now tore through Menges's cockpit, killing or at least incapacitating the young ensign. His F4F immediately stalled and drifted out of control towards Pearl City, cross-channel from Ford Island. There, at the end of a shallow dive, it crashed and exploded in flames on the veranda of Palm Lodge, a tavern at the water's edge. Palm Lodge quickly burned to the ground, but no one other than the twenty-four-year-old Menges, the very first U.S. Navy fighter pilot to die in the Pacific War, was killed or injured.

Likewise, self-sealing fuel tanks might well have given Eric Allen's Wildcat the margin of escape. As it was, its main fuel tanks apparently pierced by gunfire in the same instant as Menges's cockpit, Allen's F4F immediately erupted in flame, giving its pilot no time to climb and barely enough time and altitude to bail out. Short moments after his burning plane plummeted into the waters of Drydock Channel, Allen also hit the water hard, his fall scarcely broken by his parachute canopy. Seeing these two planes go down made Waldo Rathman, a sailor aboard destroyer tender *Whitney* (AD-4), feel that the morning's drubbing was a thing of the past. It was a thrill to see the harbor's gunnery take them down in flames. *Honolulu* sailor Claire Boggs's immediate thought was: "We got you, you little yellow sons of bitches."

Meanwhile, Fritz Hebel never made it anywhere near Wheeler. Instead, his Wildcat got into the sights of Army antiaircraft gunners north of Pearl Harbor. He opened his throttle, but the Pratt and Whitney engine merely sputtered and died. With no other landing option in sight, Hebel touched down on a sugar cane field near Aiea. Hitting hard and skidding through dirt and cane stubble, his aircraft cartwheeled and broke in two. The wreckage finally came to rest in a gully, where portions erupted in flame. Onlookers pulled Hebel—unconscious, with a fractured skull but still clinging to life—clear of the mangled cockpit.

———

With Hebel's, Menges's and Allen's Wildcats already down, Gayle Hermann's was the next to fall to friendly fire. A five-inch AA shell crashed into his Pratt and Whitney engine. While neither exploding nor wounding Hermann, the shell's impact quickly turned Hermann's plane into a seven-ton glider. On the verge of nosing into an unrecoverable stall, Hermann had little choice but to try for a dead stick landing on Ford. His plane took eighteen more hits as it touched down, bounced along the runway and unceremoniously braked to a halt on a golf course just east of the runway's apron. Hermann was still under small arms fire as he grabbed his parachute, jumped out of his cockpit and sprinted like a broken-field running back towards the sanctuary of VF-6's field hanger.

Jim Daniels and Dave Flynn were initially luckier than Menges, Allen, Hebel and even Hermann, but only to the extent that they had enough time to initiate evasive action. Before dousing his running lights, Daniels dived directly for the floodlights at the southwest edge of the field, hoping to blind or disperse the gunners. He then cranked up his wheels and headed southwestward toward Barbers Point where he marked time for about ten minutes, waiting for the firing to die down.

When he finally reestablished contact with the flight tower at Ford, Daniels received decidedly different instructions for his second approach: leave your lights off, come in low and touch down quickly. This time, flying much like a real enemy aircraft might have, darkened and hugging land and sea from the south—he nearly clipped the foretop of battleship *Nevada* (BB-36) grounded off Hospital Point—Daniels brought his Wildcat in safely. Even so, he was fired on briefly as he taxied to the field hangar. When Daniels finally cut his engine and climbed from the cockpit, Gayle Hermann—shaken, but in one piece—jumped onto a wing. The two momentarily shared their uneasy joy at being alive.

————

Off to the west and ten or so miles out to sea, Dave Flynn, the last man of Hebel's six-plane flight still airborne, faced a dilemma. With both his radio transmitter and receiver on the blink, Flynn was especially wary about flying back towards Oahu, but his Wildcat was also perilously low on fuel. Reluctantly, Flynn turned toward the shore.

When he made landfall at Barbers Point, Flynn thought better of trying again for Ford Island. Instead he banked north toward the Marine airfield at Ewa where, still several miles short of the runway, his fuel finally gave out and his Wildcat stalled. By then he was also taking ground fire, so Flynn elected to bail out. It was a life-saving decision: As he para-chuted down from 1,200 feet, his aircraft exploded in flames behind him. Tumbling hard to the ground, Flynn was eventually picked up by some passing soldiers.

———

With all six aircraft down, it was left now only to account for the fate of the ordeal's injured survivors: Fritz Hebel, Eric Allen and Dave Flynn. As perhaps just another measure of the day's confusion, Flynn, who had bailed out well west of Hebel's crash point near Pearl Harbor's northeast shore, was shuttled by rescuers to Tripler Army Hospital, southeast of Aiea, while Hebel's Samaritans took him farther north to the Army hospital at Schofield Barracks.

By that hour—now well past 9 p.m.—most of the day's thousands of casualties were crowding makeshift, understaffed facilities of every description and locale. Flynn's good fortune was that his relatively minor injuries—a wrenched back and wrist—could handle either journey, while Hebel's fate was such that he could survive neither. Never regaining consciousness, Hebel died the next day.

Earlier, Eric Allen had waged his struggle to survive by summoning the remnants of his swimmer's training and conditioning. Despite grievous internal injuries sustained during his parachute drop, Allen managed to stroke his way through the oily, debris-strewn waters of Drydock Channel up past the wreckage of battleship *California*. There, sailors from minesweeper *Valerio* (AM-52) finally plucked Allen from the ooze. He was ferried to Ford Island, most likely in one of the gigs or launches darting about like water bugs.

Conditions on Ford Island were chaotic, nowhere more so than in the barracks and mess halls serving as temporary dispensaries, hospitals and morgues. With patients overflowing onto patios and steps, many with their foreheads marked with Mercurochrome crosses to indicate they'd received morphine, Allen had to wait his turn.

It was only as medics wiped away the oil scum on Allen's torso that they realized he had taken a rifle-caliber bullet. Drained by internal bleeding, one of his swimmer-tenor lungs hopelessly collapsed, Allen died at 2 a.m. on December 8, 1941.

PART TWO

HARD PRESSED

3
PROTOTYPES

When Jimmy Collins received Jake Swirbul's call, he all but knocked over the Roosevelt Field Hotel restaurant's cashier in his haste to reach the lobby phone.

In the fall of 1933, the Roosevelt Field Hotel was Collins's home-away-from-home, as it was for a host of other freelance pilots who hung around its restaurant—talking, smoking, drinking coffee and anxiously awaiting a phone call that might bring a contract offer.

The Ohio-born Collins, fatherless at five and orphaned by his mother's death a decade later, was a product of what was then the U.S. Army Air Service's flight training program. A classmate was Charles Lindbergh who, although as rail-thin as Collins, was taller and two years older than Collins.

Collins and Lindbergh were among eighteen graduates of a class winnowed by training rigors from one hundred and four trainees. They were also among just four selected for specialized training in pursuit (fighter) aircraft. Having since left the Air Service in 1928 after stints as an instructor, Collins was already a test pilot of some repute—and some notoriety.

If his skills and daring set Collins apart from other pilots, so did his opinions and political leanings. Collins was a voracious reader who had immersed himself in the works of British philosopher-playwright George Bernard Shaw. Heavily influenced by Shaw, Collins styled himself as a pacifist and socialist—perhaps even a communist. His pacifism had spurred his decision to resign his Army commission, while his socialism and sporadic activism, not surprisingly, had made Collins anathema to the more established portions of the aviation industry.

Now to make matters worse, Collins was, like so many other boom-time aviators, suffering through a Depression era that stalled the commercial aviation industry and curtailed lucrative opportunities for even the least controversial pilot impresarios. For long stretches, as Collins ran up his hotel charges on Long Island, his wife Dee and their two infant children stayed with her parents back in Oklahoma—a way of assuring they'd at least have a roof over their heads if test pilot jobs didn't turn up.

"I've got a job for you," Swirbul announced, "a dive demonstration."

Desperate as he was for a job, Collins was immediately suspicious. Years before, during a dive demonstration for another manufacturer, the test aircraft's wings had sheared off with an explosive crack that propelled Collins's head into the instrument board. Knocked senseless by the impact, he revived just in time to parachute clear and land yards away from the flaming wreck.

"What kind of a ship?" Collins asked warily.

"It's a bomber fighter," replied Swirbul with his best chamber-of-commerce optimism. "Second model, first production job, a single-seater biplane."

Though there was some comfort in Swirbul's upbeat assertion that the ship was in production, not purely experimental, it still begged the question: Why him? Collins knew that Grumman had used Bill McAvoy, a test pilot from the National Advisory Committee for Aeronautics (NACA[1]) for demonstration of the FF-1, the company's first military model.

"What's wrong with your other pilot?" Collins asked Swirbul.

Nothing, Swirbul was prompt to assure him. McAvoy simply had other commitments that made him unavailable for the full round of demonstrations, although he would likely be on site beforehand. Roy Grumman, though a test pilot himself, was not qualified to test his own plane and none of the company's salary pilots were up to this sort of work. Besides, why should Grumman take a chance on breaking up its organization if it could call in a freelancer?

In the end, Collins had to concede that Grumman's logic was impeccable. It would be hard to keep up company morale if it put salary pilots' lives on the line for high performance test flights.

Collins was pushing thirty—no youngster when it came to these special high-paying test jobs—with a wife and family to support. Before long he'd be too old for this sort of thing and wouldn't be getting any more

---

1. NACA was the predecessor to NASA.

calls like this. And, in the meantime, Collins would be constantly battling the headwinds of his left-leaning apostasy.

"I'll take your job," Collins finally told Swirbul after the two haggled briefly over contract terms. Grumman would be in touch, Swirbul told Collins, as soon as the ship was ready.

After putting down the phone, Collins returned to the restaurant. Responding as nonchalantly as he could to the coffee klatch's inquiring stares, Collins told them about the new Grumman job. Immediately, the other freelancers began to razz him. Diving demonstration? He could have that job! What kind of flowers did he want on his grave?

Collins shot back: They should ask themselves what meal they preferred—breakfast, lunch or dinner—when they were down to one a day.

Studying his decision some months later, Collins would reflect that somehow—despite his idealism and his spiritual connection with flying—he had made a pact with ambition and money. Regretfully, the time had finally come when he "would rather eat than fly."

Now though, in the presence of his Roosevelt hecklers, Collins was more self-justifying than reflective. "Anyway," Collins told them, "I won't be dropping dead of starvation around here this winter."

———

Collins's 1933 Grumman contract specified fifteen hundred dollars plus expenses for the first ten days. After that, if the rounds of flight demonstrations continued, he would be getting a thirty-five dollar per diem. Additionally, for the duration of the demonstrations, Grumman would insure Collins life for fifteen thousand dollars and provide for disability compensation.

Because of his wife and family, the life insurance and disability compensation were just as important as the money. Collins had heard of another freelancer just like him that had parachuted from a dive demonstration. He'd survived, but only after banging into the plane's tail structure during the jump. He'd broken both legs and an arm in the process; a year later he was still hospitalized.

In the two weeks' time between Swirbul's job offer and the October day when he stepped out of a taxi in front of Grumman's Farmingdale hangar just off the Hempstead Turnpike, Collins wrestled with his usual spate of second thoughts. Not surprisingly, their origin was the dive demonstration crash he'd survived years before. Up until that incident it had never occurred to Collins that a plane he was testing might fall apart.

He knew that planes had—and would—but only with other pilots at the controls, not him.

After that one crash experience, of course, Collins knew better. Sometimes (not immediately after the crash, but periodically in the months and years ahead, and especially in the lead-up to new test jobs), he found himself startled awake at night. Collins didn't suffer vivid nightmares—rather, a vague, low-voltage jolt of fright.

The airplane Collins was to test was waiting in the middle of the hangar, suspended from a chain hoist with the wheels of its retractable undercarriage hovering just inches from the hangar's cement floor. A group of Grumman's engineers and mechanics swarmed all over the ship, which had a silver fuselage and a darker, but still gleaming, interior. To Collins's first appraising glimpse, the XF2F was sturdy and squat, almost bull-doggish in the way only a military aircraft can—and should—be.

———

Those distinctive retractable wheels were, so to speak, the "feet" in the door when it came to Grumman Aircraft's courtship of the U.S. Navy. Even before Grumman opened its own doors for business in 1930, its principals were busy scouring industry channels for contract opportunities. The Navy then had scout and observation planes, products of Chance Vought, to which it could attach centerline floats for water takeoffs and landings. What it wanted to do, however, was to add fully retractable wheels to the boat-shaped floats, thereby adapting them for land and even aircraft carrier use.

Even back then, retractable airplane wheels were not entirely new. They actually had been pioneered early in the 1920s as a means of streamlining monoplane racers. Once aloft, the wheels and wheel struts on these planes were collapsed (like card table legs or the stems of eyeglasses) and hand-cranked back into recesses in the wings. For most types of aircraft, however, the aerodynamic advantage of incorporating retractable wheels did not yet justify their engineering complexity and added weight.

Because Loening (Grumman Aircraft's precursor) had long specialized in floatplanes, Grumman designers had already mastered partially retractable wheels—but, even so, only for civilian aviation use. Thus the challenge they faced—if they hoped to snag Grumman's first Navy contract—was three-fold: conceiving a wheel undercarriage for the float that was fully retractable as well as unfailingly dependable and light enough not to compromise aerodynamics.

Aspects of the solution had first been worked on during the waning months of Loening Aeronautical's existence—when there was little original engineering to be done. By the time the fledgling company set up shop in Baldwin, chief designer Bill Schwendler thought he had the makings of a pretty workable landing gear.

Bill Schwendler was being modest. What Grumman ultimately put before the Navy's Bureau of Aeronautics (BuAer) represented not one, but several strokes of genius. In all, the company's proposed design was, by any measure, a technological breakthrough, a game changer.

Not only did Grumman's brain trust produce an aerial float with fully retractable landing gear (and with a restraining hook for carrier landing use), but, in the process, Schwendler's team also had saved enough weight to make the new float lighter than the float without wheels that the Navy already used.

The solution's overall success was attributable to the melding of genius strokes—and a willingness by its designers to take each stroke in a new direction. Cams in the landing gear retraction mechanism, for example, were configured such that the wheels and struts, rather than being hinged and swinging up in an arc, instead moved in a parallelogram-like path—first horizontally *in* and then diagonally *up*. Rather than being collapsed out of sight, the landing gear was neatly sheathed, visible like two recessed donuts, but completely flush with the fuselage. The resulting solution was at once less intricate, more efficient and more reliable: ideal, in other words, for military use. And although, as built, this mechanism required hand cranking (as did other fully retractable gear), it could easily be adapted to hydraulic power.

The key to the float's weight reduction was something called monocoque construction. Monocoque—a design approach wherein external surfaces (rather than a heavier internal framework) carry the loads and stresses—was, like retractable landing gear, not entirely new to aeronautical design. What was new was introducing monocoque, or "stress-skin," construction to airplane floats.

BuAer representatives—at this stage, in what was still naval aviation's infancy, they tended to be middle- or junior-level officers rather than top brass—were suitably impressed. Remarkably, at a cost of just thirty four thousand dollars, the small Baldwin, New York start-up had devised a solution that doubled the utility of the Navy's small fleet of Chance Vought scout planes. The Bureau soon contracted for manufacture of six of what became known as the Model A Float.

Before long, BuAer was doing some romancing of its own, asking whether Grumman might consider adapting its retractable gear for use in the Navy's Boeing biplane fighters. Both sides knew that neither Boeing— then producing the carrier-based F4B biplane for the U.S. Navy—nor any other aviation manufacturer yet built a military fighter equipped with retractable gear.

In a very real way this was the moment that Grumman's triumvirate— Grumman, Swirbul and Schwendler—had been waiting for since they'd first charted their venture. Because it held unbounded risk and unbounded opportunity, it was also a moment they simultaneously dreaded and relished.

Though they were just scant weeks into an all-important courtship, the Navy's earnest and needy new suitor marshaled its courage and balked. Bureau representatives were told such an adaptation would be impossible: The fragile Boeing fuselage simply couldn't handle the retractable gear without a complete redesign.

Besides, if Grumman gear was to be used, it should be used on Grumman planes.

It just so happened, Roy Grumman told the Bureau of Aeronautics, that his team had been working on a fighter design that incorporated the new landing gear along with other innovations.

Bureau officials, while decidedly noncommittal, agreed to take a look at the features, facts and figures of what was termed a High Performance Two-Seat Fighter. This two-seater was the FF, what came to be known in pilot circles as the "Fi-Fi" and to Grumman insiders (owing to the robust design's eventual scout and amphibious offspring) as the "Fertile Myrtle."

The FF-1, the production version ultimately acquired by BuAer (after manufacturer's demonstration flights by NACA's Bill McAvoy and the Navy's own round of tests) was gifted with features that, beyond stress-skin construction and retractable wheels, displayed Navy veteran Roy Grumman's first-hand insight into the needs—and occasional foibles—of carrier aviators. For example, the FF-1 possessed two essential features, extraordinary cockpit visibility and low-speed maneuverability, that aided rather than complicated carrier deck landings.

Less readily apparent but perhaps more important, the FF-1 also had an inherent ruggedness, an ability to "get back to base" even when mechanically or structurally impaired. Whether in peace or combat conditions, this meant a lot to carrier pilots flying (then without benefit of radios or radar) over trackless stretches of ocean and into unpredictable weather conditions.

And this factory-built ruggedness even paid dividends to bone-heads. For example, Navy pilots new to carriers, retractable landing gear or both had a frightful habit of making belly landings after neglecting to lower and lock their wheels. When this happened—as later operational experience amply demonstrated—the FF-1 could take the abuse in stride. Often, squadron mechanics could simply jack up the plane, drop the wheels, bang out the belly dents and attach a replacement propeller.

Unseen by the Navy, Grumman had even managed to streamline its internal design and manufacturing processes. Design drawings for parts and subassemblies, for example, went first to the shop as scaled sketches (rather than blueprints), enabling foremen and mechanics to evaluate and test them (sometimes even as cardboard cut-outs) before they were finalized. It fostered a productive and unprecedented give-and-take between drawing board dreaming and shop floor pragmatism.

The Navy's own XFF tests (at Anacostia, Virginia in early spring 1932) revealed a tough, fast and agile airplane which, in all but two categories (climb rate and maximum ceiling) either matched or exceeded the performance of its current Boeing model. In sea-level speed trials, the two-seater XFF's 195-miles-per-hour speed bested Boeing's one-seater F4B-4 by a full eleven miles per hour. BuAer ended up contracting for twenty-seven of the production FFs in time for Christmas—and the funding of Grumman's year-end employee bonuses. By then, prototypes for FF scout and amphibian variants were already in the works. Altogether, Fertile Myrtle had positioned Grumman as a worthy competitor to Boeing for the Navy's fighter aerial fleet.

Still, while Grumman was in the game, it was not yet the signature suitor. It would take something more to achieve that.

————

Bill McAvoy, the NACA pilot who had piloted the XFF through its successful manufacturer demonstration flights, was on hand in Farmingdale to take Jimmy Collins on a walk-around of the XF2F. As the two men circled the new plane amid the last minute primping by Grumman personnel, McAvoy mentioned that he had already flown a stress analysis on the ship, a piece of reassuring news to Collins.

With the plane dangling specimen-like from the rafters of the Grumman flight hangar, Collins could make a closer unvarnished inspection of what he was about to fly. He couldn't help but take comfort in the ship's sturdy aluminum construction and forged fittings—the attention to detail was there on display. He was especially impressed by the wires bracing its wings. They looked strong enough to hold the Brooklyn Bridge. He liked the wires a lot.

————

When Collins hoisted himself into the plane's tiny cockpit, he was confronted by new gadgets he'd never encountered before. In the past, dive demonstrations were more adventurous art than cold science. Manufacturers had once relied on the test pilot's word for what he'd seen, heard, felt and done up in the air. Not so long before, Collins knew, you could get away with certain things—at least so far as your conscience would permit.

But not anymore.

Now there was a maze of new recording and sensing instruments on each plane, all seemingly tamperproof and some even invisible to the pilot. This F2F model, for example, included what was called a vee-gee recorder. The vee-gee, Collins learned, etched a pattern on a small piece of smoked glass as the plane was flown. Afterwards, the vee-gee results told the Grumman engineers just how fast the pilot had dived, the angle of his dive, and what kind of pull-out he made. They no longer had to take the pilot's word for it. And, of course, if the plane crashed and the pilot didn't survive, the vee-gee might provide valuable post-mortem data.

There was another instrument, this one visible to the pilot, that Collins had never seen before. It looked like a speedometer but the engineers instead called it an accelerometer. From the Grumman mechanics' explanation, Collins grasped that the accelerometer somehow measured pull-out forces. Details beyond that escaped him—at least for the moment.

————

That afternoon, Collins took the little bulldog biplane for a familiarization spin. He rocked, horsed, yanked and pulled it, all the while watching the ship's silver wings, fins and wires for any telltale flexing, vibration and flutter. Back on the ground Collins gave Grumman's men his impressions. That night the ship was inspected and a few small things were tinkered with. Next morning, Collins went back at it, doing many of the same things—but this time a little further out on the edge. He applied more speed, took steeper dives and wrapped the ship in progressively tighter turns.

Finally, after several days of these familiarization flights, Collins signaled he was ready for the official demonstrations. Grumman scheduled the Navy's observers. Once they were on-site, the first thing Collins would be demonstrating was speed dives.

————

Collins was no aeronautical engineer or physicist, but he was also no stranger to the concept of terminal velocity. He knew that a diving plane actually had a speed limit. So, for that matter, did a falling man. When either built up enough wind resistance to offset its own weight, it went no faster.

A falling man's terminal velocity, Collins had heard, was about 120 miles per hour. Of course, airplane designers and engineers could do much better than that. Playing around with different combinations of airplane weight, construction, aerodynamics and engine power, they could—and were—pushing terminal velocity ever higher.

At the same time, though they could estimate what their product's theoretical terminal velocity might be, it was still the test pilot's job to find out in practice. Without, of course, demolishing the aircraft—or demonstrating his particular terminal velocity. The XF2F's terminal velocity would be one of the primary performance features determined in the days and test flights ahead.

On the first demonstration day, Collins took the Grumman plane through five test dives, interrupted by ground inspections after the first, third and fourth runs. The first four each began at fifteen thousand feet of altitude, with Collins increasing velocity—and the distance dived—for each run. During the first demonstration he reached a dive speed of three hundred miles per hour. By the fourth run Collins had the dive speed up to three hundred and forty. By then, however, he was also losing nearly seven thousand feet of altitude with each plunge.

For the fifth and final demonstration of the day, just to play it safe, Collins climbed to eighteen thousand feet. It was cold up that high and the sky was very blue. With the oxygen level so thin, he found himself breathing harder and harder. Realizing that he was apt to be addled by oxygen starvation—hypoxia—Collins made a point of being especially deliberate. He methodically checked pitch, fuel mixture, stabilizer roll and rudder tab. Then he made sure to point the ship downwind before executing a half roll that pushed him over into the dead, still drop that marked the dive's first stage.

As they had during each of the previous runs, Collins's senses sharpened to the sights, sounds and feel of this final run for the day—or for his life.

He watched the air speed indicator as it first raced around its dial and then eventually slowed to an almost imperceptible crawl; the altimeter as it wound down like a dream clock running backward, the more sensitive of its two needles (registering each hundred feet of descent) steadily outpacing the slower (registering each thousand). He heard the mounting whine of the engine and the insistent whooshes and whistles of struts and wires. He felt the stress and stiffness that permeated the entire ship as its velocity increased, then held.

Suddenly, at eight thousand five hundred feet, with the altimeter still winding down but with the air speed all but stuck at three ninety-five, the motor at peak whine, and the ship's struts and wires shivering and now nearly screaming, something popped from the instrument board and smacked Collins in the face.

It wasn't much—perhaps in the way that the first pebble in an avalanche or first drop in a downpour isn't much. Inconsequential as it might be, it also brought to mind the sickening head smack he'd experienced when his test plane fell apart years before. Instinctively fear-ridden, Collins shot a glance at his wings as his hands and arms tightened the stick and eased the ship out of the dive. The silver wings and their sturdy bracing wires were still there—and so, apparently, was he.

By the time Collins got level and got things quieted down he found he was at five thousand feet. Having planned to bottom out at eight thousand he had lost an extra three thousand to the fear and confusion of what turned out after all to be just a harmless distraction.

The glass cover had managed to vibrate off the ship's manifold pressure dial, propelling its tiny indicator needle like a dart into his cheek.

Still shivering from the ice-cold clarity that comes with a jolt of boundless fright and his inner ears bulging with pressure, Collins eased the aircraft lower and toward the runway. After turning the ship over to the Grumman mechanics for their nightly tinkering, and with bad weather looming for the next day, Collins went out to tie one on.

———

At first, the next day's skies seemed as menacing as Collins's hangover. However, by midday, the bad weather (unlike Collins's head) lifted and the XF2F was rolled out, leaving Collins no choice but to crawl into the cockpit. As he strapped himself in, Collins was reminded that this and the next day's demonstrations were about both speed and *g* forces.

In the way he knew about terminal velocity, Collins also knew the rudiments of *g* (gravity) force. He knew, for example, that in level flight *g* force equaled 1, an index number representing body weight: in Collins's case, one hundred and fifty pounds. Collins had certainly experienced multiple *g*: the mounting centrifugal force exerted by a quick pull-out from a steep, high-speed dive. At their worst, the resulting multiple *g*—in effect, added body weights—pinned him briefly to his cockpit seat.

Although Collins would be allowed to gradually build up to it, what Grumman and BuAer ultimately wanted was for him to take the plane through a prolonged ten thousand foot dive during which he would reach and hold terminal velocity before finally pulling out hard enough to register a 9 *g* reading on their newfangled accelerometer.

Simply put, the prospective buyers wanted to be sure the plane held together at—and maybe a little beyond—the bounds of aerial combat stresses. Collins quickly did the math: 9 *g* meant 1350 pounds. His head still mushy, he took to the air with only a vague notion of how pushing nine *g* might feel and might affect him.

———

During that first, hungover afternoon, Collins made two build-up runs and, in the process, learned something important: The stiffer the pull-out and the sooner the release, the better he seemed able to weather the heavy *g*.

During the first go—a pushover at fifteen thousand feet, a dive reaching three hundred miles per hour, and a pull-out (he learned later) at 5.5 *g*—Collins went momentarily (but no less completely) blind. He couldn't see instruments, wings, sky above or ground below, a sensory deprivation he'd never before experienced. It made him wonder with dread: how would he possibly survive the double dose of terminal velocity and 9 *g*?

That dread softened a tad in the next run: also begun at fifteen thousand, but this time with dive speed upped to 320. Speculating (for whatever reason, the new experience had instantly cured his hangover) that he had perhaps unnecessarily prolonged his pull-out, Collins decided this time to grab more aggressively for *g*.: in effect, taking a bigger gulp of medicine but downing it faster.

It worked. In the process, Collins even shot past a hoped-for 6.5*g* up to 7*g*. All the way through he felt as if his guts were being sucked out of him and he had to battle for both sight and consciousness, but both he and the plane emerged intact.

After a ground inspection, Collins made two additional runs. During the second of them, the speed reached an impressive 360 miles per hour and the pull-out an amazing 8.5 g. At day's end, now just a whisper shy of the demonstration goal, Collins felt both better and worse. He was elated at both his dive results and the vanishing of his hangover. But Collins also found himself drained. He was experiencing unfamiliar pains shooting through his chest and, later that night in his room, his nose bled.

———

Next morning, though, after a quiet night alone in his Roosevelt Hotel room, Collins felt altogether fine. It was crisp, golden autumn day. The skies over Farmingdale were as blue as indigo and as clear as a mountain stream. In all, it was a good day to be alive to be flying.

Supremely confident after his brush with unprecedented g force—and after discovering his little trick to counter its effects—Collins felt more than ready for his ultimate run. It turned out, however, that the XF2F wasn't quite set: During the previous day's next-to-last demonstration, the combination of speed and pull-out had flattened a portion of the plane's belly faring. The damage, fortunately, was not structural.

As Grumman personnel reshaped and braced the faring so they could proceed with the day's test, Collins chatted with a Navy commander just up from Washington. When Collins related the gut-tearing effects of heavy g, the Commander suggested yelling during pull-out. It tightens the neck and abdominal muscles, he told Collins, holding the blood long enough to delay unconsciousness and loss of sight.

It seemed silly, but the Commander was serious—as was, apparently, another onlooker who was perhaps too quick with a cautionary tale about heavy g. Several years before, the onlooker said, an Army test pilot had unknowingly pulled too many g: perhaps as many as twelve or even fourteen. That guy had ruptured his intestines and some blood vessels in his brain. He was out of the hospital now but he was no longer the same. To put it mildly, the onlooker told Collins, the guy was a little bit goofy.

Well, Collins thought to himself as he watched the repaired XF2F finally being wheeled out to the runway, you have to be more than a little goofy just to go up in the first place.

———

When he finally took to the sky that afternoon, Collins climbed the XF2F up to eighteen thousand feet. Then he rolled and pushed over. On the way down, Collins once more heard the engine's mounting whine and the intensifying whistles and whooshes of wires, wings and tail surfaces. Gasping for both oxygen and straight thinking, Collins kept his focus on the instrument panel's dials and flickering needles, all but heedless now of sky or ground.

Thirty seconds into the dive, after watching the altimeter wind down beyond eight thousand feet and the speed indicator needle's crawl towards terminal velocity, Collins shifted his gaze to the accelerometer.

Knowing he had to horse it up to 9 g, Collins used two hands to pull back at the control stick. Because of the intense vibration (so strong now both sky and ship seemed to be on the verge of imploding), the stick resisted his grasp, almost as if it were plugged into high voltage.

Collins was now crushed into his seat and his vision darkened and retreated into no more than a pinpoint. Collins had planned to yell, even scream, but now he entirely forgot to.

Before Collins's vision finally eclipsed, he thought he saw the accelerometer needle edge past 9. Collins's retreating senses signaled he was going to overshoot g.

As he let up on the control stick, Collins felt its electric pulse ease. He also felt the pure dense lead of his body lighten and, with it, the unwinding of his brain stop and his vision return, brighten and broaden. He could see the altimeter reading six thousand five hundred feet. Astoundingly, everything around and about him seemed intact.

Collins was certain he'd wrapped it. Indeed, after landing and turning the plane over for inspection and calibration, he learned he had. Even the visiting Navy commander was impressed, admitting excitedly: "Boy, I thought you were never going to pull that out!"

––––––

It would be another few mildly harrowing days before Collins finally completed his 1933 Grumman contract. Having piloted the XF2F through its manufacturer site demonstrations, Collins and his plane were next routed to Navy turf: testing facilities in DC and Dahlgren, Virginia. There Collins demonstrated takeoffs and landings, combat acrobatics (snap-rolls, spins, inverted flight, even true Immelmanns) under different load conditions and, to cap it off, two more of the 9 g pull-outs from high altitude terminal velocity dives. (Grumman and Navy personnel now seemed to assume it was just another stunt that Collins had long ago mastered.)

Although Collins flew under the scrutiny of what he knew to be Grumman aircraft's most exacting critics (twenty or so Navy aviators from an F4B squadron that might someday be flying this new fighter), all went remarkably well. When it was over, freelancer Jimmy Collins got his payday and Grumman's enduring gratitude. More important he returned to his family and his life. For the XF2F's manufacturer, meanwhile, the biggest hurdle still lay ahead. And the stakes, both in terms of money and prestige, were enormous.

————

As a stimulus to help America's industrial economy through the Great Depression, Congress had passed the National Industrial Recovery Act of 1933 (NIRA). NIRA in turn had set up the Public Works Authority (PWA), an administrative vehicle to initiate construction projects as well as fund projects by other government entities, including the military. Seven million PWA dollars would go to the Navy to procure new aircraft under a decidedly modest "1,000 plane" program.

Although the Fertile Myrtle had already garnered Grumman an important advantage, the decision on this new contract would be especially consequential. Boeing Aircraft, the manufacturer of the Navy's F4B, also had an entrant in the courtship: the XF6B. Just as Grumman's new model had been put through its performance paces at the hands of a company pilot, so had Boeing's. Now the XF2F and the XF6B were set to go head-to-head.

While Grumman engineers could reasonably point with pride to their nifty cutting-edge design, in the end it would be the visual evidence of a few moments in the skies over Norfolk, Virginia, with Navy test pilots behind the controls and BuAer's top brass looking on, that would decide the issue.

4

TERMINAL VELOCITY

In early 1934 the Navy's Norfolk Air Base was little more than an expanse of flat, grassy field. But while Norfolk lacked paved runways and all but the most basic aviation facilities, it was nonetheless the site of the high stakes showdown between the XF6B and the XF2F and, by extension, their two manufacturers. Boeing, the odds-on favorite, had a relationship with the U.S. Navy dating all the way to 1917. Grumman, the small, aggressive upstart, was challenging Boeing's near lock on the design and production of Navy fighter aircraft.

Watching intently and conspicuously from the sidelines were two men who might be most instrumental in deciding the showdown's outcome. Given the considerable contrast between the two manufacturers, it was fitting that the two men, though alike in their tall, lean frames, made their own study in champion-contender contrasts.

The older of the two was well into his fifties and wore a bespoke three-piece suit and a flat brim fedora. The younger, still shy of thirty, was bundled in shapeless flight coveralls. But while age and apparel may have accentuated their physical contrasts, it could not totally account for them. So ingrained, for example, seemed the older man's demeanor that it could only have been his birthright. Youthful ambition and stubborn pride had hardened into a regal cantankerousness with the coming of age, stature and power. His piercing stare and a way of standing and moving that telegraphed impatience made it obvious that the man seldom tolerated disagreements or wastes of his time. He had battled for power and stature. He was not about to concede what he had accumulated—and he was intent on accumulating more.

Meanwhile, his younger companion's demeanor was anything but stern or contentious—and betrayed no signs of ever becoming so. Instead, his loosed-limbed appearance seemed to be cobbled from mismatched pieces that somehow melded into a better finished product. His too-small head sat atop a frame that appeared (even padded by flying gear) too skinny. His face was pinched but easily crinkled into a winning smile. His small, angular jaw was set beneath a pair of almost plaintive hound-dog eyes. Overall, the appearance was of someone who, to the extent he succeeded in the world with what other talents he possessed, did so on the strength of his congeniality.

Outward appearances aside, the contrasts between the two men also extended to their places in the increasingly overlapping worlds of the U.S. Navy and aviation itself. Rear Admiral Ernest J. King, BuAer's newly anointed top dog, represented what the Navy had been and perhaps also what it might become when war struck. Meanwhile, to the extent that pioneers such as Charles Lindbergh and Jimmy Collins embodied the daredeviltry of pre-war flying, so men such as Navy test pilot Lieutenant John S. Thach embodied a likely—though still formative—scenario for its future. While Lindbergh and Collins were solo virtuosos, Thach was a consummate ensemble player poised, if he survived, to excel in the teamwork of combat flying.

————

Ever since his USNA days, Rey King had always seemed to gravitate to promotions and controversy. During his senior year he reached the rank of Cadet Lieutenant Commander, then the highest cadet ranking possible. But King never climbed this or any ladder by overly ingratiating himself with those above, below or even on the same rung.

During King's time Annapolis was a neglected institution with shabby facilities, dubious academic standards and a faculty—comprised mostly of junior officers fresh from sea duty—who taught their cadets by rote and seemed perpetually at odds with them. At the core of the experience—especially for first year plebes—was a traditionally harsh campaign of bullying and psychological manipulation administered by upperclassmen and the school's ominous Department of Discipline. The idea behind this Spartan regimen was to subject cadets to the kinds of intense stress experienced at sea and in wartime. Tradition held that those who didn't crack in the cauldron emerged equipped with unflinching instincts toward duty, obedience, leadership and honor. It was Rey King's type of place.

"Temper? Don't fool with nitroglycerin," the Academy's Lucky Bag annual warned about King when he graduated fourth in his 1901class. The same temper was to nag his otherwise steady climb through the ranks. He advanced—both in assignments and rank—despite his tantrums, although in the process he made legions of enemies. Later in his career, for example, when King attended the Navy's War College as part of his grooming for admiral, he resisted any inclination to soften his image, his tongue or his pen. King's thesis about the influence of "National Policy on the Strategy of War" brimmed with pedantry—as most War College theses did. But its language was also unflinching and unusually blunt.

Written during the 1932 presidential election, it decried America's "traditional (and habitual)" failure to adequately prepare for war. There was plenty of blame to go around. He pointed to American society ("the inability of the average individual . . . to understand the interplay of cause and effect not only in foreign but in domestic affairs"); democratic principle ("which tends to make everyone believe that he knows it all") and even representative government (as putting a "premium on mediocrity" and encouraging "the defects of the electorate").

Small wonder that King's reputation and opinions often clashed with government bureaucrats and elected officials. When testifying before Congressional committees, King, despite efforts to restrain himself, sometimes flew into ugly, inarticulate rage. Such incidents did him no good, either with Congress or the Navy.

When he needed to, King could muster grace and seductive charm ashore. (Off-hours he could do better—or worse. Despite a long-time marriage and a brood that included six daughters, King's bouts of "play time" drinking and debauchery bordered on the scandalous.) On balance, the storm within him seemed to blow best at sea.

This reality likely accounted for the relatively smooth velocity of King's early career when he served aboard battleships and cruisers and even captained a destroyer. Despite some telling incidents of drinking, carousing and unyielding disputes with peers and even superior officers, King was savvy and strategic when it came to garnering plum assignments. During World War I his indefatigable staff service earned a Navy Cross. King demonstrated that he was at his best with the pressure on and mannered politeness set aside.

Following the war, sensing a career opportunity in a relatively new seagoing branch, King moved into submarines. After an abbreviated training course at the Navy's New London Submarine Base, he was flag officer for a sub division before assuming command of the entire base.

King's success during this particular detour had at least something to do with the nature of the fledgling sub service: the interruptions from above were few, giving room for King to stamp his authority. But King also proved his worth in a crisis. Indeed, his greatest plaudits came in response to catastrophe: the grim, thankless and occasionally harrowing business of salvaging sunken submarines.

———

In 1926 another such opportunity presented: a chance to transfer into aviation as CO of aircraft tender *Wright* (AV-1) at the behest of Rear Admiral William A. Moffett, the first—and thus far only—Chief of the Bureau of Aeronautics. Congress that same year had passed a law requiring the COs of aviation commands to be flight-qualified. Although, as an interim measure, senior officers could qualify by taking a shortened "naval observer's course," King chose instead to earn his wings. At age forty-eight and already ranked a captain for five years, King dutifully journeyed to Pensacola for aviation training.

In fall 1909, while still an engineering lieutenant aboard battleship *New Hampshire* (BB-25), King had witnessed a demonstration flight over New York Harbor conducted by none other than Wilbur Wright. Like most of the audience on hand for the event, including Assistant Secretary of the Navy Franklin D. Roosevelt, King had been impressed. But, unlike virtually all of the much younger and more junior members of his 1927 Pensacola flight class, King was not impassioned by aviation.

Nor was he a born pilot. Instead, he went about flying the way he did everything else: by the book. He followed procedures and was ever calculating and careful. After logging the minimum total flight hours and solo flight hours needed to qualify, King received his wings of gold in May 1927. He joined the coterie of what would soon be known as the "Pensacola Admirals," brass-hat latecomers who often took seniority and position over younger airmen.

When his tour aboard *Wright* ended two years later, King fully expected to command a carrier. Instead, he went ashore and directly into the arms of controversy. Appointed BuAer's Assistant Chief under Moffett, King quickly wore out his welcome. After repeated hot-tempered disputes over bureau policy and the best use of personnel, he soon found himself shunted off to become CO of Norfolk Air Base.

Redemption at sea came the following summer when King at last received orders as CO of *Lexington*. As much as his rough demeanor ever allowed, King reveled in this particular command. Originally laid down as a battle cruiser, *Lexington* was instead refit as an aircraft carrier. It was one of the newest and mightiest ships afloat, part of a small fleet segment that now comprised *Saratoga* (CV-3)—another battle cruiser convert—as well as the aging *Langley*. King commanded and conned Lex with regal disregard for any other ships that operated with her. But he also established and rigorously enforced standards for its airmen and sailors that made the ship a taut and gleaming showcase.

His success aboard *Lexington* earned King his War College tour and with it the leisure to compose his plain-spoken thesis. But then, as if not fully heeding the lessons that Rey King's track record ashore was trying to teach them, Navy brass once more installed him in the halls of bureaucracy. King wanted to stay in aviation and the occasion of Moffett's untimely death in an April 1933 airship crash gave him a means. King's aggressive and heavy lobbying—literally during the days of his predecessor's funeral and interment—secured him the appointment as BuAer Chief. It propelled King to the top of the Navy's aviation branch and simultaneously "fleeted" him up to rear admiral. Among the rivals bobbing in his wake was another Trade School Alumnus, Captain John H. Towers. Although seven years younger than King, Towers had the distinction of being Naval Aviator No. 3.

While Towers had twenty years of operational flying experience, King, though now seven years a naval aviator, had virtually none. It was Towers who had taken King on his very first aircraft flight at a time when pilots—and passengers—sat in chairs (without seat belts) amidst fabric-covered wings, wooden frames, wire stays and the sputtering exertions of primitive piston engines.

To make matters worse (at least as far as Towers was concerned), the two men had also crossed swords. Fuming at King's typically unseemly behavior during an evening social event at the Coronado Hotel, Towers had taken King aside and directly confronted him about it.

In the years ahead Towers would bemoan it as the one great mistake of his career. Little did he understand that King never carried grudges about outrageous behavior—his or others'—during party time.

———

The 1921 creation of the Bureau of Aeronautics was due in no small part to the headline-grabbing advocacy of a relentless adversary: Colonel Billy Mitchell of the U.S. Army Air Service. Mitchell argued forcefully that future conflicts could be fought and won solely by strategic land-based bombers and he campaigned for the formation of a separate, independent air force.

While Mitchell eventually self-destructed in a court martial, Bureau status offered some insulation from the disruptive poaching of other outsiders. At the same time it also kept hostile insiders at bay, not least "Gun Club" admirals who saw aviation's value solely in being the "scouting eyes" of the Battle Force.

By 1933, BuAer, like nearly everything else about the U.S. military establishment, had fallen on hard times. The Bureau's staff was housed on two floors of the Navy Department headquarters on Constitution Avenue. Its fifty naval officers, most of them aging lieutenants, had just absorbed a 15 percent pay cut, but were glad to be employed. To remain inconspicuous to appropriation cost cutters, the Navy men usually wore civilian dress, making them virtually indistinguishable from the Bureau's one hundred civilians. Perhaps alone among them, their new bureau chief Rear Admiral Ernest J. King stood out.

Though he too wore civilian clothes in and around Washington (including a fedora to disguise his baldness), the ever-stylish King had his suits and uniforms hand-tailored by Brooks Brothers.

————

As a Navy test pilot, Lieutenant Thach had flown both Boeing's XF6B and Grumman's XF2F. Having squadron experience with earlier Boeing models, Thach was more familiar with its name brand. However, truth be told, he was more impressed with the Grumman prototype. Still, Thach knew that he couldn't let his preferences sway his work. And he also knew he didn't have to. Whether he piloted the Boeing or the Grumman, Thach simply had to fly the plane full out. The truth should reveal itself—God help them all if it didn't. Leave the bureaucratic pull and tug to Rear Admiral King and the rest of the brass.

Certainly, given the consequences involved, there was going to be some jockeying over the contract even today. In an effort to short-circuit any fuss from the Boeing and Grumman representatives about pilot even-handedness, test protocol had the pilots rotating between the two aircraft and even sitting out certain flights. Leave it up to the company men, though, to use any perceived disadvantage as a pretext to cry foul. Sure enough, during the very first demonstration, a seemingly straightforward side-by-side test to see which aircraft could take off first, controversy erupted.

Thach piloted the XF2F during this particular round and, when his plane easily beat the XF6B aloft, he should have let the result speak for itself. Instead, he surrendered to a boneheaded impulse. Rather than just circling back to land, Thach couldn't resist making a diving pass at the XF6B, then still in the midst of its takeoff. As expected, the Boeing men became unglued, howling that Thach was showing off and demanding another go. They got it—this time with Thach and the other pilot swapping places—but with the same embarrassing result.

―――――

Since beginning his test pilot tour in the summer of 1932, Thach's main responsibility had been split between rough water testing of experimental seaplanes and evaluating new carrier aircraft prototypes from an ever-changing assortment of aviation start-ups.

In the process, Thach had piloted more than his share of flying bricks. That said, the fierce competition for military dollars in lean economic times had simultaneously winnowed the manufacturer ranks while improving their offerings. Firms were now even required to conduct their own stringent manufacturer tests (under Navy scrutiny) before shipping their prototypes down to Norfolk.

Being a military test pilot meant steady work for the likes of Thach, but not necessarily less danger or hardship. Much of Thach's extra flight pay, for example, went to costly insurance premiums.

Still, there were compensating factors. Navy test pilots were positioned for better assignments later on. They also had some input on the design factors—the stall speed and turning capabilities of carrier aircraft as one example—that helped their brother pilots in operational squadrons. Perhaps most important, pilots like Thach got first crack at flying the aircraft that might someday reach the fleet.

―――――

In some ways, John Thach, a native of Pine-Bluff, Arkansas, straddled the otherwise incompatible worlds of freelancers such as Jimmy Collins and military careerists such as Admiral Ernest King.

Thach, like King, was an Annapolis graduate. So was his older brother James, a 1923 alumnus. During his own years at "Trade School" (which by then had quadrupled the size of its student body while vastly upgrading its facilities and academics), the younger Thach lived in James's shadow. Because James, a footballer, was called Jim or Jimmie during his Academy years, scrawny John—who preferred be called Jack—was promptly labeled "little Jimmie."

If Thach and Collins shared a common nickname, there were a couple of other similarities as well. Despite the stresses involved in bringing test pilot risks into a relationship, both men were married, though Thach and his wife Madalyn (the daughter of a San Diego physician) were still new-lyweds without children. The two pilots were also remarkably near in age: Thach had been born on April 19, 1905 (the third of four children born to a high school principal father and school teacher mother)—just shy of a year following Collins's April 25, 1904 birth date.

Beyond that, however, the flight paths (and fates) of the two pilots—one a civilian stuntman, pacifist and working class activist, the other an aspiring military lifer—scarcely touched. Collins's lone wolf sensibility was vastly, if not completely, at odds with Thach's already evident fascination with aerial teamwork and combat tactics.

———

Since graduating in June 1927 (by the skin of his teeth, though in an academic setting much stiffened since King's time: Thach stood 494th in a class of 579), John Thach had nursed an interest in aviation. At the time, Annapolis graduation was a primary requisite for selection to Navy flight training, but only in tandem with passing another hurdle. The U.S. Navy's prestige arm was its Battle Fleet—the battleship-cruiser Gun Club where most high-ranking admirals (among them Ernest J. King) had first cut their teeth and gotten their sea legs. Two years aboard such capital ships was the first step for virtually all Trade School hatchlings. Thach punched his own ticket with stints aboard battleship *Mississippi* (BB-41) and then *California*, his older brother's ship.

While in San Diego and still aboard *Mississippi*, Thach (who had already received some flight orientation at Annapolis) managed to obtain a slot in elimination training, so-called because it culled the few that displayed flight aptitude from the many that didn't. Jimmie Thach showed immediate potential, soloing after ground school and just six hours of instructor aerial practice.

Finally receiving orders to full flight training in 1929, Thach earned his naval aviator wings in January 1930. Soon afterwards he joined Fighting Squadron 1 (VF-1B) stationed at San Diego's NAS North Island, then a poor relation to the Army Air Corp's more spacious (and more generously paved) Rockwell Field.

Pensacola had not provided Thach (or its other graduates) with any more than cursory training in fighter aircraft and tactics. New aviators usually arrived pretty raw, leaving it up to squadron veterans to show them the ropes. But Thach, in his year and a half with the squadron, learned quickly.

At the time, the VF-1B "High Hats" were renowned for flying a nine-plane stunt formation during which the wings of their biplanes (at first Boeing single seat F2B-1s, but later Curtiss F8C-4 Helldivers) were joined by manila line. At air shows and other demonstrations, the High Hat aircraft took off, gained altitude, did loops and then landed, all the while tethered together. Its pilots had also pioneered aerial dive-bombing tactics, earning them the new nickname "Hell Divers" as well as stunt roles in a 1931 Clark Gable, Wallace Beery movie of the same name.

In many ways, "Hell Divers" was a Navy production. The film was scripted by Frank W. "Spig" Wead, himself a pioneering U.S. Navy aviator who had been paralyzed in 1926 after a fall down a staircase. Given Wead's indisputable credentials, the Navy agreed to cooperate fully with the project. At least up to a point: the film's display of carrier arresting gear and aircraft tail hooks was considered confidential and was left out of the final cut.

To his relief, given his boneheaded lapse earlier that morning, Jimmie Thach sat out what proved to be day's final test between the XF2F and XF6B. It was a carrier landing ground simulation. In turn, each plane was to approach a portion of the landing strip rigged with arresting wires. Then, with flaps down, wheels lowered, tail hook deployed and flying just above stall speed, each plane was to land within a length of strip equal to the dimensions of a carrier flight deck.

It was, of course, an indisputable test for a would-be carrier aircraft. But it was also a test with multiple dimensions: minimum distance, but also style points. Time after time, with King and Thach (both carrier air veterans) looking on, each aircraft landed within the allotted space. But in the process—also time after time—the Boeing plane scraped the ground with a wing before its wheels ever touched down.

Soon King—who was already becoming known as the "Adamant Admiral"—had seen enough. Brushing aside the pleadings of the Boeing men, he promptly climbed aboard his aircraft for the trip back to Washington. Boeing—though it would continue to produce aircraft, and especially bombers, for the Army, had fallen out of favor with the U.S. Navy.

————

In January 1935, even as the first production run of the F2F-s were being delivered to the Navy, Grumman's brain trust realized it was no time to rest on their laurels. The F2F-1 was giving the U.S. Navy just what it then needed—a fast, rugged, maneuverable, and carrier-capable single-seat fighter with retractable landing gear. The F2F's small wing span—only 230 square feet—also made it ideal for below-deck storage on aircraft carriers.

Pound for pound, the F2F-1 was the best fighter aircraft of its time. But Boeing was hardly going to give up the chase, and the production F2F had also displayed some flaws. Minor blips included its cramped cockpit and a tiny bit of directional instability. Much more troubling and potentially devastating, though, was the F2F-1's tendency to whip into a spin whenever it stalled.

At high altitude this tendency was of little immediate consequence; all biplanes could make quick recoveries when their noses dropped and speed increased. In a landing approach, however, especially onto a carrier flight deck when pilots were already dealing with so many distractions, stability just above stall speed was essential. Accordingly, as soon as the F2F-1 went to production, Bill Schwendler and his team jumped immediately to the task of removing the flaws in hopes of further cementing the Navy's hard-won allegiance.

The result was the rollout of the XF3F that same March—and with the rollout an immediate call to secure Jimmy Collins's services.

————

In October 1934 Collins had gone to Buffalo, New York to test a new Curtiss fighter-bomber for the Navy. While there he wrote a letter to his sister, out West: "I got to thinking it over," he told her, "and thought I wouldn't come back because it was a dangerous job, and then poor Archer would be out of column. So I playfully wrote one for him in case I got bumped off. Thoughtful of me, don't you think? I never got bumped off. Too bad, because it would have been a scoop for Arch."

Arch was Archer Winsten, a *New York Post* journalist (whose 'In the Wake of the News" column featured offbeat stories) who had been trying to persuade Collins to write a guest column for him. Winsten, it seemed, was an avid reader of Collins's similarly offbeat articles about aviation in the rival *Daily News*.

Jimmy Collins's entree to newspapers had come via Joseph Medill Patterson. Patterson, an enthusiastic amateur aviator who had taken flight lessons from Collins, was also the founder of the New York *Daily News* (in 1919) and the man who had first adapted Britain's racy style of tabloid journalism to American newspapers. Something of a professed socialist in his earlier years, Patterson had written muckraking articles for *Collier's*, then a prominent weekly. In 1935 Patterson even helped conceive *Terry and the Pirates*, a syndicated comic strip featuring the breathless exploits of aviators and adventurers in a smoldering Far East. Patterson may have had *Terry* already in mind when he hired Collins and gave him *Daily News* space several days a week to write features under the "Flying Stories" rubric.

Collins's Flying Stories were pithy and pungent, though sometimes outlandish. Their vignettes enabled everyday readers, many worn down by a dismal economy, to thrill vicariously to the exploits of devil-may-care adventurer-flyers. It mattered little that these men (and a handful of women) and their way of life was even then heading towards extinction.

For *Daily News* readers Collins wrote about aerial stunts, close calls and disasters; about quirky aircraft and unpredictable weather; and about starlit skies and forbidding terrain. Above all, though, Collins introduced his readers to a zany cadre of legendary aviators who—save for Collins's one-time Army flight school buddy Charles Lindbergh—were virtually unknown to the man and woman in the street.

Like Collins, each of these pilots was capable of amazing feats and outrageous behavior while venturing, every day it seemed, into the jaws of disaster. And each, like Collins, was also fatalistic about his profession and uncertain personal future.

There was, for example, Eddie Stinson, who once flew a cross country demonstration of a German aircraft being evaluated by the U.S. Post Office. Whenever Stinson thought his motor was running rough, Collins wrote, "he reached down under his seat and pulled out a bottle of gin. He took a long swig and listened to his motor again. It had smoothed right out." It took Stinson, Collins had heard, "the whole quart of gin to smooth that motor out and get that ship over the mountains and onto Curtiss Field."

Another, an old airmail pilot named Dean Smith, explained a long absence by telling how he had gotten "tangled up with a load of ice" during a flight over the Allegheny Mountains. Continuing to lose altitude no matter what he tried, Smith finally gave up:

"So I said, 'Here, God, you fly it awhile,' and turned her loose and threw my arms up in front of my face".

"I guess it must have been tough, because He cracked her up. He piled into that last ridge outside of Bellefonte."

Collins's contract called for ten manufacturer demonstration flights of the XF3F prototype from Grumman's Farmingdale field. The first eight were flown on Wednesday, March 20 and each went routinely. The plane was overall a bit larger than the F2F with a bigger engine and a number of aerodynamic refinements, including a hoped-for fix to the troublesome stall-induced spin. With Collins at the controls the ship had handled and performed beautifully. At the end of the day Collins had pointed to a few needed changes in rigging and alignment. These were made that same night and the plane was ready to go for the final two test flights on Friday.

That same day, in the latest of his Flying Stories features, Collins updated his readers on the progress of the tests. "I'll let you know how I make out."

Although Thursday was an off day, Collins again returned to Farmingdale, this time bringing his young son with him. A picture was taken with the two posing in front of the XF3F, the boy bundled in boots, a striped knit sweater and matching wool skull cap. Collins, meanwhile, is resplendent in slacks, tie and jacket, his dark, pomaded hair slicked back in movie star (or test pilot) fashion. The angle of the picture clearly shows the detail of the Grumman landing wheel undercarriage mechanism and, behind both of the Collins's heads, the heavy-duty stays that brace the XF3F's upper and lower wings. Jimmy Collins—a heavy smoker—brandishes a cigarette between the fore and index fingers of his right hand and he seems to be using the fingers to call the boy's attention to the photographer's camera.

One of the Grumman field personnel has apparently given the youngster a turnbuckle, the sort of hardware that might be used to secure a guy wire or spar. While glancing momentarily, the boy seems much more interested in the turnbuckle than he does in the camera.

Thursday's edition of the *Daily News* also includes a "Flying Stories" article and in it Collins ruminates on the ironic fate of a one-time college fraternity brother named Zep Shock. Shock, a somewhat undersized football player, liked to kid Collins about his flying ambitions. "Here's to Jimmy Collins," Shock would toast every night at dinner. "The average life of the aviator is forty hours."

"That was eleven years ago," Collins wrote in his final paragraph, "and I'm still flying. Poor Zep made the regular team the next year and got killed playing football."

———

Friday, March 22 found both Roy Grumman and Jake Swirbul in Washington on Navy business. However, head designer Bill Schwendler was on hand for what was to be, over the course of the last two flights, a series of dives and pull-outs. The day's very last evolution was to be a terminal velocity dive ending at 5,000 feet with a 9 g pull-out.

Dusk was gathering as Collins last took to the sky in the XF3F and, after climbing, kicked into his final contract dive. "It was practically right over our head," Schwendler would recall later. "The first thing we heard was the engine winding away."

The next thing the ground observers realized was that the engine had dislodged from the plane. Separately, the engine and propeller were coming down while "over there was the rest of the airplane with no engine on it."

They looked on anxiously, hoping to see Collins bail out.

———

Jimmy Collins had prefaced his "scoop for Arch"—the article he had mentioned to his sister in a letter the previous October—with the following:

"The next words you read will be those of James H. Collins, and not 'as told to' although you might say ghost written."

"I am dead," were its first words.

———

Schwendler and the others raced to the grounds of nearby Pinelawn Cemetery. "We got over there quickly and there he was."

Collins's body was still trapped in the cockpit of the XF3F, which had crashed into a stand of trees (and, not apparently, as some sources had it, into a tombstone.)

Its vee-gee recorder, later recovered, indicated that Collins had actually pulled over 14.5 g in his fatal dive. The XF3F's air frame had partially disintegrated; parts of it were found as far as five miles away. The aircraft, undoubtedly succumbing to stress, had first failed where two lower wing panels joined beneath the fuselage.

Grumman executives were devastated by Collins's death. But, grief aside, they were also rightly worried that this crash might well prove to be a fatal blow to their contract with the U.S. Navy. Those worries only seemed to deepen when, after a quick design fix (stronger engine mounts and panel fittings), a follow-up prototype failed a spin demonstration in the skies over Anacostia.

That particular plane was not seriously damaged nor, as it turned out, was Grumman's standing with the Navy. BuAer immediately requested a new prototype, which this time was design-tested using a NACA wind test tunnel—the first of its kind.

This prototype, with Bill McAvoy once more at the controls, met both the manufacturer and Navy test standards and was accepted by BuAer in June 1935. What was to become the F3F-1 matched the 230 miles per hour speed of the F2F-1 with higher range and ceiling but somewhat slower climb rate.

The F3F-1's most important advance (in a way, what Jimmy Collins had given his life for) was its aerial stability. It gave its pilot a steadier platform for aerial combat.

5

SAMURAI

In 1937, when he graduated from the Imperial Japanese Navy (IJN) Fliers School at Tsuchiura, fifty miles northeast of Tokyo, twenty-one-year-old Saburo Sakai ranked first among the twenty-five students in the Thirty-eighth Noncommissioned Officers Class. That those twenty-five graduates had been winnowed from an original class of seventy—culled in turn from a pool of 1,500 applicants—made the achievement all the more remarkable.

Sakai's keepsake from the event was an emperor's silver watch, but he saw his crowning reward as having at last surmounted the trials and personal shortfalls that had plagued his youth, brought shame to his family and, perhaps worst, betrayed his heritage.

Modest as was his family's modern day status—for several generations they had been merchants and farmers in and around the small city of Saga on Kyushu, Japan's southernmost home island—Sakai's ancestors had occupied the highest strata of the four castes dividing Japan's medieval society. They had been *Samurai*—warriors and liege servants to the feudal lord of Saga and, as a result, free from life's mundane responsibilities, including survival in the leanest of times.

That secure status eroded considerably with the nineteenth century establishment of a more western-style Japanese government and a conscripted national army. Some *Samurai* adapted to the emerging egalitarianism but many others did not. These former *Samurai*, Sakai's grandfather among them, either became destitute or eked out a subsistence living doing manual trade or farm work. Even after acquiring a one-acre farm plot, the grandfather, his children and their children struggled to sustain the humblest of livings.

Circumstances were only made worse by the death of Sakai's father when Saburo, the third of four sons (there were three sisters as well), was only eleven. Sakai's mother and older brothers were saddled with the backbreaking farm work. Meanwhile, though Sakai had excelled in his studies at the government-funded primary school, it was inevitable that he would have to end his schooling thereafter and join his family in the fields.

Then fortune smiled, or seemed to.

Sakai's uncle, a successful official in Japan's Ministry of Communication, generously stepped in, offering to adopt him and bring him to live and attend secondary school in Tokyo. It was a remarkable opportunity but, while Sakai found a loving home with his uncle's family, he also found himself struggling to adjust to Tokyo's bewildering pace while, for the very first time, falling behind in his studies in the face of much stiffer competition. Desperate to succeed, he only made things worse by falling in with a crowd of inept and unruly classmates. In time his uncle gave up on him, sending a disgraced Sakai back to his impoverished small-town home. He returned as a failure not only to his family but to the entire population of Saga.

But at just such times, when everything about his life looked hopeless and Sakai hovered on the verge of tearful despair, it was Sakai's mother, a *Samurai* in her own right, who would forcefully yank him back from the brink. "Shame on you," she would admonish him, "Do not forget that you are the son of a *Samurai*. Tears are not for you."

———

During the train ride from Tokyo back to Saga, Sakai had happened to see railway station posters calling for IJN volunteers. Although he was largely ignorant of events unfolding in an increasingly martial Japan (which was then already on the brink of a prolonged war in China), Sakai promptly made his decision. When he joined the IJN in May 1933, Sakai, then just sixteen, saw it as an escape.

Rather than providing an exit from his plight, however, Sakai's enlistment instead shackled him to an unremitting ordeal of harsh discipline and monstrous physical and psychological brutality that defied even the vilest imagination. Beatings, most often administered to bare buttocks in the middle of night by stick-wielding petty officers, were the common nostrum for infractions in discipline or training—large or small, individual or group.

The perpetrators of this "paternalistic discipline" were mostly older men with no hope of further promotion. The frustrated petty officers seemed to be channeling the very savagery they had once experienced firsthand. Meanwhile, the victims were constrained from crying out in pain by the certainty that such displays of weakness would only deepen the ordeal. Even losing consciousness was no escape: it simply meant a dousing with cold water and the continued rain of blows.

Such beatings, along with the excruciating pain, raw red welts and gruesome bruising they produced, were the most enduring aspects of what was otherwise a months-on-end blur of sleep-starved instruction, study and drill. Even for hardy recruits like Sakai, IJN recruit training was a crucible that left deep scars on both body and mind lasting far beyond the early stages of "boot camp" indoctrination. Indeed, Sakai did not finally emerge from the prolonged, all-encompassing nightmare until he became a petty officer several years later.

The experience left Sakai with an abiding hatred for senior IJN petty officers (ironically, a cohort into which he'd now been promoted.) At their hands the recruits had been turned into little more than human cattle, never daring to question orders or doubt authority—automatons who obeyed without thinking. It made him long for an environment free of such ingrained brutishness.

Now at the other end of his "training," Sakai felt he'd been entirely robbed of his youthful ego and ambition—with nothing built in its place. But, surprisingly, the crucible's scars had not entirely ruined him. Somehow, in his case anyway, it had also toughened him and called forth a will to endure that may have been at the core of his *Samurai* heritage. Most immediately, it had also recouped the stature Sakai thought he had lost forever in the eyes of his family, his village and especially his uncle in Tokyo.

His renewed pride seemed to burst all bounds when Sakai applied for flight training and learned, much to his astonishment, that he'd been accepted. Unlike many other countries' armed forces, the backbone of IJN's aviation program was its cadre of enlisted petty officer ranks—men just like Sakai. By the end of the decade, enlisted aviators would comprise more than ninety per cent of the roughly 3,500 active IJN pilots. Entering a regimen that stressed quality over quantity and was notorious for its stringent standards and high washout rates, Sakai would emerge as one of the most skilled and painstakingly trained combat pilots in the entire world.

In the spring of 1937, St. Louis, Missouri–born Edward H. O'Hare was in the final stages of what was, by any comparison, a vastly more mannered naval training apprenticeship than Saburo Sakai's. Now imbued with a much better reputation, the United States Naval Academy at Annapolis produced fully prepared officers and gentlemen, sending each of them forth on elaborate, at times insular, paths of seagoing, command, diplomatic and staff tours—the foundation for the leadership pinnacles of America's Navy.

That said, its midshipmen weren't entirely insulated from the effects of the Great Depression. Indeed, during its worst years, there was extra incentive for midshipmen (plebes and upperclassmen alike) to excel in studies, athletics and military training.

Class standing was always an important determinant of assignments, promotion dates and even choice of living accommodations; it followed a graduate as surely as his name, rank and serial number. But with military budgets tight, the consequences of tumbling into the bottom half of a graduating class could be serious. It might mean receiving an undergraduate degree but no officer's commission. Bottom-rung graduates, in other words, risked being cashiered, at least temporarily. For young men who had trained to be naval officers but instead landed "on the dole," this could be a bewildering, unsettling outcome.

O'Hare was probably better prepared than most to adapt to the Academy experience. Prior to entering Annapolis in 1933 (the same year of Saburo Sakai's IJN enlistment), O'Hare had spent his junior high and senior high years at the Illinois–based Western Military Academy. Following graduation from Western, he had also attended Cochran-Bryan, a Maryland preparatory school specializing in shoring up the faltering academics of prospective midshipmen.

Several years after his Academy graduation, O'Hare confided to his younger sister Patsy his doubts that he could ever again endure anything as grueling as plebe year; owing to his own experience, he assured her, no son of his would ever attend a military academy. Nevertheless, relying on his comradeship with a tight coterie of classmates, his penchant for aquatics (he enjoyed sailing and swimming and, for a time, was a part of the Academy's water polo team) and just enough concentration on academics, O'Hare made it through to his June 3, 1937 graduation. O'Hare's final ranking was in the perilous lower half: 255th out of a graduating class of 323 (the original plebe class numbered 417). But, with the economy showing signs of revival and, more important, the world edging closer to all-out war, he received both his degree and his commission as a U.S. Navy ensign.

———

Perhaps no one was prouder of O'Hare's graduation than his father Edgar Joseph O'Hare, known as EJ. At an age where future generations of young American males would often just be shrugging off years of parental estrangement, Edward (eventually to be known as "Butch") and EJ's relationship had always been strong—albeit competitive and sometimes physical. Adolescent wrestling bouts between Edward and EJ that left the O'Hare household in shambles (at least in the estimation of Selma, EJ's wife and Edward's mother) gave way to less combative but equally competitive hunting and fishing outings.

The father-son relationship had even survived the surprising 1932 divorce of EJ and Selma—just as Edward began his prep year at Cochran-Bryan. It had been EJ who had first steered his son into military schooling, in no small part because of EJ's own fascination with flying and the possibility that the boy might get involved in military aviation. To be sure, Edward had at first been none too enthused about the disciplined regimen or the months of separation from his family; but he had more than adapted.

By 1937, of course, EJ's own career path had been set. EJ's first-generation Irish father owned a St. Louis restaurant but, after working for brief periods in the restaurant and then the produce business (his father-in-law's profession), EJ helped establish a prosperous trucking company.

All the while, though, EJ had his career sights set higher. In March 1923, after passing the Missouri bar examination without benefit of formal legal training, EJ became a licensed attorney. While he did some trial work, EJ applied his legal skills more enthusiastically to business entrepreneurship. It was through these interests that EJ became involved in the lucrative, somewhat shadowy greyhound racing industry; at first assisting with the patent for a racetrack "mechanical rabbit," and then opening his own dog-racing business, the Illinois-based Madison Kennel Club.

It was Madison Kennel that established EJ's name and reputation, though in an arguably corrupt business milieu. Of more enduring consequence, it gradually pulled EJ ever deeper into the orbit of a younger but decidedly more influential entrepreneur: Chicago's Alphonse "Scarface" Capone, the kingpin of perhaps the biggest and most ruthless criminal enterprise of its day.

———

Saburo Sakai experienced his first aerial combat in September 1938 in the skies over southeastern China. It was a humbling event, one he was lucky to escape from alive and in one piece. And, in its own way, it revived the shame and self-loathing that had tortured him as a naive schoolboy and then as an IJN recruit.

Since his graduation from Navy Fliers School in 1937 (part of the 11th Combined Air Flotilla), Sakai, now promoted to Naval Aviation Pilot, Second Class, had rotated through service air squadrons at Oita and Omura Naval Air Bases in Northern Kyushu, where he received specialized training in carrier landings, instrument flying, aerobatics, formation flying and air combat.

To Sakai the aerobatic and landing techniques required of carrier pilots were particularly difficult to master. Although he passed minimum qualifications for both (and was astonished at the high skill levels of even those who didn't), he also understood that only the best naval pilots— most with a minimum of eight years' experience—were ever rotated to carrier duty. Still, for his part, Sakai's performance had earned him selection for ground-based fighter training, meaning that instructors judged Sakai to be particularly skilled and aggressive.

Sakai was then transferred to Formosa for the second big stage of his preparation: Joint Aviation Training with a land-based fighter group. His stay in Formosa, however, turned out to be brief. With combat in the "China Incident" raging across multiple fronts, there was a pressing demand for fighter pilots—even green ones like Saburo Sakai.

———

That demand became even more evident soon after Sakai reported to the 12th Air Group in southeastern China. The Group commander had a reputation for being openly contemptuous of inexperienced pilots and purposely excluding them from meaningful missions. That made it all the more surprising when Sakai, easily the greenest of the new fliers, spotted his name on the roster of fifteen fighter pilots scheduled for a regular patrol over a big enemy airfield near Hankow.

At the time, Japan's China War fighter pilots flew the Mitsubishi Type 96 carrier fighter plane—later identified by Allied forces with the code designation Claude.[1] The Claude was an open-cockpit, fixed landing gear monoplane, slow in speed and limited in both range and altitude.

Flying that morning through clear skies at 10,000 feet above the re-

---

1. See chapter notes for an explanation of the conventions used by the Allies for naming Japanese aircraft during World War II.

markably green landscape of Hankow, Sakai's formation was suddenly jumped by enemy fighters. Before Sakai knew it, one of them was on his tail; and all at once, exposed to the cold wind, straining for oxygen at such high elevation and his ears buzzing with the noise of his engine, the months of meticulous training that Sakai had absorbed all but flew out the window.

In the midst of his feckless, fumbling distress, Sakai could remember only one thing: stay on the tail of his wingman. Somehow he managed to strap on his oxygen mask and advance the throttle. But then, even as his engine responded, Sakai found himself still losing ground: like an idiot, he had forgotten to jettison his auxiliary fuel cell. As others of the Russian-made (and, it was assumed, Russian-piloted) fighter aircraft swooped in to fire at him, Sakai was saved only by the last-second interventions of several veteran Japanese pilots.

Even when Sakai inexplicably ended up close-in on the tail of an enemy fighter, his dormant instincts still betrayed him. Pulling the control-stick trigger to fire the Claude's two machine guns, nothing happened. Sakai cursed the guns for having jammed until he realized it was he who'd simply neglected to arm them. Somehow regaining a favorable position on the fleeing prey, Sakai again squeezed the trigger for all it was worth. This time he connected. The Russian plane first spewed black engine smoke and then dropped helplessly towards Hankow's greensward. Momentarily elated at having scored his first aerial kill, Sakai then realized to his consternation that he had taken himself out of the rest of the fight. In that one prolonged burst, he had expended all of his ammunition.

Sakai returned from his introduction to air combat appropriately humbled but still alive—thanks chiefly to the last-second maneuvers of formation veterans. In a very real way they had set him up to learn some life-and-death lessons. They'd dangled him as bait only to rescue him from the enemy predators' hungry jaws. It was a cruel initiation rite that could easily have spelled his end.

Once this latest blush of humiliation subsided, however, Sakai realized he'd also successfully passed through his baptism by fire. Not only had he survived it, he had, in the process, claimed a kill. He'd earned the right to paint a blue star on the fuselage of the Claude fighter.

The blue star was, however, a deceptive emblem of Sakai's prowess. The 12th Air Group pilots shared a pool of aircraft and enemy fighter pilots had no way of telling whether their Japanese opponent was a storied veteran or a lowly acolyte. Nevertheless, it gave Sakai great satisfaction—and set him apart.

———

That June, when Grumman's XF4F-2 prototype lost out in a three-way competition to become the U.S. Navy's first monoplane fighter, Roy Grumman and Jake Swirbul were not overly concerned. After all, it hardly signaled an end to their long-term prospects. The F3F biplane was still in production and would be for another year. The company's diversification into civilian aviation was picking up steam as the economy improved—though it brought with it the need for additional capital and the burden of outside shareholders.

But perhaps most promising was the fact that the Navy was continuing to hedge its bets. Even though BuAer had contracted for fifty-four production models of the stubby, barrel-shaped Brewster F2A-1 Buffaloes, Navy representatives insisted that work continue on the Grumman prototype. They still liked what they saw from Bethpage. For their part, Grumman and Swirbul were certain they had the better airplane.

———

The XF4F had first taken shape as a biplane, a slightly smaller, somewhat faster would-be successor to the F3F. The XF4F-1 had reached the mock-up stage when Brewster's monoplane design first caught the Navy's fancy. Bowing to the inevitable, Grumman scrapped the XF4F-1 and set off on the long, arduous process of designing, prototyping, testing and refining the XF4F-2.

The midwing monoplane prototype that first rolled out for testing in September 1937 was all metal save for its fabric-covered control services and was powered by a nine hundred horsepower Pratt and Whitney engine. During initial tests the XF4F-2 had reached a V max (the new trade name for an aircraft's highest rated speed) of two hundred ninety miles per hour, almost fifty miles per hour faster than the production F3F. And, although the XF4F-2 had a somewhat lower ceiling than its biplane predecessor, it had a better climb rate.

The XF4F-2's problem, one that dragged on for a year and nearly doomed the plane in the process, was its Pratt and Whitney engine. The fourteen-cylinder Twin Wasp, which was integral to the airplane's design, at first displayed a tendency to burn out its crankshaft bearings. But then, even as Pratt and Whitney engineers solved the crankshaft glitch, another, more fundamental obstacle emerged. The Navy, it turned out, wanted an F4F engine that incorporated a two-stage, two-speed supercharger.

———

The supercharger is essentially an air compressor that forces larger volumes of air into engine cylinders at higher altitudes, thereby increasing engine power and efficiency. Single-stage superchargers were then standard in military aircraft, but BuAer was now insisting on two-stage capabilities for different altitudes—what soon came to be called "low blower" and "high blower."

Engineering a two-stage supercharger was no mean feat. High compression raised airflow temperature and high blower settings too often caused premature detonation of the highly compressed air-fuel mixture. For a long time, Pratt and Whitney was stumped. Meanwhile, as the engine maker labored to solve the problem, the XF4F design languished.

Finally, though, in the waning months of 1938, Pratt and Whitney engineers came up with an ingenious solution. They devised the first "intercoolers," engine components that cooled the compressed air flow between low blower and high blower stages.

By the time Pratt and Whitney's new 1,200 horsepower Twin Wasp engine was ready for production, the XF4F-2 design had already been reworked to incorporate it. To account for the extra 600 pounds of engine weight, the prototype's wing span had been increased to 38 feet (from 34) and its wing tips squared off.

The revamped XF4F-2 first took to the air in February 1939 and, after manufacturer tests, was turned over to the Navy a month later. Navy tests subsequently clocked a V max of 333.5 miles per hour—three miles per hour faster than Grumman's own projections. In August 1939, fully two years after initially contracting for the XF4F-2 prototype, BuAer signed up for fifty-four production F4F-3s.

———

At 3 p.m. on November 8, 1939—a typically cool mid-fall afternoon in the Midwest—EJ O'Hare left his office, climbed into the driver's seat of his new black Lincoln Zephyr, started the engine and drove away from Chicago's Sportsman Park. On this day, EJ—then age 46—had reasons to be both proud and cautious.

Topping the list of his successes may well have been the progress made by his eldest child and only son Edward. After his 1937 Naval Academy graduation, followed by the obligatory two years of service detour into the

U.S. Navy's battle fleet, Edward was now in phase three of aviation flight training at NAS Pensacola—the acknowledged Jerusalem and Mecca of U.S. Naval Aviation. Squad III, as it was called, would entail all-weather instrument flying in monoplane trainers.

Near the end of October, EJ had received a particularly enthusiastic letter, boasting: "We made darn good time in going through II as it only took us eight weeks and it is listed as a fifteen week course." At age twenty-five, Edward was now fully on the path to the military aviation career of his— and his father's—aspirations. His next stop would be advanced training (formation flying, aerobatics, gunnery, carrier landing practice and night flying) after which he would receive the coveted "wings of gold."

But EJ, the aggressive, pragmatic businessman with an admittedly suspect past, no doubt had priorities as well when it came to his cautions. Between 1925 and 1931, EJ had operated dog racing tracks in Chicago, Boston and Miami; and during that flush period, EJ had never seemed to stray far from his secretive partner-protector relationship with the infamous Al Capone. The truth, however, was that he had strayed very far indeed: at some juncture EJ had gone undercover for the U.S. Treasury Department.

EJ's motives in collaborating with the T-Men were likely several. In 1926, he'd served several months in federal prison on a Prohibition-related charge. Although the charge was later overturned, it was clear the authorities were watching him. EJ likely also contemplated the eventual— and perhaps lethal—demise of his relationship with Al Capone, not to mention the consequences the demise might have for his family (including a son he wanted to see enrolled in the U.S. Naval Academy). Whatever the combination of reasons, EJ's covert role ultimately figured in Al Capone's 1931 conviction and imprisonment for tax evasion. Capone, set for release on parole that very November, was now ailing (he suffered the ravages of advanced-stage syphilis) and was "retiring" to Florida. But it was all but certain that he'd somehow learned of EJ's turncoat role and that revenge would top the list of Scarface's post-incarceration to-dos.

———

On this autumnal afternoon, as EJ O'Hare's northeast-bound Lincoln passed the intersection of Ogden and Talman Avenues, it was overtaken by a second, almost identical Lincoln, this one carrying two sinister men. As the two cars approached Rockwell Street, now traveling on either side of the largely deserted avenue at speeds approaching forty-five miles-per-hour, the barrel of a sawed-off shotgun edged through the window of the pursuing Lincoln. The range was so close that the double-barreled shotgun's blasts, rather than entirely shattering O'Hare's driver's side window, instead punched twin two-inch diameter holes in it. On the other side, most of the buckshot entered EJ O'Hare's head and neck.

The two cars stayed parallel for perhaps another second or two. Then EJ's car—with a dying man behind the wheel—vaulted the right hand curb, brushed a street light pole and then rolled sixty feet down an embankment into a hood- and grill-crumpling collision with a trolley pole.

That same day, EdwardO'Hare—now known as "Butch" to his friends and family—learned of his father's death by telegram and was immediately granted fifteen days' compassionate leave. The next morning, he and his instructor climbed into the dual cockpits of a Vought SU-1 biplane. After a four-hour fifteen-minute flight interrupted by a fuel stop, the SU-1 touched down at St. Louis' Lambert Field.

Butch O'Hare returned to Pensacola on November 25, but he would wait another three days before resuming his phase three training. His daily report on November 28 noted: "Refresher period after long lay-off."

———

VF-3 Flight Officer Jimmie Thach had a foolproof method for showing newly minted aviators joining the squadron that they still had a lot to learn. Absent enough suitable aircraft, available flight decks and seasoned instructors, for example, the new pilots' time in the U.S. Navy's Advance Carrier Tactical Group (ACTG) training was not all that useful. The ACTG graduates were especially deficient when it came to gunnery training—VF-3's acknowledged strong suit. In Thach's mind it took a good fifty hours of gunnery practice followed by another thirty to fifty hours of section and division-level team practice to make a pilot combat ready.

Perhaps most alarming of all, none of the new pilots seemed to grasp a fundamental—even axiomatic—truth about the physics of air-to-air combat: If one of two aircraft—each with equal performance characteristics—held altitude advantage over the other, its pilot should be able to get on the other's tail and (absent any human mistakes) win the aerial dogfight anytime.

Given such human mistakes, however (and Thach assumed they were endemic to rookie pilots and even pilot transfers from other squadrons), the reverse was also true. Experienced pilots (all aircraft performance factors equal) could give away altitude advantage and still turn the tables every time. To prove his point—and rub the veneer of cockiness off his new pilots—Thach had created the "Bitching Team," a cadre of VF-3's best and most experienced pilots.

The team's routine was simple and unvarying. Thach or another of its members—there were usually about four at any one time—would take each newcomer aloft and give him all the altitude advantage he wanted. Then, after being cued, the rookie would dive, try to get on the veteran's tail and stay there long enough to have gotten in a good shot. In a way it was like a rookie rodeo cowboy trying to ride one of the circuit's meanest bulls.

The results were always the same. Thach, or another member of the Bitching Team, inevitably reversed the advantage. At times it seemed like they could do it while munching an apple or reading a newspaper. By summer 1940, now a full year into his VF-3 tour, Thach was convinced the Bitching Team's ability to turn the tables on hotshot rookies was nearly as axiomatic as the law of altitude advantage.

The NAS San Diego-based squadron that Thach (now age thirty-five and with tours in patrol and scout planes as well as in fighters and test piloting) had joined in 1939—first as gunnery officer before moving up to operations—had a solid if somewhat meandering pedigree. Initially organized in 1921 as Combat Squadron Three, the unit had morphed through a series of name and mission changes (for example, from flying fighters to flying dual purpose fighter-bombers and then back) until, in 1937, the squadron settled into Fighting Three (VF-3).

Fighting Three took its number from the hull number for *Saratoga*, VF-3's home afloat. Despite its new "fighter only" identity, the squadron still retained its iconic "Felix the Cat" insignia: a malicious black feline (then famous in newspaper comics) toting a bomb with a lit fuse. Most recently, with Thach as squadron gunnery officer, VF-3 pilots' expert marksmanship earned them the 1939 fleet gunnery trophy (the "Top Gun" equivalent of its era) and the right to sport the E for excellence on their aircraft. At year's end the squadron had begun a transition to new aircraft. Their reliable but now antiquated Grumman F3F-1 biplanes were traded in for Brewster Buffalo F2A-1s—monoplanes with greater speed and heavier armament.

On July 1, 1940, when he walked into the NAS San Diego hanger emblazoned with "Fighting Three" and a giant depiction of Felix the Cat, Butch O'Hare reported first to Lieutenant Commander Warren W. Harvey, VF-3's CO. Harvey, known as "Sid" to his friends and most of his squadron, was respected and well-liked. At thirty-nine, however, Sid Warren (Trade School Class of 1924) may also have seemed ancient to O'Hare. If so, it was another reminder that slow promotions were the way of the pre-war Navy, even in the aviation branch.

After a quick introduction to VF-3 XO Lieutenant Charles Quinn, O'Hare's next likely stop was the hangar office of Flight Officer Jimmie Thach. Their meetings were probably more frequent, longer and more comprehensive. Thach, after all, bore responsibility for integrating new pilots into the squadron's organization as well as its training and day-to-day routine.

———

In the roughly seven months since EJ's funeral, Butch O'Hare had completed the final phases of his Pensacola flight training. After finishing Squadron III and two months of Squadron IV (service seaplanes and lumbering multi-engine "big boats"), he had moved at last to Squadron V. V was the final phase, where trainees learned the special skills of a serving naval aviator: instrument flying, acrobatics, advanced formation flying, precision landings, dive-bombing and (Thach's passion) aerial gunnery.

In reviewing O'Hare's file, Thach could see that O'Hare had learned from some of the best, including (for fighter familiarization and primary combat training) Lieutenant James H. Flatley, Jr., whom Thach knew well. Jimmy Flatley, Green Bay, Wisconsin–born and then just shy of thirty-four, was a 1928 USNA graduate. In addition to their nearly identical nicknames (Flatley's natural, Thach's more contrived but still inescapable) the two also shared very similar flight careers. Flatley's next logical move—as was the case for Thach—would be promotion to a squadron XO. Flatley even rivaled Thach's gunnery expertise.

On first assessment, Thach also detected a few things in O'Hare's personal background that resonated with his own. Thach liked that O'Hare was both an athlete and a hunter—signs not only of physical skill but also of competitiveness and persistence. Furthermore, the hunting background seemed to have paid specific dividends. While O'Hare's flight training evaluations were good but not exactly off the chart, he did stand out in one all-important area: fixed aerial gunnery.

The proof, of course, would show in the air. Thach decided right then that he would be the one to process young O'Hare through the Bitching Team grinder. Appropriately enough, they would both be "riding" Buffaloes.

———

When Saburo Sakai returned to Japan late in the fall of 1939, he was treated like a triumphant hero. Despite being wounded on the ground during a surprise enemy bombing, Sakai had climbed into the cockpit of one of the few undamaged Claudes and taken off in pursuit of the Chinese twin engine bombers. Although Sakai only managed to damage one bomber, his singlehanded exploit earned him instant acclaim.

During his first weeks back Sakai allowed himself to bask in the adulation of his family and his village. Soon enough, though, he grew impatient, both with the slow process of recuperation and with the fact that it held him back from keeping pace with his glory-wrapped comrades back in China. Most by now were combat aces with at least five aerial kills. Meanwhile, Sakai had shot down only the one Russian aircraft—and that victory was all but a fluke.

In January 1940, Sakai was finally cleared for flight status at the base in Omura. The following month he was even sent to Osaka for exhibition flights. But, after returning to Omura, Sakai became stuck in a monotonous day-to-day training routine, a process that dragged on through spring and summer. It was not until April 1941 that Sakai finally received new orders, transferring him back to the 12th Air Group, this time in Hankow. The prospect both surprised and energized him: Hankow was now Japan's main advanced air base. Being assigned there meant he'd be close to the action.

Another surprise awaited him when he reached Hankow. Expecting to see the familiar stubby, open cockpit Claudes standing on the airfield, he instead saw strange new planes. Their graceful clean lines, their enclosed cockpits and retractable landing gear made these low wing monoplanes unlike any other Japanese fighter aircraft Sakai had seen. They were the new Mitsubishi Zero fighters—Zero-sens. [2]

An eyeful even as it posed motionless near the runway, the Zero-sen proved to be an even greater marvel when it took to the air. It had almost twice the speed, climbing rate and range of the Claude. And, in addition to its cowling-mounted light machine guns, the Zero-sen boasted twenty-

———

2. See the chapter notes for more detailed information on the history and naming conventions for the Zero.

millimeter wing cannons. Most important, it was a dream to handle. The slightest finger pressure brought instant response, especially during turns. Equipped with these aircraft, it was small wonder Sakai's former comrades in China were racking up kill after kill.

To be sure, the Zero-sen's spectacular performance capabilities had required some trade-offs. Mitsubishi, in order to meet the IJN's exacting design standards for speed, endurance and maneuverability, had striven to keep the aircraft as light as possible. This meant that some weight-heavy features like armor plating and self-sealing fuel tanks—features now being introduced into other nations' military aircraft—were not incorporated in the final product. But to Sakai and the other 12th Air Group pilots, these seemed matters of little consequence. They already flew aircraft that lacked these features; the Zero-sen was, by contrast, such a vast improvement even without them. Some pilots even questioned the need for the Zero-sen's bulky and unreliable radio equipment. Their flying skills and experience, they reasoned, could easily offset the questionable value of such untested innovations, especially if they slowed the Zero-sen or compromised its stunning maneuverability.

———

The first opportunity for the Group to try out its amazing new aircraft seemed to beckon when its pilots were posted to French Indochina.[3] Japanese Army occupation troops holding key ground positions needed top-cover protection. Just getting to the scene of the action, the pilots learned, required a nonstop eight hundred mile flight to Hainan Island, an incredible cross-ocean flight for a fighter aircraft.

As it turned out, the Zero-sens, equipped with auxiliary fuel tanks, covered the distance from Formosa to Hainan easily. However, once the pilots arrived, they found disappointingly little to do. Eager to put their new aircraft to the test, Sakai and the others ran into virtually no ground or aerial opposition. Japan's military steamroller seemed all but unstoppable. It was not until the Group was finally posted back north to Hankow that brighter prospects at last seemed to beckon. China, the pilots had reason to believe, would be a more suitable arena in which to parade their fabulous—and deadly—new beasts.

———

3. Now Vietnam.

6
LOW BLOWER

LIEUTENANT JIMMIE THACH WAS ONE OF THE U.S. NAVY FIGHTING SQUADRON COs sifting worriedly through the intelligence coming out of China in the spring and summer of 1941. Much of the dope came from official reports such as the awkwardly titled yet authoritative Fleet Air Tactical Unit Bulletins (FATU). But there were also compelling eyewitness accounts from on-the-scene experts such as Claire Chennault. The former Army pilot, now an advisor to the Chinese, was assembling a mercenary fighter unit called the "Flying Tigers" to take on the Japanese.

FATU and eyewitnesses like Chennault touted a Japanese fighter far superior to anything the United States Navy or Army could put in the air. The claims for its capabilities were jaw-dropping: a 3,500-plus feet-per-minute climb rate; a blistering V max ranging somewhere between 322 and 380 miles per hour; and incredible maneuverability, especially in turns. If actual capabilities were only half of what they were hyped to be, Thach knew the Japanese plane could easily best the Brewsters the squadron flew—and even the new Grumman F4F Wildcats beginning to reach the fleet.

———

Jimmie Thach's rise in rank, first to VF-3 XO and then CO, was meteoric—for the U.S. Navy anyway—but also laden with tragedy. Thach had only recently stepped up to XO when, in October 1940, Sid Harvey died of a heart attack en route to Great Britain to observe the air war. When Thach was unexpectedly promoted to CO it made him, at age thirty-five, one of the very first 1927 Academy graduates to "fleet up" to a squadron command.

As summer began, VF-3 was just wrapping up what was to have been a three-month cruise aboard *Enterprise*. Two circumstances had presented the opportunity: VF-6, Big E's nominal fighter squadron was ashore for transition from F3Fs to F4Fs, while Sara was set for overhaul in Bremerton. Thach's pilots had looked forward to going to Hawaii but in the end the deployment had brought little beyond frustration.

VF-3's Brewster F2A-2 Buffaloes—a more powerful but heavier model than the F2A-1 predecessor—was been prone to landing-gear failures. Now, however, the planes' Wright engines were also acting up, resulting in sometimes crippling damage to master rod bearings. Halfway through the cruise, fewer than half the Brewsters were operational—and those that could fly were in no condition for tactical exercises. In the end, VF3's sea operations had been curtailed and the squadron sent ashore to Ford Island where some semblance of combat readiness could be restored.

———

Now that VF-3 was back at North Island (there to begin the switch from the now much-despised Buffaloes to Wildcats), Jimmie Thach finally had the opportunity to do more than just fret about the unsettling news concerning the new Japanese fighter. Freed for a time from the nonstop obligations that went with carrier flight ops at sea, Thach could ponder tactics at day's end and put his thinking into practice the next morning.

In what would become a nightly routine after dinner in the small rental house in nearby Coronado that he shared with his wife Madalyn and their toddler son, Thach would seat himself at the kitchen table and simulate flying formations, using matches to represent aircraft. He normally used a pile of about thirty matchsticks: eighteen to stand in for the aircraft authorized at the time for each U.S. Navy fighter squadron; another dozen or so to represent enemy fighters.

Thach realized that he and his pilots might someday soon encounter Japanese fighter pilots whose aircraft topped theirs in speed, climb rate and turning radius—the paramount variables that any fighter pilot had to work with. Although the prospects were potentially overwhelming, Thach took it a step at a time. He turned his thinking first to cruise formations, the formations flown en route to a battle. This was when fighter aircraft were most vulnerable to surprise attack. He worked well into each night, often setting the task aside only when Madalyn reminded him that he had to fly the next morning.

———

A relatively new naval aviation building block Thach could use in his thinking—and matchstick manipulation—was the two-plane section. Just that July, after two long years of fleet-wide discussion and in-flight experimentation, followed by frustrating cycles of procrastination, debate and last-minute reversals, Vice Admiral Bill Halsey, in his capacity as Commander, Aircraft, Battle Force (ComAirBatFor), ordered each U.S. Navy fighting squadron to organize itself into three six-plane divisions, each in turn composed of three two-plane sections.

This was a distinct break from the past—a holdover literally from the World War I aerial battles over the trenches in France. Up until the new mandate, U.S. Navy fighting squadrons flew three-plane sections comprised of a section leader and two wingmen flying astern of the section leader and usually flanked to either side.

Many seasoned naval aviators, among them Thach, had concluded that three-plane sections were cumbersome and dangerous for single-seat aircraft flying at ever-increasing speeds. The wingmen had to concentrate on staying in formation and avoiding collision in the event of sudden, tight turns. The threat of combat, in effect, required each pilot to have another set of eyes. Even in practice, each seemed busier avoiding the other pilots than he was looking out for enemy fighters. Pilots in two-plane sections were simply better able to execute radical turns. In combat the wingman's job became elemental: stick with his leader and protect his tail.

Beyond the two-plane section, however, not much else about combat formation flying had changed. Division-size cruising and fighting formations had remained static—albeit adapted to incorporate the new building block. It was with these six-plane formations that Thach's kitchen-table analysis took issue.

———

Thach knew that a fighter pilot had only two options when he was jumped unexpectedly by an aerial marauder: either turn and run; or turn directly *towards* the assailant, trying to fight back or spoil his opponent's aim. He also knew—or at least assumed from the intelligence he'd seen— that it would be futile to try to escape the new Japanese fighter. It was just too fast, too nimble.

The only real option then was to counterattack and fight—in the process upsetting the opponent's aim and maybe, like a gunslinger, getting in a snap shot. If this was to be so, then the six-plane (three-section) formation was fatally flawed. The formation's combat maneuvering almost inevitably turned into a strung out tail chase. Each wingman stuck to the tail of his leader and each leader was in turn pinned (at least by doctrine) to the section ahead of him. In effect the six planes became one big target snake.

Successive rounds of matchstick jockeying finally convinced Thach that better combat formations could be built around combinations of four aircraft (two mutually supportive sections) rather than six. That alone was a revelation. Thach figured he was on to something, but he knew that he had more nights ahead of him. Thach also knew that when he finally worked out a solution, its perfect test bed would be the skills of Butch O'Hare. O'Hare was, after all, the only pilot who had ever been able to turn the tables on the Bitching Team.

————

When he had first taken Butch O'Hare aloft the summer before, Thach had given O'Hare the usual altitude advantage before dropping to lower altitude to await the fun.

It never came—the fun that is—or at least not in the way that Thach anticipated.

O'Hare didn't make any rookie mistakes during the flight. Instead, he came right in on Thach's tail and stuck there. Despite trying all the tricks in his repertoire, Thach could not shake O'Hare. If this had been life or death combat, Jimmie Thach realized, he would have been a goner.

Thach (a tad humiliated but also excited about the prospects for this new VF-3 pilot) gathered O'Hare and both returned to the field. As soon as he was out of his cockpit, Thach went looking for Rolla Lemmon, VF-3's gunnery officer and a charter member of the Bitching Team. Lemmon, although just an ensign and a full decade younger than Thach, was a seasoned veteran who had earned his wings in one of the earliest classes of naval aviation cadets.

Being caught in an enemy's sights—even in practice—was an eerie new sensation. Even as he told Lemmon about the flight with O'Hare, Thach's pulse was still racing. He wanted each of the other Bitching Team members to have their own go. "He's pretty good," Thach warned Lemmon. "I'll even wager you a little bet that he'll get on your tail the first time and stay there."

"Oh, they never do," Lemmon replied with knowing resignation, thinking perhaps that the older Thach had lost his edge. "Where is he?"

Soon enough, Rollo Lemmon was back on the ground, flush-faced and marveling at O'Hare's performance. Clearly he had a good sense of timing and an innate grasp of relative motion. But it also seemed as if the rookie had been born with the ability to fly his aircraft smoothly and efficiently. Unlike any other greenie, he didn't try to bull his plane around, didn't create unnecessary drag. Each of his moves in the air was what it should be—just enough.

Eventually, perhaps to spare VF-3 veterans any further humiliation, Butch O'Hare was quietly added to the ranks of the Bitching Team.

———

If twenty-two-year old Alex Vraciu was not the most honored undergraduate in DePauw University's Class of 1941, he was arguably its most famous.

Vraciu (pronounced like "cashew") was a native of East Chicago, Indiana, a rail and steel "melting pot" city just west of Gary and the southern tip of Lake Michigan. The first-generation son of Romanian immigrants, Vraciu had enrolled in DePauw University, a small Methodist college in Greencastle, on the strength of a full academic scholarship. Throughout his time at DePauw, Vraciu had been remarkably energetic, active and involved. Helping to make ends meet by working a series of campus jobs, the sociology major also competed in track and football, and was the social chairman for his Delta Chi fraternity chapter. But Vraciu's indelible reputation owed less to these activities than it did to the visible imprint of a sophomore year prank.

A DePauw psychology professor named Paul J. Fay impressed on his students—Vraciu among them—the tricks that eyes and expectations could play. Things were not always as seen—or assumed. Inspired by the visual ruses Fay sometimes pulled on the class, Vraciu concocted one of his own. One spring day, Vraciu arranged to have his Delta Chi brothers wait with a tarpaulin below the class's second floor lecture hall. Then, in the midst of Fay's lecture, Vraciu suddenly jumped up, screamed "I can't take this anymore!" and bolted for an open classroom window.

As one coed screamed "Alex! Come back!" Vraciu hurled himself out window. After landing safely on the waiting tarpaulin, Vraciu looked up to see a crowd of horrified students—and one psychology professor—staring in disbelief. The stunt (captured on film by a DePauw public relations specialist tipped off beforehand by Vraciu) made the local newspapers and radio stations and even spilled into the Chicago media. One inspired but goofy prank had firmly cemented Vraciu's reputation as DePauw's resident jokester.

———

Across America 1941, college undergraduates were as captivated as ever by free-spirited campus pranks such as Vraciu's. But they were just as attuned to the ominous cross-currents stirring in the nation and abroad.

Alex Vraciu was no exception. The lives of students on the DePauw campus seemed to exist in what he remembered as a horrible limbo. Students sorted themselves between two camps. Some were isolationists supporting organizations like the America First Committee whose spokesman for a time was the iconic airman Charles Lindbergh. Others, stunned by the brutality of Germany's aggression in Europe and across the Channel, favored providing wartime aid to battered and embattled England.

Whichever cause their hearts supported, most students' heads aligned with the fatalistic thinking then abroad in the nation. In a 1941 Gallup poll of the nation, for example, 85 percent reported being convinced the country would be drawn into the war in Europe. In another poll, two-thirds predicted a forthcoming conflict with Japan.

For male students such as Vraciu, these survey predictions had particular impact. The year before, Congress had passed the Selective Service and Training Act, the first peacetime draft in American history, requiring all men ages twenty-one to thirty to register with local draft boards and, if drafted, to serve in the military.

In light of this, the pragmatist within the prankster that was Alex Vraciu had already taken action. In the fall of his senior year at DePauw, as a means of delaying military service until after graduation, Vraciu had declared his intention to join the U.S. Navy. Figuring that an almost inevitable war was certain to grab him, Vraciu also knew precisely where and what he wanted to be when the time came.

The previous June, foregoing his usual summer job at Inland Steel, Vraciu had instead gone cross-state to Muncie. Working nights at a Muncie restaurant to cover his expenses, Vraciu had participated in the government-funded Civilian Pilot Training Program (CPTP). Through a combination of ground school and instructor flight practice, CPTP (which mimicked similar programs already established in European countries such as Germany and Italy) enabled college students like Vraciu to earn their private pilot licenses.

Vraciu's CPTP instructor was Larry Hirschinger, a former naval reservist who was immediately impressed with Vraciu's knack for flying. After earning his private pilot's license, Vraciu saw his next step clearly. He would become a Navy fighter pilot.

———

Alex Vraciu was soon to find himself—along with so many other young men like him—in a nexus that joined the intense desire to fly with an even more intense and certainly more strategic need for talented military pilot prospects.

Even as Vraciu was beginning CPTP, Rear Admiral John H. Towers was asserting before a Navy Department press conference that: "It's the aircraft carrier that will spearhead the action in the next war."

Sensing both Tower's unease (Naval Aviator No. 3 was no great public speaker) and the sort of firestorm that such a statement might ignite in the Navy's Gun Club ranks and the halls of Congress, one reporter asked him to repeat what he'd just said. Towers promptly obliged.

It was an assertion that earned Towers (who had finally landed BuAer's top job—and his rear admiral's stripes—two years before) instant gratitude among naval aviation's restive ranks. It also garnered him a *Time* magazine cover and with it a front-row-center hot seat in the revived controversy over whether there should be a separate U.S. air force branch absorbing the aviation resources of both the Army and Navy.

Not since the days of Billy Mitchell had the controversy's smoldering "bed of coals" flared so bright. And not since then had the U.S. Navy been as concerned that its air arm might be disturbed.

Tower's press appearance was undoubtedly a staged event. Since fleeting up, Towers was back on the reservation when it came to air matters and the chain of command. His newly subdued behavior even had one probing Congressional questioner demand answers "from Captain Jack Towers . . . and not from Admiral Towers, who is taking orders from too many line admirals."

No matter. Whether he was pundit or puppet, preaching to the pews or the choir loft, Towers' press conference performance gave much-needed publicity to "the finest naval air service in the world." And it seemed to be paying off. The Navy's once starved Bureau of Aeronautics was being granted the wherewithal to play an unprecedented game of catch-up in spending, building, recruiting and training.

A 1938 fiscal year naval aviation budget of 51 million dollars ballooned to 1.5 billion dollars for 1941. With 2,500 naval aircraft on hand, 7,000 more were either on order or authorized. With six aircraft carriers in service (though split between two oceans) and a seventh almost ready for commissioning, eleven more were on order.

A lot of this, and especially the carriers, would take time. Too much time, some openly worried.

Meanwhile, however, of more immediate and direct import to Alex Vraciu (and others like him) was this: A 3,500-man naval aviator cadre at year's beginning was slated to grow to 6,000 by year's end. U.S. Navy aviator ranks were projected to eventually swell to 16,000.

———

By late summer 1941, the 12th Air Group pilots' once high hopes for demonstrating the prowess of their Zero-sens in China combat was proving to be as elusive as it had been in Indochina. The reputation of the new aircraft had clearly preceded them. Enemy pilots seemed to have lost their stomach for fighting. They eluded the Group's Zero-sens at almost every opportunity, engaging only when they clearly had the advantage of surprise or position. While this was in its way a tribute to the Zero-sen's growing reputation, it gave the Air Group pilots little solace. Hoping to somehow force the action, they found themselves foraying deeper and deeper into China.

On August 11, Saburo Sakai was assigned to a penetration mission involving the escort of seven twin-engine bombers originating in Hankow. The Zero-sen pilots linked up with the bombers in a pre-dawn rendezvous over Ichang. The bombers had left Hankow at midnight and the joint formation was next bound on a nonstop eight hundred-mile round trip flight to strike an enemy airfield in far off Chengtu.

For some time the Japanese formation flew through the darkness, using only the whitish meandering line of the Yangtze River Valley below them as a navigation guide. Not until they were over the target airfield did the sky at last begin to brighten, finally enabling Sakai to discern the Mitsubishi G4M bombers' profile. Their fuselages were fat, almost cigar-like (indeed, crewmen called them *hamaki*, "cigar"), the lines interrupted by large glassed-in nose, dorsal and beam machine-gun blisters. The G4M's wings were wide, appearing even more so because of their pointed tips.

The G4Ms were the bomber equivalent of the Zero-sens: fast and light (even with their five to seven-man crews); well-armed (four machine guns were distributed among the nose, dorsal and beam blisters with a tail-mounted 20-millimeter cannon); and capable of long range strikes. They were reputedly as lightly armored as their Mitsubishi fighter cousins; if so, Sakai knew, the G4Ms would need all the protection they could get. Unfortunately—at least as far as the Zero-sen escorts were concerned—there was no enemy fighter opposition to be seen.

————

Just then the Zero-sen flight leader dived for the airfield, the signal to strafe. Below him, Sakai could see Russian fighters moving along the runway with their ground crews scattering like ants and diving into defensive trenches off to the side.

Swooping in at low altitude, Sakai pulled in behind one aircraft just as it lifted off. It made a perfect target; a short cannon burst immediately torched the helpless fighter. Pulling out of a subsequent strafing run, Sakai lined up a shot on a second such plane. Another short cannon burst and it too was gone.

Within minutes there was nothing left to strafe. Climbing back to seven thousand feet, the Zero-sen pilots could see that each of the grounded enemy planes was engulfed in flames. In the background, the field's hangers and shops were also a fiery shambles, the result of the bombers' run. Disappointed as usual at the lack of any real air opposition, the Zero-sen pilots continued to circle the field, hoping somehow that the towering plumes of smoke might yet lure enemy fighters.

Suddenly three of the Zero-sens plunged out of formation, bound, Sakai noticed, for a brightly colored biplane flying just above the treetops. It was evident the biplane's pilot, whether Chinese or Russian, was skilled and crafty. He snapped his slow but agile plane right and left, deftly avoiding the machine-gun and cannon rounds aimed at him.

After their all-or-nothing dives, the first trio of Zero-sens had little choice but to pull up and regain altitude. Sakai and another pilot had by now joined in the melee—the mad pursuit of a mere insect that none of them seemed able to squash. For his part, Sakai had the biplane lined up in his sights and fired, only to have the adversary escape in an exquisite snap roll, spiral and tight loop.

Finally, however, as he neared the summit of a hill west of the airfield, the biplane pilot was forced into a fatal mistake: As he rolled his plane over on its back to clear the summit, he exposed its belly. Once more, Sakai had the plane in his sights. This time he loosed a few cannon rounds that tore through the biplane's floorboards, almost certainly killing the pilot. The plane at once fell off into a wild spin. Though other pilots continued to shoot, the biplane crashed into the hill and exploded.

————

It was over. Sakai had broken his long drought by downing his second aircraft (the two caught in take-off didn't count)—and his first at the controls of a Zero-sen. Hopeful it might signal further and more challenging battles, Sakai was both relieved and excited.

But also badly mistaken.

In fact, the odd episode proved to be the Group's very last combat action in China. Even after moving to a new base further into the Chinese hinterland, its pilots flew weeks of patrols without ever seeing an enemy plane.

Finally early in September 1941, all the IJN pilots stationed on Mainland China were returned to Hankow where, shortly after their arrival, they received an unexpected visit from Vice Admiral Eikichi Katagiri, the Naval Air Force Commander in China. Katagiri told the pilots they would soon be transferred back to Formosa. Without being any more specific, he also told them they would soon embark on an important mission. Sakai, like most, expected that war with the Western powers was finally about to begin.

———

Jimmie Thach's VF-3's pilots were intrigued when, in the fall of 1941, they reviewed the new tactics devised by their CO. In his write-up, for lack of a better term, Thach called it the "beam defense position." Beyond its use of the two-plane section and its logical extension, the four-plane division, the beam defense, Thach's pilots learned, relied heavily on proper aircraft positioning.

Thach had become convinced that positioning held the real key to the tactical puzzle of defending against superior aircraft in a surprise attack.

His reasoning was that in combat (at least under current U.S. Navy fighter doctrine) even four plane multiples could get in each other's way. Sometimes they flew 300 feet apart; at other times as close as 150 feet. Accordingly, they lacked room, either to maneuver or to counterattack effectively if one section or the other was bounced.

Thach had also conjectured that flying line-astern—whether in six- or even four-plane formations—might be a drawback. What, he had wondered, about flying two sections of two line-abreast? And what about spreading out those sections?

For argument's sake, why not increase the separation to the turning radius of the aircraft? In that way, at least, a counterattack would not immediately risk collision.

———

What had seemed elegant in Thach's late-night thinking seemed to make even more sense when plotted out on the kitchen table: Widely spaced and abreast of each other, pilots in each section made good lookouts for pilots in the other. Further, in line abreast, all four aircraft had clear fields of fire: they could shoot simultaneously in the event of a head-on attack.

And what about these options? What if one section, detecting the other section being bounced from behind, immediately turned *towards* the attackers?

What if other section used this very turn as the signal (no time-consuming, enemy-alerting radio warnings needed!) that they were being bounced?

And what if the section under attack at the very same time turned toward their counterattacking buddies?

It was all there to see (though still yet to try): The two sections would cross each other like scissor blades, in the process leaving the enemy attackers—their aim already disrupted—a set of bad options:

Being shot from the side if they pulled out early.

Being shot head-on if they tried to stay on the first targets.

And finally (as if more were needed!) this:

As the two sections continued to reverse turn and scissor—to weave—they made a team ever poised to foil—and to kill—their freelancing opponents.

Thach, even at the moments when Madalyn would have no more of it and ordered him to bed, was enough of a pragmatist to know that anything could happen aloft. That matchsticks and table tops—chess pieces on game boards—made one realm, pilots in fast aircraft and limitless sky entirely another.

––––––––

As they mulled over Thach's descriptions and diagrams, squadron pilots seemed to agree the beam defense position tactics were well worth testing. But "who" was going to stand in for the Japanese and where could they get the aircraft to plausibly mimic the Zero?

Thach was ready with answers for both questions. Butch O'Hare would lead a four-plane division representing the Japanese. And, to approximate the imagined Zero-Wildcat disparity, they'd just do some handicapping.

While O'Hare's "Japanese" Wildcat attackers would operate at full power, Thach's four "American" Wildcat defenders would face agreed-upon limits. A little mark was etched halfway along the throttle quadrant of each plane: Thach's formation could operate up to—but not beyond—half power.

O'Hare's pre-flight instructions were straightforward: Attack from any direction he chose and log the result. How did Thach's beam defense respond? Did it give the "Japanese" Wildcats any problems?

During the first practice flight, O'Hare pulled out the stops, leading his division in "bounces" from every possible direction, trying all the offensive tactics he knew and using his Wildcats to their best advantage. Most bounces, not surprisingly, began at high altitude and came down, attacking either astern or head-on. But O'Hare's aircraft also positioned themselves to use the sun or the shelter of clouds. And, given the presumption of more power and maneuverability, they even tried beam and belly approaches.

To Thach, always flying on the defensive, it looked like a pretty good thing. He knew it was far from being totally realistic. The airplane disparities were contrived, no shots were being fired, and his division pilots were always expecting to be jumped. Still, Thach had chosen O'Hare, VF-3's best pure pilot, to lead the "Japanese." As each attack came, the beam defense seemed to help. All of them were novices, but the weave it created both kept them on alert and ready to counter the attackers' best efforts.

When they finally landed, O'Hare, clearly brimming with enthusiasm, ran over to Thach. "Skipper, it really works!"

O'Hare told Thach that he couldn't make any attacks without seeing the nose of at least one of the "American" planes—meaning the defender could at least get in a shot. Because he was already familiar with the tactic, O'Hare was fully expecting that one of Thach's sections would turn towards him—but he couldn't tell when and he had difficulty anticipating it. Whenever O'Hare got in position to squeeze the trigger, "here you went and turned, and I didn't think you saw me."

That, Thach understood, was the real beauty of the beam defense. There was no need to communicate, no unnecessary delay. You flew along in your section, watching the other section on the beam. When they turned, you instantly realized there was a bandit on your tail. You knew you had to turn in a hurry—and you had the maneuvering room to do it.

Throughout his fighter pilot career, Thach had flown with the assumption that a superior aircraft could knock him out of the air. That was that, unless your adversary was a rookie or a stupid pilot, something you could never assume. Now, VF-3 pilots had something to work on, something to keep them—and their CO—from becoming demoralized.

When they reached Formosa in early December 1941, the pilots from the

IJN's China air groups were organized into an entirely new flotilla and at once began an intense new round of training. They were restricted to base and each day, regardless of the weather, they practiced escort tactics, mass formation flying and strafing.

After learning their targets would be on the island of Luzon in the Philippines, the pilots also confronted hurdles of distance and endurance beyond even those encountered in China. Luzon air bases like Clark and Nichols Fields were between 450 and 500 air miles from Formosa.

In light of the formidable cross-ocean distances, some thought had been given to employing three small aircraft carriers to bring the Zero-sens closer to their targets. But that idea had soon been discarded: the ships could not embark nearly enough aircraft and many of the China pilots were not thoroughly practiced in operating from carriers. Instead, tactics would simply have to be improvised to launch missions directly from Formosa.

Accounting for the round-trip flight distance, the need to be over targets to fight and the additional need to have some fuel in reserve, Zero-sen pilots would have to fly between 1,000 and 1,200 miles nonstop. The Zero-sen had been designed to remain aloft for a maximum of six or seven hours. However, that would have to be stretched to as many as twelve hours, a burden both for the aircraft and the pilots.

The measures devised—limiting cruising speed to 115 knots, cruising ceiling to twelve thousand feet, and propeller rpm's to less than 1,850—were extreme. It meant that during the entire transit, each Zero-sen would hang on the fringe of losing power, stalling, and then perhaps not being able to recover. But the measures were also proving effective. During one practice flight, for example, Sakai managed to reduce his per-hour fuel consumption from thirty-five gallons to only eighteen. The normal fuel capacity for a Zero-s+en was 182 gallons.

To a man, of course, none of the pilots—commissioned and non-commissioned officers who had been trained to obey orders instinctively and many of whom had already been flying combat for years—questioned the motives or wisdom of launching a war against the Americans. They were mostly curious about the opposition they would face. Sakai knew virtually nothing about American aircraft or the quality of their pilots. He expected, however, that both would be better than what he had squared off with over China.

———

In the days immediately after the Japanese attack on Pearl Harbor, Lieutenant Commander John Waldron drove the pilots of Torpedo 8 relentlessly. From their base at Norfolk, Virginia's East Field, the squadron's TBD Devastators flew off on twice-daily four-hour training missions aimed at mastering formation flying and torpedo attack techniques. Waldron also made them fly simulated carrier landings—"bounce drills"—at all hours, night and day.

At age forty-two, Waldron was a good twenty years older than most of the men in his squadron. He'd been born in Fort Pierre, South Dakota and raised on a government reservation where his father traded with the local Indian tribe. On his mother's side, Waldron traced his lineage to the Oglala Sioux, a heritage that earned the tall, rugged Waldron some ridicule (as the class "Redskin" and a "seagoing cowpuncher") throughout his Naval Academy years.

After his 1924 graduation and his obligatory tours at sea, Waldron went on to flight training, earning his wings in 1927. Two years later he married Adelaide Wentworth, a Pensacola native he'd met at a Navy dance. Now the mother of two young daughters, Adelaide had proved the perfect service wife: good-humored, supportive and uncomplaining through frequent relocations and long absences.

Even as John Waldron steadily advanced in his naval aviation career, he continued to weather some ridicule for his intense, hard-driving manner and maverick methods. In wartime photographs he brandished not one but two side-arms—a holstered .45 caliber pistol dangling from a web belt, another tucked in a rawhide-threaded shoulder-holster. Waldron even insisted that his squadron pilots participate in a daily physical fitness regimen.

Despite his eccentricities, Waldron was considered an exceptional air squadron commander, one who stressed readiness and stuck up for the welfare of his men. A few months after the squadron formed in 1941, a new pilot flying a worn-out Brewster trainer had been killed during a carrier landing off Norfolk. Afterwards Waldron had literally marched on Washington, telling BuAer brass he simply wouldn't allow his flyers to go up in such deathtraps. A week later new replacement aircraft began to arrive.

Even with better training aircraft, however, VT-8 still made do with grossly inferior combat planes and aerial torpedoes. Their Douglas-made TBD Devastator torpedo bombers were underpowered and embarrassingly slow: lugging a torpedo, they could scarcely break 100 knots. Lacking cockpit armor and mounting just two Colt/Browning .30 caliber machine guns—one for the pilot, another for the rear gunner—they were also nearly defenseless. Other squadron types—the fighters and dive-bombers—were well along in upgrading their aircraft: the fighter units with Grumman Wildcats, the bombing and scouting squadrons with Douglas Dauntlesses.

Grumman TBFs would eventually be replacing the TBDs, but they were only now beginning to roll off the assembly line. True to form, John Waldron was aggressively lobbying BuAer to move VT-8 to the head of the recipient line. The key question: Would Waldron's boys be able to get the new planes and train with them before they had to go into battle?

––––––

For America's aviation industry, even though the production floodgates had opened well before the Japanese attack on Pearl Harbor, there were still bottlenecks—and a lot of catching up to do. Within weeks of the U.S. Navy's first production order for F4Fs in August 1939, for example, Germany's blitzkrieg had been unleashed against Northern Europe. The Navy, at the behest of the U.S. State Department, had stepped back to enable Grumman to produce 100 carrier-based Wildcats for the French Navy. (When they were ready for delivery the following spring, France was already in German hands and the F4Fs went instead to the British.) F4F production for the U.S. Navy was now just getting back on track.

Grumman's earlier F4F bake-off loss was a thing of the past. The Navy's flirtation with Brewster Aircraft had since faded. (Owing to nagging quality and production problems at Brewster, the Buffaloes would soon no longer roam.) Grumman's Plant Number 2, the site of the truncated grand opening on December 7, had gone on line not only to relieve pressure on Wildcat orders, but also to expedite the production of the new TBFs that torpedo-bomber squadron commanders like Torpedo Eight's John Waldron were hollering for.

For obvious reasons, the new seven-ton TBF was a highly anticipated model. Its V max was a stunning 278 miles per hour and its range, even when equipped with a ton of ordnance, was slightly over 1,200 miles. Both the TBF pilot and his gunner were equipped with .50 caliber machine guns and its third crewman—a bombardier—could fire a .30 caliber belly "stinger." Employing sensitive amplidyne motors devised by

General Electric researchers, the after ball turret was even power-driven to increase response speed and torque.

———

Also solidifying Grumman's position with the Navy was a new priority system that channeled the production of various plane-builders to specific military branches. Under the system, Douglas, Grumman and Vought became prime suppliers to Navy, while Lockheed, Republic and Boeing focused on the Army.

The system was a natural fit for Grumman, which specialized not so much in designing the best possible fighter (or bomber or torpedo) plane as it did in designing the best plane that could work within carrier aviation's exacting parameters.

Even as they refined Grumman designs to push V max, range, climb rate and maneuverability, Bill Schwendler's minions learned to live with a litany of carrier air compromises: a flight deck five hundred to nine hundred feet long and just sixty feet wide; a landing-speed-without power (stall speed) of not more than sixty-eight miles per hour; a takeoff run of not over two hundred feet into a twenty-nine miles per hour headwind; a (nearly contradictory) balance of low- and high-speed maneuverability; the optimization (via short cowlings and prominent cockpits) of pilot visibility for landings.

———

Factors beyond aircraft performance presented ongoing challenges to the progress of carrier aviation. While war gaming of carrier tactics as early as the 1920s demonstrated that numbers were vital, the reality of ever bigger aircraft threatened to collide with the less malleable constraints of flight deck room and hangar stowage capacity.

Building more, larger and more expensive flattops was one way to address the problem. Another, less costly way, was to increase the flight time of existing aircraft. Efforts to reduce landing-launch intervals, for example, led to the innovation of flight deck crash barriers—in essence mid-deck fences that permitted the deck parking of planes on the bow during recovery.

But a third way was somehow to engineer the size and configuration of the aircraft itself—and especially its wings. BuAer had long made wingspan and surface area a factor in sponsoring prototypes. But because greater aircraft power and performance often went hand-in-hand with wing size, trade-offs here could only go so far. The alternative was to accept overall size while reducing storage dimensions. In other words, find ways to equip combat carrier aircraft with retractable wings.

Although compelling at first glance, this "hinging" solution (not so surprisingly) generated other problems—among them greater weight, added height and reduced structural integrity. Working out the trade-offs was a tall order, but the thinking that Grumman engineers—and especially founder Roy Grumman—brought to the situation was unique. Aircraft stowage was a carrier problem, thus a Navy problem and thus, at its heart, a Grumman problem.

Roy Grumman was an intuitive engineer—quite in the way that Jimmie Thach was an intuitive tactician. Grumman understood that the desired result was akin to the way a bird twisted and then folded its wings to conform to its body. The bird didn't hinge its wings so much as pivot them—a more complex means to a more elegant end. The engineering concept, Grumman realized, was a skewed axis—in the case of an aircraft wing, a pivot set in the wing root that jutted out and then swung backward as the wing folded.

To model the concept, Roy Grumman used something akin to Jimmie Thach's kitchen matches—in this instance a trapezoidal drafting eraser (representing the aircraft fuselage) and two metal paper clips (representing the wings.) Grumman first bent the short end of each paper clip until it was perpendicular to the body of the clip. Next, he began sticking the short ends of the two clips into the sides of the eraser (the fuselage), trying different positions until he found the one at which each clip (wing), when twisted vertically, would also tuck snugly against the eraser.

It was simple—or it finally would be when the hard engineering was worked through to ensure the mechanism was functional, strong, light enough and fail-safe (made so by having the extended wing locked into place by a series of pins backed up by a master pin). The resulting Sto-Wing became a feature of the first TBF models. Grumman also began incorporating it into the F4F series.

It turned out that the arithmetic for the F4F Sto-Wing was particularly astonishing: it decreased the Wildcat's wing span from 38 feet to just slightly over 14 feet. This meant being able to accommodate nearly twice the number of Sto-Wing Wildcats in the same space required for the lesser number of fixed-wing Wildcats.

PART THREE

A PRECARIOUS HONOR

7

SANS CELEBRATION

ON DECEMBER 8, WHEN THE NEWLY REFITTED *Saratoga* HURRIEDLY DEPARTED San Diego for Pearl Harbor, VF-3 brought aboard little more than half the complement of Wildcats it was authorized. The problem, Jimmie Thach was told, was a strike-related shortage of a small electronic device used to control the Wildcat propeller's variable pitch. Cold comfort—but with a war underway, Thach would simply have to make do.

From a personnel standpoint, at least, Thach had reason to be pleased. While VF-3 had its share of rookies, on balance the squadron was as experienced and well trained as it could be, short of war. To offset novices, Thach's stable included a good mix of promising yearlings (among them the exceptional Butch O'Hare, now VF3's engineering officer and recently married) and aviation cadet veterans such as Bitching Team stalwart Rolla Lemmon.

Besides Thach and O'Hare, VF-3 also included seven Trade Schoolers. Perhaps the best among these was Lieutenant Donald A. Lovelace, a 1928 USNA graduate with solid experience in utility, torpedo and scouting squadrons—the last as VS-41's flight officer aboard *Ranger* (CV-4). Since Lovelace had joined as XO in early 1941, he and Thach had bonded as friends, colleagues and tacticians. On December 7, for example, Thach and his wife Madalyn had been driving through Coronado headed for lunch with Lovelace and his wife when they first heard about the Pearl Harbor attack on their car radio.

Saratoga's actual stay in Pearl Harbor was short—about enough time to take in the appalling carnage and register the shaken looks on peoples' faces at dockside. It made a startling contrast to the wisecracking bravado so rife aboard *Saratoga*. The ship's sailors and airmen were with few exceptions mad as hell—eager to get out and catch the people that had done this; and supremely confident that they were going to win.

Thach, O'Hare, VF-3's crew chief Willie Williams and a few mechanics went ashore to locate more Wildcats and the spare parts to keep them flying. They found two more fighters (upping their total to thirteen) while newly sympathetic supply officers (along with a bit of midnight requisitioning by Williams' mechs) filled out most of the immediate parts needs. Meanwhile, Thach got the chance to talk with an Army pilot who'd taken on a Zero and lost. He was on the Zero's tail and ready to shoot (the pilot marveled and shook his head), when the Zero simply flipped on its back, got on the P-40's tail and opened fire.

On December 16, her hangars and decks stacked with not only the eighty or so planes of her four air group squadrons (VB-3, VS-3 and VT-3 in addition to VF-3), but also fourteen Brewster Buffaloes of Marine Fighter Squadron 221 (VMF-221), *Saratoga* left Pearl. The carrier and its air group were the centerpieces of TF 14, a fourteen-ship relief force under the command of Rear Admiral Frank Jack Fletcher (a non-aviator) bound for Wake Island. Wake, two thousand miles west and across the International Date Line, had been under siege since December 7 (December 8, Wake time). Its beleaguered defenders had already repelled one Japanese invasion attempt on December 11.

The original plan was for TF 14 ships to shuttle cargo, aviation and troop reinforcements to Wake while evacuating civilians. Given the mood of the hour, one not-so-unlikely contingency was to have seaplane tender *Tangier* (AV-8), loaded with cargo and U.S. Marine reinforcements, run up on the beach. Meanwhile, a second carrier task force—Vice Admiral Wilson Brown's TF 11 centered on *Lexington* and her air group—was to stage diversionary attacks on the Marshall Islands, the launch point of Japanese ground-based air attacks on Wake.

Even as these pieces sailed into position for a December 24 (Wake time) D-Day, momentous events unfolded back in Hawaii. Admiral Husband E. Kimmel, the Pacific Fleet commander whose misfortune it was to be in command on December 7, was summarily relieved pending a stateside court inquiry. Because Kimmel's CinCPac replacement, Admiral Chester W. Nimitz, would not arrive until the end of December, Battle Force commander Vice Admiral William S. Pye took custodial command.

Uneasy in his caretaker role but also privy to new intelligence that

Japanese carrier strike forces had moved in to hasten Wake's downfall, Pye waffled on Kimmel's original plan, first canceling the Marshall strikes, then dispatching Halsey's TF 8 (with *Enterprise*) west for added support, and finally putting the brakes on Fletcher's advance towards Wake.

At 2:30 a.m. on December 23, the Japanese played out their endgame at Wake, this time sending ashore overwhelming waves of special naval landing force troops—the IJN equivalent of U.S. Marines. By daylight, even as Japanese troops mopped up the remnants of Wake's stubborn defenses, Pye conceded the inevitable and flashed recall orders to his task force commanders.

––––––––

Thach, who'd been flying CAP when Pye's recall order came, returned to a flight deck and ready room boiling with indignation. All during transit, VF-3's aviators had made a festive mockery of counting down the "bombing days" until Christmas, but today their anger was more purposeful and their cockiness was pared back. The morning before, Thach's wingman Lieutenant (junior grade) Victor M. Gadrow had been lost at sea after experiencing engine problems, stalling and crashing. Gadrow, twenty-eight and a 1935 USNA graduate, was VF-3's first wartime fatality. In a way, giving up on Wake was cheapening Gadrow's sacrifice.

Word had it that in *Saratoga's* command spaces the mood was even fiercer—bordering, however briefly, on rebellion. Several senior officers urged immediate retaliatory air strikes in defiance of Pearl's explicit recall. Reportedly, Air Task Group (ATG) commander Rear Admiral Aubrey Wray "Jake" Fitch, one of the Pacific Fleet's few experienced aviation flag officers (and no "Pensacola Admiral"), in an effort to avoid hearing the mutinous talk, had stepped off the bridge until cooler heads prevailed. The emotions of most squadron aviators—Thach and O'Hare included—sided with the saber-rattlers. But a few, including Don Lovelace, were more circumspect. "The setup seemed perfect," he confided to his diary, "for those of us who did not have a complete picture of the strategical situation."

During TF 14's sullen return voyage, the VMF-221 Buffaloes, originally ticketed for Wake's fallen garrison, were instead dispatched from *Saratoga's* deck north to Midway Atoll to reinforce its garrison. Midway was situated a good deal closer to Pearl than was Wake, but this made it no less a cipher in the Pacific's catalog of far-flung place names.

Saratoga reached Pearl on December 29—a day ahead of Nimitz's relief of Pye—where it was apparent that sober conservatism had replaced the mood of shock, denial and full-throated anger immediately after December 7. More strategic considerations had quelled retaliatory urges—at least for the time being. Fearful of risking either undue concentration or immobilization when it came to the Navy's handful of carriers, Pye—and then Nimitz—rotated each separately into Pearl and then as quickly out to sea again. This time outbound forces were tasked with more vague and circumscribed missions: patrolling and keeping open fragile lines of communication and supply to the U.S. mainland and to regional "white man" allies such as Australia and New Zealand. The subtext was: don't get sunk.

————

After its own in-port days of resupply and lackluster liberty (in a Honolulu clamped down by martial law), *Saratoga* and TF 14 returned to sea. This time it was to guard the sea lanes to Midway. And this time, to replace Frank Jack Fletcher, who'd flown to San Diego to take charge of TF 17 and carrier *Yorktown* (CV-5) (just in from the Atlantic), yet another non-aviator, Rear Admiral Herbert F. Leary, took the helm.

A New Year's "sans celebration, sans hangover" (in the words of VF-3 aviator Lieutenant [junior grade] Onia B. "Burt" Stanley) brightened a bit on January 3 with an All Navy dispatch announcing wholesale (albeit temporary) wartime promotions. Butch O'Hare became one of the squadron's new full lieutenants while Jimmie Thach and Don Lovelace both jumped to Lieutenant Commander.

The next day, as if to demonstrate that the universe's system of distributive justice still prevailed in war, the newly-promoted Thach succumbed to a painful attack of kidney stones and checked into sick bay.

————

On December 8, when the Formosan fog finally lifted and they took off for the Philippines, the Tainan Air Group pilots fully expected heavy opposition. Even as they had waited impatiently on the ground for the skies to clear, the men heard a stirring and detailed loudspeaker account of the Pearl Harbor strike. Resounding cheers immediately rang out, but it was still several more hours before the skies cleared—and more hours still before they would reach Luzon. The Americans there must already be preparing—and might have already launched a long-range strike of their own.

Saburo Sakai's Zero-sen was one of nine planes responsible for flying ahead of the main force to sweep the skies of any American interceptors.

Leaving Formosa a little after 9 a.m., this first wave finally reached Luzon at 1:35 p.m. Opening throttles and climbing towards twenty thousand feet, the Zero-sens headed immediately for Clark Field.

Rather than being confronted by swarms of American fighters over Clark as they'd anticipated, the pilots instead saw runways lined with four-engine bombers parked wing-to-wing. It looked too good to be true. Like a pack of unsuspecting lambs. Or some sort of trap.

A few minutes later, when a handful of enemy Curtis P-40 interceptors finally did appear at lower altitude, the Zero-sen pilots at once jettisoned external fuel tanks and charged guns. For the moment, as they awaited the arrival of their own bombers, Sakai and the others could not take the initiative. That was up to the defenders but, strangely, they never did. Rather, the enemy fighters circled aimlessly five thousand feet below the Zero-sens, remaining there even as the IJN bombers swept in from the China Sea to obliterate the orderly herd of grounded American planes. It was both exhilarating and ludicrous.

Once the twin-engine G4Ms finished their bombing work, leaving Clark Field's runways in ruin, Sakai's group helped escort them back to sea. It was only when the escort group circled back to strafe Clark that a pack of five P-40s at last pounced. Instinctively and in unison, each of the Zero-sen pilots jerked back his control stick and kicked his rudder pedals to climb and bank. The maneuver—as quick as a reflex— seemed to stun the enemy pilots. All five P-40s rolled and scattered, four of them disappearing into the columns of oily smoke still pouring from Clark's runways.

The fifth, however, spiraled alone into clearer skies. Sakai at once spotted him and swung up to approach from below. Desperate now to get away, the American half-rolled into a high loop. Already, though, he was doomed. Sakai had the P-40 in his sights at two hundred yards but, after pushing the throttle forward, he steadily closed the gap to one hundred yards and then just fifty. A brief burst of machine gun and cannon fire ripped into the P-40's belly and literally blew off the plane's canopy. The plane staggered and fell back into the smoke.

It was Sakai's third enemy kill and his second in a Zero-sen. It was also his first American—something of note, but it left him perplexed all through the return flight to Formosa. This aerial face-off was so much easier than the duel with the tiny biplane over Chengtu had been. What was it with this new enemy?

Was he flying an inferior aircraft? Perhaps, but that hadn't seemed to dispirit Sakai's nimble Chengtu adversary. Was it lack of experience or skill? Again, perhaps—but the IJN pilots had expected so much more of the vaunted Americans.

Was it as Japanese leaders and propagandists said? Did this new enemy simply lack the will to fight? If so, there would be no stopping the IJN pilots . . . no stopping Japan itself.

———

Soon thereafter, however, as the Air Group began taking on the American B-17 bombers (this time aloft), Sakai's disdain for the Americans' aircraft and fighting spirit ebbed somewhat. It started with the planes.

While the ungainly-looking Boeings were huge, they were neither slow nor vulnerable. They could soar well above twenty thousand feet, where the Zero-sens' maneuverability was somewhat diminished. They were also incredibly well-armed—and especially lethal when flying in formation. During the Group's ten days of mid-December strikes against the Philippines, Sakai had managed to shoot down a lone B-17 over Clark Field, but only after a prolonged full throttle chase and repeated firing runs.

Strangely, though, at least from a tactician's point of view, the big bombers were being dispatched on futile errands. Sakai's victim, for example, was returning from trying to sink Japanese invasion shipping—unlikely sorts of targets for an aircraft flying at 20,000 feet or more.

Meanwhile, even as the conquest of the Philippines continued, the Tainan Air Group was being hop-scotched south in an effort to keep pace with Japan's lightning-fast advances to secure sources of fuel and raw materials. On December 30, in what was another test of pilot and plane endurance, Sakai and twenty-six other Zero-sen pilots flew 1,200 miles nonstop from Formosa to the Sulu Islands, midway between Mindanao and Borneo. From there they moved even further south along Borneo's east coast, first to the offshore island of Tarakan and then, in early February, to Balikpapan.

Here, the pilots came up against newer Boeing models, these ones equipped with tail guns. This fact—along with knowledge of the bombers' sturdy construction—called for new aerial tactics. Instead of coming in astern and raking the Boeings' fuselages from tail to nose, the pilots tried head-on passes. This worked for awhile until the American pilots countered with stunningly quick evasive turns to bring their own guns to bear. The Americans had adapted—a surprise in itself —but

Zero-sen pilots adapted in turn, this time diving directly down, then snap-rolling as they passed, all the while pouring in machine gun and cannon fire.

One day over Balikpapan, Sakai and his wingman came upon two four-plane sections of Boeings. The Japanese made repeated rolling dives into the big formation, each time being met by a tracer-lit blizzard of return fire.

During his second pass, Sakai saw his cannon projectiles explode along the drab green flanks of the one Boeing's fuselage, with big chunks of metal jumping outward and into the slipstream. But the big Boeing, despite the hits, remained all the while in tight formation. Its own guns never stopped blazing away at the two Zero-sens—nor did the guns from the other bombers.

Finally, after a sixth pass by Sakai and his wingman, the wounded Boeing sprouted a thin black stream of smoke from one of its engines. Seeing that the Boeing's tail gun position was little more than tangled wreckage, Sakai pressed the attack from astern. Closing to within fifty yards, he simply pressed and held his gun triggers. It took every last round, but the stricken American bomber finally dropped from formation, nosed down and disappeared.

When he returned to base, Sakai was credited with a probable killed. The other pilots marveled that his Zero-sen, after all the enemy fire, showed just three bullet holes. For his part, while he could hardly admire the American gunners' and bombardiers' skill (or the sense of leaders who sent the Boeings on such foolhardy missions), he gained new respect for the American crews' stubborn endurance—and for the sheer ruggedness of their aircraft.

Sakai had to wonder what else the Americans might have in store.

———

The torpedo that hit and exploded against *Saratoga's* port side during the evening of January 11 devastated three fire rooms and killed six sailors. The impact sent Sara heeling violently to starboard before she rocked back and listed to port as seawater gushed in. Ruptured fuel bunkers splattered oil across portions of a flight deck already littered with metal hull fragments. General Quarters (GQ) alarms sounded even as damage control personnel scrambled to shore up the gash in the hull and counterflood to correct the list.

To Jimmie Thach, still confined to sick bay, the tremendous impact and noise made it seem the very bottom of the ship had blown out. Many VF-

3 aviators were at dinner in the wardroom; they stepped over shards of dinnerware and piles of spilled food in the race to reach their ready room GQ stations.

Saratoga was then some four hundred miles southwest of Pearl and zigzagging slowly—too slowly—as it headed for a rendezvous with Halsey's TF 8. During the rendezvous, VF-3 was to swap Wildcats with VF-6. It struck VF-3 engineering officer Butch O'Hare as a particularly bad bargain. The VF-6 Grummans (export versions originally intended for the Brits and Greeks) had Pratt and Whitney engines equipped with conventional single-stage superchargers—low blowers. Pilots already bemoaning their Wildcats' limited endurance were none too thrilled at losing their more robust models, some now even fitted out with pilot armor and self-sealing tanks. While the downside of the swap scarcely compared with *Saratoga's* ruptured hull and lost lives, O'Hare, for one, was relieved when the rendezvous/swap was scratched and *Sara* instead set course northeast for Pearl.

———

Plans to repair *Saratoga* at Pearl proved unrealistic and were quickly rethought. Instead, she was cleaned up in preparation for full scale repair and modernization back in the States. The ship's February departure for Bremerton would leave VF-3 without a sea home even as interest in executing spot raids against the Japanese revived. Already, TF 8 had been dispatched below the Equator to deliver reinforcements in Samoa. Afterwards, Halsey and *Enterprise* were to link up with Fletcher's TF 17 (newly arrived from San Diego with *Yorktown*) and backtrack to stage early February hit-and-run strikes in the Gilberts and Marshalls.

On January 19 Wilson Brown's TF 11 sortied south to back up Halsey and Fletcher, only to be rerouted towards Wake. The loss of Wake had particularly stung but efforts to avenge its fall soon proved just as jinxed. On January 23 an IJN sub intercepted, torpedoed and sank fleet oiler *Neches* (AO-5), Brown's only fuel source for the mission.

Brown could do little more than reverse course for Oahu, where *Lexington's* otherwise abject homecoming did offer one opportunity. Fighting Two, an idiosyncratic squadron first organized in 1927 and still largely made up of enlisted Naval Aviation Pilots (NAP) was now the only carrier VF squadron still equipped with Brewster Buffaloes.

The Navy had all but closed the books on Brewster Aeronautical. Beset with management problems, the company never met production quotas.

Breakdowns attributable to the Buffaloes' overweight air frame and rickety landing struts were bad enough, but now some pilots suspected instances of factory sabotage. In mid-January transports arrived in Hawaii with disassembled stores of Wildcats intended as fleet replacements. With enough on hand to reequip VF-2, most of the "Fighting Chiefs" went ashore to expedite the change. Meanwhile, a small pilot contingent, headed by squadron XO Lieutenant Commander James H. Flatley (one of Butch O'Hare's Pensacola instructors), was to board *Saratoga* to supply air cover during the trip to Bremerton. All this juggling created an opening for VF-3.

Since returning to Pearl, Jimmie Thach (and his kidney stones) had been ashore, confined to a hospital bed. By the time he was released on January 17, his squadron was well along in the process of acquiring five more Grummans. This would up its total to eighteen—enough to enable pilots to fly more or less routinely in the same plane.

Aircraft, like the crews who flew them, were now building combat records. BuAer Number 4031, for example, the Wildcat whose number was most often jotted into Butch O'Hare's personal flight log, had first been assigned to VMF-211, the Marine fighter squadron wiped out in the defense of Wake. The Marines had left 4031 behind at Ewa in late November when its engine failed to start. Spared that opportunity for glory (and near certain oblivion), 4031 had somehow managed to sit out December 7 intact. 4031 was now more or less restored to fighting trim, though it still lacked self-sealing fuel tanks and pilot armor.

VF-3's full complement of pilots and combat-ready aircraft made the squadron an ideal replacement squadron for VF-2 aboard *Lexington*. On January 26, Thach was alerted to ready VF-3 for sea duty on short notice. Thach received his orders four days later and on January 31 VF-3 (along with other air group squadrons) made the short hop from Kaneohe to *Lexington's* seaborne flight deck.

JIMMIE AND BUTCH

FEBRUARY 20, 1942 (WEST OF THE INTERNATIONAL DATE LINE)

As Lieutenant Commander Jimmie Thach and his wingman, Ensign Edward "Doc" Sellstrom Jr., reached the area where *Lexington's* fighter director officer (FDO) Lieutenant Frank F. "Red" Gill had vectored them, they encountered a heavy cloud bank and rain. Going on instruments, the two pilots closed up interval and edged warily into the soup. All at once Thach found himself about to collide with his quarry, what must be a Japanese patrol plane. It even surprised Red Gill, who radioed that the three planes had merged.

"Roger," Thach radioed back. "That's because we're within about thirty-five feet of each other. You put him right into my lap."

Gill, Thach understood, could hardly be congratulated —or blamed —for matters of intercept precision. *Lexington's* "long-range" CXAM search radar only provided ranges and bearings within a limited radius of eighty or so miles. The rest (including altitude) was little more than guesswork. Gill even lacked real-time visual displays of the situation. The radar screens—repeaters—were housed in a compartment adjacent to Air Plot, where Gill was stationed. Information—radar sighting distance, bearing and time—were passed by phone for plotting on a large polar chart. Over time, the hand-plotted contact points (*x* for a bogey, *o* for a friendly aircraft) resolved into course lines and headings.

Cloud-bound as he was, about all that Thach could see was the snooper's silvery wing emblazoned with a red meatball. Soon even that disappeared as the Wildcats' speed carried them out of the cloud and back into the clear. If Thach and Sellstrom were to nail the intruder, there was little to do but circle and reenter the murk. After a few more anxious minutes of circling and groping, they finally saw the snooper break into the clear.

Identification was then easier: a big four-engine Japanese flying boat, with a strut-mounted parasol wing and twin-fin tail (a Kawanishi H6K, which Allied intelligence would come to nickname Mavis). Knowing they'd been detected, the Japanese pilots were now retreating southwest toward Rabaul. Thach and Sellstrom took off in pursuit.

The two Wildcats quickly closed the gap on the ungainly silvery bird. The Japanese pilots made no effort to evade, surely knowing it would be futile. Rather, they held a steady course, hoping their gunners could somehow fend off or discourage the pursuers.

Thach intended to corner the plane. He slid out to the right and radioed Sellstrom to "bracket." This meant that Sellstrom was to stay on Thach's wing through a first pass, only afterwards crossing to the opposite side. Instead, the twenty-five-year-old Sellstrom—still a newcomer toVF-3 and its tactics—moved at once to the left. It got him the immediate attention of the Japanese tail gunner and Sellstrom had all he could do to dodge bursts from the 20-millimeter "stinger" cannon.

Unaware for the moment of Sellstrom's plight, Thach lined up for a high-side run, his first against an actual enemy. "With all the training I've had," he thought to himself, "I'd better get it right." He did his best to keep everything smooth and easy. Making sure to line up the proper amount of deflection, Thach even checked his ball leveler to be sure he wasn't slipping or skidding.

Thach was certain his bullets hit the seaplane's two starboard engines on the first pass, but nothing seemed to happen. But then, as Thach circled back for a second run, the quarry's wing erupted and its bomb load tumbled like eggs from a basket. As he zoomed past this time, Thach caught a glimpse of the Japanese pilots standing in the cockpit. Their human predicament was a factor in the combat equation that no amount of training could have prepared him for. The crippled Mavis with its trapped crew stayed on course for a few more seconds, but finally nosed down towards the sea.

The plume of smoke from the crash was clearly visible from the decks of *Lexington* and other Task Force 11 ships, now thirty-five miles away. It was, simultaneously, Lex's, VF-3's and Jimmie Thach's first aerial kill of the Pacific War.

VF-3's January 31 deployment aboard *Lexington* was yet another improvisation in the disordered on-again off-again strategy of the U.S. Navy's first months at war in the Pacific. The wounded giant was flailing about—and none too successfully.

A factor in the flurry of January task force moves was the hope of disrupting at least the pace of Japan's relentless expansions in the Southwest Pacific and along the rim of the Coral Sea. In an effort to help the beleaguered Australia-New Zealand (Anzac) Forces stop—or at least retard—Japanese thrusts toward the New Hebrides, Nimitz was ordered to reroute Brown's *Lexington* task force (now finishing up escort duty and set to return to Pearl) south of the Equator.

Herbert Leary, who took a dose of criticism for *Saratoga's* torpedoing, had been kicked upstairs to vice admiral and shuttled down to Wellington, New Zealand to take command of Anzac. Saddled with another seemingly futile cause, Leary was understandably delighted with Task Force 11's temporary assignment and plans for an air strike on Rabaul with a possible follow-up shelling. Rabaul, which had fallen after little opposition to Japan on January 23, was already a painful thorn. Japanese aircraft based on the island's Vunakanau field were in easy reach of eastern New Guinea and the Solomons—both gateways to Australia.

Staging the strike would mean taking *Lexington* into the Bismarck Sea—and far out on a limb, in more ways than one. During the long expedition, there would be no adequate refueling or resupply port for TF 11 nearer than Pearl and no repair facility nearer than Sidney. Accordingly, TF 11's shipboard fuel supplies and stores would be stretched perilously thin.

To deepen the risks, Brown's navigation charts for some stretches of the voyage were little more than updates of surveys conducted by eighteenth century French explorers. As Brown picked his way past uncharted hazards, his ships would have to observe the strictest radio silence. Even after the strike was over, refilling bunkers would depend on finding a tanker sent to a pre-designated rendezvous point.

Finally, there were the perils of oversight. When Brown reached the South Pacific, he would be leaving Nimitz's jurisdiction, reporting instead (via Leary) all the way back to U.S. Navy Headquarters in Washington. The temperature for his hot seat would be adjusted not only by the Japanese—but by the DC Brass as well.

———

During the second week in February, Japanese reconnaissance planes flying out of Balikpapan reported heavy concentrations of fighter aircraft in Surabaya, on Java's northeastern coast, doubtless intended to stop Japan's planned invasion of the island. The Dutch bastion was a good 430-mile flight from Balikpapan, making it yet another endurance challenge for the Tainan Air Group. Accordingly, in advance of the first strike, pilots were assigned special ditching islands, surface units were positioned for rescue along the route and a fast reconnaissance plane was set to act as a pathfinder and scout for the fighters.

On the morning of February 19, twenty-three Zero-sens—one piloted by Saburo Sakai—took off for Surabaya. When they arrived overhead a half-hour before noon they encountered a sight they'd not yet seen in the new Pacific War: at least fifty Allied fighters arrayed in inverted Vee-shaped formations, sweeping counterclockwise at ten thousand feet over the port city. Most of the Curtiss P-36 Mohawks, P-40 Tomahawks and Brewster Buffaloes that now broke formation and zoomed unhesitatingly towards the Japanese bore Dutch markings. The outnumbered Zero-sen pilots, readying for the onslaught, jettisoned fuel tanks and charged guns. Already at sixteen thousand feet, they climbed for even more altitude.

―――――――

The main act of the midday melee over Surabaya lasted little more than six minutes. Sakai's first victim, a P-36 that screamed towards him only to flick into a beckoning left roll, fell during the first minute. A sharp right turn put Sakai directly on the Dutch pilot's tail. Close range machine gun fire tore away the P-36's right wing and then its left, sending the plane into a wild tailspin that dismantled the substance of its fuselage.

Returning to center stage, Sakai saw at least six more Dutch planes falling in flames with the Zero-sens zooming about like ravenous, insatiable wolves. Scanning for another opportunity, Sakai noticed the unarmed Japanese pathfinder being harried by three Dutch fighters. He dived for this ill-matched side brawl only to arrive too late. Another Zero-sen, screaming down in a power dive, had picked off all three Dutch planes in blinding succession, afterwards pulling alongside Sakai to grin, wave and climb back towards the slaughter.

Sakai finally did snare a second victim, a rolling and diving Dutchman obviously bent on escape. A hasty ill-timed burst of cannon fire at first disrupted Sakai's aim, but he recovered and, slamming the Zero-sen into over-boost, easily cut inside the frantic Curtiss pilot's escape path. Sakai now only had to wait for the P-36 to overtake him. When it did, Sakai sent two better-aimed cannon bursts into the P-36's flanks and watched it being swallowed in flame.

————

When Sakai again joined the aerial scrum, it was circling at eight thousand feet and consisted entirely of Zero-sens, about twenty of them. The Dutch fighters meanwhile registered as dark specks disappearing in the distance. Below the Japanese planes, the Dutch antiaircraft batteries in Surabaya remained strangely silent even though the skies were now clear of friendly aircraft.

His magazines still nearly full and his appetite up, Sakai set off over water towards Madura, the fingerling island whose shores bordered the northern rim of the bay into which Surabaya was tucked. There he spotted and marked on his map a small airstrip that no previous intelligence flights had reported. As he turned once more and climbed, a single P-36 passed beneath him, bound for Surabaya and apparently unaware of Sakai's presence.

Again, poor firing discipline cost Sakai a quick kill. Spotting tracers, the Dutch pilot nosed down to accelerate and escape. One of the Zero-sen's few "failings"—owing to its incredible lightness—was sluggishness in high-speed dives. The diving Dutchman was now able to gain separation on his pursuer and would have escaped had he not started his dive too soon and too low. Once his trajectory had flattened, the Zero-sen steadily gained on the P-36 as both hedge-hopped and zigzagged through a landscape of trees and low houses. Within sight of Malang Air Base, Sakai finally closed and again opened fire. Sakai's wing cannon magazines were now empty, but a concentrated stream of machine gun rounds ripped the P-36 apart. The Dutch plane plowed into a rice paddy and flipped on its back.

Sakai was the last plane to form up for the return flight to Balikpapan. When he touched down he learned that his squadron lieutenant, Masao Asai, was among the three pilots lost over Surabaya. As expected, aside from the losses of friends, the returning pilots were jubilant about the mission, claiming among them as many as forty enemy fighters shot down.

Under normal circumstances, Sakai knew enough to discount such claims by twenty to thirty per cent. This day, however, the claims seemed hardly exaggerated at all. It was by far the biggest air-to-air which he had ever seen. It was no surprise that from then on the Tainan Air Group faced little more opposition from Dutch fighter aircraft.

———

While the TF 11 raid on Rabaul had been set for early February 21, the snooper intrusions on the twentieth foreshadowed its disruption—perhaps even its demise. However, for the six Wildcat pilots circling the skies above *Lexington*, these weighty matters were of little immediate concern. For each of them (one man, one plane) the mission was in the moment—and now made only more so as Red Gill broke radio silence to give the south-southwest vector to a bogey. Butch O'Hare was thrilled, but then as deeply dismayed when Thach ordered O'Hare's and Burt Stanley's sections to stay while he and Sellstrom peeled off to investigate.

Another dose of dismay promptly followed. No sooner had Thach and Sellstrom returned from their kill (evidenced by the towering plume of black smoke), than Gill had a range and bearing on a second snooper. This time the vector went to Burt Stanley and wingman Ensign Leon W. Haynes. Neither had to be asked twice; they zoomed off to make the intercept and, minutes later, the kill of a second big Japanese seaplane. All the while O'Hare and his wingman, twenty-five-year-old Lieutenant (junior grade) Marion W. "Duff" Dufilho, were left stewing on the sidelines like third stringers.

At 12:40 p.m., there was a third customer—a bogey at the outskirts of the CXAM radar's maximum radius—but it never got closer than seventy miles before altogether disappearing. With it went the last of O'Hare's and Dulfilho's hopes for the morning. Everyone in Thach's First Division was now low on fuel. Don Lovelace's Second Division was already being spotted on *Lexington*'s flight deck for afternoon relief.

———

Despite the fact that the two *Lexington* Class carriers were virtual twins, VF-3's aviators were, without exception, happy and warmly appreciative at being cross-decked from *Saratoga* to *Lexington*. Commissioned within weeks of each other in 1927 (*Saratoga* first, despite its higher hull number and *Lexington*'s class lead status), each had been built on a commodious battle cruiser hull and engineered for long distance and 35-knot speed. And both could accommodate seventy-five or more aircraft in their hangar spaces and on their identical 800-foot-long, 160-foot-wide armored steel decks. Aside from this visible outward kinship, however, the two big ships seemed (at least to VF-3 personnel) entirely unrelated when it came to fighting spirit, morale and efficiency. *Saratoga* now appeared hopelessly jinxed after the aborted Wake mission and the sitting duck torpedo hit. It would take more than a Bremerton overhaul to remove the taint of Albatross from her decks and spaces.

Burt Stanley, for one, noted the "better spirit" that characterized *Lexington*, even in the small things. Life jackets, for example, were available but stowed away, not "omnipresent" as they had been on *Saratoga*. For his part, Jimmie Thach noted most the tremendous difference in leadership—though not necessarily at the top.

As so often seemed to be happening (at least as far as restive aviation veterans like Jimmie Thach were concerned), task force command had devolved on a member of the Gun Club. In this case it happened to be Wilson Brown. Now just two months shy of his sixtieth birthday, Brown was the oldest USN flag officer afloat; he was near—if not already beyond—his last hurrah. As if to further undercut his credibility in the eyes of the task force pilots, Brown, owing to a slight hand tremor, was nicknamed "Shaky."

But if Shaky Brown's bona fides were suspect, those of his immediate subordinates were not—and this made all the difference.

Lexington's CO Captain Frederick C. "Ted" Sherman, though a pilot of the Pensacola Admiral strain, made up for that shortcoming (as well as his explosive bouts of irritability, later attributed to painfully bad teeth) by his passion for aviation, his sense of tactics, his coolness under pressure and his pure willingness to fight. Sherman collaborated with Air Officer Commander Herbert S. Duckworth, the VF-2 Fighting Chief's former skipper (and an early adherent of the two-plane section) to ensure that priority was given to aerial gunnery and bombing practice. To Thach's mind, the Sherman-Duckworth administration seemed to run things in every way to enhance the use of the air group. To make it—as it rightfully should be—the point of TF 11's spear.

———

As VF-3 squadron personnel swilled water, smoked cigarettes and picked over a ready room lunch pieced together from *Lexington's* depleted larder, the morning's victors recounted their exploits. Thach could say with assurance that the experience was just like another gunnery training run—what they had been practicing for months now.

All the while, Thach couldn't help notice that O'Hare was fit to be tied. Moments later, when word filtered through about the fate of the next day's big strikes, the rest of them were fit to be tied as well.

Anxious about dwindling fuel and stores, all but certain TF 11 been pinpointed and reported by the two downed snoopers, and with no taste for a prolonged engagement with a fleet of land-based Japanese planes, Wilson Brown was considering calling off the entire Rabaul raid. Only after heated counter arguments from Ted Sherman and his own staff did Brown relent somewhat. Rather than withdrawing immediately, TF11 would instead, with Leary's and far-off Washington's approval, feint an attack. It would offer itself as the sort of bait that might yet lure the Japanese away from their offenses in the East Indies and Coral Sea.

Within hours the ploy seemed to bear fruit. At 3:42 p.m. *Lexington* radar detected a possible bogey or bogeys seventy-six miles to the west. Within minutes, the first substantial aerial fight between Japanese and American carrier-based planes was underway, much of it playing out well within sight of a cheerleading audience of TF 11 sailors.

————

Don Lovelace's Second Division CAP, aloft since 1:30 p.m., was getting low on fuel; the VF-3's Third Division, led by twenty-six-year-old Lieutenant Noel A.M. Gayler (and numbering two Grummans borrowed from Thach's division), was readying on deck to replace him. Even though this newest radar contact had momentarily vanished from the scope, an attack was still considered a possibility. Accordingly, Ted Sherman, on advice from Duckworth and Gill, ordered Gayler's division to launch a bit early. At 4:15 p.m. when the last of these six Wildcats took off, *Lexington's* flight personnel began an arduous re-spot of nearly thirty aircraft in preparation for Second Division's recovery. As a handful of pilots taxied F4Fs and SBDs forward, plane handlers leaned into the heavy work of repositioning the ungainly TBDs.

Unfolding events soon enough made Gayler's early launch seem prescient. At 4:14 p.m. the bogey reappeared on the A-scope, this time at seventy-two miles, bearing 270 degrees. Though it once more faded, there was enough substantiated suspicion now to warrant an intercept. Alerting Lovelace's division that their recovery had been scratched for the moment, Red Gill vectored all twelve Wildcats to the west. At 4:25 p.m. the contact was slightly more to the northwest, still forty-seven miles out. But the contact was big enough to be tagged as multiple aircraft, and these bogeys were now closing at high speed.

The pace of events persuaded Sherman to order Duckworth to cancel the full deck re-spot and instead make every effort to launch the four fighters and eleven dive-bombers that were armed and fueled. These fifteen planes were explosive liabilities while on deck, potentially decisive weapons if they could somehow get airborne.

As *Lexington* went to flank speed and the ship's company raced for "torpedo defense stations," Duckworth looked over the array of ready Wildcats and Dauntlesses on his flight deck, checked his roster of available pilots and alerted the ready rooms.

Jimmie Thach and Butch O'Hare were still in VF-3's ready room leafing through intelligence reports when the call came. They raced to the flight deck where plane handlers were still busy with the emergency respot. Thach's Wildcat was by then at the head of the pack, but O'Hare's and Sellstrom's planes were still several rows back. Even as Thach strapped in, VS-2 air crews, many of them without helmets and other flight gear, were scrambling into the cockpits of their Dauntlesses.

Thach realized that Lovelace's division was still overhead, joining in the fracas but likely apprehensive about their depleted fuel reserves. *Lexington* was now heeling to port to get the wind over her bow. As the forward edge of the flight deck swung across the mid-afternoon horizon, Thach could see the six planes of Gayler's Third Division. In their haste to respond, none of them had taken time to form up. Instead, each was flying independently, each clawing for altitude while pounding upwind towards a distant line of barely discernible specs.

Herb Duckworth, now brandishing a bullhorn, called for "Thach in 13, Sellstrom take 2, O'Hare in 15, Dufilho, 4." Once he had these four aloft, all of VF-3's sixteen operable Wildcats (and all but two of Thach's pilots) would be committed to the fight.

————

Thach was first off the deck at 4:36 p.m. Three minutes later, ten miles northwest of the task force and flying through light cloud cover at an altitude of thirteen thousand feet, Gayler's Third Division Wildcats were finally positioned for high-side runs into the heart of the enemy's "Vee-of-Vees" formation two thousand feet below.

Pilot circuit chatter had identified the Japanese formation as consisting of nine twin-engine bombers. Their wings were wide at the root but narrow at the tips; and their cigar-shaped fuselages were painted mottled brown and green. (They were Mitsubishi G4Ms, within months to be known, with respectful familiarity, as Bettys.) Somewhat unexpectedly, the Japanese planes were lining up not for torpedoing but for horizontal bombing. Over the next two minutes, lookouts spotted three of these enemy aircraft dropping out of formation, one of them being chased to the water by a lone Wildcat. To the amazement of some witnesses, the six remaining aircraft merely closed up ranks and continued on.

By 4:43 p.m. one more Japanese plane was seen dropping. Speculation had it being the flight leader; the five other enemy aircraft, seemingly disoriented, flew past the ships before finally swinging around to parallel *Lexington's* course and overtake her from astern. The task force cruisers were now firing their five-inch antiaircraft batteries but their aim was poor. Shrapnel from the time-fused projectiles appeared more a threat to friend than foe. Three minutes later, with *Lexington's* flight deck bow finally clear of F4Fs and SBDs, CO Ted Sherman turned his ship out of the wind, released his own antiaircraft batteries, and began defensive maneuvering.

As one more of the Japanese bombers tumbled (most likely from aerial attack, though cruiser gunners later claimed credit), the four survivors soldiered on towards release points. Japanese formation discipline had been eerily impressive throughout the murderous run, but bombing accuracy was blessedly not. Of the four bombs that now dropped from their bays, the nearest exploded no closer than three thousand yards from *Lexington*.

The only serious destructive threat in all this time came from one of the wounded bombers. Its pilots, struggling to keep their damaged plane aloft, flew in low on Lex's starboard bow. As the distance closed and Sherman maneuvered to keep clear, secondary antiaircraft batteries on the starboard catwalks all but ripped the plane apart. The wreckage finally crashed and burned in the big carrier's wake, just seventy-five yards astern.

At 4:49 p.m., in the midst of this valedictory brush with disaster, Lex's Air Plot had a first fix on entirely new bogeys, these thirty miles north-northeast. For the moment, however, Red Gill saw no way of interrupting the action aloft to vector an intercept.

Jimmie Thach had lacked time and altitude to get into the main event, but now, with the three Japanese survivors making for the exits, his Wildcat loaded with ammunition and fuel, and his combat appetite whetted, Thach couldn't resist joining the chase. He still lacked a wingman, but that was not an immediate concern. There were no Japanese fighter escorts to contend with and Sellstrom could catch up.

Thach's decision left Butch O'Hare and Duff Dufilho behind again as the others, like a pack of fox hounds, pursued the Japanese. Held in reserve by Gill, there was little for O'Hare to do but gather Dufilho (who'd also entirely missed the fight) and orbit the task force as the only fighter CAP.

Within moments, however, that all changed. At 4:56 p.m. destroyer *Patterson* (DD-392), dropping astern of the task force to retrieve a downed flier, spotted the new menace—a formation circling ten miles to the northeast. Four minutes later, Red Gill confirmed the sighting and dispatched O'Hare and Dufilho. He also tried recalling the distant hounds.

————

At 5:05 p.m. O'Hare and Dufilho had visual on what they reported as a formation of nine bombers a few miles astern of the task force. In truth there were eight aircraft: two three-plane Vees and an echeloned pair on the right. The two Americans were then at twelve thousand feet, about a thousand feet above the Japanese, who were in a shallow dive, gaining speed and lining up to bomb. Approaching the enemy formation head-on but apparently undetected, O'Hare and Dufilho allowed the lead Vee to pass below them before rolling in for a high-side attack on the formation's right flank.

O'Hare aimed for the outermost bomber. Always deadly accurate in practice gunnery, O'Hare's high-deflection aim was no less so here. A short .50 caliber burst pierced the bomber's wing root and starboard engine, releasing streams of oil and smoke.

The wounded plane slowed so abruptly that O'Hare had to pull up his nose to get out of its way. But even as this first victim fell, O'Hare still had a chance to aim and fire at the plane adjacent to it. This next burst hit this aircraft's starboard engine and must have also ruptured the wing tank. A thin white contrail—aviation gasoline—traced the plane's downward arc.

The end of this first pass placed O'Hare momentarily ahead and on the left side of the Japanese bomber formation. As he wheeled to port and climbed to regain altitude and again get behind the Japanese, O'Hare looked for Duff Dufilho but saw no sign of him. Dufilho, it turned out, had fallen victim to faulty ammunition belts. None of his six guns would fire and he had pulled off, desperately trying to clear his guns. O'Hare and BuAer 4031 were on their own.

————

O'Hare next targeted the left side of the formation. The Japanese pilots again seemed unperturbed, closing ranks as if the missing planes and their crewmembers had scarcely existed. This time in a flatter high-side run, O'Hare went after the rearmost plane. He aimed for its starboard wing, expecting that if his aim was off he might still hit the cockpit and the port engine. As it was, O'Hare's aim was perfect; flame erupted from its starboard engine and it dropped away.

After sidestepping this third victim, O'Hare aimed for the trailer in the formation's lead Vee. This one he caught with a longer burst to the left wing and pilot cockpit. Its port engine flamed and seized, causing the plane to stagger, lurch to port and fall.

With Dufilho out of the fight, every Japanese blister and dorsal gun that could bear was firing at the BuAer 4031. O'Hare gave the tracer streams little separate thought. He realized that even a heavy volume of defensive fire was no offset for flimsy aircraft with vulnerable fuel tanks. O'Hare concentrated instead on keeping his altitude advantage and lining up low-exposure, opportunistic bursts.

As O'Hare started his third firing pass, again on the left side, the bombers were almost over the task force. O'Hare saw puffs of antiaircraft fire but ignored them as well. For the moment at least, the rounds were exploding well below the altitude of the action.

O'Hare now set his sights set on what had become the new trailer on the left side. A short burst dispatched this plane, clearing the way for a shot at the formation's lead bomber. O'Hare's final burst on this third pass was point-blank close; his rounds hammered the enemy's port-side engine until it literally tore loose from the wing.

———

Even as the Japanese lead plane skidded towards the water, the four surviving aircraft toggled their bombs. *Lexington* was just then finishing up the recovery of Don Lovelace's bone-dry Second Division Wildcats. At 5:09 p.m., as soon as the last of these Wildcats were trapped, cleared the barriers and taxied forward, deck personnel raced for cover—just moments ahead of the bomb blasts, the nearest of which erupted barely one hundred feet from the fantail.

Meanwhile, in the skies above *Lexington*, Butch O'Hare's four-minute, one-man, one-plane rampage was all but over. Lining up a shot at a seventh victim, he managed to squeeze off about ten rounds before his magazines emptied. Minutes later, when O'Hare finally touched down on *Lexington*, a mob of joyous pilots and deck personnel (the first of many—and much larger—crowds to come) swarmed him.

O'Hare asked naively for water and refills on fuel and ammunition.

Instead, he was rushed to the bridge to receive congratulations from Brown and Sherman. A report on the day was already being transmitted to Wellington for relay to Washington. Just after dusk, with flight operations shut down, TF 11 was steering slightly south of east and making twenty-two knots. Brown's ships were putting distance between them and Rabaul, bound now for a resupply rendezvous in safer waters.

———

If TF 11's feint towards Rabaul had presented a rare opportunity to maul the Japanese, it offered little deterrent or delay to their steamroller advances in the Southwest. The seagoing naval aviation component of this steamroller was Vice Admiral Chuichi Nagumo's thirty-one-ship Pearl Harbor Task Force with its potent, coordinated Striking Force of six fleet carriers: *Akagi, Kaga, Hiryu, Soryu, Shokaku* and *Zuikaku*.

After returning to home waters in the days immediately after the December 7 triumph, Nagumo's force had taken to sea again on January 5, 1942, bound this time for the South Pacific. After neutralizing Rabaul on January 22 (and then racing east—absent *Shokaku* and *Zuikaku*—on the fool's errand of trying to overtake the American carriers that had struck the Marshalls and Gilberts), Nagumo was ordered to stage raids on Port Darwin along Australia's northern coast. His carrier forces coiled and struck on February 19.

Commanding the 188-plane carrier-based bombing mission on Port Darwin was thirty-nine-year-old Commander Mitsuo Fuchida, a longtime China veteran with over three thousand hours flight experience. More recently and more significantly, Fuchida had led the nearly two hundred planes of the vanguard Pearl Harbor strike. In fact it was Fuchida's radioman who had tapped out the momentous radio message: "*Tora, Tora, Tora*" (Tiger, Tiger, Tiger), signifying that the Americans had been caught totally by surprise.

To Fuchida, no target since Pearl Harbor had seemed particularly worthy of the offensive prowess of the Nagumo Force. That had certainly been true of Rabaul, where Fuchida's flight of ninety bombers and fighters unleashed its outsized punch against just one coastal gun emplacement, one cargo ship, two enemy planes and two dusty, otherwise deserted air fields. And now Port Darwin was proving to be much the same.

While, in contrast to Rabaul, Darwin's harbor was filled with ships, its shore installations comprised little more than a few warehouses and a single pier. Moreover its air field, though reasonably large, had only three hangars and an assortment of just twenty aircraft—all parked and waiting on the ground. Leaving his fighters to take care of the air field, Fuchida led his bombers on a shipping strike that destroyed twenty vessels.

After this series of either underwhelming or foolhardy missions, Nagumo's force withdrew to the west. After rest and resupply on the southeast coast of Malaya, the Japanese sortied to support the invasion of Java, the last remaining Allied bastion in the East Indies.

————

Although Anzac leaders believed that Java was in all likelihood going to be lost to the Japanese, there was still an outside chance of holding on if fighter aircraft could somehow reach the island. Flying them there was all but impossible. More planes and pilots had been lost during the hop from Australia to Java than in actual combat. With the Japanese now ashore on the island's north side, the one remaining possibility was to haul aircraft by sea into Tjilatjap, the only port of any size on Java's south coast. It was for this ferrying job that the former U.S. aircraft carrier *Langley* again took to sea.

After her conversion from collier in 1920, her 1922 re-commissioning as CV-1 and a two-year stint on the U.S. East Coast, *Langley* had served most of her twelve-year flattop career with the Pacific Battle Fleet. In essence, she was an unarmed test bed for new seaborne aviation concept and practices, including how to park flight deck aircraft more efficiently and launch them more quickly.

By June 1923, when *Langley* visited Washington, DC to demonstrate carrier flight operations to influential dignitaries, her successors *Lexington* and *Saratoga*—also conversions—were already in the works. Both CV-2's and CV-3's flight decks were built atop the wider, longer and sturdier battle cruiser hulls; by contrast, *Langley's* flight deck was scarcely a wingspan wide and just over half as long as her successors. (That said, some aircraft of the era were able to take off while the ship was still anchored, leading some to view *Lexington* and *Saratoga* as costly white elephants.) *Langley's* legacy had all but been eclipsed by 1936 when she was pulled into Mare Island Naval Shipyard for a second makeover, this time as a seaplane tender (AV-3).

When war broke, *Langley* had been anchored off Cavite in the Philippines, part of the Striking Force of the Asiatic Fleet (TF 5)—in truth a make-do assemblage of tender *Langley,* two cruisers and two oilers. On the evening of December 8, 1941, TF 5 fled Cavite bound for Balikpapan. As the Japanese advance continued, *Langley* retreated to Australia.

For the mission to Java, *Langley* sailed first to Freemantle to pick up aircraft and pilots. Then, paired with cargo ship SS *Sea Witch* and escorted by light cruiser *Phoenix* (CL-46), *Langley* departed Freemantle on February 22 to join a large convoy bound for Bombay, India. Thirty-three flight-ready Army P-40s were lashed to *Langley's* partial flight deck while another twenty-seven were crated and stowed below decks on *Sea Witch*.

The original plan, to detach *Langley* and *Sea Witch* well along the convoy's route and then have them backtrack unescorted to reach Tjilatjap under the cover of darkness, was scrapped in favor of a more direct expedient: *Langley's* detachment on February 23 and a mostly unescorted run directly north. This riskier track had the tender reaching Tjilatjap (now under escort) during daylight on February 27.

By the morning of the twenty-seventh, *Langley* had rendezvoused with Navy destroyers *Edsall* (DD-219) and *Whipple* (DD-217) for the final leg. Just before noon, however, trouble arrived in the form of a high-flying Japanese scout plane. Crews on the three ships rushed to general quarters just as Japanese reinforcements—a flight of land-based twin engine bombers with fighter escorts—arrived.

Although the two destroyers did their best to protect her, *Langley* was in no condition either to fight or to flee. Her best speed was little more than ten knots. Commander R.P. McConnell, *Langley's* skipper, used hard rudder turns to avoid two waves of bombs, but a third wave struck home. Three direct bomb hits and five near misses sent chains of explosions rippling through the fighters on deck. Flooding soon created a ten-degree port list. Deckhands rushed to jettison burning aircraft while sailors below counter-flooded, but, with *Langley's* steering mechanism and gyro compass knocked out, McConnell could not hope to navigate the channel into Tjilatjap. Instead, he pinned his hopes on somehow reaching Java's coast where he could beach *Langley*.

Soon even that plan proved futile. Lacking adequate pumps to stem flooding, *Langley's* main engines were soon swamped and the ship went dead in the water. Many of her crew now jumped over the side. ("Mamma said there would be days like this," the ship's chief radioman tapped out before shutting down his transmitter. "She must have known!") Finally, at 1:32 p.m., McDonnell ordered abandon ship.

All but sixteen of *Langley's* ship's company and air crew passengers, nearly 500 men in all, were pulled safely aboard of *Edsall* and *Whipple*. The Japanese were gone for the moment, but nobody was betting against their return. Standing clear of the *Langley*, now adrift seventy-five miles south of Tjilatjap, the two destroyers scuttled the Covered Wagon with torpedoes and salvos from their four-inch deck guns.

––––––

Just a few days later, 180 aircraft from Nagumo's powerful carriers—again commanded by Mitsuo Fuchida—pounced on Tjilatjap, sinking another twenty ships. Troop landings then went forward as scheduled and on March 9 the entire island was in Japanese hands.

Langley's scuttling made a little-known footnote to the fall of Java. Arguably, though, the Covered Wagon was the first—but by no means the last—carrier to be lost in the Pacific War.

9
THERE IS ONLY ONE MISTAKE

EARLY MAY, 1942

Even before the action in the Coral Sea began, Ernest King read about it in the newspapers. Douglas MacArthur's headquarters in Australia was apparently telling reporters that a major Japanese naval offensive was imminent. King was outraged. If the Japanese read such newspaper reports they could easily deduce that their secret codes had been broken. King immediately called Army General George C. Marshall, his colleague on the Joint Chiefs of Staff (JCS), to remind him that MacArthur should button his lip. Amidst this righteous indignation, however, King could hardly have lost sight of his own indiscretion and how it might impact what was about to happen.

———

King was the architect and driver of the hit-and-run carrier forays against Wake, far-off Marcus Island, the Marshalls, the Gilberts and the Bismarck Archipelago. Some forays, like Wake, had been total fiascos, while others had questionable strategic impact. Never mind, they served a purpose and King found validation of that purpose in a March 29, 1942 *Saturday Evening Post* article written by Charles F. Kettering, General Motors' research VP.

Kettering titled his article "There Is Only One Mistake: To Do Nothing"; in it he commented on the post-Pearl Harbor vilification of the military for its poor preparedness and industry for its slow mobilization. Critics—the instant experts, the second-guessers, the politicians, the public at large—are always with us, Kettering consoled. The path to success was not caving to their hysteria. Rather, it was doing what you could with the facts and resources at hand. Taking risks, even accepting intelligent mistakes with tragic consequences, was the recipe for determining and solving *real* problems amid the distractions of *apparent* problems.

King was impressed by Kettering's analysis, so impressed that he made it required reading in one of his reminders to Chester Nimitz about the importance of hitting the Japanese whenever the opportunity presented. "You are requested to read the article," he wired Nimitz on March 30, 1942, ". . . and to see that it is brought to the attention of all your principal subordinates and key officers."

———

Events had moved fast for King in the days, weeks and months since the Japanese sneak attack. In truth, the curtain had opened on the defining act in King's long career just when he despaired of ever claiming its center stage.

After his 1936 departure from BuAer, King had served next as Commander, Aircraft, Base Force (ComAirBasFor). AirBasFor was little more than a Pacific frontier seaplane command—one of just two flag-level operational aviation commands in the U.S. Navy. It took him two additional years to fleet up to the other, more prestigious one: Commander, Aircraft, Battle Force (ComAirBatFor). His tenure there saw the addition of two more carriers (*Yorktown* and *Enterprise*) to the Navy's modest inventory, but King's own time was steadily running out.

In 1939, when King lost out to a Gun Clubber (Admiral Harold R. Stark) in the race for Chief of Naval Operations (CNO), in no small part because of the cumulative ill will he had generated through the years, his career seemed over. Due to retire at age sixty-four in November 1942, King transferred to the General Board—the elephants' graveyard for aging Navy admirals.

———

But then, in 1940, King got an unexpected reprieve in the form of an opportunity to take command of the Navy's Atlantic Squadron. During that stint (which coincided with the German U-boat threat along the Eastern Seaboard and, accordingly, the elevation of the Atlantic Squadron to the Atlantic Fleet), King caught the eye of Roosevelt's new Secretary of the Navy, Frank Knox.[1]

———

1. An industrialist, publisher, passionate New Deal critic and 1936 Republican vice-presidential candidate, Franklin Knox had been astutely co-opted by Roosevelt. The cabinet post ended any of his aspirations for being the Republican presidential nominee in 1940.

In the notoriously belligerent, but always forthright King, Knox saw just what he thought was needed at the Navy's helm: a no-nonsense doer. In the wake of Pearl Harbor, even as Roosevelt and Knox tapped Chester Nimitz to relieve Husband Kimmel as CinCPac, Knox offered King the loftier and more politically perilous post of Commander in Chief, U.S. Fleet.

After some wrangling over title (the CinCUS acronym was too suggestive of the U.S. Fleet's current state) locale and scope, King became CominCH effective December 30, 1941. He would be headquartered not at sea or some far-off outpost but in Washington, DC. He would have "supreme command" of all the Navy's operating forces and even authority over its rat's maze of administrative bureaus. Most important, King would hold direct reporting responsibility to the President. The final hurdle to King's ascension—his awkward co-star billing with CNO Stark—was removed on March 12, 1942. Stark was bundled off to London to command Naval Forces in Europe and King, via Executive Order 9096, became CNO as well as CominCH.

————

Perhaps the quality that most impressed Roosevelt and Knox about their new CominCH-CNO was how, even as the Allies' defense lines in the Pacific seemed to be crumbling, King offered a definitive plan for the future—one that put the global war in perspective while showing how the Japanese could be beaten.

Britain and Russia, King understood, were committed to fighting Germany. All the U.S. could do for them in the short term was to send munitions, food and raw material.

In the South Pacific, meanwhile, the lines of supply and communication to Australia and New Zealand had to be preserved at all costs. However, once the U.S. reinforced bases along the Hawaii-Australia line, the road to defeating Japan, while formidable, was clear: an assault into the Solomon Islands, New Guinea and the Bismarck Archipelago.

————

For Ernest King, doing what could be done with resources at hand applied no less to his cadre of uniformed leaders. Because the Navy's battleships had largely been put out of the fight, the surface actions revolved around carrier aviation. The Gun Club admirals were for the first time being put into secondary roles and some of them were fiercely protesting. Conversely, senior officers with aviation training were pushing for a bigger voice in strategy and decision-making. To tackle this and even more pressing strategic matters, King arranged to meet with CinCPac Chester Nimitz on April 25 in San Francisco.

Although believing the fifty-seven-year-old Chester W. Nimitz (a submariner by trade) was still unproven as a fleet commander, King generally respected Nimitz's abilities and trusted his judgment. One expression of this respect and trust was a King-inspired directive giving Nimitz not one, but two command roles: in addition to CinCPac, Nimitz was also Commander in Chief, Pacific Ocean Areas (CinCPOA). As CinCPOA, Nimitz was in charge of all U.S. military forces across the Pacific save those (under Douglas MacArthur) in Australia, New Guinea and the Dutch East Indies. The not-too-subtle subtext was that the war against Japan would be a Navy show.

Despite all his confidence in Nimitz, however, King had one nagging point of discomfort. Nimitz had most recently been Chief of the Bureau of Navigation (BuNav), where he was responsible for orchestrating Navy personnel assignments. In King's mind this made Nimitz a "fixer"—someone too lenient on his subordinates and too willing to smooth things over. He didn't understand why Nimitz and other Navy fixers were so queasy about firing bad people—something that had to be done.

———

Of special concern to both men was the state of U.S. carrier aviation. Though the four carriers operating in the Pacific had escaped the Pearl Harbor carnage, carrier decks were in short supply. The U.S. had begun the war with just seven. Five of a new class of *Essex* carriers—bigger, sturdier, faster and in every way more capable than their predecessors—were now under construction. But it would be a long time before any of these ships and others like them, would be ready to fight.

Meanwhile, younger, more aggressive and savvier aviation flag officers were needed to make the best use of the precious carrier inventory that existed. Unfortunately, there were not enough prepared to take charge. Instead, King and Nimitz were settling for the likes of Wilson Brown and Frank Jack Fletcher, aging non-aviators at the helms of TFs 11 and 17. While these two task force admirals usually deferred to aviation-trained subordinates such as Aubrey Fitch (a Rear Admiral) and Ted Sherman (a Captain) when it came to air tactics, this was an incomplete solution.

Of more immediate import, King had little enthusiasm for either man. In February, when *Lexington*'s Wilson Brown had communicated his desperate need for re-provisioning, King had been moved to snap: "Carry on as long as you have hardtack, beans and corn willy. What the hell are you worrying about?" King had likewise chastised Frank Jack Fletcher when he suspected Fletcher of avoiding a strike on Japanese transports: "Your [message] not understood if it means you are retiring from enemy vicinity in order to refuel."

Only William Halsey, the stocky, restive and bushy eye-browed ComAirBatFor represented the ideal. Halsey was an experienced task force commander and, most critically, an inspiring and relentless fighter. King and Nimitz needed more Halseys but they didn't have them. Halsey had been slated for relief just as the war started. That move had been postponed, but now the one 'Halsey' King and Nimitz had at their disposal was being run ragged spearheading raids all across the Pacific.

––––––

Topping King's and Nimitz's April 25 agenda was the defense of New Guinea. Navy intelligence analysts were convinced the Japanese were planning to launch an invasion of Port Moresby. If the Japanese succeeded, they would control Eastern New Guinea, deepening the threat to Australia. Nimitz brought with him for King's review his plan to defend Port Moresby by confronting the Japanese in the Coral Sea.

King concurred with Nimitz's plan because it brought Navy carriers into the South Pacific where King wanted them—not held in reserve with the "pessimists and defeatists" at Pearl. At the same time, both men knew that an earlier move by King—one that had allowed an *apparent* problem to take precedence over a *real* one—put Nimitz's forces at a disadvantage.

Months before, caving to everyone's thirst to avenge Pearl Harbor, King had allowed himself to embrace a bold scheme concocted by two members of his planning staff: a bombing strike over the very heart of Japan. A Navy aircraft carrier (*Hornet*, accompanied by *Enterprise*) would launch Army Mitchell B-25 medium bombers (led by Army Lieutenant Colonel Jimmy Doolittle) against Tokyo and other big Japanese cities. Following the raid, the B-25s would fly on to safety in China.

After garnering JCS and presidential approval for the idea, King had built a tight circle of security around plan specifics. The circle was limited to King himself, his two staff planners, Nimitz, Army Air Forces Chief General Henry H. "Hap" Arnold (who would supply the bombers and crews) and the two Navy officers who would execute it—overall task force commander Bill Halsey and *Hornet* CO Marc A. Mitscher.

The problem was that the April 18 strike (announced after the fact by a jubilant Roosevelt to a morale-starved nation) violated sound strategy. It diverted critical scarce resources from the South Pacific, where King himself had argued America's current strategic interests lay—and where the Japanese were about to launch a showdown offensive.

The Doolittle raid had in effect denied Nimitz the use of *Enterprise* and *Hornet*. (Although the two carriers were hurrying back to Pearl, they could not be expected to reach the South Pacific until well into May.) Perhaps as bad, the move left Halsey, the U.S. Navy's best carrier admiral, thousands of miles from what could well be a decisive action. Instead, King and Nimitz would have to place their bets with Frank Jack Fletcher, an admiral whose judgment and fighting spirit King seriously distrusted.

––––––

On April 5, 1942, nearly three weeks before the King-Nimitz meeting in San Francisco, Japanese Admiral Isoroku Yamamoto, commander of Japan's Combined Fleet, received a phone call from his staff Operations Officer Commander Yasuji Watanabe. Watanabe, then in heated negotiations over war strategies with representatives of the Naval General Staff in Tokyo, had reached Yamamoto at his Combined Fleet headquarters aboard flagship *Yamato* at its anchorage near Hiroshima.

Watanabe updated his boss on the status of negotiations, which had been dragging on for several days. Naval General Staff representatives were adamant that their plan for a South Pacific offensive aimed at eastern New Guinea, the Solomons, New Caledonia, Fiji and Samoa should take precedence over Yamamoto's ambitions to capture Midway Atoll and thereby lure the Americans into a decisive fleet battle in the Central Pacific.

For its part, Naval General Staff was intent on neutralizing Australia as a potential springboard for enemy counter-offenses. First steps toward that end had already been taken in early March with the invasion of Lae and Salamaua on the north coast of New Guinea. Though the invasion force ships had been attacked by American carrier aircraft, follow-up plans to occupy Port Moresby on New Guinea's south coast and Tulagi in the Solomons were already in the works.

Meanwhile, Commander Tatsukichi Miyo, who represented the Naval General Staff, had been arguing vigorously that Yamamoto's proposed Midway venture was fatally flawed. After Pearl Harbor, the crucial element of surprise had been lost, at least in the Central Pacific. Moreover, it was debatable whether the Americans could be lured into a fleet engagement or whether possession of Midway itself would be of any strategic value.

After reporting the General Staff's position, Watanabe informed Yamamoto the two sides were deadlocked. He requested instructions for the stand he should take.

———

The strong-willed Yamamoto, then fifty-eight, was used to these tussles between Combined Fleet, the IJN's seagoing arm and the Naval General Staff—Tokyo–based armchair strategists led by sixty-one-year-old Admiral Osami Nagano, then Japan's highest ranking admiral (and Yamamoto's nominal superior).

Yamamoto and Nagano had been like-minded in resisting Japan's plunge into war but, once that issue was decided, the two IJN leaders had promptly parted ways on war strategy. Nagano had advocated an immediate southward thrust to secure sources of oil, while Yamamoto's proposed opening gambit was destruction of the U.S. Fleet by means of a coordinated carrier air strike on the Hawaiian Islands. Yamamoto's secret plan had prevailed (in large part because of his threat to resign if it was rejected) and its success had given Combined Fleet enormous leverage for driving future strategy.

Yet despite Pearl Harbor's spectacular results, Yamamoto agonized over unfinished objectives. The U.S. carriers were still on the loose and their raids, especially against Marcus Island, so close to the home islands, caused reverberations far beyond the damage inflicted.

Perhaps more than anything, Yamamoto was obsessed with the idea that his foremost duty was to protect the Emperor and his throne in Tokyo. Yamamoto understood that any attacks against Tokyo would have to employ seaborne aviation. Accordingly, he had taken precautionary defensive steps. These included a trap line of early warning picket boats stationed six hundred miles east of Tokyo; and the staging of daily long-range reconnaissance air patrols. The raids on the Marshalls had even prompted Yamamoto to recall carriers *Zuikaku* and *Shokaku* from the southwest Pacific to bolster home island defenses.

Still, no matter where fleet actions took him, Yamamoto never failed to ask for the latest Tokyo weather conditions. Only if conditions were bad did he feel relieved.

———

Watanabe returned to the Naval Staff conference table with Yamamoto's explicit marching orders and relayed them in no uncertain terms: The success or failure of Japan's Pacific strategy would be determined by whether or not it succeeded in destroying the U.S. Fleet. The General Staff's approach was indirect—to sever the U.S.-Australia supply lines by placing certain areas under Japanese control. The better, more direct way was to destroy the enemy's carrier strength in decisive battle. Without U.S. carriers, no supply lines could be maintained.

Yamamoto (via Watanabe) rested his case and he would not budge. Among those sitting in on the negotiations was Vice Admiral Seiichi Ito, Nagano's Deputy Chief. Ito knew full well the outsized leverage that Yamamoto possessed. When another negotiator at the table reluctantly proposed that the Naval General Staff agree to the attack on Midway, Ito quietly nodded his assent. It was as if Nimitz—Yamamoto's U.S. counterpart—had overruled King.

In the days that followed, even as formal plans and schedules were drawn up by Combined Fleet, the Naval General Staff continued to drag its feet as a way of extracting concessions. To appease them, Combined Fleet finally agreed to two subsidiary operations: first, the incorporation of a plan to attack the Aleutian Islands in concert with the Midway offensive; and second, agreement to lend carrier support to the planned early May invasion of Port Moresby and Tulagi.

————

Butch O'Hare was certain that he'd shot down six bombers during the February 1942 Rabaul mission. *Lexington* CO Ted Sherman's after-action report, however, ultimately reduced the count to five but it also recommended that O'Hare be awarded a Navy Cross. Brown's endorsement (which also included award recommendations for Jimmie Thach and five other VF-3 pilots) emphasized O'Hare's singlehanded exploit.

It was this mention that piqued the interest of Washington brass, including Navy Secretary Knox and Admiral Ernest King. Almost certainly for King, O'Hare's actions symbolized a gallant defense of Lady Lex, King's favorite ship. The two men set the wheels in motion for what they felt would be more fitting recognition.

————

On March 10, even as stateside newspaper accounts (especially in St. Louis and Chicago) touted O'Hare as the Pacific War's first Navy ace, Wilson Brown's *Lexington* task force, augmented by carrier *Yorktown*, struck at Japanese invasion beaches on New Guinea's northern coast. Just reaching targets at Lae and Salamaua from launch points in the Gulf of Papua involved cresting the sixteen thousand foot Owen Stanley Mountains— no mean feat for the bomb and torpedo-laden SBDs and TBDs—but the mission was a huge success. With the loss of a single Lex SBD, the Americans had sunk or damaged at least nine Japanese ships and possibly side-tracked Japan's plans for the conquest of Eastern New Guinea.

After Lae and Salamaua, *Lexington* made its long-delayed return to Pearl for a well-deserved period of rest and refit for many VF-3 personnel. For O'Hare, however, it meant the kick-off of a media-drenched publicity blitz and hero's tour. On April 15, when *Lexington* again set sail for the South Pacific—this time with VF-2's Fighting Chiefs restored as Lex's fighting squadron—O'Hare was en route to San Francisco by flying boat.

There followed an April 19 trip to Washington coincident with the announcement that O'Hare was to be promoted to lieutenant commander and receive the Medal of Honor—the country's highest tribute for combat valor. For O'Hare, the April 21 White House ceremonial meeting with President Franklin D. Roosevelt was awkward at best. Even as Roosevelt urged him to stand at ease, O'Hare stood rigid, his eyes blinking incessantly. When he spoke, his throat seemed as dry as it had been in the skies off Rabaul a month before.

After reading the Medal of Honor citation, Roosevelt handed the document to O'Hare and the two shook hands. O'Hare's wife, Rita, next draped the medal with its baby-blue ribbon over her husband's head. To accommodate the clamoring press photographers, she agreed to do it again.

With the formalities complete, but the press still in attendance, the President casually asked O'Hare what he would like to have incorporated in the next Navy fighter plane. Arguably more at ease with that question, O'Hare replied: "Something that would go upstairs faster."

The next day Butch O'Hare was flown to Bethpage, there to watch production of the F4F, thank the Grumman employees for their efforts and, in private, discuss the next fighter aircraft with Roy Grumman's engineers.

————

The Navy's new Grumman fighter was then still in design, but first person feedback from frontline Wildcat pilots like O'Hare gave key Grumman personnel important insights on what fighter pilots wanted—and didn't. Not surprisingly, what they craved most was speed, maneuverability and, as O'Hare had phrased it for Roosevelt and the press, the ability to "go faster upstairs." Also high on the list were firepower, cockpit visibility—you couldn't hit what you couldn't see—and better provision for auxiliary fuel tanks to increase flying range.

Pilots appreciated having things the enemy apparently didn't: pilot armor, bullet-resistant windshields and self-sealing fuel tanks. However, what they didn't like (and what they were saddled with) was the extra weight, especially without a more powerful engine to compensate for it. Unfortunately, frontline wish lists, no matter how compelling, too often fell to the bottom of the designers' in-baskets. Not because engineers didn't want to know—it was simply that they couldn't do much about them.

The accepted wisdom was that when war began, design stopped and production took over. Except for tweaks and small refinements, the Army and Navy would have to live pretty much with what was already in the pipeline—and hope it was better than what the enemy had in its. In early 1941, however, with Grumman ramping up production but formal war not yet declared, Bill Schwendler and his engineers had approached BuAer with an ambitious idea. Already working on Wildcat refinements—among them a wider landing gear stance, the Sto-Wing concept and a much more powerful engine—they realized that they were on the threshold of an entirely new aircraft. Should they proceed?

For good reason, BuAer told them to go forward with the new design and return when they had something to show. Next in the Navy's fighter pipeline was a gull-winged Vought aircraft called the F4U Corsair. Its prototype had first flown in 1940, but the loss of that prototype in a crash and a succession of other delays meant that the Corsair, despite its performance promise, might not be combat ready until early 1943. Already jittery about the performance advantages of Japan's Zero fighter, the Navy wanted insurance. Accordingly, when war broke out, Grumman design Number 50 was being built as the XF6F-1.

———

O'Hare returned briefly to Washington after the Grumman visit, but by week's end he and his wife were en route to St. Louis for a hero's parade organized for Saturday, April 25. Despite temperatures in the low fifties, a stiff wind and intermittent rain, for the parade's sixty thousand spectators it was an event to rival Charles Lindbergh's 1927 homecoming from the New York to Paris flight.

On April 28, Butch and Rita O'Hare flew back to Washington where Butch was to resume Navy duties. First on the schedule was a round of see and be seen visits to naval air stations across the country, including those at Norfolk, Miami, Corpus Christi and Jacksonville. Each stop required a recounting of O'Hare's February actions above *Lexington*—always stressful and embarrassing for the taciturn O'Hare. For the assemblies of aviator cadets, though, it was the unprecedented opportunity to see a live-in-the-flesh, certified hero—the first one wearing Navy Wings of Gold.

Whether you were hero or hero-worshipper, just looking around at the throngs of people at a Grumman plant or an NAS facility gave one a sense of the enormity of wartime mobilization. And the time, persistence and coordination required for it to succeed. (It was just as Kettering had described it.)

Congress had authorized a Navy air armada of fifteen thousand aircraft. To build its portion of that armada, Grumman was now adding a thousand new production employees per month to its payroll. With a current roster of about six thousand five hundred naval aviators, startup training facilities like Corpus Christi were tasked with closing the manpower deficit, in part by double-timing cadets through a training syllabus reduced from one year to seven months. And, of course, even when pilots were ready for planes, there was more. New squadrons and air groups had to be organized and deployed. New carriers had to be commissioned, crewed and made ready for combat.

Of course, participants' perspectives on the pace of this enormous complex of tasks depended on where they were situated. For aviation cadets such as twenty-three-year-old Alex Vraciu—one among the sea of faces staring at Butch O'Hare from the seats of the base auditorium at NAS Corpus Christi in early May—the sense was that the cadets could easily be ready to go before the planes, squadrons, air groups and carrier decks were ready to receive them.

After being called to active duty in October 1941, Vraciu had gone first to Glenview, Illinois for "E-Base" (the "E" stood for Elimination)—a program to winnow out unqualified prospects. Vraciu was next sent to Dallas, where he had to wait a month for NAS Corpus Christi's first 1942 Basic Flight training program to get underway.

Vraciu had to redo ground school (at the time, neither military aviation branch gave credence to CPTP) but, beginning in February 1942, he was flying nearly every day. By April's end, Vraciu had logged more than one hundred and twenty solo hours, all of them in the N3N Canary, the Navy's two-seat biplane trainer.

For Vraciu, seeing O'Hare in person was a source of inspiration. Vraciu had long before determined he would settle for nothing less than becoming a U.S. Navy fighter pilot. But seeing Butch O'Hare and hearing first-hand what he'd done was also a source of frustration. The pace through the pipeline seemed slow—and word had it from those even further along that there were simply not enough planes and carrier decks yet to put any of them to good use.

The snail's pace of this process would only seem to grind more slowly in the weeks ahead as news accounts told of the dramatic carrier battles being waged in the Pacific.

10

SCRATCH TWO FLATTOPS

From his vantage point at ten thousand feet, VF-42 XO Lieutenant Commander Jim Flatley had a splendid view of VT-5 TBDs as they started their torpedo runs on the Japanese carrier. Their target was heavily obscured by black smoke, but it looked to Flatley as though the ship, after already being worked over by Lex's aircraft earlier in the morning, was a goner. To be honest, the *Yorktown* TBDs and SBDs were probably just wasting their time. They should instead be expending ordnance on other ships in the formation—and probably would be if there'd been an on-the-scene strike coordinator to sort these things out.

Just to get into position, the *Yorktown* TBDs had to skirt heavy antiaircraft fire from the Japanese cruisers. It was nearing noon before they were finally zeroing in on the small slice of the carrier's starboard side not obscured by smoke. Only after the pilots had dropped their fish (they later claimed ten hits) did a couple of fighters—open-cockpit Claudes—finally converge on the TBDs. Flatley at once spotted them and took his five VF-42 Wildcats in a steep, spiraling dive to intercept.

———

When he arrived in the South Pacific in late April, Jim Flatley carried orders to assume command of VF-42—only to find that VF-42 already had a skipper. The confusion was unfortunate, yet understandable. Having never received a copy of Flatley's orders, *Yorktown's* CO Captain Elliott C. Buckmaster had stepped in to bump VF-42 XO Lieutenant Commander Charles R. Fenton into the CO slot vacated by the promotion of Lieutenant Commander Oscar Pederson to CAG.

Settling for the role of squadron XO until things were straightened out, Flatley was happy to avoid a return to the States. Indeed, when word of his new assignment arrived on May 1, just as action in the Coral Sea seemed to be in the offing, Flatley promptly lobbied Buckmaster to stay as 42's XO until the smoke cleared.

In a way Flatley's new squadron possessed the inadvertent "wrong place-right time" qualities that characterized his own arrival. First embarked aboard *Yorktown* in April 1941, VF-42 was to be a temporary stand-in for VF-5 (*Yorktown's* home team) as VF-5 pilots transitioned from Grumman biplanes to Wildcats. December 7 found *Yorktown* in Norfolk, Virginia with VF-5 not yet equipped to return, so VF-42 stayed aboard even as *Yorktown* shifted to the West Coast and deployed to the Pacific.

On February 1, VF-42 joined the action as *Yorktown* teamed with TF 8's *Enterprise* for strikes in the Marshalls and Gilberts and, on March 10, with TF 11's *Lexington* for the Lae-Salamaua raids. *Yorktown* was now set to rendezvous once more with *Lexington* in the Coral Sea.

On May 4, when *Yorktown's* air group hit a Japanese invasion force at Tulagi, strike pilots got their first high altitude glimpses of the sharp mountain ridges and dank jungle slopes of nearby Guadalcanal. During an afternoon fighter sweep, two VF-42 pilots, twenty-six-year-old Lieutenant (junior grade) E. Scott McCuskey and his wingman, twenty-two-year-old Ensign John P. Adams, got even closer. Lost and low on fuel, both set down on a narrow rocky beach on Guadalcanal's southeast coast. After making futile efforts to torch their planes, McCuskey and Adams were rescued that same night by destroyer *Hammann* (DD-412).

Yorktown met up with *Lexington* and an ANZAC surface squadron the next morning. The ships spent that day and the next refueling as they headed towards the Louisiade Archipelago southeast of New Guinea. Then, after sending fleet oiler *Neosho* (AO-23) south to safety under escort by *Sims* (DD-409), Fletcher assumed command of both task forces (as TF 17) and, based on reports of an enemy carrier and invasion force poised to strike Port Moresby, readied for battle.

The long awaited moment came at 8:15 a.m. on May 7: a purported SBD sighting of two carriers and four heavy cruisers at a position two hundred miles northwest of TF 17. Fletcher felt certain these were Japanese fleet carriers *Shokaku* and *Zuikaku*—his main objective. An hour later, Fletcher turned the reins over to *Lexington's* Aubrey Fitch, now designated TF 17's air task group commander, to launch strikes.

There was some initial confusion as to whether, given the distance involved, fighter aircraft would join in. Soon, however, Fitch confirmed that under the circumstances (what amounted to the first ever carrier-to-carrier duel) he wanted to hit with everything he had. *Lexington* launched first, beginning at 9:16 a.m., and her strike group departed for the target a half hour later. Then it was *Yorktown's* turn: VB-5 and VS-5 SBDs followed by VT-5 TBDs.

Last off the deck were VF-42's eight Wildcat escorts. The four TBD escorts were led by Jim Flatley. A mix-up during launch, however, gave Flatley an extra hand—the Wildcat flown by twenty-nine-year-old Lieutenant (junior grade) Walter A. Haas.

———

Flatley took on one of the two open-cockpit Claudes in a high-side run, pinning it so close to the water that the pilot's only hope to escape was to try acrobatics—wings, rolls, even tight loops. They were impressive but of no use. Using the splash patterns of his first machine-gun rounds to guide his aim, Flatley systematically walked his burst directly into the Claude's fuselage. As the Japanese plane crashed, Flatley instinctively used his dive momentum to pull up and regain altitude.

As the second Claude fled low off the surface, Flatley's wingman twenty-six-year-old Ensign John D. Baker latched on to its tail and set off in pursuit. Meanwhile, however, another Japanese fighter had nosed its way into the melee.

The intruder was first spotted by twenty-five-year-old Lieutenant (junior grade) Brainard T. Macomber, Flatley's second section leader. Seeing its long glass cockpit canopy as it passed beneath him on an opposite heading, Macomber mistook the aircraft for a two-seater scout bomber. The mistake was understandable: few in the squadron had yet seen, much less tangled with, a Japanese Zero.

Macomber banked, dived and set off after what looked to him like a sitting duck. But when he attacked from above and behind, his opponent turned smoothly and countered. The two planes passed nose-to-nose, exchanging fire.

Macomber then turned back, but so did the Japanese pilot—and, surprisingly, much more nimbly than could Macomber's Wildcat. After a second nose-to-nose scissoring, the Zero managed to cut inside Macomber's next turn. With the enemy plane on his tail and too low now to try diving away, Macomber had no choice but to fight it out.

Macomber's wingman Ensign Edgar R. "Red Dog" Basset also thought that Macomber's assailant was some sort of scout bomber. Bassett, twenty-eight, a veteran of the Lae-Salamaua and Tulagi raids (a free spirit and poker sharp but also a fatalist who would have bet the house on his imminent death), moved up steadily behind the distracted Japanese pilot and gave him a long burst. At the first sign of Basset's tracers, the enemy rolled out and accelerated. Seeing white smoke stream from the plane's belly, Bassett tried closing to finish it off. To his amazement, the cripple easily pulled away.

At that moment Walt Haas, Flatley's extra man, was circling above the fray, looking for an opportunity. When he saw Bassett's quarry break away and head in his direction, Haas was in a good position to take him on.

The Japanese plane had stopped smoking but its pilot was still fleeing—now just a few hundred feet above the water. Haas used dive speed to overhaul the unsuspecting pilot and got in position for a stern shot. When Haas opened fire, the nimble plane rolled into a climbing turn. This maneuver brought the enemy directly into Haas' sight. A short burst hit the enemy's fuselage, and immediately set it ablaze. The pilot stood up in the cockpit, apparently intent on jumping. He was still standing when the craft hit the water and disintegrated.

Both Macomber and Bassett were witnesses to Haas's kill. Though it went into the records as a Type 96 fighter, Haas became probably the first U.S. Navy or Marine Corps aviator to have shot down one of Japan's near-mythic Zero fighters.

———

At 12:10 p.m., when *Lexington* VS-2 SBD pilot Lieutenant Commander Robert E. Dixon sent the message "Scratch one flattop, Signed Bob," cheers erupted through decks and interior spaces across TF 17. The weather near the carriers had worsened to solid overcast by the time the strike aircraft returned, but once they were aboard, deck crews worked quickly to refuel and re-arm, having them ready within two hours. By then, however, after reviewing flight crew debriefings, Frank Jack Fletcher was not so certain the two Japanese fleet carriers had been discovered. Fletcher opted instead to conceal his forces in the squally overcast of the warm front, awaiting further developments and more information.

Information—bad information—came first: oiler *Neosho* and destroyer *Sims*, thought to be safe far to the southeast, had been attacked by dozens of Japanese carrier bombers. *Sims* had been sunk and *Neosho*, while still afloat, was listing perilously and adrift without power.

Then at 5:47 p.m., *Lexington* FDO Red Gill reported low altitude bogeys fifty miles to the southeast. Four CAP VF-2 Wildcats were sent to intercept, while both Lex and *Yorktown* scrambled seventeen more into the
overcast. Within minutes, the VF-2 CAP division led by CO Lieutenant
Commander Paul H. Ramsey bushwhacked a formation of seven unwitting Japanese aircraft, splashing five of them.

While Ramsey's division mopped up this intercept, Red Gill sent Jim
Flatley with seven Wildcats to find a new set of bogeys. Southbound and
thirty miles out, Flatley's pilots spotted a six-plane formation pass below
them heading north—it could only be Japanese. Hindered now by darkness as well as overcast, Flatley's pilots set upon the unsuspecting planes
and claimed two of them before being recalled.

During these short, one-sided duels, the Japanese apparently lost seven
aircraft with their crews while TF 17 lost two of its fighter pilots in action
(one each from *Lexington* and *Yorktown*) and a third (VF-42's John Baker)
to weather and darkness. But while the day's casualties were at an end, the
enemy presence wasn't. For the next hour, as the tense nighttime recovery of the CAP aircraft was completed, spectral intruders continued to
turn up and as quickly turn away.

Without doubt the intruders were Japanese aircraft and almost certainly, given the hour and weather conditions, they were not snooping
TF 17. More likely, the pilots were seeking their own flight decks while
returning from their attacks on *Neosho* and *Sims*.

Under the circumstances, Frank Jack Fletcher could be sure of three
things. Despite the cost and however inadvertently, the Japanese had managed to find his carriers. If these aircraft were in transit from further south,
they were well within striking range. With little doubt, Fletcher's pilots
and sailors would be in battle once May 8th dawned.

———

"Hey Rube!"

The expression, a carnival huckster's invitation to easy marks, had
been incorporated in the FDO lexicon and its meaning was precise. At
10:59 a.m. on May 8, when *Lexington* FDO Red Gill called it out, the
CAP fighters currently aloft—a division each from VF-2 and VF-42—
knew exactly what they were expected to do: return to station over their
respective carriers.

The fighters were needed there. *Yorktown* and *Lexington* radars were
both seeing a large group of bogeys coming from the north—now less

than seventy miles out. Of equal concern, these CAP divisions had already been aloft for ninety minutes. Though not yet low on fuel, they likely would be by the time the Japanese strike aircraft arrived. There was no option to recover them now. The flight deck crews were busy launching the handful of reserve fighters. The "rubes" returning to the carriers would have to wait, then fight and hope for the best.

———

Three minutes after Gill's CAP recall, and just as the *Yorktown* elements of TF 17's strike formations were beginning their attacks on carriers *Shokaku* and *Zuikaku* 170 miles to the north, Jim Flatley's reserve CAP took off from *Yorktown*. With the task force now on the southern fringes of the warm front that had hidden them yesterday, the ceiling directly overhead was unlimited. The patchy clouds to the north, however, made convenient cover for snoopers and incoming bogeys. For this flight, twenty-four-year-old Lieutenant (junior grade) Richard G. Crommelin flew on Flatley's wing while Brainard Macomber and the ever-fatalistic Red Dog Bassett comprised the second section.

Counting the eight F4Fs already aloft, Flatley's four, plus five under VF-2's Paul Ramsey launching now from Lex, TF 17 would have seventeen fighters for defense. They could only guess how many Japanese were on the way.

———

After forming up, Flatley's division circled to await Gill's instructions. Flatley kept radio silence, but soon the anticipation of the moment became too much. More than two hours before, *Yorktown* radio intelligence had begun intercepting enemy aircraft messages from a snooper dodging in and out of the clouds to the north. The Japanese knew precisely where the Americans were and their attackers were almost here. At 11:08 a.m., Flatley's patience expired. "Let's go!" he snapped at Gill.

"Climb to ten thousand feet," Gill responded tentatively, "until we see what develops."

Two minutes later Flatley's Wildcats were still climbing when Gill radioed again, this time reversing himself, though with considerably more conviction: "Vector 020 degrees, Angels 1, Buster."

Flatley didn't copy all of it. "Angels 1000 or 10000?" he asked and at once got Gill's clarification: "Sorry—Angels 1, fifteen miles."

Buster meant top sustained speed, Angels 1 (one thousand feet) that Gill must have a track on enemy torpedo planes. The four pilots swung to the specified bearing and let down, finally leveling off at two thousand five hundred feet to keep some altitude advantage. Four sets of anxious eyes scanned the skies ahead and below as they entered the fringes of the warm front.

Soon Gill was back with an all-CAP message: "Keep a sharp lookout. Agnes Red is attacking now."

Agnes Red, Flatley knew, was Paul Ramsey's VF-2 CAP. If Flatley had been sent out low, Ramsey must have been sent high. VF-2 seemed to be in the thick of it. Meanwhile, as Flatley's aircraft reached the vector boundary, there was still nothing to see.

At 11:15 a.m., Gill broke in again, this time ordering Flatley to Angels 10. Absent further clarification, Gill's abrupt redirect only compounded Flatley's confusion.

A partial transmission from Agnes Red— "We are going to chase bombers"—only added more.

At six thousand feet, as Flatley's division topped a patch of overcast, they saw what was happening on the surface. A full-scale sky-sea battle was underway: the wakes of wildly maneuvering carriers, cruisers and destroyers; barrages of time-fused antiaircraft rounds exploding at lower altitude like kernels of black popcorn; and a three-ring circus of aircraft— some in pursuit, others trailing smoke, still others falling in flames.

Flatley's division was still climbing at 11:19 a.m. With the ships they were supposed to defend falling ever more astern and with nothing visible ahead, he could no longer contain himself. "Give me something to do!" he angrily implored Gill.

"Roger," Gill answered, but this time his voice betrayed panic. Gill had no more instructions but Flatley needed none. It was time to go back.

Flatley signaled his division. The four Wildcats banked, turned south and poured on the coal.

While *Yorktown* aircraft were negotiating clouds and squalls to attack the distant Japanese carriers, Frank Jack Fletcher, Aubrey Fitch and their two carrier captains—*Yorktown's* Elliot Buckmaster, *Lexington's* Ted Sherman— had nowhere to hide their own ships. With just seventeen Wildcats aloft to intercept (and eight of those low on gas), it would come down to a battle of maneuver, of shipboard gunfire—and luck.

The opening gambit found the American formation turned southeast, making twenty-five knots—reserving full speed for when attacks commenced. To the northeast were close to seventy Japanese torpedo planes, dive-bombers and Zero escorts.

The eighteen Japanese torpedo bombers came in first, descending to four thousand feet and closing on the carriers' port sides. Most of the eighteen would head for *Lexington*, the nearer and larger of the two flattops, while a handful would veer west to take on *Yorktown*.

The bigger contingent, intending to flank *Lexington's* bow, split in two, with several torpedo planes accelerating to cross the carrier's bow and then turn to attack her starboard bow. This "anvil" tactic—used by torpedo pilots of both navies whenever possible—was designed to preclude escape. Indeed, even as the first Japanese torpedoes splashed off to port and Ted Sherman ordered full right rudder, Lex slid ominously into the paths of more to starboard. Somehow Sherman had to position *Lexington's* bow to comb some of the torpedo wakes while hoping others passed ahead, astern or beneath his hull.

Such finesse presented monstrous challenges. *Lexington's* tactical diameter (the circle her wake could carve at full right or left rudder and full speed) was two thousand yards. The Japanese fish were incredibly fast. And many were coming her way.

———

At 11:16 a.m. Commander Paul H. Ramsey's five VF-2 Wildcats were at twelve thousand feet and drawing close to the carrier formation—but still laboring to reach the higher altitude Japanese dive-bombers. Doc Sellstrom, one of Ramsey's two wingmen,[1] knew from past experience that overhauling the dive-bombers from below was impossible. So instead, at risk of defying Ramsey's orders, Sellstrom dove for the surface.

Equipped now with height advantage and speed, Sellstrom picked out one of the Japanese torpedo planes just then making a run toward *Lexington's* port side. A short, low deflection burst set it aflame and into the water. Then, when three nearby Zeros tried to retaliate, Sellstrom pressed his advantage with head-on runs and extended bursts. Finally forced to climb, Sellstrom headed first for the nearest screening ship, allowing its antiaircraft fire to brush off the Zero still on his tail. Sellstrom then made good his escape, convinced he'd shot down two fighters and a torpedo plane.

———

Lexington lookouts had called out eleven wakes before two Japanese tor-

---

1. Sellstrom was then on temporary assignment to VF-2.

pedoes finally found their mark. They exploded in quick succession at 11:20 a.m., both on the port side.

The first detonated near the forward gun gallery, buckling aviation gasoline stowage tanks, leaking volatile (and ultimately fatal) fumes into surrounding compartments. The second explosion erupted opposite the island structure, rupturing a water main, causing flooding and forcing the shutdown of three boilers.

Even as these explosions rocked *Lexington*, slowing her speed to twenty-five knots, listing her to port and leaving giant pools of fuel oil in her wake, the Japanese dive-bombers came screaming in from high out of the brilliant midday sun.

The Japanese bombers were opposed first by the four fighters stacked directly over the carrier. This over-matched handful was quickly overwhelmed by the bombers' Zero escorts. In the process, two American pilots—thirty-one-year-old Lieutenant (junior grade) Clark F. Rinehart and his wingman, twenty-two-year-old Ensign Newton H. Mason—were shot down and killed.

This left defense to the ship's antiaircraft batteries—gallery- and island-mounted 1.1-inch, 20-millimeter and .50-caliber for close range. Their gunners threw up sheets of gunfire but, hurtling in at different times and from different angles, most Japanese bombers got to their release points.

Most of the bombs, tumbling from perhaps a quarter mile above Lex's flight deck, splashed wide, though some explosions came close enough to rupture deck plates and raise huge plumes of oily-black water.

Two, however, were direct hits.

One exploded in a five-inch ammunition storage locker forward on the port side, sending up a towering sheet of flame, bulging a portion of the flight deck and killing an entire gun crew.

A second bomb hit the port side of the ship's huge smokestack, well above the flight deck. As if to proclaim her cumulative distress, Lex's emergency siren, triggered and jammed by the explosion, added prolonged shrieks to an atmosphere already thick with the mingled sweet and acrid aromas of fuel oil and gunpowder.

For his part, Elliot Buckmaster had the advantages of his ship's tighter tactical diameter and fewer torpedo attackers—and those aiming only for *Yorktown*'s port bow. At 11:18 a.m., in response to the first three of an eventual four splashes, Buckmaster throttled Yorktown to thirty knots and ordered hard right rudder. Ship and crew were untouched even as bombs began dropping at 11:24 a.m.

Immediately overhead were two Wildcats—VF-42's Lieutenant Vincent F. McCormack and his wingman Walter Haas. Positioning themselves to defend against the dive-bombing attack, both had missed the Japanese torpedo planes. Now, having climbed to thirteen thousand feet, they spotted a queue of Japanese bombers lining up to attack *Yorktown*.

McCormack rolled his aircraft and charged into the middle of the line, pouring bullets into at least one bomber. After pulling off to the side, he then approached a bomber from behind, ignoring the bullets from its rear gunner to get in a point blank burst that sent it falling away. Haas meanwhile spiraled down with some of the attacking bombers. As they slowed, Haas accelerated past, firing a burst on any Japanese plane that crossed his gunsight along the way.

McCormack's and Haas's intervention may well have disrupted the dive-bombing attack. But finally, at 11:27 a.m., one bomb connected—an armor-piercing projectile that penetrated the flight deck just inboard of the *Yorktown's* island. The bomb sliced through to the fourth deck level before exploding.

The blast tore through the decks and bulkheads of sweltering red-lit interior spaces where crewmen wore little more than t-shirts and cut-off dungarees. More than sixty of them were killed, maimed or incinerated.

———

Jim Flatley, Dick Crommelin, Brainard Macomber and Red Dog Bassett finally arrived for the closing moments of the melee. All they could see to do was shake off a pack of Japanese Zeros mauling some low-flying SBDs.

"Bandits," Flatley announced to his two sections at 11:23 a.m. "Enemy fighters down here, let's go!"

These SBDs had been Ted Sherman's brainchild—ersatz "fighters" assigned to patrol ahead of the carriers as a layer of defense against torpedoes. Once the shooting started, however, most ended up being out maneuvered and out-gunned. Zero pilots had already finished off four of eight deployed to shield Lex.

Flatley spearheaded his Wildcats in a shallow, high-speed dive, intending a series of quick hit-and-run passes. He and Crommelin were the first to engage—a high-side run on a Zero crossing from right to left at six thousand feet. Flatley triggered a short full-deflection aiming burst at four hundred yards, paused and then fired with assurance as he closed. Flatley then steepened his dive, readying to use his momentum for a recovering climb and expecting the others to follow.

Just before this first Zero spun away, Crommelin fired as well, but his two-second burst and the concentration it took made him lose sight of Flatley. His flight leader was now below and behind him, but instead of looking for Flatley, Crommelin set off after other Zeros that caught his eye.

With each of the four pilots now turned soloist, the apex of Flatley's zooming climb brought him above a new trio of Zeros. Alone now but without hesitation, Flatley dove for the formation's trailer, coming in high-side astern. Before Flatley could fire, however, the quarry—perhaps alerted—swung sharply towards him and continued into a steep, high-speed climbing turn.

Intent on following, Flatley pulled back on his stick, trying his best to haul his heavier Wildcat to keep up with the lighter, nimbler Zero. It was no use.

Crushed by overwhelming g, Flatley soon blacked out. When the fringes of his vision returned, he found himself side-by-side with the Zero. And then, just as the Japanese pilot chopped speed to drop back and line up a shot, the Grumman lost all momentum, threatening to stall into a spin that Flatley worried might mean his end.

Somehow he managed to recover into a half loop, but on its downside Flatley could see the two other Zeros, advantaged with better position and higher speed, clawing after him. It was all he could do to hold his dive right down to the wave tops and use his new reserve of speed to pull out and head for the exits. As he fled, Flatley kept twisting until he was certain his tail was clear.

Later, back aboard the damaged *Yorktown*, Flatley reflected ruefully that what had begun as a division-sized team battle had quickly devolved into an outnumbered free-for-all with no mutual support. There had to be a better way.

Minutes later, off to the north, Commander *Lexington* Air Group (CLAG) and strike leader William B. Ault had sighted one of the Japanese task force carriers through a break in the overcast. It was moving to an open space, and Ault had decided to take his command group of four SBDs and two Wildcat escorts around to the north so as to attack from a different direction than Lex's torpedo planes. Heavy smoke mingled with the overcast, evidence of the work done earlier by *Yorktown's* strike group.

As the six Lex aircraft neared the attack point, the two Wildcats, flying above and astern of the SBDs, were suddenly bounced by Zeros. The first VF-2's Lieutenant Richard S. Bull Jr. and Ensign John B. Bain saw of their attackers were the red tracer flashes passing their wings. Bull and Bain were flying so slowly—just 120 knots—and the Zeros came in so fast that there was little either pilot could do. As the Zeros climbed away, Bain lifted his nose and fired a quick burst that fell well short. Then both Zeros were gone.

Just then Ault took his SBDs into a shallow glide bomb attack, so Bull and Bain followed them in, intending to cover their withdrawal. But as they leveled off below the overcast, a second pair of Zeros went after them from above and behind. This time, however, the F4Fs had built up considerable speed and both their pilots were ready.

When Bain made a hard turn, his Zero attacker overshot him and tried a climbing escape. Bain stayed with him long enough to get in a low deflection shot at medium range. As Bain's bullets ripped into the climbing Zero, the enemy plane staggered and spun toward the water.

In countering this Zero, Bain lost contact with both the SBDs and his section leader. Bain climbed up through the overcast but when he broke into sunlight at eight thousand feet he found another Zero above and behind him. As this Zero attacked, Bain countered by turning into him, triggering a long head-on burst that caused his opponent to break away. As the Zero rolled out, Bain climbed on past him. Through scissoring sequences each tried to get on the other's tail. Bain could see the Zero was beating him on each of the turns—it was just a matter of time. Choosing discretion, Bain dropped his nose and ran for the clouds.

———

VF-2's new XO Lieutenant Noel A. M. Gayler, leading one of a pair of sections escorting the *Lexington* TBDs in their attack, also found himself outmatched by Zeros. Trying to conserve fuel as well as stay with the lumbering TBDs, Gayler and his wingman, twenty-one-year-old Ensign Dale W. Peterson, were flying at barely 105 knots. So, when several Zeros bounced them from out of the clouds, they were momentarily unable to maneuver. Within seconds, as the Zeros slashed uncontested in and out of the TBD formation, it became every man for himself.

Gayler glimpsed both planes in his other VF-2 section being chased into the clouds, each with a Zero on its tail. Gayler soon lost track of Peterson, too, and found himself cornered by four Zeros.

Gayler dove, and when one Japanese plane latched onto his tail, he opened his flaps to chop speed and disrupt the enemy's aim. As the Zero overshot his Grumman, Gayler took the opportunity to duck into a cloud. He emerged only to confront yet another Zero, but this time, as the two planes crossed head-to-head, Gayler at least managed to get off a shot. He turned hard coming out of that scissor, fully expecting to have to claw for position and cross again. To Gayler's great relief, however, the Zero was nowhere to be seen.

His close call left Gayler shaken and flushed, but on his way home he spotted a chance to get even. Happening upon an unescorted pair of northbound Japanese dive-bombers, Gayler used altitude and surprise to make several high-side passes that flamed both. If there was pleasure in revenge, however, it didn't survive the journey. Lieutenant (junior grade) Howard F. Clark, Gayler's second section leader, radioed that he was lost, out of fuel, and was ditching. Clark, twenty-seven, was never heard from again, nor, it turned out, was Dale Peterson, Gayler's wingman.

———

For TF 17 airmen and sailors there were to be two codas to the struggles and sacrifices of the day. The first came at 2:54 p.m., well after *Lexington* had recovered the last of its aircraft ever to return from the morning strike. In shaky transmissions coming from far away, CLAG William Ault had radioed that he was lost and that both he and his gunner were wounded. "From CLAG," Ault's last transmission began. "OK, so long people. We got a 1000 pound hit on the flattop."

For *Lexington*, the next toll was its own. By mid-afternoon the ship damage, once thought to be manageable, was mounting. A 2:42 p.m. explosion lifted the forward elevator a foot above the deck, coursed smoke and steam throughout the ship, and set the already-smoking hangar deck ablaze. The explosion that sealed the ship's fate came three-quarters of an hour later. Its impact blew out plates near the firerooms and damaged vital boiler uptakes. In the process, water pressure and steering control were lost. Soon ship-wide fires were reported out of control, never to be contained.

Ted Sherman would stay aboard *Lexington* until 6:30 p.m., entering the water only when he was certain no living crewman was still aboard. A whale boat from destroyer *Hammann* was soon on its way to retrieve Sherman, the ship's executive officer Commander M.T. Seligman, a Marine corporal and Sherman's dog. They were the last of 2,770 sailors and airmen picked up alive.

Lexington was then fully ablaze, visible for miles. Beginning at 7:15 p.m., destroyer *Phelps* (DD-360) fired five torpedoes into the flaming inferno. At 7:52 p.m., as the rest of TF 17 steamed south, *Lexington* rolled to port and disappeared. The tremendous underwater explosion that followed was strong enough to be felt twenty miles away.

"Congratulations on your glorious accomplishment of the last two days," read the message from Chester Nimitz to Frank Jack Fletcher with a copy to Ernest King. "Your aggressive actions have the admiration of the entire Pacific Fleet. Well done to you, your officers and men."

Nimitz's message reached King even before Fletcher's after-action report, claiming one Japanese carrier sunk and a second badly damaged. *Lexington* and *Yorktown* had been hit and damaged too, the report said, but neither badly.

Soon enough, there was more information, the worst of it being that *Lexington*—King's former command and a ship he loved—had been not just damaged, but sunk. When Nimitz nonetheless pressed to promote Fletcher to Vice Admiral and award him the Distinguished Service Medal for a "victory with decisive and far reaching consequences," King at once vetoed the idea. While intelligence suggested the Japanese had abandoned the sea-borne invasion of Port Moresby, and that one Japanese carrier had been sunk and another heavily damaged, in King's mind losing *Lexington* was neither victory nor reason to bestow laurels on Fletcher.[2] As it was, the *Lexington*'s sinking would have to be treated with great secrecy.

In the days ahead, *Lexington*'s loss continued to weigh on King, curbing his willingness to jeopardize his carriers. (He would mandate, among other things, that each flattop be equipped with an admiral and its own separate screen of cruisers and destroyers.) Though King remained convinced that Japan's next move would again be in the South Pacific, Nimitz was now touting message intercepts pointing to a late May Japanese invasion of Midway.

With this in mind, Nimitz sought to concentrate his three remaining

---

2. Fletcher would receive his promotion to Vice Admiral in August 1942.

carriers—*Enterprise*, *Hornet* and *Yorktown*—west of Hawaii. Even more, Nimitz was lobbying for the discretion to move the carriers as he thought best (just as King was giving thought to bringing some carrier aircraft ashore to bolster island defense).

Yorktown was returning to Pearl Harbor to repair the damage from Coral Sea. Halsey, with *Enterprise* and *Hornet*, meanwhile, had reached the South Pacific. King intended that they stay put and he'd told Nimitz so when they met in San Francisco. But now Nimitz urged him to reconsider. "Time and distance," Nimitz cautioned in a May 14 message, "require a definite decision in the near future."

King temporized. It was a complex problem that he needed to ponder. At the same time, though, King left room for Nimitz to press his case. While insisting to Nimitz that he still believed the Japanese would next strike in the South, King didn't rear up when Nimitz, in a May 16 note, tactfully but forcefully disagreed.

Perhaps (Nimitz suggested) if King's intelligence analysts reassessed their data, they might change their thinking. And (Nimitz assured King) Halsey could always be pulled back south if new information pointed to a different Japanese objective.

In this fashion, King and Nimitz found themselves shaping the boundaries of what was evolving into a remarkable relationship. Oddly enough, King was avoiding direct orders, instead looking for consensus through an exchange of views. For his part, Nimitz was holding his ground but being restrained and tactful about it.

After further discussions with his intelligence analysts, King finally decided that Nimitz' judgment was likely correct. On May 17 he sent Nimitz word that Halsey could indeed return to the Central Pacific.

The days ahead would be an anxious time, made even more so by distressing news about the condition of the indispensible William Halsey. When Halsey paid a courtesy call on Nimitz at Pearl he arrived looking haggard, exhausted and driven to fidgety madness by uncontrolled dermatitis. Nimitz immediately ordered Halsey to the hospital but also gave him the consolation of choosing his replacement.

Halsey's choice was Rear Admiral Raymond A. Spruance, his cruiser commander. Spruance, a 1906 Trade School graduate and Gun Clubber just shy of fifty-six, was short, wiry and energetic, an abstainer of liquor and tobacco, a connoisseur of coffee and a glutton for walking.

Spruance was known to be brilliant (though some thought too introspective and overly nuanced) and he would embark aboard *Enterprise* aided by the entirety of Halsey's seasoned staff. But still, it had to give Nimitz and particularly King pause, if for no other reason than it meant that Frank Jack Fletcher would be in overall command.

It was no surprise, then, that, as the likelihood of the battle for Midway loomed ever larger, King was exacting about the limits of risks he was willing to take. He ordered Nimitz "to employ strong attrition tactics and not—repeat—not allow our forces to accept such decisive actions as would be likely to incur heavy losses in our carriers and cruisers."

11

A BAG OF GOLD THROUGH A LONELY FOREST

June 4, 1942

At 2:45 a.m. the sound of aircraft engines roused Mitsuo Fuchida from his sick bay bed aboard carrier *Akagi*. His instincts were to rush topside but, when he tried to stand up, Fuchida found his legs still unsteady.

A week before, when Vice Admiral Chuichi Nagumo's First Mobile Force (Striking Force) had emerged from Bungo Strait and entered the Western Pacific, Fuchida was already feeling discomfort from what doctors ashore thought might be ulcers. That first night at sea Fuchida had barely dropped off to sleep before he awoke, doubled over in pain. *Akagi's* chief surgeon diagnosed it as acute appendicitis and urged an immediate operation. But Fuchida resisted, knowing it would sideline him in the coming days.

It seemed an odd twist of fate for the Pearl Harbor aerial strike commander. In the months since, Nagumo's Striking Force had covered nearly fifty thousand miles of ocean and Fuchida had led devastating air strikes on Rabaul, Port Darwin, Java, and Ceylon. No American, British or Dutch unit had been able to stop Fuchida, but now his body had.

Fuchida had no alternative, the doctor insisted: postponing treatment would undoubtedly kill him. Even Commander Minoru Genda, First Air Fleet Operations Officer (and Fuchida's classmate at Japan's Naval Academy), urged him to undergo surgery. Hadn't Fuchida himself told Genda when carriers *Akagi, Kaga, Hiryu* and *Soryu'* and their sixteen escorts sortied from the Hashirajima Anchorage that Striking Force fliers were in good shape, ready and confident?

Since the appendectomy Fuchida had been confined to sick bay, but now he just couldn't resist the urge to get topside and watch the action unfolding. Fuchida slipped out of sick bay into empty, dimly lit passageways secured for battle conditions. Before long he was bathed in cold sweat and so weakened and dizzy that he often had to stop and sprawl on the deck to rest. Once he reached his cabin, Fuchida paused to catch his breath and gather his strength before donning a uniform and going topside.

———

On Midway Atoll, some 240 miles southeast of Striking Force's carriers, TBF pilot twenty-three-year-old Ensign Albert Kyle "Bert" Earnest had also awakened to the sound of warming engines, those of Army B-17s parked on one of Eastern Island's three runways. It was 3:35 a.m. Moments later, Earnest heard the Marine pilots stirring from their bunks. He rose as well, following them outside. There was a light sea breeze and above him a sky filled with stars.

Earnest wasn't particularly hungry. So, instead of following the Marines to the mess tent, he went to check out his airplane. Earnest climbed into the TBF's cockpit, turned on his instrument lights and, as he had done many times before, went through his own pre-flight routine. Earnest, a Richmond, Virginia native, was a practical man. He took quiet pleasure in these mechanical aspects of his job—in observing and understanding why things worked. When he finished, he fired the engine, feeling the Wright Cyclone's familiar vibrations as it worked up to speed.

Ahead of him on the flight apron Earnest could discern the outline of VT-8 flight leader Lieutenant Langdon Fieberling's TBF and the shadowy movements of its crew. Earnest listened carefully to the deep, steady sound of his own engine; when he was sure it was fully warmed, he cut the power and settled back in his cockpit to wait.

———

A few minutes after he reached the *Akagi* flight control platform, Mitsuo Fuchida saw Minoru Genda slowly climbing the ladder. Having contracted a virus, Genda too was visibly ill and still dressed in pajamas. He nodded to Fuchida before gingerly continuing to the command bridge. There Genda was greeted by Admiral Nagumo himself, who wrapped his ailing staff air strategist in a fatherly embrace.

The first wave of attack planes was already lined up along the flight deck in three staggered columns. The deck, island and catwalks were hives of activity; while white-clad deckhands (in honor of the occasion, many had donned clean uniforms for the first time in weeks) tended the planes, other sailors scurried to battle stations and lookouts scanned the still dark sky. The sea continued rough, but conditions had measurably improved since Striking Force had cleared the leading edge of a storm front. The first strike wave would launch at 4:30 a.m., a half hour before dawn.

Weary and weak as he felt, Fuchida couldn't help kibitzing. He asked an officer if reconnaissance aircraft had already been launched. No, they would instead take off along with the first attack wave. Fuchida at once felt a twinge of concern. In his experience such "single-phase" air searches risked unearthing hidden threats at inconvenient, even perilous times. He shouldn't worry, the officer assured him: a second attack wave would be standing by in case the search planes discovered American ships.

––––––––

As he sat in his TBF cockpit on the Eastern Island runway apron, thirty-two-year-old Langdon Fieberling wrestled with his conscience. He simply didn't agree with Midway Marine air group commander Ira Kimes' plan to have the Navy TBFs, the Army B-26s and the Marine SBDs and SB2Us execute a coordinated strike. This tied the fate of the faster B-26s and TBFs to that of the slower Dauntlesses and ancient Vindicators.

To make the situation worse, the pilots of VMSB-24, Marine Major Lofton R. Henderson's dive-bomber squadron, were clearly raw and unready for what they were about to face. You could never doubt a Marine's courage, but more than half of Henderson's pilots had just joined VMSB-241 and none had ever flown an SBD until a few days before. Henderson would be lucky if he could organize any sort of bomb run at all, luckier still if he could bring any of his Marine fliers back alive.

And then there was the matter of fighter cover. Based on Midway CO Commander Cyril Simard's decision to use all his fighter aircraft to defend the atoll's garrison, the strike formations would be going in without escort. Under the circumstances, the TBFs' and B-26s' best defense was their speed.

––––––––

On May 31st, two days after the VT-8 TBF detachment's arrival at Pearl, Fieberling had first learned from detachment CO Lieutenant Harold "Swede" Larsen that six of their TBFs would be sent to Midway to augment the island's garrison. Fieberling would lead the flight, accompanied by five volunteers.

Although it was a long hop to an unknown island for an undefined mission, everyone in the detachment volunteered. Those finally chosen craved action, but also welcomed the chance to get away from Larsen, who was uniformly disliked. While no one doubted Swede's guts or flying ability, most believed his life centered on looking out just for himself.

In March, when most of VT-8 had deployed aboard *Hornet*, CO John Waldron had been forced to leave behind a detachment of personnel to handle a newly arrived shipment of Grumman TBFs. Larsen was put in charge and he immediately proceeded to make everyone's life miserable as they trained and prepared to deploy.

On the other hand, detachment personnel regarded "Old Langdon" Fieberling (Larsen's number two) with a mix of admiration and envy. A worldly bachelor a good decade older than most in the squadron, Fieberling was tall and slim, wore tailored uniforms, and drove an immaculate, bright-green Lincoln Zephyr convertible. Despite outward appearances, Fieberling was good-natured, free of bravado, calm, and self-contained. He never considered any job beneath his dignity. Fieberling led more by suggestion than direct order, quietly motivating others, enlisted and officer alike.

For his own part, Fieberling felt a deep personal responsibility for each of the men who'd flown with him to Midway. He was passionate about approaching the job ahead just as John Waldron would expect him to.

Among other things, the Skipper had stressed the importance of being able to fight independently. To prepare for this contingency, Fieberling had already told his pilots that if they encountered one enemy carrier, they would break into two divisions, one aiming for the carrier's starboard bow, the other for the port. If there were two or more carriers, however, then it would be up to each TBF pilot to pick a target of opportunity.

In the end, Fieberling reasoned to himself, once they spotted the Japanese, the Army, Navy and Marine aircraft would end up being on their own. It was one thing to make grandiose pre-flight plans, another thing entirely to stick to them when you were attacking under fire.

Fieberling simply wanted his own guys to have the best chance possible to complete their mission and return alive.

––––––

Forty minutes before sunup, *Akagi's* loudspeakers ordered strike aviators to assemble. After final flight deck briefings, the air crews, already sweat-drenched in heavy brown cotton flight suits, bounded towards their planes. On the bridge, after glancing solemnly at Genda and receiving a nod in return, Nagumo finally ordered: "Launch the air attack force."

As plane engines revved for take-off, white flames shot from their exhaust pipes and their blue and white wing lights blinked on. Hooded flood lamps facing inward from the deck edges were switched on, casting harsh light on the yellow flight deck and the panoply of dull green, buff and black fuselages. Virtually all the aircraft paint jobs were weather-beaten, chipped in places and mottled with grease smudges and streaks of hydraulic fluid—proof of their virtually nonstop use since Pearl Harbor.

A Zero-sen was the first to take off, beginning its run even with the bridge and gathering take-off speed through a corridor of cheering, waving crewmen. Eight more fighters promptly followed. Next to go were the dive-bombers: eighteen big, powerful Aichi D3A1 Type 99 aircraft (what the Allies code-named "Val") with their distinctive elliptical wings and "spatted" fixed landing gear. Each dangled a gray-painted 250-kilogram bomb from its belly.

In preparation for their own deck launches, Striking Force's three other carriers had widened the formation considerably—as had the escorts. *Hiryu*, though still abreast of *Akagi*, now steamed more than four thousand meters off to port. Astern of their respective carrier division mates, *Kaga* (to starboard) and *Soryu* (to port) had also opened the distance. Each carrier was contributing nine Zero-sens to the first wave. *Kaga* (like *Akagi*) was launching eighteen Vals; meanwhile, a combined thirty-six Nakajima B5N2 Type 97 dual-purpose attack aircraft (what the Allies code-named "Kate"), each equipped with a eight-hundred-kilogram bomb, were climbing from *Hiryu's* and *Soryu's* shorter flight decks.

Replacing Fuchida in overall command of the morning's attack (and personally leading the thirty-six Kates) was Lieutenant Jōichi Tomonaga. This would be Tomonaga's first sortie against the Americans, but he was an experienced flight leader and a seasoned China veteran. Indeed, nearly all the pilots boasted two or more years of flight experience.

———

Both Genda and Fuchida understood this was it. On the sortie's first day, when both were still up and about, they had jointly fretted that the decision-making and preparation for this massive operation had been too rushed. Genda had told Fuchida that Combined Fleet commander Yamamoto had bullied his way past all the skeptics, in the process saddling his subordinate Nagumo with two potentially conflicting mission objectives: to crush resistance ashore at Midway and obliterate any American carrier forces at sea and in the air. Still, Genda was confident that Striking Force was fully capable of handling its roles in the grand plan.

Genda's opinion always carried weight as far as Fuchida was concerned. Not only had Genda been the chief planner for the Pearl Harbor attack, he had been the advocate and architect of the multi-carrier task force concept as well as a driving force in persuading Yamamoto to create First Air Fleet.

Instead, it was Nagumo about whom Fuchida had considerable doubts.

Fuchida wasn't at all sure he still recognized the Nagumo he'd first met a decade before. Fuchida had then admired everything about Nagumo: his intelligence and energy, his exacting performance and leadership, his logic, his candor and, perhaps above all, his open-hearted willingness to assist younger officers. Now, while he retained his composure and friendliness, Nagumo had somehow lost much of his vigor and fighting spirit. He appeared markedly older, seemed unable or unwilling to take the initiative.

Genda could only agree. Whenever he drafted a plan, Genda confided to Fuchida, it was approved with little discussion or change. It disturbed both men that these drafts were directly transformed into formal orders that could fundamentally impact Japan's destiny. Critics, Genda knew, had come to refer to Striking Force as "Genda's fleet."

———

At 4:40 a.m., as the *Hornet* VT-8 squadron ready room teletype clacked out a message, drowsy pilots perked up and watched the screen. Torpedo-equipped PBYs from Midway (it advised them) had launched a successful night attack on a Japanese force west of Midway. The news held the pilots' attention briefly but, with no more information forthcoming, most eventually returned to what they'd been doing. Some drifted back to sleep, while others joked amiably or traded raunchy limericks.

Most of the pilots knew each other well—many from their time together in Norfolk. They were a tight-knit group accustomed to bickering and bantering caustically but good-naturedly with each other. Not surprisingly, they treated newcomers in the way any close family might act with outsiders: polite, friendly, but with more than a little reserve.

One such newcomer was twenty-six-year-old Ensign Frederick "Fred" Mears III. Few VT-8 veterans asked, knew or would have much cared that the Seattle-born, Yale-educated Mears came from a family of some prestige and influence. His father, Colonel Frederick Mears, was a brilliant Army engineer who'd overseen the construction of the Alaska Railroad and been instrumental in founding the city of Anchorage. An uncle on his mother's side had very recently made the headlines: Army Lieutenant General Jonathan Wainwright, former commander of U.S. forces in the Philippines, was now in Japanese captivity.

Mears had arrived in Hawaii in mid-April carrying orders to join VT-2 aboard *Lexington*—this despite the fact that he was carrier qualified only in SBDs. With Lex still out at sea, Mears had been temporarily assigned to VT-3, where he at least gained some actual TBD flight time. But now, with Lex at the bottom of the Coral Sea, Mears had received last minute orders to join VT-8 aboard *Hornet*.

When John Waldron, the lean, fierce-looking VT-8 CO learned that neither Mears nor the two other new arrivals had ever landed a TBD on a carrier, he said he didn't want them. Only reluctantly had he agreed to take them on as spares. Under the circumstances, there was little chance the three would be flying today. Perhaps in the third or fourth attack, but only if the *Hornet's* CO gave his express permission.

———

Once Striking Force's first wave aircraft were launched, the empty flight decks on *Akagi*, *Kaga*, *Hiryu*, and *Soryu* again began filling with planes. This time each was spotting Zero-sens for backup CAP. Meanwhile, below decks, from *Akagi's* and *Kaga's* forward magazines, armorers were already hauling torpedoes from storage racks. The new, seventeen-foot-long Type 91 torpedoes were fast, ferocious water serpents—enormously more accurate, powerful and reliable than any "fish" the Americans had.

They were to be attached to the Kates being held in reserve. Meanwhile, the reserve Vals would be armed with the same sort of 250-kilogram bombs used by the first wave's dive-bombers. The inclusion of torpedoes would make the second wave a more potent anti-shipping weapon—a contingency specified by the exacting Yamamoto in case American carriers were discovered.

Despite the bustle and semblance of readiness, Mitsuo Fuchida remained uneasy. Striking Force ships were vulnerable to a strike from Midway, but they still had no word from their own attack aircraft. Nor had they heard from reconnaissance scouts about the possibility of enemy warships. CAP Zero-sens were aloft but the rest of Striking Force's reserve aircraft were mostly hangar-bound. All in all, Nagumo's ship formation made an inviting target.

A month before, Fuchida had returned to *Akagi* from a morning air-to-ground strike on Ceylon convinced that a follow-up strike was essential. En route he had made such a recommendation to Nagumo, who ordered that second wave planes be armed with bombs instead of torpedoes. Before those reserves were launched, however, reconnaissance planes detected British cruisers advancing on Striking Force. In the midst of a botched and seemingly endless effort to re-arm the reserve aircraft, Nagumo finally dispatched just the dive-bombers to attack.

The Vals had saved that particular day, sinking the British ships—two cruisers—in a matter of minutes. However, Fuchida knew enough not to count either on good luck or enemy unpreparedness. To him, this morning's flight operations suggested a man carrying a bag of gold through a lonely forest—ripe pickings for the first robber lurking behind a tree.

———

Feeling exhausted, Fuchida had returned to his cabin to lie down, but was there only a few minutes when bugles signaled an air raid. Fuchida could feel the deck above him rumble as interceptors took off. He paused to count—nine of them. The momentary silence that followed their departure was suddenly broken by the bark of antiaircraft guns. Fuchida glanced at his watch. It was 5:20 a.m.

Once again Fuchida climbed up to the flight control platform. Air Officer Shogo Masuda informed him that the intruder was a flying boat—an American PBY. According to ship's personnel monitoring the radio frequencies, the intruder was already transmitting a lengthy coded message. All at once feeling incredibly dizzy, Fuchida slumped to the deck. An officer placed a parachute pack under his head as a pillow. Fuchida could now only stare up at the brightening sky and take in the commotion that surrounded him.

———

At 5:45 a.m. Langdon Fieberling was in Eastern Island's air operations bunker with Ira Kimes and Kimes' XO Verne McCall when one of the reconnaissance Catalinas sent an urgent, plain language message: "Many planes heading Midway bearing 320 degrees, distance 150." Fieberling dashed back to the flight line.

Bert Earnest was then still asleep in his cockpit, but a Marine officer awakened him and told him to stand by for take-off. "Attack enemy carrier bearing 320 degrees, distance 180 miles, course 135 degrees, speed 25 knots," he shouted, before jumping from Earnest's wing and leaping into a waiting jeep which raced on to the next TBF in line.

Earnest still couldn't believe they were going out, but Fieberling had started his engine, so he did, too. Soon they began taxiing out onto the runway; Fieberling first, followed in order by Earnest, Ensign C. E. "Charlie" Brannon, Ensign O. J. "Ozzie" Gaynier, Ensign Victor A. Lewis, and finally NAP Darrel D. Woodside.

The TBFs had to mark time as the Marine Wildcat and Buffalo fighters left first. At 6:15 a.m., once the runway was clear, the VT-8 planes revved engines and took off. Aloft, the six TBFs joined up into two three-plane sections. Fieberling led the first, with Earnest on his left wing, Brannon on his right. Ozzie Gaynier, leading the second section, aligned his three planes off Brannon's right wing.

Earnest looked back to Midway to see that the B-26s, SBDs, and SB2Us were still taking off from Eastern Island. The TBFs were supposed to circle and wait for the other planes to join up. Instead, Fieberling simply picked up speed and led his formation up towards the scattered clouds, all the while pointing them northwest.

Jay Darrell Manning, Earnest's eighteen-year-old turret gunner, soon broke in on the intercom: "They're hitting Midway, Skipper." At about the same time, Earnest spotted a flight of aircraft approaching Midway, each sporting big red meatballs on their wings—the first Japanese aircraft he'd ever seen. One Japanese pilot even made a tentative pass at Earnest's TBF before veering off without firing—apparently mindful of the bigger job he had to do.

———

The teletype in VT-8's ready room clacked to life at 6:10 a.m.: "Many enemy planes headed for Midway, bearing 320," the screen showed. Then: "This looks like the beginning. We are about to change course to 330."

Fred Mears realized 320 degrees meant an enemy force off to the northwest of Midway—not to the west as the earlier teletype had suggested. From that moment, every pilot eye remained glued to the screen.

At 6:15 a.m.: "8 combat patrol pilots plus two stand-by pilots man planes." Then: "All fighter pilots man planes on flight deck. *Hornet* base course 240."

Then the ready room loudspeaker squawked an all-hands message: "The enemy main body is now attempting to take Midway. We are heading toward Midway to intercept and destroy them."

Again the teletype went to work, first rattling off orders to man bombers and torpedo planes only to hastily reverse itself: "Correction, do not man planes until directed."

Almost as if chastened by its presumption, the teletype afterwards confined itself to transmitting pilot chart board data: surface wind ("126° true, 6 knots"), ship's position ("latitude 31° –368 longitude 176° –29"), enemy bearing ("239°").

The next scoop belonged to the loudspeaker and to all hands. "We plan to launch planes at 0700 (7 a.m.) to attack enemy while their planes are returning from Midway. We will close to about one hundred miles of enemy position."

Only then did the teletype chime in with its more clipped version. "Present intent to launch attack groups 0700 plus 4 sections each carrier for combat patrol. Each group attack one carrier."

———

Even as the ready room teletypes updated the squadron pilots, their leaders, Commander *Hornet* Air Group (CHAG) Stanhope C. Ring and his four squadron commanders, were conferring with *Hornet's* CO Marc A. Mitscher on the bridge.

No one present could question Mitscher's naval aviation bona fides. Known as "Pete" to his Naval Academy classmates and peers, the bone-dry, diminutive Midwesterner had won his wings in 1915 (he was Naval Aviator No. 33) and had earned the Navy Cross as part of a pioneering transatlantic flight from Newfoundland to the Azores. Mitscher had commanded *Hornet* for the Doolittle Raid and was now slated to fleet up to rear admiral.

At a planning meeting with Mitscher several days before, VT-8's Waldron had requested fighter cover for his TBDs, a request endorsed by Ring and VF-8 CO Lieutenant Commander Samuel G. "Pat" Mitchell, both of them Mitscher subordinates at BuAer. Mitscher, however, had been adamant in denying Waldron's request. *Hornet* CAP would be limited as it was. The ten Wildcats accompanying the strike mission would cruise at high altitude, sticking with the dive-bombers. Now on the bridge, just minutes from take-off, Pat Mitchell raised the escort issue one last time. Mitscher hadn't changed his mind. Without pause, he shook his head and ordered Mitchell to stay with the bombers.

With *Hornet*, *Enterprise* and their screens about to disperse for flight operations, talk turned to the choice of the outbound course. Ring proposed 265 degrees, almost due west and a full thirty degrees north of the Japanese carriers' last reported position. Waldron was quick to object, arguing instead for 240 degrees—a more southwesterly course that better estimated an enemy backtrack to the north after its early morning launch. Mitscher listened but again had the final word. Just as CHAG recommended, *Hornet's* strike group would go west, not southwest.

––––––

At 06:45 a.m. the first message from strike leader Lieutenant Jōichi Tomonaga finally reached *Akagi's* command bridge: "We have completed our attack and are homeward bound." But it was another anxious fifteen minutes before a decoded message about the actual strike itself came in.

Its assessment was blunt: Another strike was needed. As word spread on bridge and flight platform, the men knew this put Nagumo—and them—in a critical quandary. Should they launch that second strike on Midway before they received full search results from the scouting planes?

At 07:05 a.m., as Chūichi Nagumo weighed his options, bugles signaled another air raid. Fuchida hauled himself to his feet and joined the others intently scanning the southern sky. It had become, he noticed, a beautiful day. There were high clouds, but the air was clear and visibility was good.

Suddenly a screen destroyer signaled "Enemy in sight" and an instant later opened up its antiaircraft batteries. Soon Fuchida and the others could pick out the dark specks of incoming planes on the port quarter. In response, *Akagi* began angling to port, simultaneously unmasking her starboard antiaircraft batteries and narrowing her profile.

––––––

What TBF pilot Bert Earnest saw first was the wake of a ship pointing southeast, directly towards them. Even from four thousand feet he could tell it was no warship, more likely some type of transport. But then, when he looked beyond this ship to the northeast, he saw warships out on the horizon—many of them. In fact, Earnest had never seen anything like it—not American and certainly not Japanese. Regardless of circumstances, he couldn't help but be impressed by the majesty of it.

Leading the armada was something Earnest guessed to be a battleship. Beyond it were two aircraft carriers, each with cruiser and destroyer bodyguards. He was certain their flight had already been spotted. The screening ships were firing and one carrier was angling straight towards them in an effort to disrupt their attack angle. Soon, Jay Manning was on intercom: "Enemy fighters!" Sure enough, they were swarming high and low—so many that they were getting in each other's way.

When one strayed into his field of fire bound for Fieberling's tail,

Earnest pressed the button on his nose gun, but nothing happened. He tried again—still nothing. Behind him he heard Manning's turret fifty open up.

Back in the TBF's tunnel, Earnest's radioman-gunner Harry Ferrier clutched the grips of his .30-caliber stinger, waiting for a clear shot. He saw Zeros darting in from behind and below, firing quick bursts before they disappeared. Bullets began hitting the TBF's skin—it sounded like a downpour on a thin tin roof. Soon something grazed his left wrist. The impact abruptly tore his hand from the gun; the pain was fierce and red hot.

Above him, Manning's .50-caliber all at once stopped firing. Ferrier looked up to see Manning slumped in his harness. His automatic turret, meanwhile, had "self-stowed", pointing itself aft because Manning's hands no longer gripped the gun—a dead man's switch. Manning's blood was already streaming down. Through the side Plexiglas, Ferrier saw a plane swoop by on fire. As fast as it happened, he couldn't tell whether it was American or Japanese.

———

Ahead and off to Earnest's right, Langdon Fieberling was now nosing over, starting his glide approach. Earnest upped his throttle and followed. A quick glimpse showed that the others—Brannon, Gaynier, Lewis and Woodside –were still there, still in tight formation. All the way down, the Japanese fighters seemed to cling to the TBFs like barn flies to sauntering horses.

When Fieberling finally leveled off at 200 feet, he skimmed directly for the first carrier. He opened his bomb bay doors and the others quickly followed suit. It cut their speed—not that it made that much difference to the nimble Japanese fighters—but it also ensured they could drop their fish even if they lost their hydraulics. Two hundred feet at 200 knots, Earnest reminded himself.

If anything, the pace of incoming fire had by now picked up. Earnest could almost feel the thump of bullets as they pounded the pilot armor behind him. Red tracers seemed to be everywhere. Suddenly, shrapnel pierced the side of his canopy. He felt a quick rush of wind and then saw a mist of blood gloss the instrument panel. Earnest felt for the source— it was coming from his neck.

Behind and below him in the tunnel Harry Ferrier was just then readying to fire at a Japanese fighter when the TBF's tail wheel abruptly dropped in front him, blocking his field of fire. Ferrier guessed the TBF had lost hydraulics. At any rate, his stinger was now useless. Suddenly, he felt a stab of pain, this time to his head. He tried to focus, but everything then went blank.

In the cockpit, Bert Earnest noticed his plane dropping from formation. He tried pulling up, but the control stick had no effect: his elevator cables must be severed. Then more shrapnel tore into the cockpit, chewing up his instrument panel. Without hydraulics and aileron control, he, Manning and Ferrier were going down.

———

Aboard *Akagi*, as Mitsuo Fuchida watched one of the whale-shaped torpedo aircraft veer from its formation, a bridge lookout reported another flight of planes, these also to the south, but further out and approaching to starboard. Fuchida glanced away briefly to pick out this threat, but then turned back in time to witness another of the torpedo planes burst into flame and crash into the sea. A triumphant cheer went up from *Akagi's* sailors, but four of these planes were still barreling in towards *Hiryu*.

Braving the risk of Striking Force's own antiaircraft fire, several Zerosens reengaged the attackers, picking them off one after the other until they were all gone. At least two managed to drop their torpedoes, but so far out, Fuchida was sure, that *Hiryu* would easily outmaneuver them.

The same fate befell the next bunch of attackers but not before these equally strange-looking twin-engine intruders got uncomfortably close. The last of them, though badly crippled, had lunged directly for *Akagi's* command bridge. The men on the flight control platform stared wide-eyed and then ducked, certain the green bomber would hit the ship. Instead, the plane skimmed just clear of the island before cartwheeling into the sea.

Though neither attack had succeeded, their sheer ferocity seemed to make up Nagumo's mind. Having heard from Tomonaga, then having his formation torpedoed, strafed and his flagship nearly demolished by aircraft from Midway, Nagumo apparently decided enough was enough. Holding his reserve aircraft back risked wasting half of his strike capability. He was, after all, in command at the front—the best position to make a tactical decision.

At 7:15 a.m., word came from the command bridge: "Planes in second attack wave stand by to carry out attack today. Reequip yourselves with bombs."

———

Bert Earnest was determined to sink a Japanese ship before he crashed. Reaching the carrier he'd been aiming for was now out of the question, but to his left Earnest saw a cruiser firing at him. He still had rudder, so he kicked the pedal hard and the TBF skidded towards the cruiser, though all the while losing more altitude. After lining up on the new target, Earnest hit the switches to launch his torpedo. He expected the plane, lightened by a ton, to pick up speed. When it didn't, Earnest yanked the emergency release lever just to be sure.

By then the TBF was dangerously low, maybe twenty-five feet above the wave tops. With scant moments to prepare, Earnest tightened his shoulder harness and, almost without thinking, reached down with his left hand to adjust the trim tab wheel next to his seat. It was something he always did to counteract the TBF's nose-heavy tendency during landings.

This time, though, the plane's nose nudged upward and with more turns it even climbed. While the elevator control cables were severed, the trim tab cables apparently weren't. Practical as ever, Earnest figured he might be able to fly his plane if he could somehow shake off the Japanese fighters trying so hard to finish him off.

––––––––

As VT-8's Fred Mears had expected, he wouldn't be going on this strike or the second. Maybe not even the third. Instead, Mears would be a bystander, his experience limited to what the ready room teletype (plus the all-hands loudspeaker announcements) told him or what he could see for himself topside. That morning the skipper had told his pilots that, if need be, he'd run the squadron dry of gas trying to find the Japanese. "In that case," Waldron said, "we'll all sit down in the water together and have a nice little picnic."

In the skipper's vernacular a torpedo was never a torpedo—it was either a pickle, a wienie, a fish or a torpecker. "If there is only one man left," Waldron had emphasized. "I want that man to take his pickle in and get a hit."

––––––––

While Japanese carrier deckhands and armorers needed little time to ready the as-yet-unarmed dive-bombers, rearming the torpedo bombers (many of which now carried torpedoes) was more complicated. It meant both removing the torpedo and changing the mounting hardware.

In the cramped hangars, with the ordnance elevators doing double duty (lifting bombs and lowering torpedoes) and with a shortage of ordnance

handling carts, rearming each plane could easily take a half hour. Readying a combined and fully coordinated second strike (balanced deck loads
from all four carriers equipped with an anti-shipping mix of bombs and
torpedoes) could well take two or more hours. Meanwhile, of course,
deck crews would also have to contend with recovering and stowing the
first wave's aircraft.

Then, at 7:45 a.m., a bolt from the blue, a report from cruiser *Tone's*
scout plane: "Ten ships, apparently enemy, sighted. Bearing ten degrees,
distance 240 miles from Midway." It was not much to go on. A quick
plot showed the American ships to be two hundred miles from Striking
Force, but what kind were they? The presence of carriers would make all
the difference, of course.

Almost at once, Nagumo ordered a flash response ("Ascertain ship
types and maintain contact!"). There was then the wait for more news,
critical news—a period of suspense ticked off in minutes but experienced
as eternities.

At 7:58 a.m. came a follow-on message: the enemy ships had altered
course to eighty degrees—that only frustrated and enraged with its mea-
gerness.

Brimming now with uncharacteristic, barely contained impatience, and
Nagumo suspended the switch from torpedoes to bombs.

———

Earlier that morning on carrier *Enterprise*, VF-6's new CO Lieutenant
James S. Gray Jr. had spoken with VT-6's CO Lieutenant Commander Eugene E. Lindsey about the fighter cover Gray's Wildcats could provide
Lindsey's TBDs. Lindsey, Gray could see, was still suffering the effects of
a May 28 landing accident that sent his TBD crashing onto the deck and
then tumbling overboard. Retrieved by destroyer *Monaghan* (DD-354),
Lindsey's bombardier and radioman were no more than drenched and
shaken, but Lindsey's face and torso were painfully cut and bruised. Days
later, with his rib cage still taped, he moved stiffly, he'd clearly lost some
weight and his face was noticeably pale and blue-black. Still, Lindsey had
insisted on leading his squadron today.

Enterprise CAG Wade McClusky (VF-6's previous CO) had granted
Gray (his former flight officer) wide latitude; Gray had pretty much decided what he planned to do with the coverage. From talking with a Coral
Sea veteran who had just joined the squadron, Gray learned of the pounding taken by the SBDs and the success of the TBDs in using cloud cover

to mask their approach. Gray also came away from that discussion more convinced than ever of the Zero's considerable superiority over the current crop of Wildcats.

It was something Gray had harped on ever since commissioning the squadron's F4F-4 inventory back in early April. While these Wildcats' folding Sto-Wings made it possible for *Enterprise* to carry more fighter aircraft, their added weight hurt the aircrafts' climb rate and maneuverability. They were simply too heavy for their low horsepower and limited fuel capacity; they had the feel (he'd warned Halsey in the days before the Tokyo raid) of fully loaded TBDs.

Gauging what he'd learned about the Coral Sea strikes plus his first-hand knowledge of the F4F-4's performance shortfalls, Gray decided to keep his ten Wildcat escorts all together, flying at high altitude in company with the SBDs. However, should Lindsey's fourteen TBDs run into any trouble, all he had to do was radio "Come on down, Jim" and help (such as it was) would be on the way.

————

Unfortunately, Gray's plan to accompany the SBDs unraveled during launch. All the SBDs took off on schedule with *Enterprise's* first deck load, but spotting the second load, which included Gray's Wildcats and Lindsey's Devastators, seemed to take forever. By the time Gray's F4Fs were finally airborne and formed up, an impatient Spruance had ordered McClusky's SBDs to head immediately for the Japanese.

Because he was depending on McClusky's dive-bombers for navigation, this put Gray in a fix. To his great relief, Gray happened to spot a torpedo squadron below him formed up and heading out without fighter escort. Deciding they must be Lindsey's TBDs (they were not), Gray had his planes follow. Gray figured he could still catch up with the SBDs over the target, but they were sure off to a late start. It was already approaching 8 a.m.

————

Just before 8 a.m., as Striking Force's Nagumo anxiously awaited clarification on the composition of the American ship formation to the north, an *Akagi* lookout reported a new flight of enemy bombers attacking *Hiryu*, this time from high level. The men on *Akagi's* flight platform watched apprehensively as tumbling bombs raised huge geysers of water that encircled first *Hiryu* and then *Soryu*—then breathed a collective sigh of relief when the turbulence finally subsided and both ships emerged, apparently unscathed.

Eyeing the big bombers, Mitsuo Fuchida grabbed an aircraft recognition chart. They were B-17s, the U.S. Army's newest bomber model. At first, as the aircraft—fourteen in all—drifted serenely away, Fuchida wondered why the CAP planes weren't pursuing them. Then he remembered what tough opponents the heavily armed "forts" were reputed to be. They could only have flown from Midway—just one more bit of evidence backing Nagumo's original decision to rearm Striking Force's torpedo aircraft with bombs.

Just then lookouts spotted yet another flight of aircraft inbound from Midway. Fuchida counted sixteen enemy planes in this latest group. They were dive-bombers even though they were approaching like no dive-bomber should: well below the cloud cover in shallow glides. Almost at once Zeros pounced on these fat targets, setting them aflame one after another. Seeing this, Fuchida was astonished to see the remainder press on through the withering gauntlet. A few even released bombs that appeared certain to hit *Hiryu*, but, to everyone's continued relief, once the splashes and smoke cleared, the carrier again plowed on untouched. To Fuchida it seemed that Striking Force had now easily withstood every type of air attack the Americans at Midway could mount. Still, Fuchida was convinced, Midway represented the clearest present danger. If only they knew for certain what *Tone's* scout plane had discovered!

———

Miraculously, inexplicably, after one final tattoo of bullets into the armor behind him, the Japanese fighter hounds stopped firing at Bert Earnest's TBF. Sure enough, when he looked around, the sky was empty. Their pilots must have left for juicier targets—maybe the Marine Dauntlesses and Vindicators that had taken off from Midway after the TBFs.

All this time, Earnest suddenly realized, he'd heard from neither Manning nor Ferrier. He tried them now but got no answer. For all he knew the intercom connection had been shot up, like just about everything else on the plane.

He was incredibly tired, but knew he had to take stock, to focus on what to do next. There was still blood flowing from his neck but, thank God, not in spurts. If it hadn't killed him yet, it might just be a flesh wound.

Earnest kept turning the trim tab wheel until he'd climbed to what he thought was about three thousand feet. He had no way of knowing for sure because all the TBF's instruments were gone: altimeter, compass, fuel gauge, oil gauge, airspeed indicator—everything.

Without hydraulics he couldn't close the bomb bay doors. For that matter, he had no way of telling for sure whether his torpedo had released; Manning and Ferrier were the only ones in position to check, by peeking through a small spy hole into the bomb bay. However, both might be wounded, even dead.

There was no sign of Fieberling or anybody else from the flight, leaving Earnest on his own in deciding what to do next. He knew Midway was his only possible landing destination, but now he had no firm idea of where it was. Fieberling had led them up from the southeast and the attacking Zeros had chased them even farther towards the northwest. That left the Japanese fleet somewhere between him and Midway. Perhaps their advance units had already invaded the island. All in all, though, heading for Midway looked to be a better option than ditching in the Pacific.

For all the outrageous punishment Earnest's Grumman had taken, its engine seemed to be running just fine. He had the sun, up now just three hours, and plenty of daylight to help him navigate 'by guess and by God' the two hundred or so miles to Midway.

Earnest used rudder to edge the TBF so that the sun was on his left side. For the time being he would fly south to keep out of the way of the Japanese. The real trick, he knew, would be deciding when to head east.

———

Following that initial shocker from *Tone's* scout plane, Striking Force continued receiving fragmentary reports, each a small and so far inconclusive piece in a huge puzzle. And each, with its imprecision, seemed to mock the greatest hopes and direst fears of the men on *Akagi's* command bridge.

First, at 8:09 a.m.: "Enemy ships are five cruisers and five destroyers." No aircraft carriers! It meant, in so many words, that action against these ships could wait.

Then, eleven minutes later, a second devastating jolt: "Enemy force accompanied by what appears to be aircraft carrier bringing up the rear."

Even after this there was still temporizing in the men's minds—some final bargaining with harsh reality:

The identification was uncertain.

In May, hadn't Coral Sea scouts mistaken an American fleet oiler for an aircraft carrier and, without confirmation, launched a hasty, wasteful anti-shipping strike?

American flying boats had been shadowing Striking Force for hours—presumably reporting their sightings to every available American unit. If the Americans indeed had carriers in the vicinity, why hadn't Striking Force yet been attacked by any carrier-launched aircraft?

Then, at 8:30 a.m., the leaden clincher for Nagumo: "Two additional enemy ships, apparently cruisers."

Any enemy formation of that size, Nagumo seemed to realize, simply had to contain aircraft carriers.

———

At 8:25 a.m. when VF-3 CO Jimmie Thach first learned of the decision to hold six *Yorktown* fighters (along with VS-5's dive-bombers) in reserve, he was furious. This left Thach with just the six Wildcats to cover TF 17's thirty-five-plane strike force: four from his 1st Division plus two from 2nd Division. He'd immediately stormed to the bridge to appeal the decision to Air Officer Murr Arnold, arguing that his new beam defense tactics required multiples of four aircraft to be effective. Arnold listened as patiently as time and circumstance would allow, but that was the way it was—decision from the top, from TF 17's Frank Jack Admiral Fletcher. After having gone north to retrieve early morning scout aircraft, Fletcher was already late getting into the fight. But he still worried that additional Japanese carriers had somehow eluded PBY search and might yet cause him trouble.

For his part, Thach had to concede (though not to Arnold) that he'd barely had time to explain (much less practice) those tactics with his flyers.

———

The time and circumstance leading up to this moment had been especially hectic for Thach. It was already the third week in May when he learned he'd be taking his barely reconstituted VF-3 (just eleven raw pilots) and his supply of F4F-4s aboard *Yorktown* (soon to go into drydock for emergency repairs). He was somehow supposed to meld his VF-3 rookies with a nucleus of VF-42 veterans (the rest would go ashore) to build a squadron that would almost immediately go into combat.

Thach realized this next battle would be his last as squadron skipper. Already, Butch O'Hare was wrapping up his stateside victory tour; he had orders to return to the Pacific and take command of VF-3 in late June.

At the end of May Thach had the good fortune to run across Don Lovelace, his former XO. Lovelace had arrived in Pearl to take command of VF-2, only to learn that the *Lexington* survivors had been sent to San Diego. With VF-2 not set to reassemble for at least several weeks, Lovelace had volunteered to be Thach's XO for the next mission.

Tragically, Don Lovelace's timely arrival was a blessing turned to ashes. On the morning of May 30, the rebuilt *Yorktown* air group flew from Kaneohe out to the patched-up *Yorktown*. Leading the squadron's 3rd Division, Lovelace had landed without a problem. But, as he waited for plane handlers to guide him to a parking spot forward, the next F4F to land (flown by Lovelace's rookie wingman Ensign Robert C. Evans) failed to snag an arresting wire. Evans's aircraft smashed into the back of Lovelace's and its propeller sawed into the cockpit. Lovelace's skull was fractured and his carotid artery severed. He died within minutes.

———

Thach had planned for Lovelace to bring the VF-42 pilots up to speed on tactics. With Lovelace gone and the moment upon him, the best Thach could do now was take a few minutes to outline a bare-bones simple escort plan. The two 2nd Division aircraft—NAP Tom F. Cheek and his wingman Ensign Daniel C. Sheedy—would station themselves low and close to the torpedo planes. Meanwhile, Thach's 1st Division (Thach's wingman, twenty-one-year-old Ensign Robert A.M. "Ram" Dibb; VF-42 veterans Brainard Macomber and Red Dog Bassett in the second section) would fly "high escort," a few thousand feet above them.

At least the strike launch sequence and search plan determined by Fletcher, Arnold and CAG Oscar Pederson, made sense to Thach. The slowest planes (Lieutenant Commander Lance E. "Lem" Massey's twelve VT-3 TBDs) would leave first, followed by the next slowest (Lieutenant Commander Maxwell F. Leslie's seventeen VB-3 SBDs), and finally Thach's F4F-4s.

In addition, instead of a time- and fuel-wasting deferred departure, there would be a "running rendezvous." Thach's Wildcats would catch up with the torpedo planes and dive-bombers en route. The search plan meanwhile seemed to account for the enemy's most likely actions. Arnold and Pederson had updated the first sightings (now several hours old) by plotting a continued advance southeast into the wind. They also judged the most likely end position at 9 a.m., given the enemy's need to launch without getting closer to Midway.

Yorktown's strike aircraft would simply fly to that position. If the Japanese were nowhere in sight, then *Yorktown*'s strike group would point northwest—the most likely track of a Japanese retreat to home waters.

It was a plan that spoke of battle experience and battle-testing. It meant that they had actually had some chance of mounting a coordinated strike.

Provided, of course, they found the Japanese.

At 8:05 a.m., a destroyer far out on the eastern rim of Striking Force's formation signaled that it had spotted still more enemy planes. Briefly it opened fire then as quickly stopped. There were nearly a hundred planes, all of them friendly, it turned out: Tomonaga's first wave returning from Midway.

About thirty minutes later, with the returning planes orbiting and the air clear of American attackers, *Akagi's* signalmen hoisted a white flag emblazoned with a black ball—her flight decks were ready to take on aircraft. Now, well out ahead of the cold front, the wind (reduced to little more than a wispy breeze) had veered towards the east. The Japanese carriers pivoted to face it head on. The course change put *Hiryu* and *Soryu* (instead of *Kaga* and *Akagi*) in the lead.

As practiced as Striking Force's pilots were by now, Mitsuo Fuchida assumed the recovery would not take long, even accounting for damaged planes and wounded pilots. Planes short of fuel or with mechanical problems or wounded crewmen went to the head of the queue. As with takeoffs, landing decisions were pretty much up to the pilots; their only technical assistance came from deck-mounted "guidance lights" used to adjust positioning during approach.

With planes touching down on each carrier deck in twenty-five to forty-five second intervals and with relatively few interruptions (one *Hiryu* plane crash landed, while a *Kaga* fighter pilot landed despite a mortal wound) the recovery process went as smoothly as Fuchida anticipated. But Fuchida also anticipated that the post-recovery process of stowing all planes below decks could be slow, especially in the midst of arming, fueling, and spotting another flight. Not only could it impede launch, it could also leave the ship exposed. An enemy strike occurring then could both inflict serious battle damage and trigger catastrophic secondary fires and explosions.

12

RETURN BUSTER

When Harry Ferrier awoke, he was draped over the tunnel stinger, which was covered in blood. He smelled a foul coppery odor and his head throbbed. Reaching up to touch his forehead, he was stunned to feel a hole. Ferrier sat up. He could hear the TBF's engine running strong and he sensed they were flying level. He tried the intercom. "Are you okay, Skipper?"

Bert Earnest's response, though immediate and enthusiastic, also registered surprise: "I'm fine. . . . How about you?"

"Wounded in the head, but I think I'll be alright. I think Jay's dead."

After a moment, Earnest returned to the circuit: "Harry, I want you to see if the torpedo dropped. I don't want us to land with it hanging out of the bomb bay."

Ferrier crawled towards the small glass spy hole in the radio compartment deck. It was directly under the gun turret and therefore covered by a thick pool of Jay Manning's blood. Ferrier told Earnest there was no way he could see through it.

"Skipper, is it alright if I come up to the middle seat?" Ferrier explained that the stinger's field of fire was blocked by the tail wheel. "Okay, Harry," Earnest agreed, "come up."

A few minutes later Earnest finally decided it was time to turn east. It was about 8:45 a.m.—both of them knew it was a make or break moment. If they missed Midway the next landfall would be Hawaii. Right now—ahead, astern and to either side—there was nothing to see but ocean. The water surface looked calm, but if they ditched there was little chance of rescue.

VF-6's Jim Gray had to assume the TBDs below him (what he thought were Gene Lindsey's VT-6 TBDs) knew where they were headed. The planes had set out on 265 degrees—but at 8:25 a.m. they swung abruptly to the southwest and Gray's Wildcats had followed.

A while later, Gray saw these TBDs disperse into a scouting line, perhaps a sign that Lindsey was close to the target and didn't want to overshoot it. Ahead lay a low cloud bank and the TBDs soon disappeared into it. Gray's pilots now kept an eye out for the *Enterprise* SBDs.

Lieutenant (junior grade) John C. Kelley, Gray's 2nd Division leader, came on the circuit at 9:10 a.m. "There they are at one o'clock down, skipper." Beyond a low cloud bank, Jim Gray saw the distant traces of ships' wakes. Holding altitude and intent on protecting McClusky's pushover point, Gray led his flight closer.

The Wildcats circled as antiaircraft bursts—all bark, no bite—erupted far below them. Gray thought it strange that no Japanese fighters were in sight. He tried radioing McClusky but got only static and there was still no call for help from Lindsey. It seemed best to sit tight and wait, but Gray had the nagging feeling that something wasn't quite right. Meanwhile, the F4F-4 engines were sucking juice.

––––––

Off to the north with the *Hornet* dive-bombers, Pat Mitchell's Wildcat pilots were also eying their fuel gauges. *Hornet's* CHAG Stanhope Ring had been leading his strike aircraft almost due west when a few pilots noticed Waldron's TBDs veer southwest and disappear. Because visibility was none too good, Ring had his dive-bombers disperse in a broad skirmish line with Ring at its center, VS-8 on his right and VB-8 on his left. Station keeping like this, executed with a precision better suited to peacetime, burned precious fuel. Having circled the task force to await the SBD and TBD launches, and then making the climb to twenty-two thousand feet, Mitchell's planes were all low on fuel.

Not long after 9 a.m., twenty-six-year-old Ensign John E. McInerny, the second section wingman in Mitchell's division, finally took matters into his own hands. Edging past his section leader, twenty-three-year-old Ensign John Magda, McInerny pulled up alongside Mitchell and pointed emphatically towards his fuel gauge. Mitchell might have limited carrier fighter experience, but he knew a young ensign's place. He angrily pointed McInerny back to his slot. McInerny dropped back but soon returned—this time gesturing with even more emphasis.

If Mitchell was fed up with McInerny's impertinence, so now was McInerny with the Skipper's intransigence. Ignoring his CO and flight leader, McInerny turned east, Magda in tow. Eventually bowing to the inevitable, Mitchell and the rest of the F4Fs turned east, too. Having relied on the *Hornet's* bombers for navigation and with no firm idea of the *Hornet's* current locale—its "Point Option"—Mitchell's flight would have to rely on their Zed Bakers to guide them home.

———

All of the returning Japanese strike aircraft had reached their carrier decks by 9:10 a.m. The last of *Akagi's* planes, Mitsuo Fuchida noted with satisfaction, were aboard ten minutes before that: little more than twenty minutes since the landings began. Even as Fuchida watched *Akagi's* aircraft being hustled below deck, a single CAP plane touched down. Then, with flight operations over for the moment, Nagumo ordered Striking Force to take a more northerly heading. He was intent on closing the gap to the American carriers before launching a crushing strike.

Strike take-off was set for 10:30 a.m., but at 9:20 a.m., when screening ships signaled approaching enemy carrier planes, everyone knew that this might come too late. Strike preparations picked up pace even as these latest attackers appeared as tiny specks low along the starboard horizon. CAP Zeros were quick to intercept: one by one the specks burst into flame, trailed smoke and fell into the water until (the CAP leader reported) all fifteen enemy torpedo planes were destroyed.

But then, at 9:30 a.m., lookouts reported two more sets of low-flying attackers, this time heading directly for *Akagi*—one set to starboard and the other to port.

———

It was nearing 9:40 a.m. when Bert Earnest spotted a towering column of black smoke off to the southeast. It sent a shiver of excitement through him. As Earnest got closer he was sure the smoke was from a petroleum fire—it could only be Midway. He didn't know if the atoll was still in American hands and, without a radio, had no quick way to find out. He had to assume it was and, accordingly, be careful about friendly fire. Earnest wrestled the TBF through the specified recognition turns used to distinguish friend from foe. Then he approached the same north-south runway he had left three hours before.

Lacking flaps, Earnest relied on throttle for descent. As the plane neared the runway, he pushed the undercarriage lever to lower wheels. His cockpit indicators—mechanical displays—were telling him his wheels were still up, but he wasn't sure whether to believe them. Earnest tried again, this time yanking hard on the emergency release. The display indicated the left wheel down and locked, the right wheel still retracted. Earnest next tried to shake that wheel loose by adding throttle to pull up, then cutting throttle and adding throttle again.

Nothing seemed to happen, but he didn't want to risk trying it again. The choice was either ditch in the lagoon or land. Earnest had less than a hundred hours in the TBF, which made him none too confident about a one-wheel landing. Still, the plane had held up well so far. Besides, if Manning was still alive, ditching would surely kill him.

———

"It's a funny thing," a one-time carrier officer confided to *New York Times* reporter Foster Hailey, "but those screwy birds seem to think they're safe once they get in their planes and up in the air. They're more nervous than the rest of us when they're back on the ship." To Hailey, however, who had watched carrier *Yorktown*'s launch from a cruiser bridge, the distant aircraft seemed "very puny things to be sending against big Japanese carriers, battleships and cruisers."

The "screwy birds" in their "puny" aircraft had since made good progress on their flight southwest to the target location estimated by *Yorktown*'s Murr Arnold and Oscar Pederson. Visibility had improved so much that at 9:45 a.m., the time estimated for Jimmie Thach's escorts to overtake Lem Massey's TBDs, Thach had no trouble spotting them. Thach signaled Tom Cheek and Dan Sheedy to take position astern and above the TBDs, while he stationed his own division at five thousand feet—above Cheek and Sheedy but well below Max Leslie's bombers.

Knowing that Brainard Macomber and Red Dog Bassett lacked familiarity with beam defense, Thach positioned his division in a standard cruise formation. Everyone had kept their throttles at maximum cruise range during transit. Thach was sure they could fly the outbound leg, fight over the target and still have a margin to get home.

Like VF-6's Jim Gray, Thach had found the new Sto-Wing fighters less responsive than the fixed-wing F4F-3s. However, he worried most about their armament: six wing guns, but only 240 rounds per gun. Thach would have felt better with fewer guns but more total rounds.

———

Now over Eastern Island's runway, Bert Earnest glimpsed a lone figure waving a signal flag. Earnest assumed he was being warned his torpedo was still onboard. He increased throttle, climbed, circled the field and made another approach, only to see the same individual waving his flag.

"To hell with this," Earnest muttered. Out of options, he just kept coming. As the TBF set down, the left wheel touched the concrete and the plane slowed. Everything seemed smooth—a beautiful one-point landing—until the right wing dipped and scraped the runway. All of a sudden, the TBF behaved like its big, heavy self, pivoting on the wingtip and barreling towards aircraft on the runway apron.

Earnest braced for disaster, but instead of crashing, the big Grumman ground to a halt just short of the coral. Though his cockpit switches were inoperable, Earnest clicked them off anyway. For a moment, except for the ticking of hot metal, quiet settled over everything—as if the universe had exhaled. Earnest was unbuckling his seat harness when he heard a siren's wail. A crash wagon and a crowd of Marines were racing along the runway.

Out of the cockpit, Earnest slid off the wing to land on wobbly legs. The first thing he wanted to see was the bomb bay. It was empty—just the torpedo mounting cables still dangling. His worries about it had been all for nothing.

Harry Ferrier was down on the ground, too, but barely able to walk. Two Marines helped him to an ambulance. Other personnel were draping Manning's gun turret with a huge canvas tarpaulin. When Earnest tried to get nearer, one stepped firmly in his way, saying "You don't want to go back there, sir."

Earnest surveyed the field. There were no TBFs. Soon the landing officer ran up, telling him excitedly that they'd been trying to reach him by radio. "We thought bailing out would be your best chance." Lacking the energy to explain that his radio had been shot up, Earnest asked if any of the other TBFs were back.

"You're the only one so far," he said.

———

At 9:56 a.m., Jim Gray radioed TF 16 that his F4Fs were circling over "six destroyers, two battleships, two carriers." Fuel levels were below halfway and falling.

There'd been no word yet from either McClusky or Lindsey. Faced with the possibility of turning back without getting into the fight, Gray considered his options. There were no Japanese fighters to engage. He could strafe but that wouldn't accomplish much without McClusky's bombers along—and it would also lose him altitude advantage. Getting back to refuel seemed his best option.

"This is Gray," he radioed at 10 a.m. "We are returning to ship due to lack of gas."

———

By the time Jim Gray's VF-8 fighters turned east, Pat Mitchell's were already an hour into their journey back to *Hornet*. The strike aircraft with the least fuel capacity, Mitchell's Wildcats had nonetheless been the first *Hornet* aircraft launched. They were all now about to run out of juice.

The ten F4Fs were grouped in two ragged formations. John McInerny was in the lead with his section leader John Magda close behind. The main group of eight, led by thirty-year-old Lieutenant Stanley Ruehlow, followed astern and off to port. Each pilot tried to keep his fuel mix as lean as possible while holding enough altitude to pick up the homing signal. All were Zed Baker novices —relying on the signal mostly for direction, not distance.

Just after 10 a.m., pilots in the larger group sighted wakes off to the north. They presumed it was the Japanese carrier force but now, lacking fuel to attack, they simply continued on.

Soon, twenty-one-year-old Ensign Humphrey Tallman—last in the formation—witnessed the first loss: a Grumman ahead of him slowed, stalled and nosed over. Tallman was too high to see the splash. Up front, Stan Ruehlow knew the victim was twenty-three-year-old Ensign George R. Hill. Ruehlow had been keeping an eye on Hill's plane, watching it fall back several times, then catch up. Now Hill was nowhere to be seen.

———

Yorktown's strike force was still on its outbound leg when, a few minutes after 10 a.m., Jimmie Thach noticed Lem Massey's TBDs swing to the northwest. Sure enough, maybe twenty to twenty-five miles away, Thach discerned smoke and wakes: the Japanese fleet.

As they closed, Massey's planes climbed a bit. Dirty-gray puffs of antiaircraft erupted in their path, most likely rounds from a cruiser or destroyer meant to alert the formation and its CAP aircraft.

Then, all at once, the sky around Thach's planes filled with Zeros—so many, thought Thach, their pilots would have to take a number just to attack.

Even as this queue formed, Zeros were jumping out of it to pounce on the Grummans. First to be hit was Brainard Macomber's wingman, Red Dog Bassett, out on the port side. Japanese fighters cornered him from above and behind and quickly had Bassett's engine smoking. As the Wildcat dropped way, Thach saw it totally enveloped in flames. Bassett never had a chance.

Macomber was hit too—bullets raked his tail section, tattooed his cockpit armor and killed his radio—but he somehow managed to keep flying. Thach's first instinct was to nose over and gain speed to catch up with the torpedo planes. But the Zeros' numbers, teamwork and firing discipline made this impossible. Instead, the three Wildcats, now strung out in single file, could only maneuver defensively.

Thach's first maneuver was a sharp turn to the right, away from the closest attacker. This made Macomber, whose plane was farthest astern, the Zero's target, though of a difficult—and errant—deflection shot. The line-astern formation enabled Thach's trio to stay together without colliding, but it also presented an easy target.

Thach wanted to get Macomber to split out to the left—it would give them all more maneuvering room and a chance to use beam defense tactics. But Thach couldn't raise Macomber by radio and realized anyway that he didn't know the tactics. Instead, even when Thach tried to wave him back, Macomber merely tightened the interval.

———

Several thousand feet below Thach, Macomber and Dibb, Tom Cheek and Dan Sheedy were also fighting for survival. When a phalanx of Zeros jumped Massey's TBDs from cloud cover out ahead, Cheek noticed one Zero swoop in for a head-on firing pass at the lead planes and then, seemingly heedless of Cheek, curl into a steep climbing turn to line up a second go. Cheek simply nosed into a climb and pulled the trigger, watching bullets tear into the Zero's belly and set it afire. The plane stumbled and spun out.

Next, he saw a pair of Zeros dart for the TBDs' left flank and once more jump the lead torpedo planes. Cheek was then too far away for a good shot, but he triggered an arcing tracer stream that chased the attackers away.

Massey's formation was still ten miles shy of the release point. The TBDs poured on what speed they could. As their pilots jinked up and down to avoid being hit, Cheek swung to either side of the formation, hoping to discourage more attackers.

———

After trying single sharp turns—hard right or hard left—to disrupt the Zeros' aim, Jimmie Thach tried two reversing turns in quick succession, the first to disrupt aim, the second to fire on the attacker when it blew by. On one try, banking first right and then reversing left, Thach got lucky: the Japanese pilot tried to pull out too soon, giving Thach a close, low-deflection shot from astern. The .50-caliber rounds jerked the Zero into a stall and sent it plummeting—a dead man at its controls. Thach calmly etched a check mark in the notebook strapped to his knee.

Still unable to shake Macomber loose, Thach instead radioed Dibb, sending him out on the right beam, just as though he were a section leader. Because he was Thach's wingman, "Ram" Dibb was among the few in the squadron who was well-practiced in beam defense. Rogering his skipper, Dibb pulled into position several hundred yards out to starboard.

As if on cue, the next Zero took aim at Dibb's solitary Wildcat. "Skipper, there's a Zero on my tail!" Dibb radioed Thach when the enemy reached his six o'clock. "Get him off!"

As Dibb turned hard left, Thach turned hard right—leaving Macomber behind and bringing Thach head-to-head with both Dibb and the trailing Zero. Thach bore in until finally—with just feet to spare—he dipped down, passed beneath Dibb, and promptly nosed up to aim for the Zero.

Thach pulled the trigger, letting the converging fire of his wing guns stitch bullets into the Zero's engine and belly. The Zero jerked up when the bullets began hitting, but too late. Its engine ignited and the plane fell, wreathed in flame and black smoke.

———

All this time Dan Sheedy had been trying to catch up with his section leader Tom Cheek. Just as he had him in sight, a Zero suddenly dropped in behind Cheek and right in front of Sheedy. Sheedy drew a bead but, finding both aircraft his in his sight, settled for firing wide and brushing off Cheek's assailant.

Massey's TBDs by now had all but disappeared below a cloud bank. When Cheek last saw them, the formation was still intact, except for one plane that had spiraled in. Cheek entered the same cloud, hoping to pick up the TBDs on the other side.

Even as he again lost sight of Cheek, Sheedy became the target of a Zero's high-side run. Small caliber bullets pierced Sheedy's canopy, wounding him in the ankle and shoulder and tearing up much of his instrument panel. Big holes also opened up in his wings as tracer rounds the size of oranges flashed by on either side of his cockpit. Sheedy's only thought was to shake his attacker by following Tom Cheek into the cloud.

———

While Ram Dibb resumed his interval out on Thach's starboard side, a confused Macomber closed again on Thach's wing. Thach watched Dibb's tail, and whenever a Zero encroached, the two Wildcats would scissor. Most often the Zeros didn't take the bait; even so, scissoring invariably brushed them away like flies.

Once, however, an enemy pilot made another fatal mistake. After aborting an attack to avoid being scissored, he slowed his Zero prematurely before pulling up. As Thach hurtled past Dibb, he found himself lined up on the Zero's tail. Thach hit the Zero with a concentrated, near point-blank blast that notched another kill.

As occupied as he was in the battle with the Zeros, Thach simply lost sight of Leslie's SBDs. At 10:20 a.m., Lem Massey could be heard by some radioing for fighter down on the deck, but Thach was in no position to help. He could only hope Tom Cheek and Dan Sheedy were doing what they could to protect Massey's TBDs.

———

Just as Dan Sheedy dipped into the cloud, Tom Cheek emerged below it and dove for the water to locate the TBDs. What he found instead was another swarm of Zeros. Four, all headed the same way, virtually surrounded Cheek, while a fifth came at him head-on.

Cheek lined up a shot on this Zero, pressed his trigger and then immediately rolled out to the left. After dodging debris—ragged chunks of the Zero's engine and cowling—Cheek charged after another Zero from the side. A well-timed deflection burst raked the enemy plane from nose to tail, clearing the way for Cheek to once more run for cloud cover. When he reached it, Cheek abruptly reversed course to cut off pursuit. The next time he broke into the clear, Cheek saw no sign of Massey's TBDs. Cheek instead saw three Japanese carriers—two ahead on his left, a third off to the north.

By then Sheedy was out of the clouds, too, but with a new pair of Zeros latched to his tail. Lowering his nose to gain speed, Sheedy tried to run for it only to find a third Zero blocking his path. Wildcat and Zero were both now low off the water and, as they closed, their two pilots traded shots. Trying to avoid a collision, the Zero pilot dipped a wing, caught a swell, and cartwheeled to his death. Sheedy barely avoided the Zero's splash. Now low and in the open, Sheedy saw Japanese carriers off to his right.

_____

Everyone aboard *Akagi* had been in breathless suspense as the two sets of enemy torpedo planes approached on either side of the carrier's bow. Soon though, these planes were also under attack by the Zero-sens.

Cheers and whistles rang out as half the attackers to either side were picked off. Mitsuo Fuchida watched amazed as the survivors kept coming.

Shipboard antiaircraft fire and *Akagi's* maneuvering were all that stood in their way, but when they reached what should have been their release points, they didn't drop torpedoes. Instead, they pulled off and turned north, evidently making their way towards *Hiryu.*

It was 10:20 a.m. Nagumo had already given the order to launch, but for the moment attention was focused on distant *Hiryu.* Six to eight Zeros had resumed the chase despite the antiaircraft fire and they were slashing at the slower torpedo planes from all directions. The long run to the north roughly paralleled the Japanese formation's base course, giving the Zeros ample opportunity to hound the Americans.

At 10:24 a.m., eyes and anticipation turned back to *Akagi's* flight deck. The first strike force plane—a Zero-sen—was gathering speed and about to take to the air.

_____

Throughout the fight with the CAP Zeros, Jimmie Thach had kept glancing down at the Japanese carriers. The air battle had taken Thach's three Wildcats northwest, edging them closer to at least one of the flattops— though it was hard to get a complete look because of intervening clouds.

The fighting had never eased up and after seeing Bassett go down and losing track entirely of Cheek and Sheedy, Thach thought it unlikely any of them would survive. But now, unexpectedly, the action slackened. Some Zeros dropped away entirely while others, though still lurking overhead, seemed to hold back.

By 10:30 a.m. they were all gone and, with time now to survey the scene, Thach understood why. Explosions had erupted on three of the carriers, with flames and smoke now engulfing their decks. Above the turmoil, Thach could pick out the steep dives of what must be U.S. Navy SBDs.

_____

At 10:25 a.m., when a lookout on *Akagi's* island screamed "Hell-divers,"

Fuchida looked up to see the silhouettes of three dive-bombers plunging towards the flagship. Some of the antiaircraft batteries began firing, but it was already too late. Fuchida saw bombs in freefall, every one, it seemed, heading directly towards him. Instinctively he dived and crawled for cover.

Sprawled, head down, Fuchida first heard the metallic scream from the Dauntlesses' dive brakes then a mighty explosion—a direct hit, he was sure. Next a brilliant flash followed by a second explosion, both louder and deeper, and a blowback rush of hot air.

There was a third explosion—a near-miss, Fuchida assumed—followed by a deathly quiet. No planes, no bombs, no guns. When Fuchida finally crawled to his feet, the sky was empty and the planes were gone, but there was destruction everywhere. The amidships elevator, twisted like molten glass, was drooping down into the hangar below. Many deck plates were twisted upwards and distorted into grotesque shapes. Deck-spotted aircraft, meanwhile, belched smoke and livid flame. Fires were spreading quickly, threatening both more fires and secondary explosions.

"Inside! Get inside!" Air Officer Shōgo Masuda was yelling. "Everybody who isn't working, get inside!" Fuchida's own escape route took him first below to the ready room, now jammed with badly burned victims from the hangar deck. More explosions soon erupted, coursing so much smoke from the hangar and adjacent passageways into the ready room that personnel fled.

Climbing back to the bridge, Fuchida was shocked to see that distant *Kaga* and *Soryu* had both been hit and that each was gushing columns of black smoke. *Akagi*, meanwhile, had suffered two near misses and a direct hit to the flight deck. A near-miss close astern had raised a water column large enough to warp a portion of the flight deck overhang while simultaneously disabling the ship's rudder. Fire was already spreading on the aircraft then positioned on the flight deck p. Of more consequence, flames escaping from huge hangar-level conflagrations were even now threatening to reach the command bridge.

———

By 10:45 a.m., Pat Mitchell, Dick Gray and Stan Ruehlow were the last three VF-8 escorts still aloft. Mitchell's plane was the first of these to run out of fuel; after stalling and hitting the water, it quickly sank. He was lucky to escape, as was Ruehlow, who gashed his head on his gun sight when he crashed, but still somehow managed to retrieve his life raft. Still aloft, watching the plight of the other two, Dick Gray took time to crank down his landing gear before easing into the sea. Gray was also able to grab both his life raft and his emergency rations. Gray and Ruehlow brought their rafts together and soon picked up Mitchell.

Under the circumstances, had Mitchell followed naval flight doctrine, he should have ordered all his aircraft to ditch in one locale. Instead, in the fifteen minutes or so since George Hill had gone down alone, six more VF-8 pilots had dropped in scattered pairs. McInerny and Magda were the first two, followed next by twenty-six-year-old Minuard F. Jennings and his wingman, twenty-one-year-old Ensign Humphrey L. Tallman. Last to go before Mitchell, Ruehlow and Gray were Gray's wingman, twenty-five-year-old Ensign C. Markland Kelly Jr., and Mitchell's, twenty-one-year-old Ensign Johnny A. Talbot.

While still aloft, Kelly reversed course, heading northwest—seemingly for the ship formation they'd bypassed earlier. Talbot followed, trying to warn Kelly not to ditch downwind, but it was too late. Kelly's plane crashed and sank, all in an instant. Moments later, Talbot landed nearby, escaped his cockpit and launched his raft.[1]

Akagi's CO and staff officers had been imploring a reluctant Chuichi Nagumo to leave the bridge by the only escape route possible: a rope suspended from the shattered front windows, thence via a gallery-level catwalk to the anchor deck. He'd resisted, but at 10:46 a.m., finally conceding the inevitable, Nagumo was assisted down the rope. Minutes later, he left aboard a waiting cutter dispatched from cruiser *Nagara*.

Mitsuo Fuchida remained for the moment on the command bridge in the company of Shōgo Masuda, *Akagi's* captain, the ship's navigator and a handful of sailors. But with flames igniting flammable bridge fixtures, the situation became so untenable that Masuda urged Fuchida to escape.

Several sailors assisted Fuchida to the dangling rope, but when he reached its end he found himself still ten feet above the flight deck. A secondary explosion finally shook Fuchida loose and he tumbled to the deck, in the process shattering both ankles. Fuchida lay helpless and unconscious on *Akagi's* flight deck for several minutes before several escap-

---

1. Talbot, along with Mitchell, Ruehlow, Gray, McInerny, Magda, Jennings and Tallman would eventually be rescued from the chilly Pacific waters northeast of Midway Atoll. The remains of Hill and Kelly were never found. The ships they had bypassed as they flew northeast turned out to be part of TF 16.

ing crewmen carried him to the anchor deck. There he was strapped to a bamboo stretcher and lowered into *Nagara's* cutter.

The ship Nagumo, Fuchida and (later) Genda left was impossible to save. Flames had already reached the lower hangar deck and electricity had failed, depriving the ship of both illumination and power-driven water pumps. Damage control personnel still were fighting courageously, even resorting to hand pumps to stream water onto raging fires. But each secondary explosion penetrated to the deck immediately below, spreading the conflagration. Because of fires on the middle decks, all communications between topside and the engine rooms had been severed. Soon, heated air from the upper deck fires would begin invading lower compartments through air intakes. Men would suffocate there as they stood resolutely at their stations.

Conditions were no better on *Kaga* or *Soryu*. *Kaga*, hit at more or less the same time as *Akagi*, had taken direct bomb hits on the forward, middle and after sections of her flight deck. A bomb landing near the bridge had wiped out most of the ship's command staff. *Soryu*, meanwhile, had also taken devastating flight deck hits that spread fire to fuel tanks and ordnance magazines. With the ship's main engines stopped, steering control lost and fire mains destroyed, her captain had already ordered abandon ship.

Only carrier *Hiryu* remained undamaged. Command of air operations had passed to Rear Admiral Tamon Yamaguchi. Already, he had organized a retaliatory strike comprising eighteen Val dive-bombers and six Zero-sen escorts. They had begun taking off from *Hiryu's* deck at around 10:50 a.m.

———

When Jim Gray's ten VF-6 escorts entered *Enterprise's* landing circle at 10:50 a.m., they were the first aircraft to return safely from the morning mission. Helped by strong Zed Baker homing signals, the pilots had gradually descended from twenty-two thousand feet for an uneventful ride home. Miles Browning's air staff personnel were eager to debrief Gray and his men. Gray's radio transmission an hour before had turned out to be the first definite word to reach TFs 16 and 17 that strike planes had actually sighted the enemy.

Confusing snatches of strike aircraft radio transmissions hinting at disaster for the Japanese had since been reaching the American carriers and anticipation was running high for eyewitness information. Gray, however, could tell them little more than what he'd radioed then. He and his pilots had never gotten into the action and never met up with VB-16 and VS-16 over the target.

To learn more, they would have to await the return of McClusky's dive-bombers.

———

At 11:33 a.m., just as carrier *Yorktown* turned eastward to launch ten VS-5 SBDs to search north and northwest for remaining enemy flattops, VF-3's Thach, Macomber and Dibb finally spotted home base. Their recovery delayed by the hurried launch of twelve CAP Wildcats, the three VF-3 pilots finally got the signal to approach the landing circle at 11:50 a.m. During this interval, Tom Cheek, returning by himself after losing track of Dan Sheedy, managed to rejoin them and form up on Brainard Macomber's wing.

Thach was the first of the four to touch down. After taxiing forward of the barriers, he jumped from his cockpit and ran to flag plot to fill in Fletcher and his air staff on what he'd witnessed. Behind Thach, both Dibb and Macomber made uneventful landings. But when Tom Cheek's wheels first hit the deck, something was wrong. Instead of grabbing a wire, his hook bounced entirely over them, sending Cheek towards a barrier crash.

Desperate to avoid the sort of accident that had killed Don Lovelace just days before, Cheek immediately jammed his control stick forward and tucked himself into a ball, his head close to cockpit deck. The F4F's nose dipped, its propeller grabbed a barrier wire, and the entire plane cartwheeled onto its back.

Unhurt but trapped, Cheek feared an explosion. "Get this thing the hell off me!" he yelled to the flight deck crew. Pulled clear within seconds, Cheek was rushed to the flight surgeon, who pronounced him okay.

Flight operations were suspended as some crewman fixed the barrier and others hoisted Cheek's inverted Wildcat for removal to the hangar deck.

Meanwhile, as Thach briefed Fletcher on the good news, air plot had a fix on bogeys to the west, distance thirty-two miles, climbing and closing fast on *Yorktown*.

———

At 11:56 a.m., when CAG/FDO Oscar Pederson first transmitted intercept vectors on the new crop of bogeys, the twelve CAP aircraft just launched from *Yorktown* were still low on the water and just beginning to climb.

Worse, few had located wingmen or divisions. Instead, each pilot was hauling back on his stick, clawing for altitude.

When he reached ten thousand feet, VF-3's Scott McCuskey was the first to confront enemy planes: two nine-plane Val formations, one formation ahead of the other. McCuskey immediately swung to his left, positioning his F4F for a flat-side beam run on the lead formation's outboard Val. He triggered a short, high-deflection burst to get this first Val and, as the Japanese bomber dropped in flames, McCuskey threaded his way astern of the remaining eight. It took finesse to negotiate the tight corridor between the two ranks of dive-bombers. Dipping a wing in order to pull clear, all that McCuskey could manage was a quick parting shot at the last Val in line.

Then, as he regrouped for a second pass, McCuskey was startled to see a pair of Vals from the lead row break ranks, turn and go after him. Relying on instinct, McCuskey managed to cut inside their turns only to end up head-to-head with still other Vals. When McCuskey opened fire to clear a path, his tracers scattered the Vals like bowling pins. McCuskey succeeded in pushing through, but in the process he expended his last rounds.

Then McCuskey heard an ominous "ping" on his left wing. Swiveling his head, McCuskey spotted a new pair of Vals poised to reprise the attack. All he could do was take the F4F into a diving spiral, using speed to shake his attackers. When McCuskey finally pulled up near the water, his tail was clear. He raced for *Yorktown's* flight deck in hopes of re-arming but was waved off. All he could do was get out of range and watch what happened.

————

Lieutenant Arthur J. Brassfield witnessed Scott McCuskey's chaotic joust with *Hiryu's* dive-bombers. The thirty-one-year-old Brassfield (like McCuskey, a VF-42 Coral Sea veteran now assigned to VF-3) was flying a thousand yards to the right of the enemy dive-bomber formation that McCuskey's run had disrupted. At 12:03 p.m., as other CAP aircraft pursued individual Vals, Brassfield set his sights on three dive-bombers heading in a loose line-astern directly for *Yorktown.*

Once he'd gotten within shooting distance, Brassfield rolled into a high-side run on the lead plane. Alerted, the Val pilot broke into a tight climbing turn, his wingmen following. Using momentum to zoom climb after them, Brassfield squeezed off a long, well-aimed burst that flamed the leader. Pressing on, Brassfield executed a violent wingover to set up a beam attack on the second Val. At close range he poured rounds into this Val's fuselage and wing root. When it exploded, Brassfield dove for the final Val, using speed to cut off its escape to cloud cover. Locked to its six o'clock, Brassfield set the Val ablaze with a quick pull of his trigger.

————

Fred Mears was on *Hornet's* flight deck when the last of Air Group 8's returning SBDs touched down at 12:09 p.m., most still carrying their bombs. As the SBDs were being spotted aft and their pilots headed for ready rooms. Mears learned that none of them had found—much less attacked—the Japanese. Waldron's torpedo planes, meanwhile, were still MIA. In less than an hour's time, given what Mears knew about their fuel capacity, they would either be aboard or in the water.

"Jap planes approaching from astern." *Hornet's* loudspeaker suddenly called out—and then: "Standby to repel attack."

Those watching from the flight deck could easily see the planes off the port beam. For no reason that made sense—Mears loosened the flap on his pistol holster, withdrew his .45-caliber Colt, cocked its hammer and took station along the edge of the flight deck. But instead of heading for *Hornet,* the Japanese planes flew on towards *Yorktown,* over the horizon on *Hornet's* port quarter. In the distance Mears soon saw a couple of smoke smudges where planes had crashed in the water. The rest of the enemy planes were well out of sight when two more columns of smoke burst up over the sea.

————

Post-action estimates had it that VF-3 CAP aircraft splashed at least seven Vals and a Zero within minutes of interception. It was good, timely shooting, but in the end not nearly good enough. Beginning at 12:09 p.m., *Yorktown* lookouts sighted as many as seven Japanese dive-bombers closing in on the ship's starboard quarter through high clouds and blinding sun.

At 12:11 p.m., the first of three Vals to score direct hits came in steeply from astern. Though withering antiaircraft fire chopped the Val into three pieces, its bomb fell clear of the wreckage to strike *Yorktown's* flight deck aft of the island and near the No. 2 elevator. It exploded on contact, opening an eleven-foot hole in the flight deck, igniting a fire in the hangar deck below and killing or wounding virtually all the gun crews in the aft 1.1-inch gun mounts.

Three minutes later, a second bomb penetrated the flight deck amidships just inboard from the island. This bomb exploded deep inside the hull, damaging fireroom uptakes in three boilers, and altogether disabling the other three boilers.

A third bomb hit just a minute later. Piercing the No. 1 flight deck forward of the island, it too went deep before exploding to ignite raging fires that eventually forced the flooding of a main magazine.

With only one ship's boiler still operating, *Yorktown* lost headway, as clouds of black smoke billowed amidships.

———

Around 12:25 p.m., *Hornet* launched a fresh four-plane CAP and made ready to recover three more. Joining the returning *Hornet* in the landing circle was the F4F piloted by *Yorktown's* Dan Sheedy. The VF-3 aviator had painful wounds in his ankle and shoulder from his Zero duels and his fuel tanks were close to empty. At 12:29 p.m., with the carrier's deck ready to receive him, Sheedy made his approach.

Fred Mears was standing near the starboard rail as Sheedy's wheels touched down and skidded to the right. The landing impact buckled the Wildcat's right landing gear. As Sheedy's tail hook snagged a wire and slewed to a stop, the right wingtip collapsed to the deck, and all six wing guns cut loose with a disastrous two-second burst of automatic fire.

The bullets ripped into the island and scattered spectators. Five were killed and twenty wounded.

As soon as the shooting started, Fred Mears dropped to his back. He was not hit but a sailor nearby caught some shrapnel in the knee. It was not a bad wound, but after dragging the sailor to safety, Mears found himself covered in blood. Then he saw the body of a dead sailor who had been hit directly in the face and a badly wounded Marine sergeant being carried on a stretcher. The Marine's arm was torn from shoulder to elbow, exposing a mass of red blood and white muscle. What startled Mears most was the sight of torn, naked flesh. It was nothing at all like the movies, where bloodshed always seemed to be concealed under clothing.

Lost in the moment's torment was the fact that Sheedy's F4F was the last aircraft to return from a morning strike that had succeeded in triggering the destruction of three Japanese aircraft carriers. Over the next hour, as the two American task forces took time to tally their decimated aircraft inventories, however, they learned of their own staggering losses: a total of twelve fighters, nineteen torpedo bombers and thirty-seven dive-bombers (and perhaps as many or more crewmen) were not coming back.

———

By 2:30 p.m., carrier *Yorktown* was on the threshold of resurrection. No longer a drifting derelict, she was a combat establishment about to re-open for business. With smoke-filled firerooms cleared and the three dis-abled boilers back on line, her speed had been worked back up to nineteen knots. In recognition, CO Buckmaster had ordered a brand new battle ensign raised. Spotted on *Yorktown's* flight deck well abaft the island, shorn of all unnecessary weight and being refueled (now that shipboard fires had abated), were eight VF-3 Wildcats. As wind speed over the deck increased, their eight pilots—led by VF-3 CO Jimmie Thach—climbed into cockpits. TF 17 (*Yorktown* plus her screen of four cruisers and seven destroyers) now lay forty miles west of TF 16 (*Enterprise* and *Hornet* with their screens). Overhead circled six CAP aircraft dispatched from *Enter-prise's* flight deck—three each belonging to VF-3 and VF-6.

An hour before, Frank Jack Fletcher had shifted his flag from *Yorktown* to cruiser *Astoria* (CA-34) (part of the TF 17 screen), in the process pass-ing control of flight operations to *Enterprise's* Raymond Spruance. As Spruance waited word from his aerial scouts on the location and dispo-sition of additional Japanese carriers, *Enterprise* and *Hornet* were re-spot-ting their flight decks with dive-bombers. Although these two flattops held a combined total of thirty fighter aircraft in reserve, none of these F4Fs would be available until the SBDs were aloft.

With little doubt, the small force of torpedo-bearing Kates and Zero escorts just then approaching TF 16 was looking for undamaged CVs. If so, their crews could be forgiven (though not in history's pages) for not recognizing *Yorktown* as the same ship bombed to near-extinction by *Hiryu's* Vals earlier that very afternoon.

Angling in from the north and maneuvering for an anvil attack on *York-town's* bows, five Kates aimed for the port side, while the others branched left, intending to sweep astern of the carrier and reach attack position to starboard.

After refueling, re-arming and gulping down lunch aboard *Enterprise*, VF-3's Scott McCuskey had talked his way into leading a CAP mission over TF 17. Since reaching position at 1:56 p.m., the division (McCuskey plus three pilots from VF-6) had been orbiting at ten thousand feet under FDO Oscar Pederson's control. When the new bogeys were first detected, Ped-erson had immediately vectored McCuskey's division northwest.

Still holding at ten thousand feet and flying through intermittent cloud cover, the pilots assumed they were looking for Vals and Zeros when Pederson suddenly came on the circuit: "Return, buster, you have passed them!"

All but certain nothing above or below had escaped their notice, the pilots nonetheless reversed course. Pederson implored McCuskey to look to his left. The bogeys, Pederson warned, were already between McCuskey's Wildcats and TF 17.

———

At 2:40 p.m., *Yorktown's* flagman was hurrying Thach's eight F4Fs off the patched deck in ten-to-fifteen second intervals. Refueling had been suspended as soon as the new bogeys were detected, leaving Thach's and wingman Ram Dibb's F4Fs as the only two with full tanks. But, whatever the fuel status, the job before each of them was formidable. Launched into the eye of a developing aerial torpedo storm, each would have to fight alone, at low altitude and slow speed while dodging antiaircraft rounds from every ship in the formation.

First off the deck, Thach banked right as *Yorktown* began a turn to starboard. Gaining altitude on one inbound Kate, Thach rolled into a flat-side run from the right, accelerated to get in close, and squeezed off a long burst. As he swung by, Thach saw flames on the enemy plane's left wing burn away the metal skin to expose the wing ribs. The left wing soon buckled, and the Kate spun into the water—but not before launching its torpedo towards *Yorktown's* starboard bow.

Next aloft was twenty-five-year-old Lieutenant (junior grade) William N. Leonard who, as he turned left, spotted a Kate trying to cross ahead of *Yorktown's* bow to reach her starboard side. The Kate's course took it along screen destroyer *Balch* (DD-363)'s starboard flank, so Leonard's flat-side beam pass carried him from port-to-starboard just above *Balch's* decks. As Leonard's shell-casings clattered on the tin can's forecastle, the Val pilot hastily dropped his torpedo and tried to escape, with flames and smoke streaming from the underside of his fuselage. Leonard turned, caught up with, and finished the Kate with a no-deflection burst to its belly.

Taking off just after Leonard, VF-3's Johnny Adams found he had neither time nor position to execute a decent firing pass. Adams did get in a quick desperation shot at a Kate apparently bound for *Yorktown's* starboard side. The shot may have induced the Kate's pilot to instead drop his torpedo prematurely on *Yorktown's* port beam. At any rate, Adams had the satisfaction moments later of seeing the Kate explode and disintegrate—perhaps a victim of his bullets, though more likely of shipboard fire.

There was some promise on *Yorktown's* starboard flank: Three torpedoes had been launched—all errantly—by Kate pilots who never lived to tell about it.

———

Racing back from the north but now too late to cut off either the starboard or port side Kates, Scott McCuskey noticed two Zeros below him at 2,500 feet. In a steep dive, McCuskey singled out one of the enemy planes, but his victim detected him and quickly hauled into a tight climb and high loop. Employing a zoom climb to hang on the Zero's tail through the loop, McCuskey pressed his trigger even as he hung from his shoulder straps at the loop's apex. The Zero—shredded and in flames—spun into the water just as McCuskey's Wildcat lost momentum and stalled.

After recovering from the resulting spin, McCuskey climbed to regain altitude. Minutes later he executed a high-speed pass on another Zero, only to find the Zero's wingman latched to his six-o'clock. The Zero pilot was in position for an easy shot—and would likely have taken it—had not Ensign Melvin C. Roach, McCuskey's twenty-four-year old VF-6 wingman, rushed in for a shot that dislodged and chased the enemy fighter.

———

McCuskey's pick-up division would tally two Zeros and crippling damage to a third—all but eliminating fighter cover for the Kates lining up on *Yorktown's* port bow. Seeing the Grummans and fearing for their own destruction before they could launch torpedoes, these torpedo planes had sought cover in nearby clouds.

Emerging from hiding at about 2:42 p.m., the five planes flew through openings in the screen and descended for their wave-top release points. Just before reaching them, they were taken under fire by VF-3's Walt Haas, the seventh of eight *Yorktown* CAP pilots. Haas was near to being the final defensive obstacle between the carrier's port side and the inbound Kates. He made a flat-side run at three or four of them and thought he winged one but never saw it splash.

The last VF-3 pilot to try to intervene was twenty-two-year-old Ensign George A. Hopper Jr. Having entered the arena last and with the Kates already over their drop points, Hopper had all he could do to avoid colliding with screen destroyer *Balch*. As he pulled up and pushed his wing over, Hopper was promptly blindsided by a Zero whose pilot hit him with well-aimed head-on burst. In an instant, Hopper's plane plowed into the water and broke apart.

By then, four of the five port-side Kates had dropped torpedoes. Sometime between 2:43 and 2:44 p.m., after tracking unerringly across the seven hundred yards that separated them from *Yorktown's* port side hull, two of the torpedoes hit. The blasts flooded three firerooms and the forward generator room. Boilers failed and power was extinguished across the ship. With her rudder jammed, *Yorktown* was soon dead in the water, listing ever more to port.

The 2:44 p.m. explosions sealed *Yorktown's* fate. Abandon ship would be called minutes later, though it would take hours (stretching into days) of indecision and struggle before *Yorktown* finally sank.

But a sighting in the very next moment would seal Japan's fate in this unprecedented carrier-to-carrier battle. At 2:45 p.m., a VS-5 SBD crew called in the course, bearing and distance to carrier *Hiryu* and her consorts. This sighting was the prelude to devastating air strikes two hours later by SBDs from *Enterprise*, *Yorktown* and *Hornet*. *Hiryu* would be sunk; with her loss would go Japan's last, faint hopes of averting utter defeat at Midway.

————

Even though he had not flown that day, VT-8's Frederick Mears watched with fascination as pilots (most from *Hornet* but some as well from *Yorktown*) returned from strike and CAP missions. After making their reports, the pilots invariably headed for the "admiral's pantry" one deck down from the flight deck. Gulping coffee or lemonade out of paper cups, they stuffed sandwiches into their cheeks, all the while yammering and gesturing about their adventures.

With helmets off, their hair was matted. Their faces were dirty and their flight suits were streaked with sweat. A cup in one hand, a sandwich or two in the other, each pilot would still employ those same hands to demonstrate incredible in-flight maneuvers, kills and hair-breadth escapes. Mears could tell they were having a hell of good time. They had fought, they were still alive and each seemed ready to go out again.

It was ridiculous, Mears realized, but also fun to watch and he couldn't help catching some of their enthusiasm.

Left to right:
Grumman Aircraft
Engineering's Leroy
Randle Grumman,
William T. Schwendler
and Leon A. Swirbul.
The Grumman Story

Aircraft landing on USS Langley (CV-1) in October 1931. *National Archives*

Grumman FF-1 (called the "Fi-Fi" or "Fertile Myrtle.") in flight on Nov 22, 1932. *National Archives*

Grumman F2F-1 in flight April 14, 1936. *National Archives*

USS *Lexington* (CV-2) and USS *Salt Lake City* (CA-25) at sea on May 20, 1930. *National Archives*

USS *Saratoga* (CV-3) March 24, 1930. Both *Lexington* and *Saratoga* were battle cruiser conversions. *National Archives*

Commander John H. Towers, USN, Naval
Aviator No. 3. *National Archives*

Jimmie Collins posing with his son next to the Grumman
XF3F on March 21, 1935. *The Grumman Story*

XF3F crash scene, March 22, 1935. *The Grumman Story*

Saburo Sakai as a petty officer-pilot during his time in China.

Mitsubishi A6M2 carrier "Zero" fighter. *Naval Historical Center*

Mitsubishi land-based "Betty" bomber. *Naval Historical Center*

F3F-1 aircraft of U.S. Navy Fighting Squadron Four in formation flight. *National Archives*

DePauw University
sophomore Alex Vraciu
jumps from the second floor
of a lecture hall onto a
tarpaulin held by his Delta
Chi fraternity brothers. *Photo
courtesy of Alex Vraciu*

Admiral Ernest J. King, USN. *National Archives*

Secretary of the Navy Frank Knox. *National Archives*

VF-3 F4F Wildcats piloted by Lieutenant Commander. J.S. Thach, USN (foreground) and Lieutenant Edward H. O'Hare, USN (upper right) on April 10, 1942. *National Archives*

Alex Vraciu (back row, fifth from right) during "E-Base" at Glenview Illinois. *Photo courtesy of Alex Vraciu*

Bombing attack on Japanese carrier Shokaku on May 8, 1942. *National Archives*

Left to right: Lieutenant Commander J.H. Flatley (VF-10), Lieutenant S.W. Vejtasa (VS-5) and Lieutenant (junior grade) J.A. Leppla (VS-2), heroes of Coral Sea Battle. *National Archives*

Then-Lieutenant J.H. Flatley being decorated by Vice Admiral William F. Halsey. *National Archives*

Midway, with Eastern Island in foreground, November 1941. *National Archives*

Bert Earnest's VT-8 TBF after its return to Midway on June 4, 1942. *National Archives*

Japanese aircraft attack Guadalcanal-Tulagi invasion force on August 8, 1942. *National Archives*

Photographed from a Japanese cruiser during the Battle of Savo Island, August 9, 1942. Cruiser USS *Quincy* (CA-39), burning and illuminated by Japanese searchlights, was sunk in this action. *Naval Historical Center*

Guadalcanal's Henderson Field (looking north), August 23, 1942. *National Archives*

Rear Admiral Richmond Kelly
Turner, USN (left), and Major General
Alexander A. Vandegrift, USMC at
the time of the Guadalcanal-Tulagi
operation, August 1942. *National
Archives*

Lieutenant
Commander Eddie
Sanders taxis a
captured Imperial
Japanese Navy Zero
fighter at Naval Air
Station San Diego,
California in
September 1942.
National Archives

Vice Admiral Frank Jack Fletcher,
September 1942. *National Archives*

USS *Wasp* (CV-7) after being torpedoed, September 1942. *National Archives*

Pilots of VF-10 attached to the *Enterprise* (CV-6). Back Row (left to right): Lieutenant M. Kilpatrick; Lieutenant (junior grade) R. L. Reiserer; Ensign R. R. Witte; Lieutenant E. J. Murphy; Lieutenant L. E. Harris; Ensign P. M. Shonk; Ensign W. B. Reding; Ensign L. P. Heinzen; Ensign A. G. Boren. Middle row (left to right): Ensign H. C. McClaugherty; Lieutenant (junior grade) R. M. Voris; Lieutenant A. D. Pollock; Ensign R. G. Taber; Ensign H. J. Boydstun; Ensign W. R. Harman; Lieutenant S. E. Ruehlow; Ensign F. T. Donahoe; Ensign D. Gordon; Lieutenant (junior grade) J. D. Billo; Ensign L. E. Slagle; NAP R. F. Kanze; Ens. S. E. Hedrick; Lieutenant F. L. Faulkner; Lieutenant S. W. Vejtasa; and Ensign M. P. Long. Front row (left to right): Ensign W. H. Leder; Ens. E. L. Feightner; Ensign E. B. Coalson; Ensign S.G. Kona; Lieutenant Commander J. H. Flatley; Lieutenant Commander W. R. Kane; Ensign L. W. Gaskill; Ensign M. N. Wickendoll; Lieutenant J. C. Eckhardt and Ensign R. T. Porter. *National Archives*

An Air Group 10 TBF prepares to take off from the deck of *Enterprise* (CV-6) for an attack on Japanese carriers during the Battle of Santa Cruz, Oct. 26, 1942. *National Archives*

Japanese aircraft attack the USS *Hornet* (CV-8) during the Battle of Santa Cruz, October 26, 1942. The dive bomber in the upper left center crashed into the signal bridge of the carrier. *National Archives*

Lieutenant Commander J. S. Thach on September 29, 1942 as he tells Washington newspaper reporters that only-carrier-based air power can clear the way for invasion and defeat of Japan. *Acme Photo*

USS *Independence* (CVL-22). *Official U.S. Navy photo courtesy of Ray E. Boomhower*

A TBF flies on anti-submarine patrol above ships of U.S. task force en route to Wake Island, September 1943. *National Archives*

VF-6 pilots photographed in Maui, July 1943. Top row (left to right): John Stanizewski, John Johnston, Robert Hobbs, Ashton Roberts, George Rodgers, Harvey Odenbrett, James Nichols, Robert Locker, Charles Palmer, Edward Philippe, Sy Mendenhall and Charles McCord. Third row: Bayard Webster, Thomas Hall, Robert Merritt, Bascom Gates, Clifford Seaver, William Davis, Donald Kent, John Benton, Herschel Pahl, Robert Klinger and Lindley Godson. Second row: John Ogg, Thomas Willman, Wilton Hutt, Thaddeus Coleman, Allie Callan, Alex Vraciu, Richard Trimble, Albert Nyquist, Malcolm Loesch, William Rose and Howard Crews. Front row: Richards Loesch, John Altemus, Foster Blair, Henry Fairbanks, George Bullard, Butch O'Hare, Paul Rooney, Joe Robbins, Alfred Kerr, Robert Neel and Cyrus Chambers. *Photograph courtesy of Alex Vraciu*

VF-6 pilots (left to right) Alex Vraciu, Butch O'Hare, Sy Mendenhall and Willie Callan aboard *Independence* on September 6, 1943. *Photograph courtesy of Alex Vraciu*

Alex Vraciu on October 5, 1943 after scoring his first aerial victory. *Photograph courtesy of Alex Vraciu*

U.S. aerial raid on Rabaul in November 1943. Picture taken by a plane from the *Saratoga* (CV-3) showing ships in the harbor maneuvering under attack. *National Archives*

VADM Marc A. Mitscher and Commodore A. A. Burke. *National Archives*

Aboard USS *Intrepid* (CV-11) air squadron VF-6 receives instructions before leaving to take part in the attack on Roi, Marshall Islands. Alex Vraciu is seated on the second row aisle. *National Archives*

USS *Intrepid* (CV-11). *National Archives*

F6F landing on flight deck of *Intrepid* February 1, 1944. *National Archives*

Two Japanese ships being bombed during attack on Truk. The photo was taken by an *Intrepid* aircraft pilot, February 16-17, 1944. *National Archives*

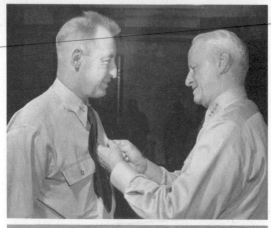

Admiral Chester W. Nimitz, USN (right) presenting the Distinguished Service Medal to Rear Admiral Joseph James Clark "for distinguishing himself by exceptionally meritorious service as Commander of a Task Group of carriers and screening vessels in the operations against Jap forces from April through June 1944." *National Archives*

USS *Lexington* (CV-16). *Photograph courtesy of Alex Vraciu*

Pilots of Lexington's Air Group 16. Alex Vraciu is standing seventh from the left in the third row. *Photograph courtesy of Alex Vraciu*

A Hellcat landing aboard the USS *Lexington* (*CV-16*) during the Battle of the Philippine Sea, June 19, 1944. *National Archive*

After landing aboard *Lexington* on June 19, 1944, Alex Vraciu signifies his aerial victories. *Photograph courtesy of Alex Vraciu*

A Japanese dive bomber crashing in the water aft of USS *Bunker Hill* (*CV-17*) on June 19, 1944 as seen from the flight deck of USS *Cabot* (*CVL-28*) *National Archives*

Japanese aircraft carrier *Zuikaku* and two destroyers maneuver to avoid attacks by U.S. carrier aircraft during the Battle of the Philippine Sea on June 20, 1944. *Official Navy photo courtesy of Ray Boomhower*

Lieutenant Ronald P. "Rip" Gift relaxes with other pilots in a ready room on board USS *Monterey* (CVL-26), after landing on her at night following strikes on the Japanese fleet, 20 June 1944. *National Archives, courtesy of Ray Boomhower*

Alex Vraciu and Marc Mitscher in a June 23, 1944 photo. *Photograph courtesy of Alex Vraciu*

Alex Vraciu during a parade and award ceremony in his home town of East Chicago, Indiana. *Photograph courtesy of Alex Vraciu*

Admiral Ernest J. King (center) with Admiral Chester W. Nimitz (left) and Admiral Raymond A. Spruance (right) in July 1944. *Naval Historical Center*

Operation Air Show, over Tokyo Bay, September 2, 1945. *National Archive*

PART FOUR

BLUE SKIES, GREEN HELL

13
GET DOWN TO WORK

After Midway, when they went ashore on liberty in Honolulu, Navy pilots either checked into the Moana Hotel or the Royal Hawaiian. The Royal Hawaiian, though a beautiful facility commandeered for exclusive Navy use, forbid women in its rooms and clamped down on rowdiness. By contrast, circumstances at the Moana were almost too accommodating for men intent on a spree. Most of the pilots, therefore, including VT-8's Fred Mears, gravitated to the Moana—a big Army and Navy fun house.

The pilots' nighttime routines at the Moana consisted of moving from room to room in search of liquor, all the while talking, arguing, fighting and smashing furniture. Some sought the company of women, but most chose to vent their pent-up emotions by being as mean as possible. Good friends would brawl to bloody collapse. Some tried to throw each other out the hotel's windows. The blacked-out Moana's eerily dim hallway lights gave the goings-on a savage aspect—like some tribal ritual.

Fights between Army and Navy personnel were particularly brutal. The Navy pilots were sure they'd won the Battle of Midway, but the Army had somehow grabbed all the headlines with stories of how their B-17s had blasted the Japanese fleet. To Navy pilots who had lost friends in low-level bombing and torpedo missions, glorifying Army fliers who had dropped bombs—mostly wide of the mark—from twenty thousand feet was infuriating.

Mears had never gotten into the aerial fight and, like most, he had no firm idea what—other than a huge American victory—had actually happened. Still, he felt deeply about the loss of so many VT-8 personnel who'd left the *Hornet* ready room on the morning of the battle, never to return. Mears and Robert "Andy" Divine, another new pilot who had not flown that day, had the disheartening job of inventorying the personal effects of the missing pilots. Each of their private possessions—a battered cap, a girl's photo, a wallet—was a potent reminder of how much each man would be missed at home. Worst of all was skimming (and censoring, where necessary) the last-minute notes the airmen had written to their next of kin just before going into battle.

During his stay at Moana, Mears ran into a number of pilots he knew but had not seen in a while, including several he thought were missing or dead. All the familiar joy had been sapped from a few of these combat veterans, while others tore full throttle into Moana's floating ruckus. Among those Mears encountered were Bert Earnest and Tex Gay—the survivors, respectively, of the Fieberling and Waldron flights. Gay, having already told his account to hundreds of people, looked particularly tired and thin, so Mears refrained from asking him anything about it.

———

During his long sea voyage back from the South Pacific following Coral Sea, Jimmy Flatley had thought long and hard about fighter tactics. His most immediate interest was to draft a combat doctrine manual for VF-10, his new squadron. But, when he set up shop at North Island in June, he also had the opportunity to read and reflect on the war of words being fought between the Pacific fleet aviators and BuAer over the events at Midway.

It was clear that fighter squadron COs were angry and distraught about the performance of their aircraft and the sometimes deadly consequences for their pilots. In a post-action report written on the day of battle (from a state room aboard *Enterprise* where he landed after *Yorktown* closed for business), Jimmie Thach was particularly scathing in his descriptions of VF-3's harrowing morning escort mission and the futile efforts to shield *Yorktown* that afternoon. "It is indeed surprising," Thach concluded, "that any of our pilots returned alive. Any success our fighter pilots have against the Japanese Zero fighter is *not* due to the performance of the airplane we fly. . . . " To prevail, his pilots either had to be individually superior to their Japanese counterparts or operate as a team. The alternative—pinning their hopes on enemy stupidity or poor marksmanship—was a recipe for disaster.

Thach's was hardly the only fighter pilot voice crying from the wilderness. On June 9, VF-6 CO Jim Gray sent a letter through channels reiterating earlier criticisms of the F4Fs' shortcomings and beseeching BuAer to prod Grumman to deliver an F4F with a better climb rate. The pilots would then at least be able to dictate the terms of combat.

Chester Nimitz, for his part, after reviewing and forwarding these arguments and ripostes, sent his own summary to Ernest King. While conceding the Wildcat's inferiority to the Zero, Nimitz tempered pilot criticisms by pointing to overall results. After all, three Zero kills had been claimed for each Wildcat loss and part of that differential could well be credited to better "armor, armament and leak proof tanks."

Nimitz felt there were plenty of improvements to be made with the weaponry and resources immediately at hand. "In most engagements" the key disadvantage was that "our fighters were outnumbered." That could and would be remedied, in part because of the F4F-4's Sto-Wing capability. With carrier fighter squadron aircraft complements expanded, other improvements would fall into place. For instance, the number of strike fighter escorts could be increased. Additional CAP aircraft, "stacked" at different altitudes, could offer more in-depth protection for the carriers.

––––––

Flatley's take on these controversies had its roots in his own experience at Coral Sea. When battling Zeros, the performance differences between F4F models mattered hardly at all. Neither the heavier F4F-4 nor the lighter F4F-3 was a match for the Zeke in dogfighting. In fact, classic dogfighting—the extended fighter-versus-fighter duel—was obsolete. Instead of individual combat (which pitched the inferiority of a lone Wildcat against the superiority of a lone Zeke), the focus should be on formation tactics, on teamwork and mutual support.

Flatley ended up adding his own voice to the controversy in a lengthy June 25 letter titled "The Navy Fighter" and directed to Commander Carriers Pacific (ComCarPac, Flatley's temporary boss) with copies to BuAer, COMinCH, and CincPac. "The Navy Fighter" both championed the F4F and, owing to Flatley's combat credentials, helped clear the air.

In Flatley's mind, the Wildcat's minuses were offset by plusses, not least of them the quality of the pilots who flew them. The bottom line: "It shoots down the enemy and gets most of us back to our base." Badmouthing the F4F was just hurting fighter pilot morale—telling pilots in effect that "they can't lick the enemy in those planes." The answer was "teaching them some tactics"—not to give them a false sense of security, but to equip them with tools that could make all the difference.

Flatley knew that VF-10, his own squadron, would go into combat with some version of the F4F. In his opinion it was time to "get down to work and quit griping about our planes."

———

In a June 19 ceremony at NAS Kaneohe Bay, Lieutenant Commander Butch O'Hare took command of VF-3 from Jimmie Thach, his former CO. The next day, at the controls of an F4F-4 for the first time, O'Hare led his squadron ninety miles south to NAS Maui at Puunene, a newly commissioned base. Puunene (the base would subsequently be renamed NAS Puunene) had facilities to accommodate an entire carrier air group; it also afforded uncluttered air space and generally better weather conditions than Oahu in which to train.

As July approached, the results of the battles at Coral Sea and Midway were having profound effects on Navy fighter squadrons. Most prominent, of course, was the loss of two carriers: there were simply not enough flight decks to go around. For the time being, with newly arrived VF-5 taking Fighting Three's accustomed slot aboard *Saratoga*, VF-3 would be staying ashore.

But also, and perhaps equally important, the shapes, sizes and uses of carrier fighter squadrons were being fundamentally re-thought. The expansion of squadron complements to twenty-seven and then thirty-six fighter aircraft meant a huge reshuffling of both planes and squadron rosters. The manpower winners in this (at present) zero-sum game, not surprisingly, were the squadrons assigned to carriers. For other squadrons—VF-8, for example, which had made such a poor showing at Midway—it meant being disbanded (the official term was decommissioned). But even for going concerns like O'Hare's VF-3, there was relentless cannibalization.

In relatively quick order, O'Hare would lose pilots to VF-5 (*Saratoga*), VF-6 (*Enterprise*) and VF-72 (*Hornet*, replacing VF-8). Among the transferees were Marion Dufilho, O'Hare's February wingman, to VF-5 and Ram Dibb, Thach's wingman at Midway, to VF-6. By mid-July, VF-3 would be down to eighteen Wildcats—and that would be only the beginning.

———

When the PBY carrying Chester Nimitz touched down in San Francisco Bay on June 30, 1942, it hit a log and capsized. Nimitz (who had never felt particularly at ease in the air since his first white-knuckle ride in one of the Navy's earliest biplanes) was nearly killed. As it was, badly shaken up, Nimitz was relieved to learn that his meeting with Ernest King had been postponed: King had been detained in Washington negotiating JCS approval for his plan to launch a counteroffensive against the Japanese.

Watchtower and Pestilence—as the operations to capture Tulagi and occupy the Santa Cruz Islands had been code-named—were King's rebuttal to a grandiose plan hatched by Douglas MacArthur to seize Rabaul. Rabaul was too heavily defended, King and his staff countered, and it would expose the Navy's precious few carriers to sustained land-based air attacks. They instead proposed an indirect approach via the Eastern Solomons.

King, it turned out, had already taken steps to force the issue by ordering Nimitz to begin preparations for a seaborne invasion of Tulagi. It was a brazen step, but two months earlier, a cagy King had gotten Roosevelt and JCS approval for a limited CinCPOA offensive in the Solomons if the opportunity presented. Confronted with a fait accompli, Marshall and MacArthur quickly concurred—with the proviso that MacArthur command the operations.

King had no intention of putting his carrier task forces in MacArthur's hands. But he also realized George Marshall (who had endorsed MacArthur's Rabaul plan) was in a tight spot. Marshall had been a lowly colonel when MacArthur held sway as Army Chief of Staff and King suspected Marshall was loath to go toe-to-toe with the old warhorse. Though mostly unsympathetic to Marshall's predicament, King proposed an expedient to get Marshall off the hook: the western boundary of Nimitz's authority would simply be enlarged to include the eastern Solomons. By means of this sleight of hand, King got the green light, not only for Watchtower and Pestilence—called Task I—but also for Task II (the taking of Lae, Salamaua and other parts of northeast New Guinea) and Task III (the capture of Rabaul itself). King's and Marshall's gerrymandering had placed Task I in Nimitz's bailiwick, while Tasks II and III (assuming they came about) would be MacArthur's.

King considered the heavy lifting done—and his players in place. On the Fourth of July, when he finally convened with Nimitz in San Francisco, King outlined the objectives for Task I, including, most prominently, the invasions of Tulagi, Florida and Guadalcanal Islands in early August 1942.

An amphibious force commanded by Rear Admiral Richmond Kelly Turner (also on hand in San Francisco) would land 1st Marine Division troops at Tulagi and Lunga Point on Guadalcanal (code named Cactus). Turner was to unload his transports during the day of the landings and withdraw them that same night. Meanwhile, the carriers (Fletcher's TF 16 with *Saratoga*; TF 11 with *Enterprise* under new task force commander Rear Admiral Thomas C. Kinkaid; and TF 18 with *Wasp* [CV-7] under Rear Admiral Leigh Noyes) were to provide three days of fighter cover— two days leading up to the invasion, the invasion itself and then, if possible, the withdrawal of the transports. Execution of the offensive would be the immediate responsibility of Vice Admiral Robert L. Ghormely, newly installed in June as Commander South Pacific Area (ComSoPac), reporting to Nimitz.

Discussion of Task I ended with Turner's departure, leaving King and Nimitz time to turn to other matters, including personnel. A still-ailing Halsey was to be relieved as Commander Carriers. But the Pacific now also had an expanded array of Rear Admiral-grade carrier task force (CTF) commanders: Pete Mitscher, George D. Murray, Ted Sherman, Noyes and Kinkaid. The cascading effect of this was the elevation of a fresh crop of carrier captains: aviation career officers such as DeWitt W. "Duke" Ramsey (*Saratoga*), Charles P. Mason (*Hornet*), Arthur C. Davis (*Enterprise*) and Forrest P. Sherman (*Wasp*).

As Nimitz went back to Hawaii and King back to Washington, it was as if the Solomons campaign, now decided, had been removed from their minds. The commanders were in place, the forces assigned and the timetable laid out. There was nothing more to say.

———

On July 10, 1942, a Navy PBY Catalina piloted by Lieutenant William "Bill" Thies had become lost while patrolling the Aleutians Islands east of Dutch Harbor. Relieved to spot the familiar shapes of the Shumagin Islands, Thies decided to return to Dutch Harbor by the most expedient route—across tiny Akutan Island.

It was above Akutan that Thies' plane captain Albert Knack caught a glimpse of what looked to be an aircraft wreck. Thies circled the site, noted its map position, and, after touching down in Dutch Harbor, convinced his VP-41 CO, Lieutenant Commander Paul Foley Jr., to let him return for a closer inspection.

Slogging next day through a muskeg quagmire, Thies and his crew, accompanied by a photographer's mate, discovered an upended but otherwise intact single-seat Japanese combat aircraft, complete with the rotting corpse of its pilot still strapped inside the cockpit. The plane's undercarriage was pocked with bullet holes, a sign the plane had been hit by ground fire. Its pilot had apparently tried a wheels-down emergency landing, mistaking the deceptive patina of Akutan's lush midsummer grass for a firm surface. He'd paid dearly for the misjudgment: the landing gear had abruptly locked in the boggy ground, the wheel struts had snapped, his plane had flipped and he had died of a crushed skull, a broken neck, or both. Because diminutive Albert Knack was the ground team's smallest member, he was the one who was sent into the plane to release the dead man's safety harness.

Postwar records would identify the Japanese pilot as Flight Petty Officer Tadayoshi Koga, one of three pilots launched from Japanese carrier *Ryūjō* for a June 4 raid on Dutch Harbor. This day, however, after tumbling to the ground in a malodorous heap and having his flight suit searched for identifying information, Koga came up nameless. Out of necessity as much as respect, the salvage team interred his corpse in a shallow grave nearby.

As word of the find filtered up the chain of command, salvage efforts kicked into high gear. A beefed-up team descended on the site the next day to give the Zero's still-anonymous donor a proper military burial and await the arrival of heavy-duty salvage equipment. Finally, five days after it was first spotted, Koga's Zero was hoisted from the muck and placed, still inverted, on a waiting barge. When the barge reached Dutch Harbor, the Zero was righted and carefully hosed down. Closer inspection revealed Koga's aircraft to be a type 0 model 21 Mitsubishi A6M Zero manufactured in Nagoya, Japan in February 1942.

On July 14, word reached CinCPac and BuAer that an "only slightly damaged" Zero had been found and that "with care and some luck" it could be returned to flyable condition. Washington was delighted: it was precisely the elusive—and intact—Zero fighter aircraft that Allied intelligence analysts had been desperate to get their hands on.

Emphasizing by radio that "flight test of airplane of highest importance," Washington first wanted to know whether the plane contained any pilot armor. Its custodians responded that it had neither armor nor self-sealing tanks.

Because inspection also revealed that aircraft's wings were integral to its overall construction, shipping the Zero by rail to the East Coast would be impossible. Instead, the plane was winched aboard transport USS *St. Mihel* for the journey to San Diego via Seattle.

Being transferred to VT-3 was, for Fred Mears, like coming home. Attached to *Yorktown* during Midway, VT-3 had lost nearly as many personnel and planes as had VT-8, including its skipper Lem Massey. In the aftermath, VT-3, now commanded by Lieutenant Commander Charles M. Jett, was left to reconstitute itself around a nucleus of pilots like Mears and Bob Divine who had not flown at Midway.

VT-3 was being equipped with Grumman TBF Avengers. The plane seemed so big when compared to the TBD that pilots at first called it the Monster. Although the Monster had a few faults—not enough firepower forward and stiff stick control— it was nonetheless a pure joy to fly. Everything in it worked hydraulically or electrically; once mastered, the cockpit controls were as simple as a one-way street. Moreover, the Avenger seemed able to out-climb, out-dive and even turn inside its Wildcat fighter counterpart—though, to be honest, the F4F still held the overall edge in maneuverability.

On July 15, VT-3 went aboard *Enterprise*, where Mears happened to know a number of bomber and fighter pilots. Mears liked the ship and the squadron; he also liked the two men assigned to fly with him. His turret-gunner was Harry Ferrier, Bert Earnest's radioman-gunner at Midway. Ferrier still bore the scars of that experience. On the right side of his scalp, just above his forehead and visible underneath his close-cropped hair was a shiny half-dollar size expanse of skin—the point where a bullet had nearly reached his brain.

Ferrier was understandably subdued. He was also frank. "I have no hankering to be an ace gunner and shoot down fifty Japs," he told Mears. "All I want to do is put enough .50-caliber slugs in the air to keep the Zeros off my tail." Aloft, Ferrier seldom talked on the intercom; instead he sat hunched up in the "goldfish bowl"—the after turret—with his knees under his chin and smoking cigarettes. Quietly glad, Mears suspected, just to be alive.

Mears's radioman-gunner was a new man, Warren Deitsch. Although Deitsch lacked combat experience and showed a streak of stubbornness, Mears liked him as well. Deitsch was thorough and conscientious; besides, his stubbornness might pay off in combat.

Eleven days out of Pearl, the *Enterprise* task force rendezvoused with the *Saratoga* and *Wasp* task forces south of Fiji. For the purpose of Watchtower, now set to kick off on August 7, TFs 11, 16 and 18 would combine into TF 61. Watchtower's amphibious landing and supply counterpart was Richmond Kelly Turner's TF 62.

The proceedings over the next days, as Watchtower rehearsals were conducted on and around Koro, a small island in the Fijis, had aspects—at least to some pilots—of a Gilbert and Sullivan production. On July 27, for example, when Watchtower bigwigs convened aboard *Saratoga*, Rear Admiral John S. McCain, who headed South Pacific land-based aviation (ComAirSoPac), took an unceremonious saltwater dunking when he lost his footing on Sara's port sea ladder. Soaked to the waist, red-faced, and sputtering, the feisty McCain was one mad little admiral.

But top brass weren't the only clowns. One morning another carrier sent a pilot over to *Enterprise* in an effort to secure a crate of eggs. His wardroom was running low, the pilot pleaded, and they wanted omelets for lunch. On another occasion, when *Enterprise* got separated from the other two carriers, a VF-5 pilot sent out to locate *Enterprise* got lost as well. Thinking he was over his own carrier, he landed to report that there was no sign of *Enterprise*. Flying back to *Saratoga* with *Enterprise's* whereabouts understood with embarassing precision, the pilot was escorted by two Big E dive-bombers. As the next morning's edition of *Saratoga's* all hands news summary put it: "A child who knows not its own mother is not so smart."

Even in tragedy there was the sense of a comic opera. On August 3, *Enterprise* fighter pilot NAP Clayton Allard was dispatched to drop a message aboard *Saratoga*. Returning home and waiting to land, he tried a low level roll off Big E's starboard side. Allard almost pulled it off, but while he was flying inverted his engine smoked and lost power. There was an explosion and a flash of fire as the aircraft disintegrated about a hundred yards from the ship. All Fred Mears could see from his vantage was a circular patch of burning aviation gas to mark the spot.

None in the air group criticized Allard for his fatal stunt. Pilots, after all, and especially fighter pilots, were supposed to have enough steam in their breeches to try such things. In a way, not making it was his own business, though as one of Mears' squadron buddies was moved to remark: "Well, I'm convinced the airplane is here to stay, but I'm not so sure about the pilot."

At noon on August 5, TF 61 turned north and by sunset Tulagi lay less than four hundred miles away. August 6, the crucial day of approach, brought deep fog and haze—ideal conditions to proceed undetected. By sunset, the south coast of Guadalcanal was only eighty-five miles to the northeast.

That night, as carrier deck crews began spotting first-wave aircraft, ships' companies cleared for action below. All bedding was stacked on deck in the middle of sleeping compartments, loose items were secured and flammables were stowed in steel lockers and cabinets.

––––––

After their February triumph above Surabaya, the Tainan Air Group's Zero-sen pilots were sent to Bali, a lush tropical island just off the eastern tip of Java. Their stay there was idyllic but all too brief. A few pilots were rotated home to Japan, but most, including Petty Officer First Class Saburo Sakai, were instead transported by freighter to Rabaul, 2,500 miles east. The dusty, volcanic island was hardly a paradise but, with a constant influx of personnel and new bomber and fighter aircraft, Rabaul was fast becoming an impressive fortress.

Early in April, Sakai joined a handpicked contingent dispatched to Lae to support Japan's push to capture Port Moresby. The contingent's aerial opponents were mainly American, Australian and Dutch P-39s and P-40s, inferior aircraft flown by courageous but inexperienced pilots. Already credited with thirteen aerial kills when he arrived at Lae, over the next four months Sakai ran his total up to fifty-nine, making him one of Japan's top three fighter aces.

At the beginning of August, the Lae pilots were recalled to Rabaul. They were glad to return to more secure surroundings. Successful as they had been at Lae, that base was coming under increased Allied pressure, with nightly bombing attacks by B-17s that disrupted any hope of sleep. During the first few days after the return, the pilots flew reconnaissance and fight sweep missions, but on the morning of August 7, a routine patrol was abruptly called off.

The Tainan Air Group pilots were instead ordered to the island's Command Post, where there was a flurry of activity. When their squadron commander emerged angrily from Rear Admiral Sadiyoshi Yamada's office, he spread a chart on a large table and began poring over it, plotting a course with a compass. He then told the pilots that they had a new mission. An American amphibious force had just put troops ashore at Tulagi and at Lunga on Guadalcanal. They would be attacking the enemy forces on the beaches.

As the pilots studied the charts, they soon understood that such an attack would involve a 1,100-mile round-trip flight. It would undoubtedly be the longest distance fighter operation ever.

———

By 8:30 a.m. the seventeen Guadalcanal-bound Zero-sens were airborne with twenty-seven Mitsubishi twin engine bombers ahead of them. As he took up his escort position, Saburo Sakai was surprised to see the Bettys carrying bombs rather than torpedoes. It seemed a poor choice of ordnance for an attack on shipping.

Three hours into the flight, the planes crossed the Russell Islands at twenty thousand feet; Guadalcanal still lay fifty miles ahead of them, but already they could see flashes of yellow flame in a sky full of cumulus clouds. In the channel between Guadalcanal and Florida Island were the crosshatched wakes of what seemed to be fifty or more enemy ships.

As the formation neared the island, the twin-engine bombers swung slowly into their runs against the channel shipping. Suddenly six American fighter aircraft emerged from the sun's glare. Ignoring the Japanese escorts, the fighters dived down towards the bombers. The planes were distinctively chubbier than any American fighters Sakai had ever seen—they had to be the new Wildcats.

———

It had been a hectic morning for the fliers and flight deck crews of *Enterprise*, *Hornet* and *Saratoga*. In the pre-dawn, Kelly Turner's invasion forces snaked around Cape Esperance, the western edge of Guadalcanal, split into two components and headed for stations off Tulagi and Lunga Point. On blacked-out flight decks, a dawn strike of close to one hundred Dauntlesses and Wildcats was readied. In rough seas, under the light of a quarter moon, and with heavy clouds towering off to the northeast, pilots manned planes at around 5:00 a.m. and began taking off at 5:35 a.m.

In the dim light and with the three carriers operating so close together, there was confusion from the start. Flight echelons intermixed; pilots joined the wrong formations; instead of rendezvousing, flights split into small independent groups. In general, flight leaders gathered whom they could and headed for assigned targets—*Wasp* planes over Tulagi, *Saratoga* and *Enterprise* planes over Guadalcanal. For the most part, the attacks—on flying boats, float planes, motor boats, fuel barges, gun positions and camps around Tulagi; on airstrip runways, structures, trucks, piers and small boats on Guadalcanal—were lightly contested.

Nearly all aircraft had returned to their decks by 7 a.m. After 9 a.m., when the 1st Division Marines stormed ashore, the carriers settled into a routine of almost constant CAP (over both the carriers and amphibious force ships), submarine patrol and ground support missions to help the Marines advance. Despite heavy Japanese ground resistance at Tulagi, the invasions seemed to be going well. Still, everyone wondered when Japanese aircraft would show up.

Their answer came at around 11:30 a.m., when TF 61 radiomen copied three messages. The first, from CinCPac, warned that Japanese bombers and fighters were taking off from Rabaul, apparently aiming for Guadalcanal (but also within striking distance of the carriers just sixty miles south-southwest of Lunga.) The next message, copied nine minutes later, alerted that Japanese submarines were headed for Tulagi. The third, and most actionable, came in plain language from an Australian coast-watcher hiding atop a jungle hill in southern Bougainville: "24 bombers headed yours."

The 11:30 CAP consisted of twenty-four F4Fs circling the carriers. Sixty miles away, fourteen more F4Fs covered the invasion force in Sealark Channel, but all these were low on fuel and set to return. Their replacements, a reduced contingent of eight F4Fs, would take another half hour to reach station. The next *Saratoga* fighter launch, scheduled for 12:03 p.m. was slated to include eight CTF CAP and four invasion force CAP. Now added to this was another Wildcat component: four VF-5 Wildcats led by thirty-year-old Lieutenant James J. Southerland to bolster TF 62's defenses.

————

At 1:15 p.m. Southerland —universally known as "Pug" because of his boxing prowess—was flying above Savo Island when he spotted the attack force of Japanese Bettys descending through the cumulous cover, gathering speed to unleash bombs. "This division from Pug," he alerted his pilots, "put gun switches and sight lamps on. Let's go get 'em boys."

With no time to climb, Southerland could only drop into a low-side run to harass the lead division of Bettys with quick bursts. Behind him, Japanese fighters zoomed in to scatter Southerland's division. The division trailer, twenty-six-year-old Lieutenant (junior grade) Donald A. "Stinky" Innis, managed to climb, scissor and trade head-on shots with five Zekes before escaping into a cloud. The other two, twenty-three-year-old Ensign Robert L. Price and twenty-six-year-old Lieutenant (junior grade) Charles A. Tabberer, never escaped the ambush.

———

Fighting alone now, Southerland crossed behind the line of Bettys, aiming for a bomber flying in the center of the formation's left-most V. In a low-side approach, Southerland riddled its fuselage just forward of its open bomb bay doors. The bomber, wreathed in flames, immediately nosed down—the U.S. Navy's first aerial victory in what would prove to be a long, vicious and costly Guadalcanal campaign.

The effort cost Southerland a bullet-cracked windshield and a fuselage smoldering with incendiary rounds. He ignored the acrid smoke to line up a deflection shot on a second Betty, this time a trailer on the far right. What Southerland suspected to be his last rounds got the bomber smoking, but he knew it was time to fold his cards.

———

As Zero escorts raced into hammer Wildcats, the bombers toggled their bombs. Saburo Sakai, then flying above the port quarter of the bomber formation, watched as the explosives tumbled and splashed far off target. The Mitsubishis then banked left, picking up speed to return to Rabaul from what had been a fruitless mission.

After escorting the bomber formation as far as the Russells, the Tainan Group Zero-sens swept back over Lunga looking for combat. When a group of Wildcats attacked from out of the sun, Sakai hauled his fighter into a steep evasive climb. Having lost track of his wingmen in the process, he saw what appeared to a lone Grumman mixing it up with three Zero-sens. Two looked to be his wingmen, so Sakai dived towards the pack.

———

Intent on escape, Pug Southerland had been flying near Savo at 11,500 feet when a Zero jumped him from behind. Hunkering low in his seat so his cockpit armor could shield him, Southerland also recharged his guns in hopes that he might yet trigger a few rounds.

When the enemy fighter moved to his starboard quarter, Southerland sensed an opening. Lowering his nose as if to dive away, Southerland immediately pulled out, cracked flaps and chopped throttle, causing the Zeke to overrun him. The Japanese pilot tried to recover with a climbing turn to the left, but Southerland easily turned inside him. Lining up for a close range shot, Southerland squeezed his trigger.

Nothing happened.

Left now with just the Wildcat's maneuverability and his own savvy, Southerland found himself beset by two more assailants, each taking turns on his flanks. Southerland's only option was to guess which Zero pilot would next attack and then turn towards him to disrupt his aim.

It was Southerland's desperate maneuvering that led Saburo Sakai to think the Grumman was attacking three Zeros.

As he descended, Sakai triggered a distant burst whose tracers prompted Southerland to snap roll right and climb. Sakai had never seen an opponent do anything like it. It was a tactic he'd so often pulled: reversing the advantage and firing up into an enemy's belly. Only now the tables were turned. Sakai was the predator turned prey.

Sakai countered with his own snap-roll but it failed to shake Southerland. Only by cutting throttle was Sakai able to throw off the American's timing. As Southerland's Wildcat pulled back in an awkward turn, Sakai added throttle. Then, just to be sure he'd shaken Southerland, Sakai rolled three more times, dropped into a spin and came out in a left vertical spiral.

The Wildcat was still there.

The American had matched Sakai maneuver for maneuver—almost as if they were an acrobatic team. Their left wings now both pointed to the water, their right wings to the sky as they extended to spiral. *G*-forces built until a grey film clouded Sakai's eyes. But he held on: if the American could take the punishment, so could he.

Only on the fifth spiral did the Wildcat at last seem to skid. Sakai thought he had him at last, but then Southerland deftly dropped his nose, regained speed and was back in control as the spirals continued. This was a terrific pilot.

In the long g-heavy dance of diving spirals with Saburo Sakai, Pug Southerland realized that he was fast running out of altitude. Sakai had not yet fired, but with each spiral he was getting ever closer on the Grumman's tail. Finally out of options, Southerland broke into level flight.

Sakai knew he had his man at last. He closed in on the Grumman's tail. Admiring the American plane's fit and finish, Sakai took time to snap a photograph with his handheld Leica. Finally, from little more than fifty meters distance, he loosed a long machine gun burst. The rounds stitched into the Grumman's distinctive fuselage and shredded its rudder until it looked like an old torn piece of rag.

Finally releasing the trigger, Sakai's was amazed to see the Grumman still flying along. It was punishment that no Zero-sen pilot could have hoped to withstand. Momentarily dumbstruck, Sakai unwittingly overran the slowing Grumman, leaving Southerland an opening for a shot. To Sakai's great relief, no bullets came.

Sakai dropped back wing-to-wing with the tenacious American and opened his cockpit to get a closer look. Southerland looked big and several years older than Sakai. His khaki flight suit was stained with blood and he appeared to be hunched over as if in prayer. Southerland even seemed to give Sakai a weak wave. Sakai at once felt empathy for the man but also excitement at the prospect of scoring his sixtieth aerial kill.

———

Southerland, it turned out, actually had no time for prayers. At that moment he was busy preparing to bail out: disconnecting his radio cord, undoing safety belts and securing the open canopy. He knew he was wounded but he had no sense of how badly and took no time to check.

The after part of the F4F's fuselage was holed like a sieve and the incendiary rounds inside were burning. There were gaping cannon-caliber holes in the wings; the instrument panel was shot up; the radio was out; the Plexiglas windshield, the rearview mirror, even his flight goggles were either bullet-riddled or shattered outright. Yet the Pratt and Whitney engine—in low blower, full throttle, low full pitch—was still performing strong.

Just then Sakai's Zeke made a firing run from the port quarter. Cannon fire into left wing root set off an explosion, most likely from fuel fumes. Southerland was ready. He climbed from the cockpit, stepped onto the starboard wing and dove over its trailing edge.

When Southerland's parachute eased down into the treetops along a jungle slope, Southerland loosed his straps and lowered himself to the ground. He started running and kept running until he found adequate cover. Only then did he stop to count wounds. There were eleven of them, the worst in his right foot, plus burns on both arms.

———

After finally dispatching Southerland's Wildcat, Saburo Sakai gathered his wingmen and cut across Sealark Channel to catch up with the bombers. As they climbed through cloud cover at seven thousand feet, a single bullet pierced Sakai's rear canopy glass, barely missing him. Angered at being caught unawares, Sakai quickly spotted the culprit, a lone SBD.

After first accelerating to open the range, the three Zero-sens swooped back to make a high-side run. A short burst from Sakai's guns caused the SBD (an aircraft from carrier *Wasp*'s VS-71) to stall and fall away.

Suddenly, Sakai saw what looked to be a tight formation of eight Grummans—a target begging for ambush. The three Zero-sens charged after them. Strangely, the Grumman pilots, instead of scattering, merely tightened their formation. Too late into a stern attack, Sakai realized he'd been fooled—and was about to pay for it. The "Grummans" were instead Dauntless bombers, each crewed by a rear gunner, and each rear gunner equipped with twin machine guns. The muzzles of the sixteen guns now swiveled and opened up on the Zero-sens.

One .30 caliber round shattered Sakai's windscreen, tore into his skull, and blinded him. His wingmen at once broke off the attack as the Dauntlesses edged into the clouds. The Tainan pilots were convinced Sakai was mortally wounded.

———

Despite blindness and excruciating pain, Sakai managed to grab his control stick, recover and pull out just above the water. He then tried to advance his throttle to gain more power, but his left hand wouldn't move. When only his right foot could reach the rudder pedal, Sakai realized his left side was paralyzed. As tears flowed from Sakai's eyes, some blood was washed away, at least enabling him to see—though only through the left eye.

Sakai struggled to stay conscious. His thoughts came and went, but he knew that as long as he could control the plane with his good hand and foot he would try to reach Rabaul. The Zero's engine was a steady drone. Thankfully, there was no smell of gasoline—no damage to the engine or fuel tanks.

As he flew on, Sakai tried to assess his wounds. Shaking off his flight glove, he moved the fingers of his right hand over his helmet. It was sticky with blood and there was a deep fissure at the top of his skull. He probed his face: his cheeks felt puffy and the flesh was ripped. Once the force of the wind dried the blood on his face, the bleeding there stopped. But the top of his skull still felt wet, greasy; he worried about bleeding to death. Thrusting his control stick into the crook of his right leg while lowering his head, Sakai used his right hand to squeeze his flight scarf between his helmet and his bleeding skull. That seemed to control the bleeding, though his head throbbed without mercy.

Again and again, Sakai found himself drifting away and losing control of the aircraft. Sometimes he would find his plane inverted or diving close to the water. Sakai took to slapping his face hard whenever he sensed he might succumb to sleep. Eventually, though, even his brutalized face lost sensation. All he could do to keep awake was to scream and curse into the pounding wind.

Several times, when despair overwhelmed him, Sakai turned the Zero towards Guadalcanal, hoping at least to be able to crash an American ship as he died. It was during the last of these detours that his head finally began to clear and the drowsiness subsided. He didn't need to crash. He could reach Buka, maybe even Rabaul.

When Sakai leaned close to his instrument panel to check his compass, he realized that all the turns and emergency recoveries had gotten him disoriented. Instead of heading toward Rabaul, he was pointing straight north into the Pacific. All Sakai could do was make a ninety degree turn and head west, hoping for the best.

Sakai's next crisis came when his main fuel tank emptied. He found that the automatic fuel transfer pump was not functioning. Only a savage working of the emergency pump got the auxiliary tank flowing. Fortunately, the exertion helped stimulate his senses. Using all he'd learned about optimizing fuel consumption, Sakai adjusted his propeller pitch and his fuel-air mixture. Still, he figured it gave him less than two more hours of flying time.

An hour later, Sakai spotted something on the water. An apparition? No, it was an atoll. He checked his map. It was Green Island—meaning he was only sixty miles from Rabaul. New Ireland's steep hills appeared next, but with clouds and squalls threatening, Sakai was forced to detour south of them, chewing up precious flight time. Soon he saw two ships— two Japanese cruisers apparently headed for Guadalcanal. He thought briefly about making a water landing, but decided to keep going.

Finally he spotted the familiar volcano that marked Rabaul. He had made it!

He had only to land.

Sakai considered ditching just off the beach rather than trying for the base runway, but quickly discarded the idea. The water landing might kill him.

As Sakai got nearer to base, the coconut trees edging its landing field loomed before him. Once he'd cleared their tops Sakai could see the runway ahead. He lowered wheels and flaps, switched off the plane's ignition and, as the Zero's wheels hit and bounced along the ground, pulled the control stick all the way back.

Sakai's Zero-sen finally rolled to a halt near the Command Post. He tried to grin at the pilots rushing towards his plane, but a wave of blackness swept over him.

14

IT ISN'T GOOD

EARLY IN THE MORNING OF AUGUST 12, 1942, ERNEST KING'S DUTY OFFICER George Russell entered the admiral's sleeping cabin on USS *Dauntless* (PG-61), the converted luxury yacht that served as both King's flagship and (aside from Sunday visits with his family at his official residence[1]) his home. King rarely was disturbed after he turned in, for the simple reason that there was little he could do in the middle of the night that would impact events thousands of miles away. Bad news usually waited until he awoke—but not this time.

"Admiral, you've got to see this," Russell said, after waking King and turning on the light. "It isn't good."

For days, reports from the South Pacific were incomplete and confusing, owing to what Nimitz had described as "extreme communication difficulties." Now King held in his hands a communiqué directly from invasion force commander Richmond Kelly Turner. The gist: In a night action near Savo Island, the Japanese had sunk or damaged five cruisers and four destroyers. There were heavy Allied casualties. Meanwhile, all Japanese ships had apparently escaped without damage. Because of "impending heavy attacks," transports supporting the Marines ashore were retiring from Guadalcanal.

In those first groggy moments King was in denial, going so far as to insist the message must be in error and demanding that it be decoded again. When the news finally sank in, however, he realized that at one stroke the whole future of the Pacific War had turned unpredictable. The understrength, inexperienced forces being employed in the Solomons might suffer defeat—and with that defeat the Allies might once more surrender the initiative against the Japanese.

---

1. The Naval Observatory

During the next hours, as fuller details of the debacle came through, King made two decisions. One was to dispatch a team of investigators to the South Pacific. The other was to suppress news of the disaster. It was well into August before King supplied full details even to Roosevelt, Knox and Marshall. For the most part, war correspondents returning from the Pacific knew more about what had actually happened than did senior military and political leaders.

With a struggle that was, at best, just beginning, King understood that his policy of constant attack had suffered a terrible setback. He wasn't at all sure whether there were enough resources in ships, aircraft and men to prevail in an extended struggle.

———

Two days of aerial combat had exacted their toll on the *Saratoga*, *Enterprise* and *Wasp* squadrons —and especially the fighters. Plagued by poor positioning and failure to achieve tactical concentration, small and isolated F4F divisions and sections had been mauled by more maneuverable Zeros flown by arguably the best fighter pilots in the world. By day's end on August 8, VFs 5, 6 and 71 counted losses of fifteen aircraft—nine of them, along with six of their pilots, to aerial combat. It was these casualties that weighed on Frank Jack Fletcher's mind when, at about 5:00 a.m. on August 9—more than three hours after the fact—the first scraps of information about Savo Island reached TF 61.

In a message sent August 8, Fletcher had advised Turner and Ghormley that, with his fighter strength substantially reduced and his ships' fuel supplies critical, he planned to withdraw his carriers a day early. That prospect had angered Turner then—even though it was in line with Turner's original timetable. However, there were extenuating circumstances. The August 7 Japanese air attack had disrupted an off-loading process already well behind schedule. Turner needed air cover extended—not curtailed.

At 11:14 a.m., Fletcher finally received a message Turner had sent more than two hours before: "Unable to depart because insufficient supplies have been landed. Request cover for attack on enemy surface force this area."

Finally, Fletcher and his staff began to piece together the fragmentary news of the devastation that had been visited on Turner's screening ships. This latest setback, as awful as it would turn out to be in lost lives and sunken and damaged ships, altered neither TF 61's own losses nor its need to re-provision.

Fletcher gave some thought to turning back toward Guadalcanal to launch a retaliatory strike, but the Japanese ships were doubtless long gone. Pursuing them might invite a major air strike from Rabaul—or from the Japanese carriers that might already be stalking TF 61. Either possibility would require high speed operations using aircraft and fuel reserves that Fletcher's COs told him they didn't have. Hired to operate carrier task forces, Fletcher intended to preserve his decks and remaining aircraft until he could confront the Japanese flattops.

Finally, at 3:15 p.m., Fletcher radioed Ghormley, referencing Turner's appeals: "Movements require protection that I am unable to provide." Ghormley's response that evening was equivocal: Fletcher should provide Turner such air cover as he could without interrupting the refueling.

In the end, Fletcher held to his intention to withdraw his carriers southeast toward safer waters and a rendezvous with fleet oilers. For TF 61 pilots near exhaustion after three days of nonstop flight operations, it represented a chance to rest, have their aircraft repaired, and get their first full meal in days. For Fletcher, however, who was to be reviled by Richmond Kelly Turner, Marine Corps Major General Alexander Vandegrift and every grunt on Guadalcanal, it represented the single most controversial and second-guessed decision of a nearly forty-year naval career.

After the long back-and-forth struggle ended, some bitter 'Canal veterans devised a sardonic "campaign medal" depicting an arm bearing admiral's stripes dropping a hot potato into the hands of a kneeling Marine. The motto: "Faciat Georgius"—"let George do it." The message: the chickenshit Navy had bugged out on the troops ashore.

―――――

VF-5's Pug Southerland was spending the night in a small village near Guadalcanal's northwest coast when he and his native hosts heard the deep percussive rumbling of pre-dawn gunfire in the direction of Savo Island. When the sun rose on the 9th, it was clear that the American cruisers and destroyers had pulled out. After witnessing the savage tumult of the past two days, the natives were understandably edgy.

Southerland had first encountered his benefactors, two Guadalcanal natives named Jonas and Joseph, while scouting an abandoned coastal village on August 8. Parlaying with Southerland in Pidgin English, Jonas revealed that he was originally from Malaita and that he worked for an Australian coast watcher. The two men had offered Southerland the sanctuary of their village. Later, as he ate and rested, Southerland was scrutinized by a steady parade of wide-eyed villagers. They all were curious about him and most were friendly, although one elder made it clear that he was more accustomed to eating white men than sheltering them.

On the eve of the Savo battle, Jonas had assured Southerland he would take him next day by canoe to Kukum, a coastal village near Lunga Point. What he had since heard and seen, however, gave Jonas pause—and sufficient reason to delay. Finally, though, at dawn on August 10, Southerland, Jonas and two other natives set off in a large canoe, paddling east. After skirting a Japanese encampment near the mouth of the Mantanikau River, the party reached its intended destination. When they were approached by soldiers in green fatigues, Southerland at first feared he was being delivered to the Japanese. Instead, the soldiers were U.S. Marines of the 1st Division's 5th Regiment.

Two days later, after having his wounds treated, Pug Southerland climbed aboard a Navy PBY for evacuation to the New Hebrides. Of the six Navy pilots downed over the Solomons in the first two days of aerial combat, Southerland was one among a fortunate four who eventually emerged alive.

––––––

On August 12, when the Japanese Zero retrieved from Akutan Island in July finally reached San Diego, it was hauled to a remote and closely guarded hangar at NAS North Island. The restoration specialists assigned to inspect the long-awaited prize quickly found themselves in luck. Aside from a severed oil line, the Zero's engine was in pristine condition. The balance of the restoration work looked to be mostly cosmetic: patching bullet holes, removing dents and kinks from the aircraft's vertical stabilizer, rudder, wing tips, flaps and canopy; re-dressing its three-blade propeller; and reconstructing sheared-off landing struts. It would take about six weeks to do the work. Then, after replacing the red meatballs on its wings and fuselage with American insignia, the prize would be fit and ready to fly again.

On August 22, BuAer assigned the Zero project to Commander Frederick M. Trapnell, chief of the flight test section at NAS Anacostia. Trapnell's deputy, Lieutenant Commander Eddie R. Sanders—a veteran test pilot—was set to arrive at North Island in mid-September to conduct flight tests.

––––––

When wounded Tainan Wing fighter pilot Saburo Sakai returned to Japan in mid-August, he was stunned by the bright signs and lights and by the bustling crowds of people dressed in light and colorful summer clothing.

Radio newscasts trumpeted tremendous victories in sea battles against the Americans off the Solomons and periodically played a strident patriotic song called the "Warship March." The nation seemed drunk on false victories.

Sakai spent the night at his uncle's Tokyo home, then left by train for the Yokohama Navy Hospital. After checking in and having his deep skull wound cleaned and dressed, Sakai was examined by an eye surgeon. The surgeon, a civilian drafted into naval service, was frank in his prognosis. Sakai needed immediate treatment. Worse, the delicacy of the procedure the surgeon had in mind prohibited the use of anesthetics. Restoration of even some of the vision in Sakai's right eye hung in the balance.

That same day, strapped to a high bed, with his arms, legs and head pinioned by hospital orderlies, Sakai was instructed to keep his eyes open and fixed on a red light suspended from the ceiling. For the next thirty minutes, as the surgeon poked and probed with steel instruments, the pain was so excruciating that Sakai wished he'd taken his own life instead of persevering to reach Rabaul.

But even the surgery's raw pain scarcely compared with the lingering torture that followed. Sakai was told that although the vision in his left eye in time would fully return, the vision in his right would never be more than a blur. Realizing his fighter pilot career—his passion, the one thing he knew how to do—was at an end, gripped Sakai with bottomless despair.

———

Early in the afternoon of August 24th, twenty-three bomb-laden *Enterprise* TBFs and SBDs were launched to comb north of the Solomons for a Japanese carrier originally pinpointed that morning by PBY searches. Two of the aircraft, TBFs flown by VT-3 CO Charles Jett and his wingman, Ensign Robert J. Bye, were responsible for scouring a "pie slice" of ocean bearing 320–330 degrees, two hundred fifty miles out from *Enterprise*. At about 2:40 p.m., Jett spotted ships on the western horizon—what looked to be one carrier screened by three destroyers, with two more cruisers some distance off to starboard. After Jett's radioman-gunner Aviation Chief Radioman I.H. Olson broke radio silence to send in a contact report, Jett and Bye headed north and climbed, intent on getting into position for a hit-and-run bombing attack.

———

In the roughly two weeks since distancing themselves from Guadalcanal, the ships of TF 61 had hewed to a conservative routine that largely kept them out of striking range of Rabaul: covering the Espiritu Santo-Nouméa lines of communication; escorting Allied ships bound for the 'Canal; and supporting Tulagi and the 'Canal against daytime incursions by enemy ships. Whenever possible, Fletcher tried to keep a safe distance from the Solomons, moving north during the day but retiring south each night.

CinCPac intelligence, meanwhile, warned of a carrier striking force being assembled in Japan's home waters. The force—organized around fleet carriers *Shokaku* and *Zuikaku* and light carriers *Ryūjō* and *Hōshō*—was estimated to reach the Solomons via Truk by August 19. On August 17, anticipating that move (and straying somewhat from King's mandate that at least one CTF stay close to Hawaii), Nimitz sent TF 17 with *Hornet* (Rear Admiral George D. Murray—former *Enterprise* CO—in command) south as reinforcement. The same day and the next, TF 61 ships topped off their fuel tanks from oilers *Platte* (AO-24) and *Kaskaskia* (AO-27).

Intelligence on August 18 had it that two enemy convoys had departed Truk the previous day, one loaded with Japanese naval landing forces, the other with army "shock troops" originally ticketed for Midway, and both convoys had rendezvoused with a cruiser-destroyer flotilla. An attack, CinCPac advised, could come as early as August 20.

The 19th found Fletcher's task force meeting up with the small auxiliary carrier *Long Island* (ACV-1) about four hundred fifty miles southeast of Guadalcanal. *Long Island's* flight deck and hangar were packed with thirty-one Marine Corps F4Fs set to be flown ashore—the first sizeable contingent for the 'Canal's Advanced Base Air Force Cactus (Cactus was Guadalcanal's call sign and Cactus Air Force became the unit's familiar moniker). They would be flying out of what was now Henderson Field, named for the squadron CO who had died leading the Marine SBD strike from Midway.

The Marine aircraft launched at 1:30 p.m. on August 20—but not before the Americans were "snooped" by a Japanese Kawanishi. VF-71 F4Fs from *Wasp* gave chase, but the snooper fled north and out of reach.

The Americans had been spotted and were again on the 22nd—though that day's crew paid dearly for the intrusion. A VF-6 division led by twenty-eight-year-old Lieutenant Albert O. "Scoop" Vorse Jr. caught up with the four-engine Kawanishi. "Look at her burn," Vorse radioed the FDO after a single high-side firing pass.

Vorse's exuberant kill call was the first made in what had been (for the carrier pilots, anyway) two weeks of scarcely interrupted South Pacific boredom. CinCPac assured Ghormely and Fletcher that major Japanese action against Cactus was still pending, though now not likely before August 23 and maybe as late as August 26. Even when the offensive was unleashed, its air component might come from Rabaul, not Japanese carriers.

The August 24 search effort in which Jett and Bye took part was TF 16 Commander Thomas Kinkaid's idea. Kincaid had also urged a strike targeting the morning PBY sighting, but Fletcher was not so sure. Back in May, to his continuing regret, he had snapped at Japanese bait in the Coral Sea, shooting his bolt against small carrier *Shōhō* but failing to detect two Japanese fleet carriers poised to retaliate. Fletcher's impulsiveness at the time had contributed to the loss of carrier *Lexington*.

Actions taken on August 23 compounded Fletcher's wariness. First, he had dispatched thirty-seven SBDs and TBFs led by *Saratoga* CAG Commander Harry D. "Don" Felt after a formation of Japanese cruisers, destroyers and transports reportedly advancing on Guadalcanal. Their futile hunt (the Japanese had reversed course) had stretched beyond twilight, forcing the pilots to take refuge at Henderson Field. Then, to compound his vulnerability, Fletcher had released carrier *Wasp* and her consorts south for refueling.

In the end, however, Fletcher acquiesced to both the searches and the strike urged by Kincaid. Another Midway lesson (learned at the expense of the Japanese) was not to hold fueled and ordnance-laden strike aircraft on deck for too long. Accordingly, Don Felt's *Saratoga* strike was launched at 1:45 p.m.

At 2:55 p.m., as they circled out to the west to attack with the sun at their backs, VT-3's Jett and Bye were finally spotted by the Japanese ships. The destroyers and cruisers opened fire on the TBFs, while the Japanese carrier scrambled interceptors. Three minutes later, Jett and Bye each dropped two five hundred-pound bombs. The carrier simultaneously turned hard right and the bombs converged into one big splash about one hundred fifty yards astern.

Five minutes later, search TBFs piloted by Lieutenant John N. Myers and Naval Aviation Pilot Harry L. Corl (one of VT-3's three Midway survivors) spotted one of the Japanese cruisers sighted earlier by Jett. After beginning his bombing run, Myers noticed the carrier, now ten or so miles in the distance. Myers and Corl aborted their runs and broke for the bigger target, only to be cut off by two Zeros. After a head-to-head firing pass at Corl, the two Japanese concentrated on Myers, who managed to escape. The Zeros then returned to resume their attack on Corl, who dove for cover in the clouds. The overcast momentarily shielded the TBF, but when Corl let down to the water, both Zeros found him again and pounced. Only Corl's radioman-gunner Radioman Third Class Delmer D. Wiley survived the ordeal.

It was about thirty minutes after Myers's and Corl's engagement that Don Felt's *Saratoga* strike group sighted the carrier and its consorts. Felt had copied Jett's contact report putting the carrier farther north than expected. Felt turned north briefly, then swung west again. There were the Japanese: distant wakes attached to tiny ship specks.

Felt radioed his instructions: Nineteen SBDs and six TBFs were to take on the carrier, while the rest were to hit a big cruiser. Upon "Execute," the SBDs and TBFs climbed to the north, planning to approach out of the northeast. As Felt's aircraft got into position, the Japanese ships readied their defenses. The carrier swung into the wind to add CAP fighters to a quintet of Zeros already circling. The screens—the cruisers and destroyers—already widely spaced, opened intervals even more.

———

Fifteen or so minutes after Felt's strike group left *Saratoga* air space, Fletcher had reason to second-guess his decision to send them. He had a new PBY sighting—only the second of the day to pinpoint a carrier. This carrier might well be the same as reported earlier, but it concerned Fletcher that it was positioned sixty miles northeast. It might be a different carrier.

If Jett's sighting (received at 3:00 p.m.) quieted this concern, what came next deepened it. Though the reception had been extremely poor, both *Saratoga* and *Enterprise* copied portions of a transmission from one of the *Enterprise* scouts. The vitals of position, bearing and course did not come through, but one thing did: the presence of two Japanese carriers somewhere to the north.

———

The first of Felt's dive-bombers pushed over on the Japanese carrier at 3:50 p.m. No Zekes intervened at higher altitude, but the carrier's maneuvering was effective. From his vantage above the action, Don Felt saw at least ten bombs fall wide of the mark. After ordering his remaining aircraft to divert to the carrier, Felt himself pushed over. His run produced a near miss, but the SBDs that rallied behind him scored three hits, all on the carrier's starboard side.

Even as Felt's SBDs dropped the last of their bombs, five TBFs staged an anvil attack on the smoke-shrouded carrier. Two torpedoes aimed at the port side missed, but one of three aimed to starboard slammed home. Its explosion breached the hull aft, knocking out starboard fire and engine rooms and crippling steering control.

After sending the balance of his strike planes home to *Saratoga*, Felt lingered in the vicinity to witness the outcome. As the other Japanese ships turned north, the stricken carrier continued circling to starboard before finally coasting to a stop with a heavy starboard list. The smoke billowing from her decks subsided, only to belch forth again. She seemed finished.

———

As *Saratoga's* Don Felt watched the death throes of what proved to be light carrier *Ryūjō*, his own carrier's radar was picking up a distant contact bearing 320 degrees. *Enterprise* spotted it as well, and though it soon faded from both ships' screens, it looked to be the real thing. Ten VF-5 fighters were dispatched for the distant intercept. At 4:10 p.m., Fletcher ordered Kincaid, whose TF 16 was then ten miles northwest, to launch the *Enterprise* strike aircraft, vector them to the Jett sighting and then close with *Saratoga*.

At 4:18 p.m. the bogey reappeared on *Enterprise's* radar, still bearing 320 degrees but much closer. "Many bogeys ahead," Lieutenant Henry A. "Ham" Rowe, Big E's FDO, radioed a VF-6 CAP section lead by thirty-seven-year-old Lieutenant (junior grade) Harold E. Rutherford. "Get up high."

Even as Rutherford (a Fighting Chiefs' veteran) and his wingman took the vector, Rowe was busy committing other resources. As finally deployed, the fighter shield would comprise an outer shell of twenty-seven F4Fs forty or so miles off to the north, plus an interior reserve of twenty-six more. This made fifty-three fighters in all—enough for the job if they could just head off the Japanese.

———

"Tally ho! There are about . . . 9 bogeys unidentified about 12,000 feet, 300 [degrees]. . . . Many ahead of those. . . . They're dive-bombers."

The first sighting report, from twenty-nine-year-old Naval Aviation Pilot Charles E. Brewer, a VF-6 second section leader, came at about 4:30 p.m. The Vals were in a shallow dive but still higher than the *Saratoga* F4Fs and about to get between them and home base.

"Don't let them get away!" Rowe exhorted.

Brewer's division was led by thirty-year-old Ensign Doyle C. "Ted" Barnes. He, Brewer and their section wingmen—Ram Dibb (first section) and twenty-two-year-old Lieutenant (junior grade) Douglas M. Johnson (second section)—reversed course and pushed throttles in a valiant effort to catch up with the Vals.

———

"Zero right above us, Scoop." The warning came at 4:33 p.m. from thirty-year-old Naval Aviation Pilot Howell M. "Muscles" Sumrall to his VF-6 division leader Vorse. Sumrall saw the Zeke—the trailer in a quartet of bandits, its pilot apparently itching for a kill—roll over on his back several times to keep the F4Fs in view.

Vorse's division, like Barnes', was climbing in pursuit of the Vals. The Zekes were undoubtedly meant to run interference for the dive-bombers, but this ass-end-Charlie was clearly looking for a straggler—so Sumrall obliged.

As Vorse's division climbed past ten thousand feet, the hungry Zeke pilot waggled his wings and rolled into a steep dive for Sumrall. To counter, Sumrall dipped his right wing and kicked full left rudder. It ruined the Japanese pilot's shot; as the Zeke zoomed past him, Sumrall reversed his turn and got off a snap burst. The Zeke dived to escape, but Sumrall kept track of him. When the Japanese pilot recovered and pulled into a climb, Sumrall was prepared. He nosed over and fired into his opponent's fuselage and wing root. The Zeke still carried its auxiliary belly tank; Sumrall's incendiaries torched it.

As Sumrall's victim dropped like a comet, Sumrall's wingman, twenty-four-year-old Lieutenant (junior grade) Francis R. "Cash" Register, got it in his mind to chase the doomed aircraft. An angry Sumrall ordered him to rejoin so they both could catch up with Vorse's section, now chasing the bombers.

Meanwhile, the sight of Sumrall's lone Wildcat soon proved too inviting for another of the Zekes, who came in for a high-side run. Sumrall, still decoying, was tracking this Zeke when another Wildcat—it turned out to be Vorse's—snuck behind the bandit for a flat-side pass. Caught by surprise, the Zeke tried a steep climb, but Vorse had the speed to stick with him.

Nearing a stall, the Zeke spun out and dropped into a whirling, dead-man's spin—what proved to be a showy performance rivaling Sumrall's. The Japanese recovered at three thousand feet. Above, Vorse and Sumrall were left with neither a kill nor a ghost of a chance of overtaking the Val bombers before they reached *Enterprise*.

———

It was now 4:38 p.m. and TF 16, the task force closest to the impending action, was bracing for attack. Its ships circled wagons into what was called a 1-Victor formation: *Enterprise* at the center, a cruiser on either bow, battleship *North Carolina* (BB-55) directly astern and the six destroyers posted to an evenly spaced outer ring.

The Japanese had sent twenty-seven dive-bombers to take out the American carriers. Even as a third of these Vals broke to the east, bound for *Saratoga* skies, *Enterprise's* would-be assailants veered due south. The eighteen Vals lowered gradually towards pushover altitude, re-aligning themselves as they advanced: The vee-of vees first lengthened into a column of vees—a sort of moving arrow. Then this column narrowed into a lengthy single-file queue—with individual Vals spaced tail-to-nose at roughly one hundred-yard intervals.

As *Enterprise* CO Davis curled his ship to starboard, ordered up speed and fled, the Vals were set to come down on the carrier's port quarter. Sun at his back, each Val pilot jockeyed to keep his place in the queue, waiting for the bomber ahead to push over.

Below, in *Enterprise's* Air Plot, frustration and exasperation held sway. FDO "Ham" Dow was doing his best to orchestrate his suddenly overmatched fighter assets using a single undisciplined radio frequency. Pilots crowded the circuit with transmissions inspired by adrenaline, exuberance and terror. Dow ("sweating like a Turk" in the estimation of one of his assistant FDOs) tried desperately to break in with updates and instructions.

Topside, TF 16 lookouts and gunners squinted into the afternoon sun, eager to pick out targets. With their ship's fire control radar system on the blink, *Enterprise* five-inch gunners were at a crucial disadvantage. But at 4:40 p.m., at least one portside gallery 20-millimeter battery commander—a sergeant in the ship's Marine detachment—glimpsed a dive-bomber and ordered his guns to fire. Thin tracer streams reached up like sparks on kindling. Within the minute, most of the formation's 1.1-inch, 20-millimeter and five-inch batteries had joined in.

———

Despite the uncommon ease with which the Japanese dive-bombers had skirted the outer fighter screen, the target path to *Enterprise* was by no means clear. The two dozen Wildcats left behind in the race were quickly catching up and the two dozen inner screen Wildcats barred the way. Wildcards for Big E's defense (they had the potential either to help or complicate) were two flights of SBDs and TBFs—one inbound (the search group launched earlier and now returning), one out (the just-launched strike group).

From his position about five miles astern of *Enterprise* and flying northwest, Lieutenant Richard E. "Chick" Harmer spotted the Vals dropping into their dives. Harmer, VF-5's thirty-year-old XO, led a Wildcat division that had been aloft for three hours and was now, to a man, short of juice. Nonetheless, Harmer's pilots poured on such fuel as they had into a parabolic, five thousand foot climb designed to put them on the Val's tails.

Harmer's wingman, twenty-four-year-old Lieutenant (junior grade) John B. "Jughead" McDonald Jr. was the first into the fray, jumping line to take after the formation lead. His wing guns blazing, McDonald followed the Val into the heart of the antiaircraft fire. The Val pilot toggled a bomb that splashed well wide of *Enterprise* before dodging his plane low off the water through the cruiser-destroyer gauntlet.

Harmer took on the second plane and, like McDonald, dove into the antiaircraft vortex, all the while trading bursts with the Val's rear gunner. This plane escaped, too, but not before dropping another errant bomb.

The third intercept—by Harmer's second section leader, twenty-eight-year-old Lieutenant Howard W. Crews came out better all around. Crews's first bullets tore into the Val's wings and fuselage; a second and longer burst got its cowling and engine. As Crews finally pulled out at three thousand feet to avoid friendly fire, the Val hurtled down. In a premature release, its bomb dropped to a towering but ineffectual splash two hundred yards wide of *Enterprise*'s port quarter. The flaming Japanese dive-bomber, meanwhile, crashed in water six hundred yards off her port beam.

―――――

"OK," Ted Barnes radioed his VF-6 division pilots. "Let's go give them hell."

It had taken Barnes's four Wildcats all this time to catch up with the Japanese dive-bombers. They arrived overhead while Chick Harmer's division was battling the head of the Val queue. Barnes and wingman Ram Dibb came in astern of the rear-most Vals. Second section wingman Douglas Johnson did the same, but his lead Chuck Brewer charged after two Vals already into their dives.

In the skies above Brewer, Ram Dibb smoked one of the lined-up Vals, only to watch in horror as Barnes's F4F was hit and blown apart by a five-inch round from below. Meanwhile, even as his tracers ignited one Val, Brewer was busy catching up with the second. Its pilot jockeyed to give the rear gunner a better shot at the Wildcat, but Brewer riddled this dive-bomber, too, pulling off only when the antiaircraft fire became too dense. As Brewer retreated, his second victim staggered aflame into the ships' crossfire. The Val's bomb tumbled and splashed just clear of Big E's starboard quarter. The pilot, meanwhile made a desperate suicidal lunge for Big E's flight deck, only to overshoot and douse his plane off the port side.

If VF-6 and VF-5 pilots seemed to be feasting on the *Enterprise*-bound Vals, those defending (knowingly or unknowingly) *Saratoga* were having even more success. Indeed, their meal was almost complete.

The reasons were simple enough. Only a third of the Vals were after *Saratoga*—nearer now to *Enterprise* than before, but still ten or so miles southeast. Of more consequence, what was the inner circle of *Enterprise's* defense was essentially the outer circle of *Saratoga's*. The skies there were filled with Wildcat soloists, sections and divisions converging on the Japanese from the north and east. Of most consequence to the *Saratoga*-bound Vals, their escorts had joined the hives in collision over Big E.

These eastbound Vals were thus few, isolated and undefended: cold meat for VF-5 Wildcats piloted by thirty-one year-old Lieutenant Hayden M. Jensen, twenty-seven-year-old Ensign Carlton B. Starkes and twenty-two-year-old Ensign John M. Kleinman.

Jensen led his two wingmen in for a high-side run on a formation already strung out in single file. After dropping the line's center plane with an opening high-side deflection burst, Jensen used the "lazy side" of his swooping pass to blast the line's trailer.

Just as Jensen flamed this ass-end-Charlie and zoomed into a recovering climb, Carlton Starkes passed overhead, working his way one by one up the line of Vals, sending two down in flames. Kleinman, flying just astern of Starkes, did the same to two more Vals while Jensen bagged his third (the trio's seventh kill overall) in a second pass.

Not surprisingly, the surviving Japanese abandoned any thought of reaching *Saratoga* and turned instead to the bigger, more profitable fight above *Enterprise*.

As it had been before for the fighter interceptors and the ships' gunners in these carrier-to-carrier battles, the tenacity of the close-in defense was impressive, even majestic—but not nearly good enough.

Upwards of seven Japanese dive-bombers had fallen. Most had toggled bombs only to have them fall wide. But, at 4:44 p.m., the first of three connected, striking a corner of *Enterprise's* number three elevator and slicing its way down to chief petty officers' quarters on the third level. The explosion spread a welter of damage and death.

A second bomb, impacting less than thirty seconds later, also aft but closer to the starboard deck edge, did its worst topside, especially to the starboard gun gallery. The bomb's explosion, coupled with flames and secondary explosions from ready ammunition caches, killed more than three dozen sailors and Marines manning gallery antiaircraft batteries.

A close miss—amidships, just off to starboard and drenching *Enterprise's* island—was followed, at 4:46 pm, by the finale: a contact explosion that opened a ten-foot crater in the flight deck just aft of the center elevator.

————

As *Enterprise's* sailors tended to her agonies, the Japanese pilots who had inflicted the wounds and were still alive to tell about it were trying to flee north with vengeful F4F pilots in pursuit.

"All planes get over the ship," Ham Dow implored at 4:53 p.m. "Don't bother those getting away."

Dow had legitimate concerns—no Japanese torpedo planes had yet been spotted, but surely they were somewhere about. But for the moment it was like trying to call off stalking cats that not only had the prey's scent, but also some of its blood and feathers in their teeth.

Two of them, VF-5's Chick Harmer and wingman Jughead McDonald, tangled with three Vals low on the water. McDonald flamed one with a full-deflection shot and Harmer staggered another. But the third got on Harmer's six-o'clock, peppering Harmer's cockpit, and wounding him in both thighs and one ankle.

Another, VF-6's Charles Brewer, was lining up for a head-on pass against a Val when a Zeke jumped his tail. Brewer coolly hammered the Val, then chopped throttle, pulled up and swung around towards the Zeke. After flashing overhead, Brewer reversed course to take down the Zeke with a full deflection shot.

As Brewer claimed this Zeke, another was lining up above and astern

VF-6's Cash Register. Register shook this assailant loose with a tight wingover. After hurtling past, the Japanese pilot made a clumsy roll out to the left that only caught him in the cross-hairs of three other Wildcats. He promptly panicked into a climbing turn that returned him to Register's sight line. After one last cartwheeling reverse, the Zeke stalled, smoked and plummeted—a goner.

"All planes, please keep quiet." Ham Dow's sharp edgewise plea broke through the celebratory circuit chatter. He spoke now for a ship and crew locked in a struggle for survival—a struggle far from complete. "There may be more bogeys and we have to give orders, so keep quiet."

———

At about this time, VT-3 TBF pilots Weasel Weissenborn and Fred Mears approached *Enterprise's* landing circle. Weissenborn and Mears were returning from the afternoon search mission which, for them at least, had been uneventful.

In fact, the first indication to Mears that something was amiss was the sight of cruiser *Atlanta* (CL-51) immersed in smoke. At first Mears wondered if the cruiser had sustained damage, but quickly realized it was firing its antiaircraft batteries. Then he saw the other ships were firing as well—black and white puffs of smoke that dotted the afternoon sky. Astern of *Enterprise*, *North Carolina's* barrages lit up the battlewagon like a Christmas tree.

Just then Mears heard on the circuit: "All friendly planes keep clear during the attack."

For the moment Weissenborn and Mears retreated to the formation's far side. Mears became so wrapped up in the action he almost forgot to keep flying.

"SBDs attack the torpedo planes." The message ended Mears' reverie. That's our meat too, Mears thought as he pulled away from Weissenborn to head for *Enterprise.*

Within moments, however, Mears found himself under the guns of two aggressive Val pilots. It was as close as he'd ever been to an enemy aircraft and soon Mears was retreating towards Weissenborn, who by then had joined VT-3 CO Charles Jett's TBF. Weighing these odds, one Val pilot disengaged, but the other seemed determined to take them on.

Mears watched in fascination as the Val went into its first run. Its mottled camouflage—brown mixed with white, emblazoned with the red meatballs on wings and fuselage—looked like a bad paint job. When the

Val opened fire, two long yellowish streamers of smoke came out of its cowling. "Jesus," Mears thought, "I don't want him to shoot me." Then, as the Val zipped overhead, Mears raised his nose and fired his .30 caliber. Nothing happened—nor did anything happen during the Val's six remaining passes. On each run, the Val fired and the three TBF tail gunners opened up in return. (It was somehow ridiculous, Mears thought later: everyone fired like mad but nobody got hurt.)

When the attacks finally ended, Jett, Bye, Weissenborn and Mears circled the carrier. Soon they were joined by Myers, whose TBF had lost nearly half its tail section. Myers grinned at Mears and put his fingers to the corner of his eyes—the Japanese were responsible.

When the circling bombers got word to drop remaining ordnance, Mears left the formation, flew out about five miles and dropped his two five hundred-pounders. He felt the whoof of their explosions beneath his plane as he returned to land.

Mears intended to get aboard *Saratoga*, but when he noticed that *Enterprise* had reopened for business, he headed there instead. It was almost dark when Mears caught a wire. A bandage swathed the head of the plane handler who taxied him up.

————

The next morning, Mears and another pilot went up on *Enterprise's* flight deck to view the damage first hand. Near the after elevator, where two big bombs had hit, there was a small hole where one of the projectiles had penetrated. Looking through the hole, however, Mears could see men working knee-deep in water and debris.

There were still sailors' bodies in the chaos of the starboard gun gallery. Most of the men had died from concussions but then been roasted. Many were in one piece, blackened but not burned or withered. They looked like iron statues: smooth limbs and rounded heads without hair.

Their postures were either normal or grotesque. One gun pointer was still in his seat, his arm leaning on his sight. Other men lay outstretched, face up or down. Several seemed to be shielding themselves, arms bent at the elbows and hands to their faces.

During the funeral service on August 26, one of the hundred or so ship's fatalities was committed to the sea near the second elevator on the hangar deck. The symbolic body was "properly enshrouded" in a canvas sack atop a pantry board. At the end of the brief ceremony, four sailors upended the board and the shrouded body slid from under the American flag and into the ocean to the sound of taps. The other bodies, however, were thrown over the fantail.

————

The next morning, the VT-3 pilots who had made it back to *Enterprise* settled into their cockpits and readied to launch. While the carrier would be going in for repairs, the aircraft would be flying to a field in the New Hebrides to await assignments.

As the morning breeze blew in the pilots' faces and they felt the sea moving beneath them, it had the aspect of a final farewell.

"This is the air officer speaking," the deck amplifier squawked. "Give 'em hell."

Then: "This is the assistant air officer. Stand by to start engines."

No sentiment from him, Mears thought to himself, and laughed.

Mears was the first to leave. When the fly one officer gave him the thumbs-up signal, smiled and waved him off, Mears made a straight run at full throttle down the deck.

15

THESE HAVE GOT US

ON SEPTEMBER 3, 1942, FRED MEARS AND TWO OTHER VT-3 PILOTS FLEW NORTH to Espiritu Santo to join up with VT-8, Mears's former squadron. Their first stop in the New Hebrides had been little more than a narrow dirt strip surrounded by jungle. The Espiritu Santo facility was not much better, but at least there were friends waiting to greet them—including Bert Earnest and Andy Divine. VT-8's pilots and crews had taken refuge in the New Hebrides for the same reason VT-3 had: their carrier, the no-luck *Saratoga*, was again out of action after a submarine torpedo hit three days before.

Bert Earnest had been sleeping soundly when the early morning explosion awoke him. "Oh shit," was his first thought and sure enough, about five minutes after the blast, *Saratoga* slowed to a stop with its engines shut down. The carrier wallowed in the ocean swells for about forty minutes—the time it took for her engineers to finally get up steam. Three hours later Sara was barely making six knots and beginning to list when she broke down again.

It was enough to convince Frank Jack Fletcher to send at least some aircraft ashore. Earnest, Divine and the other pilots chosen were instructed to pack their TBFs with personal gear, supplies and ammunition.

Shortly after 1:00 p.m., *Saratoga* was taken in tow by cruiser *Minneapolis* (CA-36). Using the combined speed from her restarted engines and the *Minneapolis* tow, *Saratoga* finally worked up enough headway for launch. Even so, the planes that took off were so heavily loaded that most were lucky just to clear the deck and stay airborne. One TBF pilot took off unaware that there was a still a torpedo in his bomb bay. Carrying this extra two thousand pounds, the TBF flew all the way to Espiritu Santo scarcely thirty feet above the water.

After the planes departed, a contingent of VT-8 mechanics and administrative personnel was high-lined to destroyer *Grayson* (DD-435) for transport to Espiritu Santo. *Saratoga*, meanwhile, was bound north for dry dock in Pearl Harbor. Vice Admiral Fletcher, who had sustained a head gash when the torpedo exploded, went with her. It marked the black shoe admiral's retirement from his short but eventful career as a carrier task force commander.

Now only two carriers, *Wasp* and *Hornet*, remained in the South Pacific.

————

On the day of Mears' arrival, VT-8 personnel were still busy setting up camp on a hill behind the Espiritu Santo airstrip, clearing and burning brush, pitching tents and setting up cots with mosquito nets. In the weeks ahead, as they waited for what they hoped would be a return to a carrier, Mears and a handful of others put their energies into camp improvements, including a shower fabricated from two water-filled oil drums perched atop a log stand.

Whenever a pilot flew in from the 'Canal, the camp inhabitants pressed him for news. One dive-bomber pilot revealed a lot just from his appearance. Aboard *Enterprise*, Mears recalled, the pilot was a walking recruitment poster, but now he looked awful: exhausted, disheveled, unshaven and malnourished.

The word from these Guadalcanal emissaries was pretty much the same: American Marine, Navy and Army pilots ruled the Solomons by day. Thanks to timely warnings from coast watchers installed on islands in the northern and central Solomons (supplemented in early September by the installation of a big air search radar system on the main field), they usually had time to gain altitude and be ready to bushwhack incoming Japanese bombers and Zeros. At night, however, when no one dared light up Henderson Field, Japanese cruisers and destroyers routinely bombarded the American positions—the targets lit up by flares dropped from Japanese aerial snoopers.

Meanwhile, the Cactus pilots lived miserable existences. They routinely flew six to eight hours a day and were on standby even when not flying. Living quarters were tents and the diet was meager—gruel or hard biscuits during the day, at night a meatless stew or rice and fish captured from the Japanese. If the pilots were there for extended stays, most eventually succumbed to dysentery and sometimes malaria. Between the nighttime shelling and nuisance bomb runs by other Japanese planes (the residents gave them names like "Washing Machine Charlie"), nobody on the island got much sleep.

————

Mears' first up-close look at Guadalcanal came during an in-and-out torpedo delivery trip with five other VT-8 pilots. Their TBFs arrived about two hours before sunset. To their relief, nobody took potshots at them as they made their approaches and landings.

Henderson Field was larger and more fully developed than Mears had anticipated. The main airstrip—captured from the Japanese on August 7—was about four thousand feet long, with dispersal and taxi ways along its northern edge. Marston matting (perforated steel planks) was laid down on some trouble spots at the center of the field, but otherwise Henderson's main runway remained a dirt strip atop a gravel base. Navy Construction Battalions (Seabees) were busy cutting palms and blasting stumps to create additional space for the main field and a separate strip for fighter aircraft. Dominating a hill about two hundred yards north of the runway was a wooden building of vaguely Oriental design constructed by prior tenants. Everyone called it the Pagoda.

It was impossible not to notice the Cactus Air Force's losses. There were shallow bomb craters everywhere and close to some rickety wooden hangars on the south edge of the runway was a "boneyard" dotted with airplane carcasses. Other than the TBFs the VT-8 pilots had just flown in, there were no flyable aircraft in sight. Instead, they were dispersed and hidden in jungle revetments.

During this short visit (aside from the airfield damage) it was difficult for Mears to associate the island with war. Several Cactus pilots showed the visitors the beach, where they could look out across a beautiful stretch of water to see small islands fringed by the distant outline of Malaita, another of the Solomons' principal islands. At sunset, visitors and hosts stood at the edge of what, before the war, was the Lever Brothers Coconut Grove. From that vantage they watched the setting sun light up the clouds above mountains off to the west.

Harry Ferrier had accompanied Mears on the flight and during their stay both men chatted with Bert Earnest, already assigned to the 'Canal. Earnest and Ferrier, of course, had in common their shared ordeal at Midway. They trusted each other and had good reason to. Earnest asked Mears if he might get Ferrier back—he needed a good man in the turret now that he was back in combat. Mears was glad to oblige and let Ferrier stay behind.

"These have got us," blurted a young ensign standing right next to Rear Admiral Leigh Noyes on carrier *Wasp*'s Flag Bridge. Both Noyes and the ensign had just heard a lookout yell, "Torpedo wake!" Now they saw three wakes off to starboard, barely a hundred yards away. All Noyes could do was brace for the detonations.

Early that September 15 afternoon, the *Wasp* and *Hornet* task forces had been steaming about 250 miles southeast of Henderson Field, positioned to shield Rear Admiral Turner's TF 65, a formation of transports and escorts en route to deliver 7th Marine reinforcements to Guadalcanal.

It was breathtakingly clear day, but a twenty-knot trade wind blowing up from the southeast was whipping the sea into white caps—perfect conditions for the concealment of submarine periscopes.

At 1:42 p.m., after completing recovery of morning CAP and search aircraft, *Wasp* CO Captain Forrest Sherman had turned his ship to starboard to resume a westerly base course. Three minutes later, with *Wasp* still turning, lookouts had spotted the torpedo wakes. With the rudder already at right standard, Sherman's only option was to order right full rudder.

The first submarine torpedo exploded against *Wasp*'s starboard bow, rupturing aviation fuel storage tanks and flooding a five-inch gun handling room and powder magazine. Seconds later, the second fish erupted just forward of the island structure, tearing open more aviation fuel tanks and flooding bomb magazines. A third explosion triggered twenty seconds later by fuel vapors propelled itself up through the bomb elevator and onto the flight deck.

The three explosions rocked *Wasp*. Flight deck aircraft, many armed and fueled, were tossed into the air only to drop onto collapsed landing gear. Leaking fuel ignited planes forward of the number two elevator. Volatile paint that should have been scraped from ship' bulkheads—but wasn't—accelerated small fires into infernos. Smoke flooded the hangar deck, where several planes lashed to the overhead had tumbled atop other planes below. All lighting was lost in the forward half of the ship and damaged fire mains there lacked water pressure.

Fires forward were soon out of control, setting off explosions of ready ammunition, fuel and bombs. Flames billowed from both sides below the flight deck, sprouting out black streamers of smoke and scattering little fires on the surrounding water. Sprays of red, yellow and green from exploding signal flares shot out like Roman candles.

Wasp was not the attack's only victim. The wakes of torpedoes that had missed the carrier and the rest of TF 18 skimmed northeast in the direction of TF 17. One hit destroyer *O'Brien* (DD-415) at 1:51 p.m., another battleship *North Carolina* (BB-55) a minute later. Neither ship was in imminent danger[1], but TF 17 beat a hasty retreat east, hoping to clear the sub threat.

Behind them, meanwhile, the fight for *Wasp's* survival was steadily being lost.

———

At 2:05 p.m., a huge explosion erupted forward of *Wasp's* island structure, flooding the bridge with burning gasses and heaving the number two 1.1-inch mount completely off its base. Because staying on the bridge was no longer possible, CO Sherman made his way to Battle II, the secondary control and command center. Soon he was joined by Rear Admiral Noyes, who had sustained burns from the latest blast.

At 2:10 p.m., still another explosion was triggered. This one dislodged the number two elevator, popped it into the air and, in the process, crushed an entire repair party. Just ten minutes later—and just thirty-five minutes after the first torpedo hit—*Wasp's* Sherman ordered abandon ship.

By then, sailors were already over the side, many after being cornered on the forecastle by the fires and explosions on the bow. Now the rest of the crew queued up on the flight deck waiting to go down lines or jump over the side. Below them some patches of water were thick with oil and fire. But circling close by were their sanctuaries: cruiser *Juneau* (CL-52) and destroyers *Farenholt* (DD-491), *Lansdowne* (DD-486), *Laffey* (DD-459) and *Lardner* (DD-487).

———

One of the men supervising the evacuation astern was *Wasp* LSO Lieutenant David McCampbell. The thirty-two-year-old Alabama-born naval aviator was an Annapolis product who had channeled most of his undergraduate energies into intercollegiate diving. McCampbell eventually won Eastern Collegiate and AAU championships, but his academics put him in the bottom half of his graduating class, delaying his commission.

After his obligatory fleet tour, McCampbell had pursued naval aviation with a passion, only to be repeatedly disqualified by Navy flight surgeons

1. *O'Brien* subsequently sank while en route to Pearl Harbor.

because of hyperphoria—a rare eye condition. To achieve his goal, Mc-Campbell even had himself examined—and cleared—by a famed civilian ophthalmologist, but to no avail. It took him another six months before he finally found a flight surgeon who would give him the okay.

McCampbell had joked to his buddies aboard *Wasp* that if the time ever came to abandon ship he would do it in style—using one of his championship dives. When the moment actually came, however, McCampbell was more circumspect. After coaxing upwards of two hundred sailors over the side on life lines, McCampbell climbed onto the LSO's platform, pinched his nostrils with the thumb and index finger of one hand (to shield his sinuses) and, cupping his genitals in the palm of the other, plunged feet first into the Pacific.

———

On September 17, VF-3's Butch O'Hare turned over the last of his F4Fs to Jimmy Flatley's VF-10. For the next months, he and his few pilots would have to settle for flying SNJ trainers and Grumman amphibious utility planes.

Flatley's squadron had arrived—sans aircraft—at Maui on August 20, a little over two months after its June commissioning at North Island. Flatley had nicknamed his squadron "The Grim Reapers"; its squadron insignia was a flying skeleton wielding a scythe with the accompanying motto: "Mow 'em Down!"

Using O'Hare's aircraft and Maui's good weather and uncluttered air space, the Grim Reapers were finally able to get in extended tactical training, including some radar-directed intercept practice with students at Oahu's Fighter Director School.

The twenty-eight-year-old O'Hare, once the thirty-six-year-old Flatley's Pensacola pupil, was now his peer—both in rank and squadron CO stature. As a true Jimmie Thach disciple, O'Hare used the time at Maui to persuade Flatley of the virtues of four-plane divisions and beam defense.

O'Hare had flown against Thach when the tactic was first tested and he had been a true believer ever since. For his part, "Reaper Leader" Flatley, having just authored a widely distributed proclamation ("The Navy Fighter") touting the need for tactics, was open to ideas that he once discounted in stateside debates with Jimmie Thach himself.

One item that caught Flatley's attention was that in his beam defense tests, Thach had restricted throttle settings in the 'friendly planes' while allowing O'Hare's 'enemy planes' to fly full throttle. At a minimum, then, the beam defense tactic might be a way to conserve fuel. As it was, Flatley instructed his flyers to keep their engine rpms at cruise setting as much as possible, even in combat.

Flatley had long favored six-plane divisions but now, in training flights over Maui, he saw some of their inherent problems—especially the difficulty of keeping track of the third section. Accordingly, Flatley experimented with four-plane divisions and he increasingly bought into the concept. In fact, by the end of September, the stubborn iconoclast had been converted. Flatley adopted the four-plane division and even began instructing his VF-10 pilots in the use of the beam defense.

In two weeks time Flatley was scheduled to take his squadron aboard the hastily repaired *Enterprise*—and their destination would be the South Pacific.

On September 20, Lieutenant Commander Eddie R. Sanders taxied the Akutan Zero onto a North Island runway and took it aloft for the first time since it had been in captivity. It was just a familiarity hop—formal test flights were not set to begin until September 26. Sanders's job would be to fully evaluate the aircraft for BuAer, documenting its characteristics and capabilities and comparing those side by side with what was in the Navy's aerial arsenal now—and what was in the pipeline. But the subtext of his job was also to pinpoint the Zero's in-flight fallibilities— the quirks, shortcomings and Achilles' heels that every combat aircraft, no matter how fabled and formidable, possesses.

Just three days into his tests, Sanders had already worked up a preliminary assessment for his boss in Anacostia, Commander Frederick M. Trapnell. Aside from its lack of pilot protection, Sanders wrote, the Zero was a carefully constructed and well-equipped fighter. Sanders also provided a summary of "pertinent" comparisons to the F4F—although he cautioned that they were based on incomplete data.

Sanders found the Zero to be several knots slower than the Wildcat (a finding that combat pilots would hotly dispute when the information finally came out). Moreover, while the Zero had superior climb and maneuverability, especially at lower speeds, its ailerons (the hinged components on the trailing edges of wings that control aircraft roll) stiffened considerably as speed increased. At 200 knots, for example, the Zeke's roll capability was slightly less than the Grumman's. At 250 knots, though, rolls were "physically impossible" for the Japanese fighter.

Another of the Zero's competitive disadvantages was in quick pushovers where the Zero's otherwise fine engine had a tendency to cut out momentarily. In simplest terms—and based on just preliminary data—an F4F pilot caught in a fight with a Zero could shake his opponent by accelerating into a dive and rolling and twisting at high speed.

Trapnell was quick to circulate Sanders' memo. By October 1, it reached Vice Admiral John Towers, then taking charge as Commander, Air Forces, Pacific Fleet (ComAirPac) in Hawaii. Within days it was accessible to Hawaii-based squadron COs such as VF-10's Jim Flatley and VF-3's Butch O'Hare.

––––––

As far as Grumman Aircraft executives and engineers were concerned, the timing of the capture, restoration and flight testing of the Akutan Zero could not have come at a more crucial juncture. Although it's unknown whether Roy Grumman, Jake Swirbul and Bill Schwendler were immediately privy to Eddie Sanders's first take on the Zero, they were going full bore to prepare an aircraft designed to meet what they understood to be the essential needs of the Pacific War's Navy fighter pilots.

Months before the Akutan Zero was unearthed, Grumman had already manufactured two F6F Hellcat prototypes. On June 26, 1942, three weeks after Midway and two weeks before the Akutan discovery, Grumman test pilot Robert L. Hall had taken the XF6F-1 up for a twenty-five-minute test. Hall, a six-year company veteran with 1,300 flight hours, likely hadn't seen the Sanders analysis either. But, having made the first tests of the Wildcat, he knew what this new bird needed—and lacked. It was obvious that the XF6F-1's installed engine—a Wright Aircraft engine producing 1,600 horsepower—was not going to do the job either in speed or rate of climb.

Grumman executives acted quickly on Hall's report, suggesting to BuAer that the Hellcat be equipped with the same engine that was going into the Vought Corsair: the Pratt and Whitney eighteen cylinder, two-thousand horsepower R-2800-8 Double Wasp. Adapted for the Hellcat (using water-injection to boost combat performance), the Double Wasp could churn out 2,200 horsepower.

Configured with the Double Wasp, a new prototype—the XF6F-3 (the "dash three") emerged for its first test on July 30, an eleven-minute hop just to try out the new engine. The dash three's life span was short. During an August 17 test flight, the Double Wasp inexplicably shut down in mid-air, forcing Hall to make a dead-stick landing into a Long Island bean patch. No matter; BuAer (which already considered the Pratt and Whitney Double Wasp an incredibly reliable, rugged and easily maintained power plant) ordered the F6F Hellcat into immediate production.

At this stage of the war, regardless of BuAer's backing, getting a new weapon of any kind into production was no easy matter. Grumman, like every other manufacturer, had to stand in line just to get the necessary materials to put a new factory online. Simply put—no factory, no aircraft.

Here, Jake Swirbul put on another not-so-uncommon display of his ingenuity and resourcefulness. Casting about for materials, Swirbul learned he could purchase the scrap-pile remains of New York City's old Second Avenue elevated railway. The Second Avenue El would, in effect, become the backbone of Grumman's hastily constructed Plant Number 3. On October 3, 1942, the first production model of the F6F Hellcat was taken aloft by Selden "Connie" Converse, another Grumman test pilot. In the months to follow, mistaken lore would have it that the Hellcats themselves—rather than the factory—were fashioned from Second Avenue El rails. This would only add to the Grumman mystique—and burnish the reputation of its soon-to-be legendary fighter aircraft.

––––––

Even as the first production Hellcat was taking to the sky, VT-8's Fred Mears was setting out on his first full-fledged strike mission from Henderson Field. Mears had taken up residency on Guadalcanal two days before, arriving near sunset as a passenger in a Flying Fortress.

As Mears encamped in his new surroundings, five VT-8 TBFs were still out on a strike against four Japanese destroyers near Gizo, a small island near New Georgia in the western Solomons. Two of the planes returned about 9 p.m. but the others, including a TBF piloted by Mears's friend Andy Divine were reported missing. Mears went up just after sunrise on October 2, circling the island in search of the lost planes. He never found them (the next day all three crews were reported safe and unhurt aboard a destroyer), but he did see the wrecks of a few Japanese bombers and Zeros and the remnants of a Grumman Wildcat strewn along a beach.

Mears's next sortie—on October 3—was as part of a strike group of three TBFs and seven SBDs. They'd taken off without fighter escort, so when he learned of Zeros operating in the vicinity, Mears got so nervous that he wished he could somehow get up and walk around the cockpit. To calm himself, he made sure that his guns were charged and his bombs armed. He told Deitsch to remind him to open the bomb bay doors when he started his dive.

They caught sight of the Japanese ships at 5:30 p.m.—a cruiser sandwiched by two destroyers. The cruiser, apparently hit, was smoking. As the ships veered into evasive turns, the strike aircraft overtook them and got ready to attack out of the sun. George Hicks, Mears's new turret gunner, came on the intercom to report two float-type biplanes flying below them. Mears was worried about Zekes, not biplanes, so he felt much relieved.

———

The Dauntlesses went in first, diving from nine thousand feet at the cruiser. None of their bombs hit the ships, but the first two TBFs did a little better. One scored two near misses on a destroyer, the next a near miss just astern of the cruiser.

When Mears's turn came he pushed over into a sixty-five degree dive. Guadalcanal dust that had settled in the TBF's cockpit covered him like a tiny cloud, initially making it impossible to get his eye on the sight. When the dust cleared, Mears could see the smoke from the cruiser and he set his sight on its bow. He pressed the bomb release three times just to be sure. As he pulled up, Mears glanced at the altimeter—two thousand feet.

Then off to the left Mears saw one of the biplanes getting close. He kicked into a turn and all at once felt the vibration of the turret gun firing. Hicks broke in to say he'd shot him down and that one of their bombs had hit the cruiser aft of its stack.

Circling past the lead destroyer, Mears considered what to do with his remaining two bombs. The destroyer was firing broadsides at him, but they were missing. Wheeling past the cruiser again, it occurred to Mears that he could hide himself in its smoke to drop his remaining bombs at low level.

Just then they were only eight hundred yards from the cruiser, with Hicks strafing. Suddenly, the cruiser gunners found the range. Tracers looped toward the TBF and it felt to Mears as if the tail section was being slapped around.

"Mr. Mears!" Hicks shouted. "Deitsch has been hit! I think we are hit badly! Let's get the hell out of here!"

Mears at once turned and fled, flying low off the water with antiaircraft rounds now bursting ahead of him. When they were finally in the clear, Mears told Hicks to go down and help Deitsch. He set course for Henderson, staying low on the water, opening his throttle and radioing Henderson's tower he had a wounded man aboard. Hicks came back on the intercom. Deitsch looked bad—they'd have to hurry if they wanted to save him.

After covering about one hundred miles in forty minutes, Mears reached Henderson at twilight and Deitsch was soon on his way to base hospital. He'd been hit on the right side of his head—a little round hole about the size of nickel. Deitsch was breathing easily then, but he was cold and wan.

The next day when Mears went to visit him, Deitsch was lying in the middle of the hospital's operating shack. He was semiconscious, pale and already jaundiced. The surgeon said Deitsch had three pieces of shrapnel in his brain and he gave him very little chance to survive. Deitsch, however, put his stubbornness to good use and was eventually evacuated.

———

On October 8, Mears went on a strike mission led by VT-8 CO Swede Larsen. The four TBFs, seven SBDs and four F4Fs were sent to attack a cruiser and four destroyers inbound for Guadalcanal—another delivery by the "Tokyo Express."

The afternoon sun was already low when the Japanese ships were spotted. The TBFs—armed this time with torpedoes—circled off to the side at ten thousand feet as the dive-bombers went in first. When it was the torpedo planes' turn, Mears and Earnest followed Larsen into the attack, all the while taking antiaircraft fire from the cruiser and two of the destroyers.

The cruiser was already smoking heavily from a bomb hit as the TBFs approached on the port quarter. As Mears broke formation to start his torpedo run, the cruiser's bow was just poking through the smoke, making it seem like a dragon's snout poking out from a cave. By then the antiaircraft fire was appalling and Mears could see that one dive-bomber was down in flames.

As Mears dropped his fish and turned off the cruiser's bow, he heard four large cracks—bullets snapping by his face. The gunfire chased them for another five miles and Mears didn't ease up on the throttle until he was certain they were clear.

When he checked the intercom, Mears learned that an ammunition canister had dislodged and broken the leg of Deitsch's replacement, a small soft-spoken sailor named Struble. Mears high-balled it back to Henderson to get treatment for Struble. Everything seemed fine until the TBF touched down. Then its wheel undercarriage slowly collapsed, setting the plane flat on its belly.

Struble, his leg in a cast, was evacuated the next day. To the good wishes written by others on the cast, Mears added: "Good luck for a good gunner."

"Jump?" The feeble voice of F. E. Taylor, the young sailor riding in the back of Ensign Alex Vraciu's SNJ trainer, was barely audible over the intercom.

"Yes!" Vraciu shouted, meanwhile giving the plane full rudder to avoid a fatal spin. "Get the hell out of there!"

Just minutes before, Taylor, like so many San Diego-based sailors, had been hanging around NAS North Island hoping to catch a joy ride with one of the pilots at the base's advanced carrier training school. October 14 looked to be Taylor's lucky day when Vraciu, one of three pilots going up to practice formations, agreed to give him a ride. Taylor had never flown before, so Vraciu gave him a parachute and a quick lesson on how to use it.

Vraciu, though still not fleet qualified, was by now a fairly experienced pilot. He had logged about three hundred solo flight hours during his nine months at Corpus Christi. (In August, Vraciu had received his instrument rating and had reported to North Island after a home leave.) That being said, while Vraciu had flown every variety of Navy trainer (the monoplane SNJ being the most advanced), the closest he had ever gotten to a Grumman fighter aircraft was some cockpit time in an F3F—the long-outmoded biplane. If Vraciu was closer to the war with Japan, it was only in the sense that he was flying over the shores of the Pacific rather than the Gulf of Mexico.

The three SNJs—a pilot and novice passenger in each—were cruising at about four thousand feet in clear skies over the Southern California town of Lemon Grove as they practiced rotating positions in echelon formation. Vraciu was the vee formation's left trailer when the right trailer, flown by Ensign W. L. Gleason, started shifting over into left echelon. It was a simple move, but as he crossed the formation, Gleason lowered his aircraft too soon and his prop or right wing tip clipped Vraciu's tail section.

So great was the resulting damage to the SNJ's elevator and rudder surfaces that Vraciu had to fight with all his strength to stay in control. Within seconds, it seemed as if he was only delaying the inevitable.

Vraciu did manage to jettison the canopy and his frantic intercom orders finally convinced his passenger to jump. With the back seat empty, control returned momentarily, along with the prospect Vraciu might yet avoid the stigma of losing the SNJ.

By the time Vraciu concluded there was no hope, however, the plane was in a full spin at low altitude. Unhooking his harness, Vraciu was literally thrown clear. He pulled the ripcord and the parachute opened— just long enough for Vraciu to swing twice in the harness before he tumbled into the branches of a lemon tree. The SNJ had already crashed in a smoking heap not far away.

Vraciu escaped injury—as did Taylor, who parachuted safely and Gleason who brought his SNJ (and his passenger) in for an emergency landing. When a Navy ambulance reached the scene, the flight surgeon was surprised to see Vraciu alive and unhurt. "Too many of you pilots," the surgeon told him, "try to be heroes and bring the planes back. Too many crash and lose their lives along with the planes."

When he got back to North Island, Vraciu presented Gleason with a large lemon as a souvenir.

———

On October 16, VT-8 managed to arrange for the evacuation of six of its most shell-shocked personnel aboard a destroyer leaving Guadalcanal. By then, for all intents and purposes, the squadron had ceased to be operational. After two daytime bombing raids on October 13, VT-8 was down to two operational TBFs.

After darkness on the 13th, Cactus personnel first heard ominous new sounds—the "whoo" of a shell whistling through the air followed by a sharp "whump" as the shell exploded on the main field. The Japanese had managed to station heavy artillery in the surrounding hills.

Soon after midnight, squadron personnel were roused from their cots and chased from their tents by the most intensive offshore shelling yet. Fred Mears, still dressed in pajamas, crowded into a foxhole along with five others. Again and again, they saw salvo flashes light the sky, then heard whistles and finally the terrible "crack-crack" sound of explosions. Coconut trees split and crashed to the ground, sprays of shrapnel flew overhead and sometimes heavy-footed duds bounded through the undergrowth. "Hell's fire," a chief petty officer cried when one round exploded, then "Holy balls" or "A red-ass mule" after the next.

After an hour or so there was a brief lull during which the men climbed out of the foxholes determined to evacuate the camp area. About seventy of them climbed into the back of a large squadron truck while others crowded into jeeps or took off on foot—all of them heading for the big bomb shelters on the beach.

As the crowded truck set out, the shelling resumed and made it the wildest ride that Mears could ever recall. Men were yelling, crying, even trying to hide behind—or underneath—one another. "They're taking us down to be killed!" one man wailed repeatedly until another man threatened to throw him off. As the truck with its crazed passengers lurched past the hospital area, doctors could be seen still operating even as blasts erupted. Nearer the beach it was almost possible to make out the forms of the ships out on the water and the muzzle flashes of their guns.

When the truck halted, Mears and the other occupants streamed into the woods towards the bomb shelters, occasionally flattening themselves or leaping into ditches when they heard an incoming round. The shelling finally stopped at about 3 a.m., only to be replaced at fifteen-minute intervals by the sleep-stealing drone of Washing Machine Charlie.

Late that morning, when the VT-8 personnel finally straggled back to the bivouac area, they found their camp no longer existed. One tent was entirely gone, another had collapsed and all the rest had been riddled, tangled and scattered by shrapnel and explosions. Butt plates of fourteen- and eighteen-inch rounds lay everywhere.

With the last of their aircraft out of commission, squadron officers decided it was time to leave the area and move in with the Marines. After arrangements were made to evacuate shell-shocked personnel, guns and ammunition were issued to everyone remaining. Taking only the belongings and supplies they could carry, the men moved to the hills and settled in a gully with a Marine special-weapons unit.

———

William Halsey, who had been recuperating after his hospital stay in June, was expecting to resume command of TF 16 with *Enterprise* as his flagship. He began his return to the South Pacific as a member of an inspection team led by Raymond Spruance, CinCPac's new chief of staff (and, after Midway, a rising star in the Pacific.) However, by the time Halsey's PBY set down in Nouméa harbor on the afternoon of October 18, those plans had changed dramatically.

With the Japanese fleet operating at will near the Solomons and a new offensive push against Guadalcanal almost certainly in the offing, Chester Nimitz was giving serious thought to removing Vice Admiral Robert Ghormley as Commander South Pacific (ComSoPac) and replacing him with Halsey.

Nimitz had long suspected Ghormley of seeing the 'Canal as a lost cause, but after reading a Ghormley dispatch that decried his forces as "totally inadequate," Nimitz knew a change was overdue. He swiftly got King's approval for the change. Thomas Kinkaid would retain TF 16 and, as senior CTF commander, would reassemble TF 61 with *Enterprise* and *Hornet*.

"Jesus Christ and General Jackson!" was Halsey's first quotable reaction to the news that he would relieve his old friend Ghormley (they'd played together on the same Annapolis football team). Halsey brought with him a new sense of grit and confidence, but he also faced formidable challenges—not least of them a crisis in ground-based air strength. Guadalcanal's aircraft losses had spiraled during the previous month. Its inventory, after losing 131 fighters, dive-bombers and torpedo planes to combat and other causes, was down to just seventy-four. The pace was killing: fully half of all replacement aircraft were expended within ten days. And the sources of those replacements—bases at Espiritu Santo, Efate and New Caledonia—were drying up as well.

Nobody was sitting on his hands: new supplies were being scrounged in the states. At Grumman, for example, emergency production teams working virtually nonstop had assembled twenty-four additional Wildcats from spare parts inventories. As important as these additional supplies were, they would not be shipped until the beginning of November. In effect, Cactus was on its own until those aircraft arrived.

––––––

Warned that his recuperation would take months, Saburo Sakai transferred in October to the Sasebo Naval Hospital. That it brought him closer to his childhood home was little consolation. During the train ride out of Yokohama, Sakai could see that Japan, despite the war, was as beautiful as ever. The torrid summer had been replaced by a glorious autumn weather. Three hours out of Yokohama the majestic sight of Mt. Fujiyama swam into view. Its graceful lines curved up towards a summit shrouded in mist. It was all stunningly beautiful, but none of it could lighten his depression.

Sakai realized now that he wasn't inviolate, at least in the way he had once thought—or acted. The enemy, once so inferior, had now taken its turn. A man, he reflected, sees the war differently after having rotten flesh scraped from his skull, after having splinters dug from his body—after being 'comforted' with words that meant death-in-life: "You are only half-blind."

ATTACK! REPEAT, ATTACK!

AT 7:14 A.M. ON OCTOBER 26, READY ROOM TELETYPES ON *ENTERPRISE* AND *Hornet* tapped out word that an enemy carrier had been sighted bearing 302 degrees, distance 196 miles. It was the news that the pilots and crews had been waiting for. The night before, TF 61's Thomas Kinkaid and his staff had reviewed what they knew. Two separate Japanese battle groups had been spotted by land-based air: an advance force of battleships and cruisers; and, eighty miles behind them to the north, two carrier formations. Well before dawn there'd also been an unequivocal message from Halsey: "Attack. Repeat, Attack!" Kinkaid had his orders and now, he thought, a definitive target.

———

Kinkaid and TF 17's Rear Admiral George Murray had first learned of Halsey's audacious plan on October 22, two days before *Enterprise's* and *Hornet's* rendezvous northeast of the New Hebrides. Beginning October 25, TF 61 was to prowl north of the Santa Cruz Islands—waters not ventured into since August—then turn southwest towards San Cristobal. Japanese actions were to decide what happened next. If no Japanese offensive threatened, TF 61 might thrust west to launch air strikes on enemy shipping off southern Bougainville.

But even as this preliminary scheme unfolded, new CinCPac intelligence pointed to an imminent offensive against Guadalcanal sometime over the next several days. CinCPac sources definitely placed just two carriers—*Shokaku* and *Zuikaku*—in the South Pacific, but Washington estimates had it that as many as four might be near the Solomons. Even with these estimates in hand, Halsey adhered to the original plan. As he later expressed it to Nimitz, "I had to begin throwing punches immediately."

———

At 7:47 a.m., *Enterprise* turned into the wind and launched a CAP of eleven VF-10 F4Fs, followed, three minutes later, by a modest *Enterprise* strike contingent. Led by CAG-10 Commander Richard K. Gaines, the strike force comprised nine TBFs (including the one piloted by Gaines); three SBDs; and Jimmy Flatley's eight VF-10 F4Fs, each equipped with an auxiliary fuel tank.

The bulk of the strike force came from *Hornet*, which had launched her first deck load about ten minutes earlier: fifteen VS-8 and VB-8 SBDs, six VT-8 TBFs and eight F4Fs led by Lieutenant Commander Gus Widhelm, VS-8's no-nonsense CO. A second strike was being readied to follow the *Enterprise* launch.

Now, as each *Enterprise* pilot taxied his plane up to the deck launch officer at fly one, a deckhand displayed a slate reading "*Proceed* without Hornet"—in effect telling Gaines's group to proceed independently. Overall, there was an air of haste and improvisation about the entire launch process—as if it were more about getting planes off the deck than organizing them for coordinated attacks. When he saw the placard, Flatley, who was flying the mission despite a broken bone in his foot, thought it was a bad idea.

———

At about 8:30 a.m., the seventy-five American strike aircraft—*Enterprise's* component sandwiched between *Hornet's* leading and trailing elements—were between sixty and seventy-five miles northwest of their carriers when a *Hornet* Wildcat pilot happened to see planes slightly above and off to starboard. Headed in the opposite direction, they could only be Japanese. The sighting and the count were relayed to the flight's escort leader, VF-72's CO thirty-four-year-old Lieutenant Commander Henry G. "Mike" Sanchez. "24 dive-bombers RED BASE," Sanchez radioed TF 61. "Standby for bombing attack."

Big E's twenty strike aircraft were then slightly east and five minutes behind the *Hornet* vanguard. They were spearheaded by a trio of SBDs, followed by eight VT-10 TBFs, split into two divisions. Jim Flatley's eight F4Fs—also split in two four-plane divisions—flanked the TBFs. Flatley's division flew to starboard, and to port flew a division led by twenty-six-year-old Lieutenant (junior grade) John A. Leppla, a Coral Sea SBD veteran. Gaines's aircraft—the ninth Avenger—brought up the rear.

Strict radio discipline was being maintained—many pilots had not yet turned on their radios nor, for that matter, tested their guns. None of the

Hornet planes copied Sanchez's alert. Lines of tracers streaming through the formation were the first warning anyone had of the oncoming Japanese fighters.

First to be hit was the lead TBF flown by VT-10 CO Lieutenant Commander John A. Collett, a Flatley Trade School classmate and close friend. With his engine and cockpit on fire, Collett stood, stepped onto his right wing and jumped, never to be seen again.

Horror brought instant alertness. Fifty caliber tracers from the TBF turret gunners converged on a Zeke diving in on the starboard quarter. The Japanese fighter—already ablaze—pulled up within feet of a TBF before disintegrating in a huge fireball.

Ensign John N. Reed's TBF was the next to go. Reed's turret gunner, Aviation Radioman Third Class Murray Glasser, saw pieces of canopy blow by and then heard Reed's intercom scream: "Bail out! Bail out!" Grabbing a chest-pack parachute, Glasser tossed another to the radioman before backing out of the escape hatch and pulling his ripcord. Glasser was the TBF's sole survivor—but was soon to end up in Japanese captivity.

———

Out on the port side, John Leppla was the first escort pilot to notice the marauding Zekes. Signaling his division to drop auxiliary tanks, Leppla pulled a hard right turn towards the TBFs. Leppla and his wingman, twenty-two-year-old Ensign Albert E. Mead, aimed for the trailing Zekes, just then recovering from their first swipes at the formation. Leppla and Mead bounced the trailers, only to be bounced in turn by other Zekes. Outnumbered and pinioned by alternating attacks from head-on and astern, both Wildcats were soon in desperate trouble. Leppla's F4F dropped—a dead-stick water crash with no chance of escape. Mead did a little better: splashing one assailant before crippling damage to his aircraft and painful wounds through both thighs and an ankle forced him to ditch. He escaped to his survival raft—only, the very next day, to be plucked from the sea by the crew of a Japanese destroyer.

———

The twin calamities of Collett's TBF in flames and Leppla's division dropping back finally alerted Jimmy Flatley to the devastation. Spotting a Japanese fighter banking for a shot at the remaining TBFs, Flatley dropped his tank and rolled into a diving turn to cut off the menace. Flatley and his division mates each snapped full-deflection shots at the Zeke, which countered into a climb. Transferring their dive momentum into a climbing chase, the four Wildcats topped out together above the smoking Mitsubishi and then dispatched it with a precise sequence of high-astern passes.

Their devastating efficiency brought a sudden end to a sudden ambush, but two TBFs were already down and two others so badly damaged they were forced to turn back. Flatley knew he couldn't justify doubling back to help Leppla. The *Enterprise* strike force, once twenty aircraft-strong, was reduced to just twelve. Five TBFs (including Gaines's), three SBDs and four F4Fs pressed on toward the objective.

"Launch all planes immediately," ordered TF 61's Kinkaid at 8:37 a.m., breaking radio silence over the Talk Between Ships (TBS) circuit. "Jap planes coming in." Kinkaid was reacting to Mike Sanchez's distant heads-up: although the bogeys should by now have been close enough for *Enterprise* and *Hornet* radars to detect them, neither system had.

"Look for hawks [dive-bombers] on port bow and port quarter," *Enterprise*'s new FDO Commander John H. Griffin cautioned CAP pilots. "Angels probably high. Look south." Griffin was relaying the information at hand, but this last was a bum steer—Griffin's misreading of radio traffic from outbound strike aircraft. (Though formerly CO of the U.S. Navy's Fighter Director School on Oahu, this was Griffin's first shift in the FDO hot seat.)

It was 8:55 a.m. before Griffin finally got something on radar. "Large group now twenty miles from base," he radioed two VF-10 CAP contingents, vectoring them west and up to twenty thousand feet.

"Tally ho, dead ahead, Angels 17," came the call four minutes later from twenty-two-year-old Lieutenant (junior grade) Thomas J. Gallagher Jr., one of eight VF-72 CAP pilots bustering to cover *Hornet*. "I think they are hawks."

In front of Gallagher and his squadron mates, arrayed in a compact column of vees, were fifty or more Japanese fighters, dive-bombers and torpedo planes.

To conserve their fuel and oxygen, Griffin had stacked Big E's CAP at ten thousand feet. "Climb, climb!" he now implored the Reapers as the *Hornet* pilots readied to square off.

As the big Japanese strike formation dispersed for attack—the torpedo-equipped Kates angling to bracket *Hornet*'s bows; one flock of bombers nosing down for her flight deck while a trailing flock peeled east towards *Enterprise*—the VF-72 F4Fs were the first to go at them.

Hoping to disrupt the entire dive-bombing attack, Gallagher's division leader, twenty-nine-year-old Lieutenant Edward W. "Red" Hessel singled out the lead Val in the first vee. As Hessel banked hard left for a flat-side run at this hawk, Gallagher swung towards the one just behind.

While Hessel and Gallagher hounded these two Vals, Hessel's second section—twenty-six-year-old Lieutenant Claude R. Phillips and twenty-three-year-old Lieutenant (junior grade) John R. Franklin, his wingman—fanned out to tear into the next vee. Phillips quickly smoked an outside trailer, but after a follow-up pass on another he found himself behind the action—and out of touch with Franklin. Scanning the skies, Phillips spotted a lone Wildcat being swarmed by Zekes and opened throttle to close. Phillips finally got on the six-o'clock of one of Franklin's assailants only to have his own aircraft ripped by twenty-millimeter cannon. Despite damage and choking smoke, Phillips managed to shake his wingman's Zeke loose, only to find that Franklin was a goner. Phillips followed Franklin's plane all the way to the water, but Franklin never bailed.

While Zekes battered Phillips and shot down Franklin, Hessel and Gallagher were barreling head-on toward another Val that seemed determined to fight back. Guns blazing, all three held their runs until the very last instant. Finally, though, the two F4F pilots caved—Hessel zooming over, Gallagher under and the Val barreling through to split the difference. Rattled, but brimming with adrenaline, Hessel and Gallagher came back around intent on resuming the fight. Ahead of them, however, the Val pilot made no move to counter. Instead, the hawk nosed over and crashed—proof that a dead man never bluffs.

———

By 9:05 a.m., when *Hornet* lookouts finally sighted Japanese aircraft, VF-72 had already paid dearly in her defense. Two divisions had splashed three hawks and severely damaged several more, but a trio of F4Fs had been shot down and two pilots killed.

Two other CAP divisions, posted to the northeast, were now needed overhead, but were much too far away. *Enterprise* FDO Griffin, sensing that *Hornet's* survival now hung in the balance, vectored seven Reaper F4Fs towards TF 17.

Griffin planned to reserve the rest for Big E's defense, but the pilots aloft saw what was happening and had other ideas—all broke west towards *Hornet*. Events, however, were already outpacing their intentions and their closing speeds. The hawks had reached angels seven, their path unimpeded by fighter opposition.

———

At 9:10 a.m., six Vals were plunging single-file for *Hornet's* deck. With *Hornet* turning southeast and pouring on speed to escape, each pilot adjusted the angle of his dive—the first quite steep, each subsequent approach more shallow.

The first of these hawks' bombs drifted wide, eventually hitting the water off *Hornet's* starboard bow. But the next, an armor-piercing projectile, hit the flight deck squarely abeam of the island, drilling through timber and three levels of steel deck to an explosion that wiped out a repair party.

A second hit followed, though this one exploded at flight deck level close to the after gun gallery on the starboard side. Its blast opened a huge crater in the deck planking and, worse, loosed a dragon's breath of flame that incinerated thirty men.

The next bomb—the third—struck very soon after and not that far from the spot of the second. Like the first, however, it was armor-piercing. The projectile penetrated four lower decks before erupting in the chief petty officers' mess compartment.

Hornet, though staggered, was not slowed by the three bomb blasts. Now, however, she had to reckon with the fish—the Japanese torpedo planes.

———

Murray's earlier course change had left one group of Kates astern, but these were beginning to catch up. Formed into ragged right echelon, the fish accelerated along *Hornet's* starboard side to get in position for a beam attack. To counter, Murray turned northeast.

Murray's turn to port bought *Hornet* time in her reckoning with the fish, but it could not fend off potential counterblows from a half dozen determined Vals. Survivors of the dustup with VF-72's fighters, the six hawks—the trailer badly damaged—had regrouped and cut north where, taking advantage of Murray's maneuver, they lined up to dive-bomb *Hornet's* port beam.

It was not an entirely clear shot. Twenty-eight-year-old Lieutenant Stanley W. "Swede" Vejtasa, one of the VF-10 CAP flight leaders that FDO Griffin had implored to climb, had finally gained enough altitude to try to interpose. Spotting the straggler, Vejtasa torched the damaged hawk with a short, high-side burst. This eliminated one hawk outright and efforts by other Reapers effectively spoiled bomb releases by four others, but the sixth Val was poised for a spectacular, suicidal strike.

————

This last hawk was already trailing flame as it came in on *Hornet's* starboard quarter. Its pilot, likely dead or dying, never toggled his bomb. Instead, the Val lunged towards *Hornet's* island complex. Its starboard wing hit first, slicing signal halyards and scraping the stack on the way down. Then, as the Val fuselage caromed off outcroppings on the island structure and nosed into the flight deck, fuel from its ruptured tanks ignited. The wreckage nearly penetrated to a squadron ready room, prompting a handful of SBD pilots to flee for their lives. As it was, burning gasoline scorched the signal bridge, killed seven signalmen and severely burned other bystanders. The devastation's only saving grace—though a huge one—was that the Val's bomb (which finally dislodged to rumble back and forth across the deck of a deserted passageway) was a dud.

Even as damage control parties fought to suppress the fires triggered by this Val's collision, *Hornet's* fate seemed to hinge on outwitting or outlasting the low-flying fish. In truth, the Kates were having a hard time. The ones angling for *Hornet's* starboard bow from the southeast were kept off balance by Murray's ever-tightening turn north. A second group to the north and east, meanwhile, came under the guns of a VF-72 F4F flown by twenty-seven-year-old Ensign George L. Wrenn. Wrenn, who'd been buzzed and chased to lower altitude by a nimble Zeke, unexpectedly found himself in perfect position over six low-flying fish. In short order Wrenn set two of them ablaze, breaking off only when the converging antiaircraft fire became too dense.

Eventually, however, three pilots from the nearer group of Kates settled for torpedo launches off *Hornet's* starboard quarter. Two were promptly gunned down by gallery batteries as they tried to pull away and—to many *Hornet* witnesses—it seemed the Japanese pilots had traded their lives cheaply. But as the torpedoes powered along just below the surface and *Hornet* leaned its mass into keeping clear, their trajectories became less and less improbable.

The first wake streamed past *Hornet's* bow—but just barely. Then, within seconds of the Val suicide crash topside, one torpedo stabbed *Hornet's* starboard beam and exploded just aft of the island. Twenty seconds later, a second torpedo explosion—this one on the starboard quarter—

ripped into engineering spaces. Almost at once, all of the ship's power and communication failed.

Taking a starboard list, the darkened, silenced *Hornet*—now pointed northwest—began to lose headway. But even as the crippled carrier slowed, a smoke-wreathed Val was approaching in a shallow dive astern. *Hornet's* beleaguered gunners hammered the plane until its trail of smoke turned to flame. The pilot toggled his bomb, but because his angle of descent was so shallow and the ship was moving so slowly, the projectile, instead of dropping, hurtled clear of the ship to land in the water ahead.

Meanwhile the pilot, who certainly must have been wounded, pulled out beyond *Hornet's* starboard bow and then reversed course. Sweeping back in a slow, fiery glide, the plane crossed in front of the bow before the pilot banked sharply and nosed into the port forward gun gallery. The Val's burning wreckage tore through the gallery deck before slamming into the forward elevator pit.

————

"Contact bearing about 345." Jimmy Flatley recognized Gus Widhelm's voice. It was 9:15 a.m. and somewhere ahead of them *Hornet's* strike group had apparently found the target carrier. Five minutes later, he heard Widhelm's confirmation: "I have one in sight and am going after them."

It was a morsel of encouragement in a steady diet of frustration. *Enterprise's* strike group was down eight aircraft, including four of Flatley's F4Fs. Moreover, Flatley's fighters had jettisoned their auxiliary tanks during the ambush. Having already fought and flown far, they had farther to go and might have to fight again.

Lieutenant MacDonald Thompson, now leading the TBFs after Collett's loss, soon spotted wakes off to the west. "There is another group of ships 270 [degrees] over there," Thompson radioed. "Let's go." As Thompson's TBFs veered west, Flatley's F4Fs and Gaines's TBF—but not the three SBDs—followed.

To their disappointment they found Japanese cruisers and destroyers, but no carriers. Thompson radioed Flatley. Could the F4Fs go further? No, Flatley replied, they didn't have enough fuel.

————

"*Hornet* hurt," was Kinkaid's concise and cogent 9:49 a.m. update to ComSoPac. To sailors aboard TF 16 ships that had turned southeast for sanctuary in a line of squalls, *Hornet* appeared a distant and diminishing pillar of smoke.

"Operate from and in positions from which you can strike quickly and effectively," was a restive Halsey's advice to his task force commanders. "We must use everything we have to the limit."

For the moment, "everything" amounted to an unescorted strike of ten *Enterprise* SBDs to go after the Japanese cruisers. Preparing for a 10 a.m. launch, crews re-spotted Big E's flight deck and began arming and fueling strike aircraft. So as not to open range on *Enterprise's* and *Hornet's* returning aircraft, Kinkaid, for the time being, put TF 16 on a southwesterly heading.

Although radar scopes aboard *Northampton* (CA-26) and *South Dakota* (BB-57) had been picking up bogeys as early as 9:30 a.m., they first showed on *Enterprise's* balky radar at 9:53 a.m. They bore 340 degrees, forty-five miles and closing. Their proximity put the 10 a.m. launch on hold (but with several armed, juiced and perilously exposed SBDs sitting topside.) Instead, TF 16 turned further to starboard and braced for the onslaught.

————

"Look for bogeys approaching from north and northeast, angels probably low."

For some minutes *Enterprise* FDO Griffin had been beset by confusion—both about the approaching bogeys and the resources he could muster against them. Griffin first vectored a Reaper CAP division led by thirty-one-year-old VF-10 XO Lieutenant William R. "Killer" Kane northwest, only to retrieve him minutes later.

Now this latest information, transmitted at 10:07 a.m. to the twenty-one *Enterprise* CAP aloft—the majority circling at low altitude—sent them stalking in the wrong direction at the wrong altitude.

At 10:15 a.m., *Enterprise* lookouts had visual spots on a line of bombers to the west—some already diving out of the sun. As *Enterprise's* antiaircraft guns (including sixteen powerful new intermediate range forty-millimeter Bofors) opened fire, her CO, Captain Osborne B. Hardison, ordered hard left rudder.

"Reapers look for planes in dives," was Griffin's abrupt new admonition to his out-of-position CAP. "Look for bogeys diving on port bow."

————

Though there were no fighters in place to block their way, the hawks faced withering barrages of antiaircraft fire, perhaps the most intense that any had ever experienced. Of the first seven Vals to attack, four were shot down as they came in off the starboard bow—and none dropped their bombs with any accuracy.

Two minutes later, a second group of hawks dropped from cloud cover to angle towards *Enterprise's* starboard quarter. Most of these were also either shot down or detoured, but three survived the gauntlet to deliver damage. The first blow, at 10:17 a.m., was a bomb hit to the flight deck well forward. After piercing the lip of the deck, the projectile dropped down through the forecastle and exited through the hull before exploding in midair ahead of the bow.

The blast effect blew an SBD spotted forward clear off the flight deck and into the water—taking with it to his death the rear gunner, just then firing at the Japanese. The impact also tossed Lieutenant (junior grade) Marshall Field Jr., out of his perch in an antiaircraft gun director. Field, heir to the Chicago newspaper and department store fortune, flew high and dropped hard to the flight deck, unconscious and riddled with shrapnel wounds. Seeing another flight deck SBD on fire, a gang of volunteers rushed forward in the heat of the attack to shove it over the side.

The second bomb, striking a minute later, also punched through the flight deck, this time astern of the forward elevator. Hitting a girder, the bomb split in two and triggered two distinct explosions—the first, at the hangar level, killed several personnel and torched several planes; the second, erupting at the third deck level, severely burned or outright incinerated most of a thirty-six man repair party.

The third bomb triggered a near-miss explosion off the starboard quarter. Tearing at waterline hull-plate seams, it opened a ragged, fifty-foot long, inches-wide gash to the sea. The blast damaged the ship's main turbine bearing and, worse, ruptured a fuel-oil bunker. *Enterprise* now trailed a conspicuous stream of thick bunker crude.

———

This Japanese dive bombing attack was over by 10:30 a.m. Too distant or too low to have been of much help in this round of the fight, many Big E CAP aircraft were now too low on juice, ammo or both to fly much longer. Nevertheless, concerned that more hawks might still be lurking, FDO Griffin directed those that were able to climb.

Indeed, just minutes later, *Enterprise* picked up a contact to the northwest that soon resolved into a bogey or bogeys bearing 330 degrees, angels twelve. Killer Kane and his wingman, twenty-seven-year-old

Lieutenant Leroy E. "Tex" Harris, were vectored to investigate. Though not directed to, Swede Vejtasa's division followed.

Pondering the nature of the advancing bogeys, FDO Griffin played a hunch: "Look out for fish," he warned at 10:44 a.m. "Fish bear about 330 degrees from base."

This time, at last, Griffin had his CAP in position ahead of the incoming raiders.

———

"Tally ho nine o'clock down," called out twenty-four-year-old Ensign William H. "Hank" Leder, the wingman in Vejtasa's second section. Leder and section leader thirty-year-old Lieutenant Stanley E. Ruehlow were at thirteen thousand feet and ten miles northwest of *Enterprise* when they banked and dove for a pair of Zekes several thousand feet below them.

Less than a minute later Vejtasa and Harris encountered the main serving: eight dark-green fish descending in a column to reach *Enterprise* from astern. The two fighters charged in for a high-side run from the left. Accelerating to 350 knots, Vejtasa and Harris combined to blast at least one Kate.

The Kates were then loosening their formation and descending into dark storm clouds. Recovering from his first pass, Vejtasa saw the F4F flown by his friend twenty-seven-year-old Lieutenant Albert D. "Dave" Pollock Jr. work onto the six-o'clock of another Kate and blast its tail at point-blank range.

Even as Pollock's fish dropped away, Vejtasa set after a fresh group of Kates, chasing them through the murk and firing at close range into the tail of each. He thought he got three, but had no time to linger.

———

As Leder, Ruehlow, Vejtasa, Harris and Pollock pummeled the Kates and Zekes miles to the northwest, a second, unescorted contingent of eight fish had hidden themselves in the squall line in order to sneak in against *Enterprise* from the west. Letting down to wave-top level, these Kates bore in at Big E's starboard side. Circling there, low on fuel and hoping to land, was VF-72's George Wrenn.

When the lead Kate swept by him, Wrenn (who had earlier shot several Kates over TF 17) at once turned onto his tail. Ahead, the Japanese aircraft was approaching the port bow of screen destroyer *Maury* (DD-401). Caught in a withering crossfire of *Maury*'s twenty-millimeter cannons and Wrenn's .50 caliber wing guns, the Kate soon shed its port wing, rolled, split the waves with its remaining wing and finally flopped into the water.

This fish went down at 10:46 a.m., but its fate hardly deterred the others.

One toggled its torpedo—a miss—against *Enterprise*'s port quarter while the rest swept past *Maury*'s bows seeking a better angle. Two gave up on hitting *Enterprise*, instead turning sharply left to aim for the thundering bulk of *South Dakota*. (At 10:48 a.m., one of the pair lobbed a torpedo so close to the battleship's port side that it sailed entirely over the main deck before splashing off to starboard.)

Captain Hardison was on the starboard wing of the *Enterprise*'s navigation bridge when he spotted three oncoming torpedo tracks. Hardison at once ordered right full rudder and bridge personnel waited with pounding hearts in heaving chests as Big E's big hull turned just inside the closely spaced parallel wakes and combed them to starboard.

———

Off to the north, VF-10's Swede Vejtasa had just then broken off pursuit of a Kate set ablaze by *South Dakota*'s antiaircraft fire. The crippled fish was falling fast, but its pilot managed to overtake destroyer *Smith* (DD-378) and nose his aircraft into her number two five-inch mount, just forward of the deckhouse. After rolling and exploding atop the number one mount, the wreckage dropped overboard, but not before depositing its torpedo warhead on *Smith*'s forecastle. Minutes later, a massive explosion forced *Smith* to fall off sharply to starboard.

By then the last of the Kate survivors had fled out of antiaircraft range. As they high-tailed it west low off the water, however, several CAP fighters, including Swede Vejtasa's, were waiting to cut them off. Vejtasa chased and emptied his magazines into one plane, which caught fire and staggered a few more miles before finally crashing. As witnessed and later confirmed by George Wrenn (who claimed five kills of his own), it was the seventh aerial victory of Vejtasa's eventful CAP mission.

———

"Remain close to base; no definite bogeys now." Griffin's 10:58 a.m. update to his fighters failed to mention that *Enterprise*'s radar was on the blink. Pilots flying the thirteen VF-10 and five VF-72 F4Fs still aloft were going nowhere. Guns were so dry and juice levels so low that most wished only to land. They had plenty of company: homeless *Hornet* strike planes, most from the second wave, had strayed in out of the west to join Big E's crowded landing circle. Deck crews worked furiously to clear debris, re-spot aircraft and clear a jam in elevator number two.

Finally, at 11:15 a.m., *Enterprise's* flight deck opened for business but, as it did, radar—repaired by the radar officer who had literally lashed himself to the sweep antenna while he fixed a faulty motor—detected a cluster of bogeys twenty miles to the north. Realizing the landing circle was crowded with *Hornet's* and *Enterprise's* own planes, Griffin's words were tentative: "They may not be friendly."

He was right. At 11:21 a.m., a line of Japanese hawks tumbled out of a thick cloud layer and bore down towards *Enterprise's* stern.

"Bandits reported above clouds." Griffin's words were hasty but authoritative. "All planes in air standby to repel attack approaching from north. Above clouds! Above clouds!"

———

Of all the morning's attacks—from what was later determined to be four Japanese carriers—this latest, for *Enterprise* at least, was the shortest and most easily defended. Because the clouds lay so low, the Vals were forced to make unusually shallow dives and became inviting targets for ship's gunners. Antiaircraft fire torched the first hawk and chopped the tail of the second while the third, though not visibly damaged, plunged straight into the water. It took a fourth incoming Val to inflict the only new damage to *Enterprise*, an underwater bomb explosion just off the port bow that dented more hull plates and opened more seams.

VF-72's George Wrenn was in a landing approach just as *Enterprise* curved into an evasive turn. It threatened his chance to touch down, but knowing he had only enough juice for this one pass, Wrenn kept on coming. To his surprise and relief, the LSO gave him a cut. After a plane handler released his hook, Wrenn had to wait uneasily in his cockpit as the flight deck tilted and the gallery guns roared. For the moment, no one else dared venture out to chock his wheels.

The morning's final attack on TF 16 was soon to end, but not before *South Dakota* suffered a bomb hit to the heavily armored top of her forward-most sixteen-inch gun turret and cruiser *San Juan* (CL-54) a stern blast that jammed her rudder and briefly sent her churning in circles. With *Smith* and now *San Juan* out of step, TF 16's formation station keeping was a shambles. Of as much concern, so was formation firing discipline. Returning strike aircraft were taking pot shots at retreating Japanese fighters, hawks and fish, while shipboard gunners, desperate to lock on suspected targets flitting in and out of low clouds, were firing indiscriminately at anything airborne.

Thomas Kinkaid's TBS plea—"Do not fire at chickens. Bogeys coming in now, also friendly aircraft"—only seemed to describe rather than reign in the mayhem.

––––––––

Mindful of their own critical fuel status, but sensing the chaos that might consume them if they edged closer now, Jimmy Flatley's four VF-10 F4Fs and MacDonald Thompson's five VT-10 TBFs stayed out on the rim of the task force.

Flatley knew the best that could be said of Big E's morning strike remnants was that they had survived a futile, nightmarish mission. After the ambush on the outbound leg, there had remained the prospect of settling the score against the Japanese carriers. They eventually had to settle for trying to sink a Japanese heavy cruiser but even this effort failed. During the TBF attack only two of four torpedoes launched successfully and neither one hit. Flatley's fighters had strafed, but he doubted they'd done much damage.

––––––––

Then, at 11:35 a.m., just as the ruckus above TF 16 was playing out, Flatley spotted outbound Zekes. The Japanese had altitude advantage while Flatley's F4F, its fuel and ammunition seriously depleted, was in no condition to fight. Knowing the others were in equally bad shape, Flatley radioed his wingman, twenty-two-year-old Lieutenant (junior grade) Russell L. Reiserer and second section leader, twenty-four-year-old Ensign Roland R. "Cliff" Witte: "Let's line abreast. Keep sharp lookout. If you see anything, start weaving. . . . Cliff, stay on line abreast and keep your eyes open."

Though they'd practiced it numerous times on Maui, this would be VF-10's first combat use of Thach's beam defense—the real test.

Flatley and Reisserer looked to be sitting ducks when a Zero dived for them, but each time the Japanese pilot got on the tail of one Grumman, he at once found the other Grumman threatening. After repeated tries, the Zekes—themselves likely low on fuel and ammunition—broke off and headed home.

Thach's idea worked just as advertised—about the only aspect of the mission that had. "It is undoubtedly," Flatley later wrote in reports about the encounter, "the greatest contribution to air combat tactics that has been made to date."

Beam defense offered the best way to protect both the bombers and the escort fighters. If his fighters had been out ahead and arrayed in line abreast (Flatley reflected ruefully), they could well have mounted a better defense against the day's ambush.

In reporting his experience and its costly lesson, Flatley would also give the beam defense tactic a new name: the Thach Weave.

————

At 12:22 p.m., when VF-72's Swede Vejtasa took the cut from *Enterprise's* exhausted LSO, there was scarcely room on the flight deck to park, never mind land. However, using consummate finesse, the new ace hooked the number one wire. After Vejtasa lifted his hook, the deck crew chocked his wheels right precisely where they stood—there was simply no more room.

This still left twenty-one TBFs aloft and in the next minutes, as crews scrambled to strike planes below and make room, a number of them would end up ditching. That said, in the roughly forty minutes since the last of the surviving Japanese hawks, fish and bandits had pulled away, forty-seven of the seventy or more returning aircraft in the landing circle had been brought in. At 1:18 p.m., after a CAP launch that included F4Fs flown by Red Hessel, Dave Pollock and George Wrenn, Big E's flight deck reopened. Ten more TBFs set down, bringing the recovery total to fifty-seven.

While every returning pilot and crewman had a story to tell, bragging rights belonged to the VS-8 and VB-8 SBD crews of Gus Widhelm's flight. Roughly two hours into the mission (after passing two groups of enemy destroyers, cruisers and battleships—among them the cruiser attacked by Thompson and Flatley), Widhelm had taken his Dauntlesses on an evasive turn to starboard to avoid some Zeros. The turn had separated the SBDs from the *Hornet's* first wave TBFs and F4Fs, but it ended up being fortuitous. Five minutes later, Widhelm spotted distant wakes. As the formation drew closer, the pilots saw two Japanese carriers, one of which was already burning—the result of an (as yet unreported) early morning attack by a VS-10 scout bomber.

Bypassing the burning ship—it was light carrier *Zuiho*—Widhelm and his bombers set their sights on the second and bigger flattop—identified later as *Shokaku*. After his SBD was shot up en route by a Zeke, Widhelm was forced to ditch short of the target (he and his gunner were later rescued by a PBY). But the remaining SBDs pressed on until, at about 9:30 a.m. (ten minutes after the Widhelm radio report copied by VF-10's Jimmy Flatley), they scored several devastating bomb hits on *Shokaku*.

The SBD bombs' explosions ignited tremendous fires on the carrier's mostly empty flight deck. Benefiting from the lessons of Midway, *Shokaku* (whose Vals, Kates and Zeroes were even then pounding *Hornet*) managed to stay afloat. Still, as the SBD pilots fled for their lives, it seemed certain that she was out of the battle.

———

In the end—which finally came at 1:30 a.m. on October 27, after determined but insufficient scuttling attempts by U.S. ships—it took four Japanese destroyer torpedoes to at last dispatch *Hornet's* ghostly, burning hulk to the bottom of the Pacific. American efforts to save (rather than sink) the crippled carrier had ended at 3:43 p.m. on the 26th when, after his ship took her third torpedo hit and her list increased to twenty degrees, Captain Charles P. Mason finally ordered abandon ship.

At about the same time, a directive from ComSoPac Halsey ordered all task force commanders to retire southward. By then, of course, *Hornet* was in no condition to comply but, after picking up survivors, the balance of TF 17's ships did. Ahead of them, *Enterprise* and her screens were already well on their way to a refueling rendezvous northeast of Espiritu Santo.

———

On October 27, all but a handful of VT-8's flying personnel were evacuated from Guadalcanal by transport plane. As they prepared to leave, a pilot who had just touched down at Henderson Field brought with him word that *Hornet* had been sunk. Though Fred Mears had also spent some time aboard carrier *Enterprise*, *Hornet* was the putative home of VT-8. Her sinking—which was soon confirmed—brought to mind the ghosts of Waldron and the other fifty VT-8 pilots and air crewmen who had perished.

The day before his departure, Fred Mears and one of his buddies went out to the front lines to talk with some of the Marines. Since moving in close to Marine positions, many pilots, including Mears, had lost all doubt as to which side would prevail. (Others, however, remained edgy. The face of one SBD pilot Mears knew would tense up automatically whenever gunfire erupted. "Are those our guns? Are those are guns?" he would cry as he jumped to his feet, as alert and anxious as a hound dog.)

To be sure, everyone was anxious on the 25th, when the Japanese had started what looked to be all-out sea, air and land offensive. There must have been a Japanese carrier in the neighborhood. The Zeros buzzing overhead seemed to linger longer than they would have if they'd taken off from a distant land base. And while the Zekes kept the Cactus fighters busy, an unprecedented number and variety of Japanese aircraft flew in to strafe and bomb Henderson.

But then the skies suddenly quieted. Whatever had happened was over and they were still more or less in one piece—though not so the Japanese soldiers who assaulted the Marine defenses.

In talking with the Marines, Mears and his buddy got a vivid idea of what the ground pounders had endured during those same days. "I had my machine gun in a perfect position," one Marine gunner told them. "There were Japs on all sides of me. All I had to do was swing the barrel in a circle."

––––––––

Events in the closing months of 1942 alternately conspired to lift and then deepen Saburo Sakai's depression. First, in November, he learned he'd been promoted to warrant officer—virtually unprecedented for someone who had enlisted in the IJN as a seaman recruit. It seemed a hollow victory, but there were compensations. Sakai was able to leave the naval hospital for thirty days' home convalescence. His stay at his mother's house in the Fukuoka suburbs proved remarkably restorative. And then, after his return to Sasebo, Sakai had an unexpected and welcome visitor: Hiroyoshi Nishizawa, another veteran of the Tainan Air Group. Sakai and Nishizawa had first met when Nishizawa was just a rookie, but from the first, Sakai considered him a pilot of true genius.

It was a wonder to see his friend not only alive but totally unscathed after the months of combat over New Guinea and the Solomons. Assigned briefly to the Yokosuka Wing as a flight instructor, Nishizawa had managed to agitate his way into another combat assignment. He was just about to leave for the Philippines.

For the moment, Sakai found himself basking in the memory of his aerial triumphs and the warm camaraderie he'd experienced as one of the elite eagles of the Tainan and Lae Air Groups.

But that momentary sensation vanished when he asked about their cherished compatriots and saw the abrupt change in Nishizawa's laughing, blustery demeanor.

"Dead," said Nishizawa. "They are all dead. You and I, Saburo. . . . We are the only ones still alive."

––––––––

In the early afternoon of February 1, 1943, Solomon Island coast watchers and scout planes from Henderson reported a score of enemy destroyers north of Vella Lavella and coming down the Slot at high speed. Because it looked like another attempt to land troops, Henderson's SBDs, TBFs and F4Fs were immediately scrambled. When the forty Marine aircraft swooped in on the convoy at 6:20 p.m., they met unusually stiff resistance from dozens of Zekes. Although a bomb hit stopped one of the destroyers, the other nineteen pressed on.

This latest Japanese venture seemed a worrisome departure from the more recent trend of events in the continuing struggle for the 'Canal. It had been mid-November when the Japanese made their last concerted effort to bolster their garrison: eleven troop- and supply-laden transports with escorting destroyers dispatched from Shetland Harbor near Bougainville. The convoy had been hounded and pounded along the route to its final destination, the Guadalcanal shoreline west of Lunga Point. In the end, only four transports made it—and these, along with their human cargo, had been massacred from the air on November 15. Although hard ground fighting had continued ever since, the final conquest of the 2,500 square miles of island miasma seemed just a matter of time.

When Henderson's planes broke off action on February 1, a collection of American destroyers and patrol torpedo (PT) boats were dispatched for what was hoped to be a surprise nighttime surface strike against the convoy. As with most engagements on and around Guadalcanal, this one didn't work out as planned. Night-flying Japanese planes kept the tin cans so occupied that they never managed to get into the fight. The small, thin-skinned PTs did get in, though with more brio than offensive punch. The next morning, February 2, found the Japanese destroyers outbound from the 'Canal, eighteen under their own power, one in tow.

Though what the Japanese were actually up to remained a mystery for nearly a week more, the first definitive clue was stumbled across that same day. When American troops captured an enemy base near Tassaforanga, they unexpectedly met no Japanese resistance. Instead, Army GIs found a large radio station, an undamaged machine shop and ten working artillery pieces.

Over the course of three nights—February 1st, 4th and 7th—the Japanese managed to evacuate the remnants of their starved and beleaguered garrison, nearly twelve thousand men in all. It was not until February 9, at the conclusion of a ground forces pincer from west and east that found no trace of Japanese troops, that the Americans finally sensed what had happened.

At 4:25 p.m. that day, Army Major General A. M. Patch radioed Com-SoPac from a small village on the Tenamba River: "Am happy to report . . . 'Tokyo Express' no longer has terminus on Guadalcanal."

Task One had been accomplished.

PART FIVE

THE HOP SUPREME

YOU LOOK GOOD OUT THERE, HONEY

KENNETH A. JERNSTEDT, A FORMER MARINE CORPS AVIATOR WORKING FOR Republic Aviation, was one of many test pilots who swapped rides with industry counterparts. It was not at all unusual, say, for Grumman's Connie Converse to drop by Republic's Farmingdale facility when a new version of the P-47 Thunderbolt was being evaluated. So it was hardly out of the ordinary that Jernstedt turned up at Grumman's Bethpage airstrip one morning in early 1943 to take a turn flying the latest F6F model. Or that while he waited, Jernstedt happened to run into another holidaying busman—a tall, middle-aged Corsair test pilot who contracted with both Chance Vought and Pratt and Whitney (two other regional industry neighbors of Grumman).

Though Jernstedt was ahead of the other pilot on the flight list, he offered to swap places. The other man demurred, but Jernstedt, who lived close by, insisted. It was getting late. He'd be able to drive home after the flight, but the Chance Vought man, who'd flown in by Corsair, would still have to fly to his final destination.

"Well," the other pilot finally said, "to tell you the truth, I really would appreciate it."

As the Chance Vought pilot neared completion of his twenty-five-minute hop, however, Jernstedt had reason to rue his graciousness. As he readied to land, the pilot radioed the Bethpage tower saying that the Hellcat's landing gear wouldn't go down. Excitement and fear spread through the facility as Grumman engineers and mechanics crowded into the control tower to try to solve the problem. They hoped to avoid a crash—and a high-profile fatality. It took three sharp dives and pull-outs before the man finally managed to lock down his wheels and come in for a safe landing.

Because of the close call, remaining hops were scratched for the day. It hardly mattered to Kenneth Jernstedt. After having nearly contributed to the death of Charles A. Lindbergh, Jernstedt was content just to get into his car and drive home.

————

The easygoing cordiality among rivals like Jernstedt, Converse and Lindbergh was part and parcel of the war effort. These men were the professional—and spiritual—descendants of "prototype" pilots like Jimmy Collins. They piloted cutting edge aircraft well before the aircraft were accepted for military use. They weren't flying in combat (though many had, like Jernstedt—a Flying Tigers veteran before being felled by malaria), but because they put their lives on the line in unproven aircraft, they faced risks and pushed performance envelopes in ways that many front-line fighter pilots never actually did.

For the most part, such teamwork and camaraderie were also the norm across war industries' shop floors, displacing the jealousy and workplace infighting that inevitably took over in more mundane—and leaner—times. For Grumman's employees, the F4Fs, TBFs and F6Fs that rolled out of the production bays took on new and vital lives. They were not being flown off into anonymity but into a life-and-death struggle. To these workers, the fortunes of the planes and the men who flew them mattered as much or more than production figures.

Still, as the pressures of wartime demand in general (and crises like Guadalcanal in particular) demonstrated, production mattered a great deal. So much so that even as Grumman hired one to two thousand people a month, and Jake Swirbul's minions scoured the countryside for real estate and construction materials to house them, the Navy's needs for combat staples like the Wildcat and Avenger seemed insatiable.

Ironically, the pressures only escalated as the vaunted F6F neared the production stage. In the short-term at least, the Hellcat's rollout would in no way put a dent in the demand for F4Fs and TBFs. It would take more than one-off production stunts (like the extra twenty-four F4Fs assembled in response to the attrition on Guadalcanal) for Grumman to meet its production commitments.

A substantial, if initially unappealing, solution came from the challenging wartime transformation that mighty General Motors was undergoing. With civilian automotive production at a standstill, GM had shut down a string of East Coast plants and furloughed the plants' workers. Seeing an opportunity to get a foothold in the Mid-Atlantic's burgeoning military aviation industry, GM lobbied Washington hard to put the idled factories and employees to use in fabricating aircraft.

Thus it was that Grumman executives, after heavy jawboning by the Navy and the federal War Production Board, entered into an uneasy partnership with the automotive behemoth. (It was one thing for the Navy's Ernest King to commend the management ideas of GM's Charles Kettering to his Pacific War admirals and something else entirely for Roy Grumman and Jake Swirbul to subcontract with a car maker to assemble high performance aircraft.) Under the terms of the negotiated alliance, GM created a new division called Eastern Aircraft and reopened five plants in New York, New Jersey and Maryland to produce Wildcats (designated FMs) and Avengers (designated TBMs).

The marriage had all the potential for unfettered discord. Each partner used vastly different production methods to meet vastly different requirements—and each thought it had a lot to teach the other. While the demands of consumer mass production drove engineering at GM, at Grumman precise engineering requirements drove design. While weight and tolerances were minor considerations for GM autos, they were major obsessions for Grumman aircraft. And while GM geared production to the capabilities of semiskilled and unskilled workers, Grumman's was a "fit-and-finish" culture executed by artisans—or at least by workers painstakingly schooled in the Grumman Way. Indeed, perhaps the greatest obstacle to the Grumman-GM partnership was the intense personal pride Jake Swirbul's workers took in their products. It was hard—at all levels—to consign even off-brand versions of those critical products to a soulless mass producer.

In the end, to make it work, Grumman personnel had to ease their defensiveness and GM personnel their tendency to patronize. And in truth, for GM, the concessions went far beyond that. The company had to abandon entire production lines and extensively retool its Eastern Aircraft plants. Technicians had to be cherry-picked and transferred in from GM plants across the country and GM had to invest in worker training as never before.

In retrospect, Eastern Aircraft (which produced its first FM Wildcat in August 1942, its first TBM Avenger five months later and turned out a combined total of more than thirteen thousand Grumman-designed aircraft during the war) became more like Grumman than GM—at least for the duration. One emblematic bridge between the two manufacturers was a set of ten Wildcat and Avengers furnished to Eastern by Grumman before full-out production began. Because they were assembled using Parker-Kalon temporary fasteners, these Wildcats and Avengers were called PK planes. If everything else (detailed engineering studies, process sheets, time studies, routing sheets, photographs, sketches, memos, meetings, phone calls) failed, workers at the Eastern plants could easily take the PK planes apart in order to study how they were put together.

––––––––

If unprecedented cooperation within and across traditional industry settings was a byproduct of the war, so were some intriguing collaborations between the military and the arts. The seed for one such offbeat co-venture was a chance conversation between Jimmy Flatley (then at San Diego's North Island organizing, equipping and training VF-10) and Walt Disney about the possibility of using filmed animation in fighter training.

Many pilots, including Flatley, had used combat gun camera footage for front line training. But live action flight training films—whether they involved actual combat or dramatizations—had their limitations, especially with novice aviators. Aerial tactics, in particular, involved spacing and distances that were difficult to capture within the frame of a motion picture camera.

In late summer 1942, following up on Flatley's initial contact, Lieutenant Commander Jimmie Thach visited with Disney before heading east for his new assignment at the Naval Air Operation Training Command in Jacksonville. Disney, the creator of Mickey Mouse, Donald Duck, and feature-length animated films such as *Snow White and the Seven Dwarfs*, was more than willing to help

NATC Jacksonville's primary function was to prepare new pilots for the planes they would fly in combat. Close to eleven thousand Navy pilots would be trained in 1942 and that number would likely double in 1943. Any imaginative tool that could condense or accelerate the process (in this case by presenting the essentials of aerial combat) was worth trying. Before the end of 1942, contracts were approved for what became the "Jacksonville Project": a series of ten thirty-minute training films (with titles like *Gunnery Approaches*, *Snoopers and How to Blast 'Em*, *Group Tactics against Enemy Bombers* and *Defensive Tactics against Enemy Fighters*) for which Disney produced the animation and Warner Brothers produced the live action sections.

In Burbank, Walt Disney provided a three-story building and scores of artists to work on the Jacksonville Project. Thach's initial role during production (he usually spent two weeks in California for every three in

Florida) was to demonstrate with hands, models and cutouts what the planes did and how they moved in three-dimensional space. Top animators took lead responsibility for illustrating the critical maneuvers, while less experienced artists drew the progression sequences.

Everything had to be precise: the look of the aircraft, the backgrounds, the angles, the relative positions, the approaches and recoveries. For Thach it was in a way like teaching the Disney cartoonists to fly. Many got so involved that the studio spaces came to have the feel of squadron ready rooms, with artists talking like pilots and excitedly using their hands to describe tactics. When auditions failed to come up with a credible narrator, Thach reluctantly took over the task. He was, after all, someone who could use the right emphasis in explaining tactical problems and solutions. His was also the voice of real experience—someone who could credibly convey to the films' viewers a sense of what they'd actually face during aerial combat.

––––––––

When Saburo Sakai was finally discharged from Sasebo Navy Hospital at the end of January 1943, he was ordered to report to his old outfit, the Tainan Air Group of the 11th Air Fleet, now stationed at Toyohashi in coastal Honshu. Of the original 150 pilots assigned to the Group when it first formed on Formosa in 1941—and flew off from there confident of conquering the Pacific skies—only twenty now survived. These pilots (some of them disabled like Sakai) formed the nucleus of an organization replete with novice pilots rushed through a training regimen that was, by any measure, inferior and inadequate.

As an officer, Sakai was now privy to the IJN's secret combat reports. From them he first learned of Japan's final evacuation of Guadalcanal in early February—a calamitous defeat that included the annihilation of two Army divisions and, for the Imperial Japanese Navy, losses equal in scope to the IJN's entire pre-war strength: two battleships, an aircraft carrier, five cruisers, twelve destroyers, eight submarines and hundreds of fighter and bomber aircraft along with their pilots and crews. The defeat at Guadalcanal was all but matched in ignominy by the earlier calamity near Midway. In one sense, Midway had been even worse: Guadalcanal's agony had been prolonged and fiercely contested. By contrast, Nagumo's staggering losses—four carriers, three hundred aircraft and nearly that many skilled pilots—had been rung up in a matter of hours.

Under such dire circumstances, Sakai knew there would be few qualms about him once more taking to the air—which he did within a day after arriving. Finally back in the cockpit and at the controls of a Zero, Sakai was joyously drunk with the air again.

But the intoxication of flight soon enough gave way to the sobering task that confronted the cadre of air combat veterans. The young pilots reporting to Toyohashi, though eager, serious and undoubtedly brave, lacked any semblance of fighter pilot skill and temperament. In their current condition they would be no match for the American adversary's experienced pilots and vastly improved aircraft. And though Sakai and the other veterans worked them hard, trying to instill the lessons, tricks and small advantages that the veterans had used to triumph and survive, there was simply not enough time to nurture promising acolytes—nor to weed out the inept before they lost their lives in flaming crashes.

Abruptly in late March—scarcely two months into the training program—word came that the Air Group would be transferred to Rabaul in hopes of bolstering the once-formidable fortress's weakened defenses. Even though Sakai believed this rush to the front lines could only end in folly, he fully expected, despite his diminished abilities, to accompany the Group. Just days ahead of the move, however, a flight surgeon prevailed on the Tainan Air Group commander to leave him behind. Aerial combat over Rabaul was no place for a one-eyed pilot—not yet at least. To Sakai it seemed like a case of saving a lone tree in the midst of a raging forest fire. Indeed, he learned that within a week of Tainan Fighter Wing's first Rabaul combat sorties, not less than forty-nine of its planes had been lost to enemy fighters and antiaircraft fire. By then, Saburo Sakai was on his way to his next assignment: as a flight instructor at Omura Air Base near Sasebo.

———

"Things are looking up," Butch O'Hare wrote to his family in a letter dated March 2, 1943. "We have quite a few pilots and a third of our planes and they really are good ones this time."

O'Hare's outlook had a lot to do with finally getting away from Maui, where VF-3 had languished through the fall and early winter of 1942, as little more than a reserve pool for South Pacific-bound squadrons. In January 1943, even when the Pacific War's deepest crisis looked to be easing, O'Hare was still forced to relinquish nine of his pilots. VF-3 seemed relegated to the backwaters of the Pacific War.

To be sure, life on Maui was far from punishing. A local couple, Frank and Ethel Hoogs, had extended O'Hare the use of a small beach cottage and a station wagon. The cottage soon became the center of squadron social life and the base camp for fishing trips, horseback riding and pheasant hunting forays into the Maui hills.

But in mid-February the exile on Maui finally ended. VF-3 turned in its remaining aircraft and shipped back to San Diego to become part of a new carrier air group. After home leave (O'Hare had a new daughter, Kathleen, whom he'd never seen), O'Hare set up shop in a hangar at South Field on North Island.

———

The planes that helped restore Butch O'Hare's enthusiasm were a dozen factory-fresh Grumman F6F-3 Hellcats. Three days before his letter home, O'Hare took his first Hellcat ride—in Bureau Number 04827, the fifty-second F6F-3 accepted from Grumman by the U.S. Navy.

O'Hare had been anticipating the event ever since his visit to Bethpage nearly a year before—and he wasn't disappointed. The Hellcat seemed to possess the same ruggedness and flight stability as the Wildcat, but its Double Wasp engine (O'Hare had flown Double Wasp-equipped Corsairs while in Maui) made a huge difference in speed and climb rate, even though the new plane was almost twice as heavy as its predecessor.

And there was more: The knock-kneed, hand-cranked retractable wheels of the Wildcat had been supplanted in the Hellcat by gear that folded smoothly—and hydraulically—into the largest wings thus far fitted on an American single-seat fighter aircraft. There was also added firepower: the Hellcat wings mounted six .50 caliber Brownings but with magazines expanded from 240 to 400 rounds per gun—close to a thousand rounds more. And, not least, was greater endurance. The Hellcat's internal fuel capacity was 250 gallons, versus 144 for the Wildcat. In addition, the use of a belly-mounted 150 gallon drop tank (versus the 58 gallon drop tank used on the Wildcat) greatly increased the Hellcat's fighting range.

By then, O'Hare had in hand the full results of the tests run on the Akutan Zero, published by BuAer the previous November. Because, at the time of publication, the Corsair was further along in the pipeline than the Hellcat, the F4U performance specs were profiled side-by-side with the Zeke. The Corsair, BuAer tests demonstrated, outmatched the Zero in level and diving speeds at all altitudes and climb rates at sea level and above twenty thousand feet. If surprised, the Corsair pilot could resort (as could the Wildcat pilot) to a pushover or twisting rolls. Pilots, however, still could not expect to turn with a Zero.

The essential advantage was that a Corsair pilot (and presumably a Hellcat pilot) could choose the terms of combat. He could out-climb ("go upstairs faster," as O'Hare himself had described it to FDR and the press) the Zero to high altitude where he would have the edge in speed. For now, of course, none of these advantages had been demonstrated in front-line combat. Until they were, hit-and-run attacks and mutual defense tactics (the Thach Weave) were still the way to go.

———

If O'Hare's enthusiasm about new aircraft was justified, his rosy outlook on personnel proved premature. In his time at Maui, O'Hare had built up a nucleus of veterans for VF-3. Some, like Lieutenant (junior grade) Sy E. Mendenhall, were not yet battle-tested. But others, like twenty-six-year-old Lieutenant (junior grade) John P. "Johnny" Altemus and Francis R. "Cash" Register were. Register, in fact, had six confirmed aerial kills—one more than his new CO. But then, at the end of March, to O'Hare's frustrated resignation, nine of his pilots (including Cash Register) were dragooned to fill Wildcat slots in Composite Squadron 21 (VC-21), then training to go onboard escort carrier *Nassau* (CVE-16).

In some cases the transfers would be temporary—but in others tragic. In late April, *Nassau* sailed north for the May 11th amphibious invasion of Attu. Alaska's rough seas, thick fog and strong winds made for abysmal flying conditions, especially during ground support missions. On May 14, VF-3's Lieutenant Douglas Henderson was killed during a strafing run into what was called Massacre Valley. Two days later, Cash Register went down with his plane near Holtz Bay.

The loss of veterans, whether temporary or permanent, frustrating or tragic, put added pressure on the squadron CO and his depleted leader cadre. They had to work doubly hard to pick up the slack and to integrate the constant influx of squadron rookies. By the spring of 1943, at least, there was no lack of new prospects. Freshly qualified naval aviators, all of them eager and some with genuine promise, were descending in hordes on West Coast staging points like North Island. The problem was to sort out the best from the rest—and more quickly than ever. The Pacific War was heating up.

———

When the showroom-new Cadillac came to rest in the sand and scrub flanking a dirt road north of Phoenix, the driver and the two groggy passengers in the back seat checked their limbs and skulls.

It could have been disastrous. The driver had failed to navigate a tight left turn and the sleek Caddie behemoth had rolled over and over—something it hadn't been built to do. Fortunately, other than being rudely awakened, shaken up and having their uniforms caked with dust, none of the three were seriously hurt. The car, though now on its roof, wheels in the air and in need of repair, wasn't really in such terrible shape either—although its Chicago dealership and its California owner might beg to differ. All the three young Navy officers could do was to retrieve their luggage from the trunk and flag down the next westbound vehicle.

Lieutenant (junior grade) Alex Vraciu scarcely knew the other two Navy aviators. What they had in common was that each had finished carrier qualifications (from the flight deck of the USS *Wolverine* [IX-64], a converted paddle-wheeled passenger liner operating in the confines of Lake Michigan) on the same day and received orders directing them back to North Island and squadron assignment. They'd agreed to travel together and one of them (not Vraciu) had talked a Chicago car dealer into letting him transport the Cadillac to a customer in Southern California.

The accident interrupted but barely delayed their plans. Indeed, the balance of the trip was comparatively smooth—a brief stopover in Phoenix to alert the dealership (Vraciu heard nothing more about the accident)—and hitched rides the remaining 350 miles to San Diego.

After reaching North Island, Vraciu went to the ComCarPac detailing office—a sort of hiring hall for shorthanded West Coast squadrons. For green fighter pilots, at least, timing and luck as much as skill or service record determined your assignment. In the case of Vraciu and another pilot, it was a toss-up between two opportunities—one in a composite squadron aboard an escort carrier (CVE) heading for the Solomons, the other a CV fighter squadron billet at North Island's South Field.

The Solomons' reputation for dysentery and malaria made it no one's first choice assignment. Vraciu, winner of the toss, chose what turned out to be VF-3. It was only when he reported to South Island that Vraciu realized VF-3's CO was none other than Butch O'Hare, the Medal of Honor recipient he'd first seen while in Basic at Corpus Christie.

———

Vraciu's assignment to VF-3, although a small, routine event in a massive war, was nonetheless representative of the turns the conflict in the Pacific was taking in 1943. He was one more drop in a flood tide of arms, manpower and offensive initiatives.

New campaigns were getting underway across the Pacific. In the South the Halsey-led drive into the Northern Solomons was poised to begin, using Guadalcanal as a springboard. In the Southwest, Douglas MacArthur had kicked off efforts to capture key bastions on New Guinea—although it was still slow going. Both campaigns were preludes to bigger ambitions: the conquest of Japan's formidable fortress at Rabaul. Both as well were battle environments where aviation support would be predominantly land-based. The U.S. Navy's carriers had shown their vulnerabilities in the confined waters off the Solomons and New Guinea, where the Japanese possessed strong island bases (in essence, unsinkable carriers) and their fleet choked the approaches. Those waters were the graveyard for *Wasp* and *Hornet*. No one wanted to revisit those agonies.

The Central Pacific, on the other hand, offered promise for an entirely new avenue of advance. Here a revitalized U.S. Navy fleet could draw Japan into battle away from its land bases, opening the way for a punishing offensive against the very heart of the Empire.

The lure of the Central Pacific, however, also heralded another back seat role for Douglas MacArthur. To no one's surprise, he objected. In MacArthur's mind, the best use for Nimitz's carriers was to guard his flanks as he drove up the New Guinea coast. That spring, however, sentiment grew for a strategic shift from the Southwest to the Central Pacific. The notion got the endorsement of the high-level Joint Strategic Survey Committee, which in turn prompted the Joint Chiefs of Staff to decide that in the fall Navy-led Central Pacific forces would attack the Gilbert Islands, an equatorial atoll chain west of the International Date Line. The two primary spearheads would be the fast carrier task forces and the Marine Corps amphibious assault force (what would become the Fleet Marine Force under the command of Richmond Kelly Turner).

What had swayed the vote of Army Chief of Staff George Marshall was the much-anticipated arrival of an impressive new armada of fast carriers—a potentially game-changing force that could not be allowed to molder or be sidetracked. For its part, however, King's Navy would have to demonstrate not only that this armada could hit and run—but also hit and stay.

———

The American fast carriers being commissioned and going through shakedown in the spring of 1943 would eventually rank high among the most important weapon systems ever in America's seagoing arsenal. Their top-of-the-line models were the twenty-seven thousand-ton *Essex*-class fleet carriers, the CVs. The potency of the CVs was not so much a matter of size—ships of the *Essex* class, although larger than predecessors such as *Enterprise*, were actually smaller than the *Saratoga* —as it was a matter of speed, resiliency and technology.

Advanced communications capabilities were built into the *Essex* line: Position Plan Indicator (PPI) radar to enable high-speed station keeping at night or in foul weather; Dead Reckoning Tracer (DRT) radar for navigation; improved Mark 4 and Mark 12 aerial radars; and secure four-channel very high frequency (VHF) radio circuits to help carrier FDOs coordinate fighter defenses. The advances made multi-carrier operations both feasible and potentially more devastating.

As to size, the dimensional and structural differences in these ships were evident where they mattered—as enhancements to flight operations. The *Essex* strength deck was the hangar deck rather than the flight deck, a design feature that lowered weight distribution and allowed for smaller, lighter supporting structures. The combination of hangar strength and flight-deck capacity (a lengthier and wider flight deck with an innovative deck-edge elevator) expanded aircraft capacity to ninety—including thirty-six fighters.

The construction, commissioning, shakedown and operational fine-tuning of these mobile behemoths was hardly instantaneous. While a total of twenty-three were either on order or in the works by August 1942, *Essex* (CV-9), the class lead, was not formally commissioned until that December. *Essex* was not to reach Pearl Harbor until May 30, 1943 and the next two, the new *Yorktown* (CV-10) and *Lexington* (CV-16), not until late summer.

This arrival pace could not have sustained the Navy's Central Pacific ambitions had it not been for the near-simultaneous introduction of new smaller carriers—improvised *Cleveland*-class cruiser conversions made it even more necessary by 1942's devastating carrier attrition at Coral Sea, Midway and Guadalcanal. *Independence* (CVL-22), the namesake of this make-do carrier class, also reached Pearl Harbor in summer 1943. *Princeton* (CVL-23) and *Belleau Wood* (CVL-24) soon followed.

The CVLs both looked and performed like stopgaps. They displaced only eleven thousand tons and could accommodate only about thirty aircraft. Their short, narrow flight decks; high, slender hulls; and generally tight interior quarters made conducting flight operations routinely perilous. One pilot summed up the experience as "hitting a splinter with a bolt of lightning."

If their cramped features did not make CVLs the favorites of hotshot carrier aviators, neither did their intended use. Because of the CVLs' limited aircraft capacity, its squadrons (proportional versions of CV squadrons, at least initially) would mostly be relegated to defense—CAP, and anti-submarine patrol work. Indeed, the one feature that recommended the CVLs was speed—they could keep pace with the rest of the new crop of ships assigned to the fast carrier task forces.

────────

The arrival of new ships for the fast carrier task forces heated up the ongoing debate over carrier doctrine and leadership. Senior naval aviators believed that their time had come—that no one other than flag level aviators should command the CTFs. But in the end these decisions would be made by Chester Nimitz.

Nimitz was the architect of the crowning victory at Midway, and his new chief of staff, Rear Admiral Raymond A. Spruance, had gotten the lion's share of credit (along with the staff he'd borrowed from Bill Halsey) for its execution. In their time of direct collaboration, Spruance had demonstrated two things to CinCPac—his superb strategic thinking and his ability to reason in concert with his boss. So it was not terribly surprising that when the Central Pacific Force (later designated the Fifth Fleet) was established as the reporting umbrella for new ships as they reached the Pacific, Nimitz chose Spruance to take command.

To ComAirPac Vice Admiral John Towers, who carried the banner for naval aviation, Nimitz' choice reeked of holding fast to the status quo. Towers and the growing cadre of aviator admirals were adamant that carrier operations were at once highly specialized and integral to overall fleet operations. Senior commanding officers of large naval forces should either be aviators or have chiefs of staff who were. The flyboys had a strong bargaining position—one that got ever stronger as more carriers, squadrons and aircraft arrived in the Pacific and became the wherewithal for Central Pacific campaigns.

Though the matter of Central Pacific Force leadership was nominally settled with Spruance's elevation, the ongoing dispute over how the fast carrier task forces should be employed was not. The aviation admirals' stance was firm and unwavering: the fast CTFs should be long-range mobile striking forces, attacking the enemy on land and sea as the principal offensive foundation of the fleet. For their part, however, Nimitz, Spruance and Kelly Turner were more equivocal. If the objective of Central Pacific campaign was to conquer island outposts, then the primary function for CTFs should be to protect and support amphibious invasions. Nimitz, Spruance and Turner wanted amphibious forces secure on the beach before fighting any fleet engagement.

To be sure, these simmering brown shoe-black shoe tensions pointed to a day of reckoning. But, given present circumstance, that day was not nearly at hand. After all, the new *Essex*- and *Independence*-class carriers were just now involved in training exercises. The new Hellcat fighters had not yet been battle-tested nor had their green pilots been under enemy fire. Most immediately there would be warm-ups—small CTFs staging late summer and early fall hit-and-run raids not (except for their punch) unlike those in the earliest days of the Pacific War. And against two of the same enemy outposts: Marcus and Wake.

As these plans went forward, not only the disputatious principals, but also the entire cast of airmen and sailors could take pride in what had been fashioned. In Hawaii there was collective relief, disbelief, and simple awe at the nonstop influx of ships, aircraft and men. Not that long before, a good portion of the Pacific Fleet had been resting in Pearl Harbor's muck. Now, on August 22, 1943, as new carrier *Yorktown* steamed towards Hospital Point on its way to a rendezvous with *Essex* and *Independence* for the raid on Marcus, the Ford Island tower blinked out an admiring Godspeed message: "You look good out there, honey."

———

With some alliterative license, U.S. Army Air Corps Sergeant Merle Miller, a staff correspondent for *Yank* magazine (and later a bestselling biographer of Presidents Harry Truman and Lyndon Johnson) described them as "Butch's Busy Babies." Writing from "Somewhere in the Pacific" (in reality NAS Puunene on Maui), Miller described how the "'babies,' many of them veterans of a year or more of Pacific combat with Zeros and bombers to their own credit expect to repeat the skipper's 'luck' with aerial-combat techniques so new they won't even discuss them. 'And they're ready' O'Hare will tell you. 'Damned if they're not.'"

Veterans aside (Miller wrote), there were also many young squadron rookies: "One is only nineteen, several are just beyond their twentieth birthdays, more than a third are only twenty-one. They are called the 'embryos' by the 'old men' among the lads—those who are in their mid-twenties. O'Hare himself is twenty-nine."

Using the *Yank* reporter's age categories, it would have been hard to classify Alex Vraciu, who, when VF-3 pulled up stakes at North Island's

South Field and departed for Pearl Harbor (and ultimately NAS Puunene) on June 15, 1943, was already twenty-four. Vraciu was not yet a combat veteran nor was he, by any stretch, among the very youngest—somewhere, then, between 'embryo' and 'baby.'

But Vraciu was also, in the eyes of his squadron CO, a fighter pilot of considerable promise. Vraciu took his first hop in a Hellcat over North Island on April 4. By the end of the month he had logged twenty-nine-and-a-half F6F flight hours—and a combined total of four hundred seventy hours of solo flight time. By the end of May (still at North Island), Vraciu's Hellcat cockpit time had vaulted to eighty-five hours and he'd received a prestigious, shoulder-heavy assignment—to be Butch O'Hare's wingman.

It was a big responsibility—he would have O'Hare's back in the heat of combat—but also a big opportunity. It was not as though O'Hare (or any squadron veteran) withheld training or mentoring from other squadron members. Rather, it was that there was special value in being privy to constant, hands-on, real-time coaching from a genuine hero—an almost venerated master. The lessons—how to conserve fuel and ammunition; when to open fire and where, precisely, to aim; why, when and how to be especially alert—had special resonance.

O'Hare's practical, soft-spoken approach to the job at hand also taught Vraciu to temper his eagerness and ego. Once, sensing that O'Hare was about to latch onto his tail during aerial combat practice (an extension of Jimmy Thach's "Bitching team"), Vraciu in desperation pulled up into the sun. It was a successful but dangerous gambit—one that could have easily ended in a collision. When the two landed, O'Hare, in his quiet but no less impactful way, made it known that killing them both with stunts like that would not help the war effort. Vraciu should save it for the Japanese.

———

On June 26, 1943, Lieutenant Fred Mears took off in a TBM Avenger from North Island. Mears was leading a three-plane formation as part of training exercise with VC-18, his new squadron. The squadron, based out of Seattle, was detached to North Island to practice dive-bombing tactics.

Ever since returning stateside with the remnants of VT-8, Mears, as with so many other Pacific War naval aviation veterans, understood he was destined to return to frontline flying. They were in it for the duration. It was still a young war and Mears—although having undeniably paid his combat dues—was still a young man.

During his home leave in Seattle, Mears took it upon himself to write up some of his Pacific War reminiscences. It may have been a lark for the benefit of his family and close friends, but when his sister Betty, herself a writer, read them, she urged him to submit several chapters to an editor at Doubleday, Doran publishers. Mears took her advice and the editor almost immediately expressed interest in publishing the final manuscript.

Mears worked on the manuscript even as he joined VC-18 and resumed training. He finished it in less than three months and Doubleday enthusiastically agreed to publish the book, to be titled *Carrier Combat*, in early 1944. The editors also expressed hope for a second book based on Mears's forthcoming experiences.

The June 26 flight out of North Island was to be a routine bombing exercise. But then, above Otay Mesa, site of a practice range near the California-Mexican border, something went terribly wrong. As Mears attempted to pull out of a particularly steep dive, a portion of the TBM's tail surface unexpectedly peeled away. Its left wing soon followed, sending the plane spiraling completely out of control. The TBM crashed and blew up on the desert floor, killing Mears and his two enlisted crewmen, Jack Booth and Joe Daniels.

A later accident investigation report concluded that Mears had been diving too fast. Flying, in other word, at terminal velocity and with steam in his breeches.

———

On October 5, 1943, a group of *Yorktown* VF-5 Hellcats, part of the first wave of a multi-division, multi-carrier strike force bound for Wake Island, encountered Zeke interceptors. The combined strike group—from TF 14 carriers *Essex, Yorktown, Lexington* and *Cowpens* (CVL-25)—had been launched in a predawn gloom a hundred miles north of the three-island atoll. The darkness, combined with a strong fast-moving squall, had already contributed to the loss of one VF-5 Hellcat during launch and disrupted pre-departure rendezvous. What was planned as a surprise attack clearly was not. Two dozen Zero defenders were already aloft at 5:45 a.m.—ready to take on the incoming Grummans.

What followed were the first sharp, probing jabs in what would, during the course of the next two years, number thousands of aerial bouts between the vaunted Zekes and the new Hellcat challengers.

VF-5 Hellcat pilot Ensign Robert W. Duncan was the first to engage the Japanese fighters. Duncan turned directly into several attacking Zekes and drew a bead on the nearest. An accurate, full deflection burst into the Zeke cockpit at once set it aflame—a brilliant beacon lighting up a still-dark sky.

Duncan went next after a Zero that had climbed on another Hellcat's six o'clock. Duncan shook it loose, but at the cost of hits to his own fuselage just aft of the cockpit. As his assailant climbed out of a firing pass, Duncan set after him, keeping close even as the nimble Zeke went into a loop. Matching him stride for stride to the top of a loop—where, for a moment, both fighters seemed to hang suspended and motionless—Duncan got in a shot that finally torched the Zeke and sent it spinning into the water.

These two Zekes were not the only VF-5 aerial tallies during this first wave of the Wake raid. A third Zeke and a Betty were shot down by other VF-5 first-wave pilots, and, pulling out after a strafing run, Duncan and his section leader Lieutenant Melvin C. "Boogie" Hoffman combined to take down a fourth Zeke. But, by most accounts, Duncan's brace of Zekes represented the first aerial conquests of Mitsubishi A6M2 fighter aircraft by a Grumman F6F Hellcat. More important at the time, when Duncan touched down on *Yorktown*, he claimed a prize offered on the eve of the raid by Air Group CO Commander Charles Crommelin: a bottle of Old Crow to the first Air Group 5 pilot to shoot down a Japanese plane.

————

Later that same morning, as TF 14 cruisers *Minneapolis*, *New Orleans* and *San Francisco* (CA-38) skirted Wake's eastern reef line steaming south, eight Hellcats led by VF-6's Butch O'Hare took off from carrier *Independence*. Their responsibility was to cover the cruisers' approach to bombardment positions off the main island's southwest shore. The main island—Wake Island—is shaped like a tilted "V" pointing southeast. Looking to starboard as they flew, the pilots could see the devastation wrought by task force bombers and fighters from the first waves: tall pillars of smoke climbing from the airfield, adjacent building, supply dumps, a complex of roads and some rainwater catchment areas.

At 11:45 a.m., the ships were still on the eastern side of the V when *Minneapolis*'s FDO Lieutenant (junior grade) Nelson H. Layman called out a bogey twenty-nine miles due west—what appeared to be several aircraft near the airfield. O'Hare's two divisions were at eight thousand five hundred feet; once they had cleared the island's southeastern tip, Layman vectored them west. At 12:05 p.m., about fifteen miles west of the cruiser formation, O'Hare spotted them ahead: three mud-colored Zekes arrayed in a loose vee headed north at about five thousand feet.

O'Hare moved his Hellcats into position, hoping to jump the unsuspecting Japanese pilots before they knew what was happening. At long last it looked as though Evil I's long-suffering fighter pilots were about to get into some real action.

———

Virtually every U.S. Navy ship acquires a nickname that comes to define the vessel's (and crew's) reputation. For good ships the names are inspiring or affectionate (Lady Lex, Big E, for example) but for bad (or hard luck) ships they can be pointedly disparaging. "Evil I," carrier *Independence*'s nickname, might have been open for interpretation, but, at least for her aviators, the moniker stood for all the things that could go wrong in carrier-based aviation.

Early in August, when Butch O'Hare first learned that VF-6 (the designation change from VF-3, made in July, reflected the squadron's Air Group 6 affiliation—though O'Hare made sure to hold tight to the squadron's emblematic Felix the Cat identity) was being assigned to *Independence*, the reaction was mixed: they were leaving the air group they'd trained with, but joining to a ship rumored to be heading for action. Then, in mid-August, when AirPac reconfigured CVL aircraft allotments, O'Hare learned VF-6 itself would be split: three divisions, including O'Hare's, would stay aboard *Independence* while three divisions (and their planes) went to *Princeton*.

This blow to squadron cohesion was only one aspect of the problem. *Independence*'s air operations were, to put it mildly, ragged. Once, during a dusk recovery while training west of Hawaii, the ship's LSO—a man known more for his dedication than skill—misplaced his illuminated signal wands. By the time he found them, the ship's radio transmitter broke down. The snafus forced three VF-6 pilots, all low on fuel, to head for shore. One pilot, Ensign Henry T. Landry, crash landed in the mountains near Kamuela and was seriously injured.

Another time, when a Hellcat rolled into a catwalk during touchdown, O'Hare learned the ship wasn't equipped to hoist the plane back on deck. Flight operations had to be canceled and the ship slouched back to Pearl with the toppled Hellcat visible for all to see.

The August 31 Marcus raid—the rumored early action that had softened the blow of being assigned to *Independence*—in the end held little excitement for VF-6. The raid itself was a great success (according to TF 15 commander Rear Admiral Charles A. Pownall, the Japanese were caught "with their pants down in the cold grey dawn"), but while fliers from

Yorktown and *Essex* had a field day, Evil I's aviators were consigned to duty carrier tasks: CAP and air-search. And while O'Hare's division (with Alex Vraciu on his wing) did manage to latch on to *Essex*'s last strike of the day, the most significant target encountered was a small Japanese fishing boat. Perhaps emblematic of Evil I's participation in the Marcus mission was the spectacle of her skipper, Captain George R. Fairlamb, Jr. (formerly CO of the Lake Michigan-bound *Wolverine*) losing his lunch—and his composure—on the ship's bridge.

Upon Evil I's return to Pearl in on September 7, even as the freshwater-going Fairlamb was being quietly and unceremoniously relieved of command, O'Hare received additional doses of good and bad news. The good (tinged with envy) was that the VF-6 contingent operating from *Princeton* had drawn first blood. On September 1, while flying CAP, Lieutenant (junior grade) Richard L. "Dix" Loesch had downed a Kawanishi H8K1 flying boat (code name Emily). Then, two days later, Lieutenant (junior grade) Thaddeus T. Coleman Jr. had bagged another. (While Loesch's downing of a slow-flying Emily didn't compare with Robert Duncan's Zeke deuce a month later, it was, nonetheless, the first aerial conquest for an F6F.)

The bad news was another round of squadron musical chairs. O'Hare lost a half a dozen planes and pilots to carrier *Cowpens*, newly arrived at Pearl. At the same time, the *Princeton* VF-6 detachment, rather than rejoining, was "cross-decked" to *Belleau Wood*. Thus, when VF-6 left Pearl en route to Wake Island, "Butch's Babies" were no longer a painstakingly melded fighter squadron. Instead, they were three separate guerrilla bands.

———

With his radio on the blink, second section leader Alex Vraciu had kept an especially close eye on O'Hare's F6F. Vraciu hadn't heard Layman's bogey vector but, when he noticed O'Hare seemed to be stalking a target, he assumed something was up. Sure enough, there were three Zekes heading north as O'Hare's Hellcats approached from the east.

O'Hare's turn to starboard put Vraciu and Ensign Allie Willis "Willie" Callan Jr., Vraciu's wingman, on the inside track. After months as O'Hare's wingman and now his second section leader, Vraciu knew exactly what was expected. O'Hare and his wingman Hank Landry (newly recovered from injuries sustained in his August crash-landing) would take the outside Zeke in the vee, while Vraciu and Callan would concentrate on the inside one.

———

O'Hare had set up his division for a steep high-side run and when they broke, O'Hare, with Landry tight on his wing, dove steeply toward the most distant Zeke. Increasing speed as he sliced in almost perpendicular to the Zeke's starboard flank, O'Hare loosed a full deflection shot and held his shooting angle as he passed astern. It was a solid punch, with rounds pounding the Zeke's cockpit and cowling. Its pilot slumped forward, smoke streamed from its dying engine, and the plane dipped its battered nose in a downward swoon towards a cloud layer.

While Landry—in the heat of the moment forgetting his wingman propers—chased after the fatally-stricken Zeke, O'Hare shifted his aim to the vee's leader. He briefly climbed onto his tail but was going too fast now to stay there and get in a shot. Its pilot had apparently spotted O'Hare's tracer overture. As O'Hare's F6F high-balled past, the Zeke rolled into a tight evasive turn. Knowing enough not to compete with a Zeke in a turn, O'Hare instead climbed to get in position for another pass.

Vraciu, meanwhile, had drawn a bead on the inside Zeke and ripped into its cowling and wing root with a sustained burst from above and to the right. Like O'Hare's victim, this plane's cowling began to stream smoke but then quickly burst into flame. Fragments of engine and fuselage, sucked into the Zeke's fiery slipstream, flew right in front of Vraciu's windscreen as he completed his run.

There it was—his first kill, the culmination of months of training.

It was thrilling—enough so to turn Vraciu heedless and careless, forgetting in a flash what all the hours of training reminded him to do next. At Marcus, he had briefly succumbed to unbridled emotion—breaking from O'Hare's wing to make an impromptu firing pass at the troublesome little Japanese fishing vessel. The CO had promptly chewed Vraciu for that indiscretion and the memory stuck.

This time Vraciu—as he was supposed to—climbed above the clouds to reestablish contact with his division leader, but O'Hare was nowhere to be seen. Willie Callan, meanwhile (after taking pot shots at O'Hare's doomed Zeke and—it turned out—at Sy Mendenhall's second division Hellcat), had broken off the fight to join up with his section leader. When Vraciu spotted a lone Zeke racing for Wake's airfield, the two set off to get him.

Vraciu and Callan caught up with the Zeke just after it touched down. Sensing what was about to happen, the Zeke pilot taxied his plane off the runway, leapt from his cockpit and bolted for cover. Swooping down on the vacated Zeke, the two Hellcats quickly torched it and then, zigzagging across the field, did the same to a parked Betty.

With still no sign of Butch and with both planes low on fuel and ammunition, Vraciu and Callan flew northeast towards the Evil I.

———

"Tally ho," O'Hare radioed *Minneapolis* as he and wingman Landry got back on station above the cruisers. "Shot down two, other one not sure."

It was now around 12:20 p.m. and another bogey had been picked up, this one tracking south of Wake. Landry gave the vector to O'Hare and, twenty miles out, he and his wingman found the culprit. It was a Betty, the first that O'Hare had seen aloft since his eventful ace-making encounter in February 1942.

When O'Hare fired after making a high side head-on run, he found that only one wing gun was working. Still, some bullets had hit and done some damage to one of the Betty's engines. Landry followed with another high side firing pass, but his took him astern of the Betty, where the tail gunner lobbed cannon rounds until Landry ducked out of the way.

By then, however, O'Hare was in position for his second, one-gun pass. Aiming unerringly for the wing root, O'Hare deftly took the crippled Betty out.

———

A picture of O'Hare taken on the flight deck of *Independence* that day shows a happy, if weary squadron CO. He is still wearing his flight suit, though his Mae West collar is hanging down and he (or someone) has plopped a steel helmet—facing backwards—atop his head. O'Hare displays a thumbs-up, and with good reason. The Wake raids were going well (so well, that they would continue for a second day), and his boys, though split among three carriers, were doing their share (combined, their aerial claims would total four Zekes, one Betty and one Nell[1]).

From a personal standpoint, O'Hare also had every reason to be pleased—perhaps even relieved. By sundown that day, he would log 7.8 hours of combat flight time—a lot, but his escapades no longer threatened to thrust him into the spotlight. Perhaps best of all, his composure, his flying skill, and his aim were all intact. O'Hare's minutes over the Lexington a year-and-a-half before were no fluke.

Butch O'Hare had chalked up his sixth and seventh kills—and had every reason to expect he would get more.

———

1. Mitsubishi G3M Type 96 land-based attack aircraft

18
BUTCH MAY BE DOWN

On November 18, 1943, when the VF-6 pilots set out for Tarawa on a pre-dawn fighter sweep, they pretty much knew what to expect and what to do. After all, they'd been seasoned: at Marcus in September, Wake in October and Rabaul just days before.

Not that Butch O'Hare wasn't missed. Since first joining the squadron, Alex Vraciu had either flown wing or second section lead for O'Hare. The frustration of having the squadron detached from Air Group 6 and then chopped up among several CVLs had been eased by O'Hare's steady presence. Still, it was the nature of the war. Some people went down while others moved up, out or both.

The change had occurred immediately after Wake. Instead of flying to Maui with his three divisions, O'Hare had ridden *Independence* all the way into Pearl where his new orders were waiting. On October 13, back at Puunene, O'Hare assumed overall command of Air Group 6. There'd been no opportunity to congratulate him—or for that matter to say goodbye.

The promotion left O'Hare a CAG without a carrier until *Enterprise* returned from a Bremerton refit. Air Group 10, Big E's home team for the past year, would arrive with her but be pulled ashore for more training at Maui while Air Group 6 took its place. Any plan O'Hare might have had for bringing VF-6 back into the fold was not to be. *Enterprise* was not due at Pearl until early November and the VF-6 detachments would be put to use well before then. Divisions I, II, and III, for example, were readying to leave aboard *Independence* on October 21, bound for the South Pacific. Instead, O'Hare had to settle for VF-2, the only squadron available. No longer the legendary "Fighting Chiefs" (that squadron had been disbanded), VF-2's "Rippers" were mostly rookies, part of a newly-constituted Air Group.

———

The darkness was the most dangerous element. Until there was some glimmer of morning light, Vraciu had learned, the mission wasn't about blasting the enemy. It was about finding the rest of your division and taking proper station in the strike formation. With running lights out and radios silenced, the best—often only—identification markers were the telltale engine exhaust flares.

It was the eerie black void that made the sudden flash of tracer rounds so frightening. Bodies tensed, pulses raced and heads swiveled. Then, as abruptly as it started, the firing stopped.

It turned out that VF-6's new skipper, Lieutenant Commander Harry W. "Stinky" Harrison Jr., had chosen the moment to test his guns. Even with the mystery solved, everyone (except perhaps Harrison) stayed on edge. It was something that Butch's Boys would never do, especially in pitch-black conditions like these.

———

The softening-up of Tarawa's beachheads by *Essex*, *Bunker Hill* and *Independence* aircraft raised the curtain on Galvanic—code name for the Gilbert Island amphibious invasions scheduled for November 20, 1943. Galvanic in turn marked the unveiling of the Central Pacific multi-carrier, multi-group task force. Indeed, by mid-November, the pace of new arrivals in the Pacific was such that three-carrier divisions (CarDivs, unimaginable luxuries just months before) no longer qualified as full-scale task forces. Instead they were designated Carrier Task Groups (CTG), smaller subsets of a vastly expanded Fifth Fleet. CarDiv 12's *Essex*, *Bunker Hill* and *Independence*, for example, were the core of CTG 50.3.

TF 50, Galvanic's umbrella organization, consisted of four CTGs with a combined total of eleven fast carriers. CTG 50.3, designated the "Southern Carrier Group," was assigned to cover Tarawa. Its Makin counterpart, the "Northern Carrier Group," was CTG 50.2—CarDiv 11 carriers *Enterprise*, *Belleau Wood* and *Monterey* (CVL-26). CTG 50.1, a third group centered on *Yorktown*, *Lexington* and *Cowpens* (CarDiv 3), and designated the "Carrier Interceptor Group," was to take station between the Gilberts and Marshalls, ready to intercept Japanese air attacks from the north. A final group, CTG 50.4—CarDiv 1's *Saratoga* and *Princeton*—was to be a

"Relief Carrier Group," held in reserve near the Solomons but ready to race north if help was needed.

The new groupings brought with them the idiosyncrasies of two familiar command names: 50.1's pleasant, affable, battle-skittish Charles A. "Baldy" Pownall; and 50.4's Frederick C. "Ted" Sherman, of the painful teeth and worse temper. But there were also a couple of new personalities: 50.3's Rear Admiral Alfred E. "Monty" Montgomery, fifty-two, a migraine sufferer who was brusque, impatient and unpopular but well-respected; and 50.2's Rear Admiral Arthur W. "Raddy" Radford, just forty-seven but an aviator since age twenty-four, known to be quiet and slow of speech but also brilliant, decisive, innovative and tough-minded.

––––––

The Gilberts were not entirely terra incognita to the Navy, the Marines or select elements of TF 50. In August 1942, a small group of Marine Raiders launched offshore from two submarines had staged a commando raid on Makin, overrunning a small Japanese garrison before withdrawing. Meant as a ruse to draw attention away from Guadalcanal, the raid produced unintended consequences. Alerted to their vulnerability in the Gilberts, the Japanese turned previously unoccupied Tarawa—the other Galvanic objective—into a heavily defended fortress.

Tarawa and Makin had also been the focus of a September 18 practice raid—a follow-up to Marcus, a prelude to Wake. Aircraft from *Lexington*, *Princeton* and *Belleau Wood* (then constituted as TF 11 under CarDiv 11's Radford), following pretty much the same procedures employed at Marcus, took swipes at Tarawa's airfields and anchorages before doing the same to Makin.

Not surprisingly, the September raid once again stirred the enemy hornet nest. On the day of the strike, Japan's Mobile Fleet—three carriers with escorting battleships, cruisers and destroyers—set sail from Truk to intervene. They got as far as Eniwetok in the northern Marshalls on September 20, but, with the American carriers already long-gone, they returned to Truk.

Concern that the Japanese might sortie again weighed on the minds of Raymond Spruance and Richmond Kelly Turner, Galvanic's top commanders. The prospect influenced their planning and particularly how they would use—in the aviators' minds, misuse—Galvanic's carrier riches.

––––––

Not long after carrier *Enterprise* left Pearl en route to the Gilberts, CTG

50.2's Arthur Radford met in Flag Plot with Big E's new CO 46-year-old Captain Matthias B. "Matt" Gardner and new CAG Butch O'Hare.

Radford, a Navy wunderkind who had reached flag rank in 1943 without ever commanding a ship, was worried. Galvanic called for the assignment of CTGs to restricted defensive sectors, an arrangement, Radford told Gardner and O'Hare, he considered dangerous. While at Pearl and in company with Pownall and Montgomery, Radford had presented his concerns directly to Spruance, arguing that a better use of the CTGs was to untether them to launch peremptory strikes at Japanese air bases in the northern Marshalls. But Spruance, ever cautious and precise in his planning, refused to budge.

Radford also showed Gardner and O'Hare dispatches just in from the South Pacific which, to all appearances, contained terrific news. On November 11, Monty Montgomery's CarDiv 12 carriers *Essex*, *Bunker Hill* and *Independence* had savaged Fortress Rabaul and afterwards handily repulsed daylight retaliation raids by land-based aircraft—in the process splashing upwards of eighty enemy aircraft.

Japanese air commanders in the Marshalls, Radford was certain, must have been appalled by such devastating daytime losses. They had to realize their best hope against Galvanic's carriers were hit-and-run aerial torpedo attacks, especially at night.

If they launched such attacks, their job would only be made easier by Galvanic's tight rein on TF 50's carriers. The sector idea, Radford was certain, made the CTGs "little more than sitting ducks." For his part, though, Radford did not intend to act like one—relying solely on maneuvering and shipboard antiaircraft gunnery to defend his carriers. He ordered O'Hare to stitch together a night-fighting capability from the resources on hand.

———

Beyond the damage inflicted on the Japanese at Marcus, Tarawa and Wake, the Central Pacific warm-up raids had been opportunities to test carrier task force tactics. Cruising groups of different sizes had been used. New ship handling techniques had been practiced and refined. And circular formations of two-, three- and even six-carrier task groups had been tried out. The warm-ups had been useful, but if there was an operation that truly showcased the power and mobility of the fast carrier task forces, it was the early November pummeling of Fortress Rabaul.

On November 1 (even as the Central Pacific admirals debated and fretted over the use of carriers in Galvanic), William Halsey had sent troops ashore at Bougainville, his last substantial objective in the Solomons. To support the invasion, aircraft from Ted Sherman's carriers *Saratoga* and *Princeton* (then under Halsey's TF 38 banner) had struck Japanese airfields in northern Bougainville, but they had kept well to the west in open waters and then quickly withdrawn.

Halsey's new offensive at once triggered Japanese actions to reinforce nearby Rabaul. Hundreds of carrier-based aircraft had been shifted to its air bases and a cruiser-destroyer flotilla was dispatched from Truk. When long-range search planes pinpointed the Japanese warships in Rabaul's Simpson Harbor, Halsey realized his Bougainville foothold faced a considerable air-sea threat.

True to character, Halsey decided to use Sherman's carriers to pummel the enemy cruisers while they still lay at anchor. Doing so, however, involved two huge risks. First, it would put *Saratoga* and *Princeton* easily within range of Rabaul's beefed-up air forces. Second, the planned strike would require all of TF 38's roughly 100 carrier aircraft. In the meantime, carrier defense would fall to land-based fighters from airfields in the southern Solomons.

———

In the end, Halsey's gamble paid off handsomely. At 9:00 a.m. on November 5, 23 TBFs, 22 SBDs and 52 F6Fs set out for Rabaul. Leading the escort fighters was VF-12 CO Commander Joseph C. "Jumpin' Joe" Clifton. Air Group 12 had yet to see any action, but Clifton had thoroughly trained his fighter pilots to stick with their charges like fleas on a hound. Clifton's philosophy was: "...get them in there, get them out and get them home—no dogfighting."

As the American aircraft approached Rabaul, the Japanese were waiting—dozens of Zekes circling the fringes of a cauldron of flak. But the defenders below also evidenced surprise. Some ships were just pulling up anchor, while others were maneuvering erratically.

Down came the strike planes—and right with them Clifton's single-minded escorts. The Japanese fighters circled, waiting for the Hellcats to break off and head their way. Instead, Clifton's pilots stuck to the bombers and torpeckers all the way down, through and out of the gauntlet. (Indicative of the punishment withstood by Clifton's boys, the VF-12 Hellcat covering CAG Commander Howard H. Caldwell's Avenger returned to *Princeton* pocked with 200 bullet holes.) The Zekes, meanwhile, unable to lure the Hellcats but unwilling to risk friendly fire, were left out of the action.

Of the 97 strike planes sent, only eight (five of them Hellcats) failed to make it back. They left behind them a crippled Japanese surface force: at least six damaged cruisers. "A glorious victory," an elated Ted Sherman scribbled in his war diary as TF 38 high-tailed it south, "a second Pearl Harbor in reverse."

But there was more. Answering Halsey's pleas for more carrier support, Nimitz had dispatched Monty Montgomery's CarDiv12, which arrived in the South Pacific on November 5, ready to lend a hand. Ted Sherman, who had never imagined a gathering of five carriers, was eager to use them all at once for another go at Rabaul from the south. Halsey was eager as well, but added a twist: Routing Sherman to the south of Rabaul while dispatching CarDiv 12 to the north, Halsey ordered combined November 11 strikes aimed, as later described in his memoirs, at changing "the name of Rabaul to Rubble."

On the morning of the strike, aircraft from *Saratoga* and *Princeton* battled heavy weather to make the first hits. Planes from *Bunker Hill*, *Essex*, and *Independence* had better luck in the afternoon, torpedoing and sinking a Japanese light cruiser, bombing and sinking a destroyer. VF-6's Alex Vraciu, who flew a TBF cover mission and got in some strafing on a cruiser, watched in disbelief as Zeke bystanders once again flirted unsuccessfully for the Hellcats' attention.

———

"Man your guns and shoot those bastards out of the sky!" Monty Montgomery's exhortation to his gunners via *Bunker Hill's* loudspeaker announced the Rabaul mission's moment of truth. Having absorbed punishment in the morning and early afternoon, Rabaul had launched an afternoon retaliatory strike of more than one hundred fighters and bombers aimed directly at CarDiv12.

Already, forty miles to the south, CAP aircraft from five fighter squadrons (Hellcats from CarDiv 12's three VFs plus Corsairs from two land-based Marine Corps squadrons) had worked over the assailants. Now the bogeys were approaching and waiting for them, along with the ships' five-inch, 40- and 20-mm gunners, were even more American fighters.

The carrier captains held their own during the afternoon duel (clocked at 46 minutes), successfully maneuvering *Bunker Hill*, *Essex* and *Independence* clear of torpedoes and bombs. Pilots and ships' gunners, meanwhile, claimed the downing of an additional two dozen enemy aircraft—in exchange for eleven American losses.

After having returned from Rabaul to rearm and refuel aboard *Independence*, Alex Vraciu's Hellcat was among the CAP aircraft sent aloft in the waning moments of the air-sea battle. He got two vectors—one to a patch of empty sky, the other to what proved to be a twin-engine friendly. To his frustration and disappointment, Vraciu never got in a shot.

The experience of the fast carriers at Rabaul had lessons to teach. Gambling on the advantages of offensive mobility, Halsey had deployed carriers to take on a major Japanese fleet and air base. In the process, not only had he wrought havoc on that base and successfully defended his carriers, but he had secured his original offensive objective—the conquest of Bougainville.

Unfortunately, as compelling as the lessons seemed to the aviators, on Spruance's and Turner's part there was neither time nor inclination to consider, argue or adopt them. Galvanic's die had been cast. With Montgomery's TG 50.3 already at sea (and racing north to take station off Tarawa), the balance of TF 50's carriers and escorts had sortied from Pearl on November 10.

Using fighter aircraft as night interceptors was neither a new ambition nor an entirely new reality. As early as 1915, Britain's Royal Flying Corps had launched nighttime "cat's-eye" missions in which fighters, aided by ground searchlights, countered German zeppelin raids. Similar tactics were used during the Battle of Britain, although searchlights increasingly gave way to the use of radar technologies.

Ironically, it was Guadalcanal's "Washing-Machine Charlie" that galvanized the U.S. Navy's interest in aerial night-fighting equipment and tactics. Rear Admiral John S. McCain (grandfather of the future U.S. senator and presidential candidate), ComAirSoPac during Cactus' first days, was livid that nothing was done about Charlie's nighttime forays except cower in foxholes and bunkers. What made it all the more infuriating was that the Japanese had no airborne radar. Instead, they depended on ingenuity, employing pathfinder aircraft (the sailors called them "Lamplighters") and relatively simple illumination devices such as parachute flares and (over water) floating lights to reveal target course.

When he became BuAer's head, "Slew" McCain spurred Radford (then still in charge of stateside naval aviation training) to look into night-fighting options. But he likewise turned to Grumman, which, before the war, had developed a promising experimental twin-engine aircraft (a potential rival to the twin-boomed Lockheed P-38) called the XP-50. Using the XP-50 concept as a foundation, the Iron Works set to work producing the prototype of a fast, heavily-armed, radar-equipped night fighter—the XF7F-1. The new aircraft, its long, slender nose crammed with radar gear, showed true promise, but it would not be ready for its first flight until December. On a different track, Commander Gus Widhelm, the dive-bombing hero of the Battle of the Santa Cruz Islands, was experimenting with a detachment of five radar-equipped F4U Corsairs. But, like the XF7F-1, Widhelm's equipment and tactics were still in the incubator stage.

Absent these options, what Butch O'Hare had at his disposal was a jury-rigged combination of human effort and still-rudimentary ship and aircraft technologies. Newly installed aboard *Enterprise* was a height-finding radar system (designated SM) used for tracking low-level aircraft. With practice, the SM could be used in tandem with longer-range SK aerial search radar equipment. Aloft, O'Hare could choose between two radar-equipped "hunters": VT-6's TBF-1C Avengers or VB-6's SBD-5 Dauntlesses. Both were equipped with primitive short-range radar— called the ASB-1—designed to find surface targets. The ASB-1 used two wing-mounted antennae, and its operator searched manually, one side (wing) at a time. Because of its greater endurance, O'Hare chose the TBF as his night "hunter." The Avenger would be teamed with two fast, lethal but night-blind Hellcat "killers."

For a host of reasons, O'Hare's night intercept concept looked like an effort based more on wishful thinking than certainty. Night flying was inherently risky and night fighting took the risks to a new plateau. The plan was being thrown together from scratch, in a hurry and with no opportunity to confer with BuAer or even fellow-experimenters like Gus Widhelm.

Success depended on complex on-the-fly teamwork among many players: the FDO, Lieutenant (junior grade) George P. Givens, a veteran of the Battles of the Eastern Solomons and Santa Cruz Islands; the Combat Information Center (CIC) personnel manning the SM and SK radars; the TBF pilot and his radar operator; and, of course, the F6F triggermen. Task force radio silence and overall operational secrecy made practice nearly out of the question. (One ace-in-the-hole, known only to Radford, was the ability of a small radio intelligence unit aboard *Enterprise* to eavesdrop on Japanese aircraft radio traffic.) O'Hare's best chance was to find and snuff out Japanese shads (shadowers)—thereby preventing the attacks altogether.

Though its concept and resources were shaky, the need for the night fighter capability was only too apparent. On November 13, in the very type of pre-dawn attack anticipated by Radford, light cruiser *Denver* (CL-58), steaming off Bougainville, was struck and damaged by an aerial torpedo. Then, after dark on the 18th, Montgomery's Southern Carrier Group was stalked, first by a shad and then by two bogey formations of ten to fifteen aircraft. Most of the enemy aircraft flew entirely past the task group, but not before one—a Betty—was engaged and torched by ship gunners.

The Japanese indeed seemed intent on slipping in after dark to take out the American flattops.

————

BOOM! The torpedo explosion that erupted on carrier *Independence*'s starboard quarter near dusk on November 20 reverberated through the length, breadth and depth of the ship. The accompanying sights, sounds and sensations were frightening, even sickening. But, for virtually all the ship's crew, the distress was at least coupled with things that had to be done—usually vital things.

Topside, gunners still had to fire away at the low-flying torpedo-laden Bettys. Below decks, damage control parties had to rush to the scene of the explosion to douse fires, shore bulkheads and contain damage. Simultaneously, medical personnel and ship's chaplains had to plunge into the chaos to minister to the agonies of wounded, dead or dying shipmates. Electrician's mates, machinist mates, communications and radar technicians, ship fitters, quartermasters and compatriots in a host of other specialty ratings had to quickly alleviate or adroitly reroute the explosion's damage to the Hydra of functions, systems and capabilities that kept the ship afloat and functioning.

The danger to each man was usually not directly less because of what he was doing individually in this all-hands effort. (Though certainly the fate of all might well depend on what he accomplished.) But just as important for the moment, his effort could—and often did—displace his fear.

In that sense at least, it was the dismounted aviators waiting in the squadron ready rooms who had the most susceptibility to free-floating fear.

Many had flown earlier in the day. Alex Vraciu had been relaxing in the ready room after completing a CAP mission and scoring a kill—his second confirmed—on a fleeing Betty. Other squadron personnel had been topside when the fireworks started, but as the attack intensified, most had retreated to the ready room. Now, in the aftermath of the jolting explosion, Vraciu watched with some interest the expressions and actions of the other fliers—men who seldom registered fear in grueling aerial combat or difficult carrier landings. Most faces—not least Vraciu's—betrayed the understandable unease of being on the interior of a ship that even now might be in danger of sinking. A few not wearing their Mae Wests went to retrieve them.

To Vraciu's great surprise, however, one of the squadron's senior lieutenants immediately dropped to his knees, clasped his hands together, raised his eyes to the overhead, and began praying—aloud and with unrestrained supplication.

––––––

In contrast to the deceptively uncontested opening hours of the Guadalcanal landings (up until the morning of November 20, 1943, the U.S. Marine Corps' only substantial experience with amphibious warfare), the first hours of the November 20th Tarawa invasion were no stroll on the beach for the men of the 2nd Marine Division. By the time the first three waves stepped ashore on Betio, a tiny island in the atoll's southwest corner, the Japanese defenders—later estimated to number some five thousand men—were out of their reinforced shelters and relentlessly mowing down the invaders with volleys of rifle and machine gun fire.

By early afternoon, an equal number of Marines had landed, but with so many casualties that they were vulnerable to counterattack. The Japanese should have struck that night, but they too were prostrate. Half of the enemy garrison was dead by nightfall, and Japanese communications had been knocked out by naval gunfire and aerial assault.

The outcome was likely decided then, but it would take another four days—at a cost of a thousand Marine fatalities—to secure Tarawa's few acres of coral. Meanwhile, 105 miles to the north, the operation to secure Makin, while considerably less costly—GIs of the U.S. Army's 27th Division confronted under a thousand defenders, most of them Korean labor troops—took virtually the same amount of time.

And, through it all, the TF 50 carriers stayed in their defensive sectors and sparred with intruders lunging for them in the dark.

––––––

On the evening of November 20th, as the exhausted 2nd Division Marines clung to their Tarawa beachhead and the torpedo-stricken carrier *Independence* withdrew south to sanctuary in the Ellice Islands, the Northern Carrier Group's Arthur Radford approved the first of what would be three Butch O'Hare-devised night interceptor plans.

The initial plan showed an abundance of caution. It restricted night flights to a window between midnight and dawn—a means of ensuring the aircraft had enough fuel to stay aloft until sunrise. During that window, TBFs would launch if ship's radar detected bogeys, with Hellcats to follow only if an attack was imminent and weather conditions permitted.

It didn't take long, though, for some of the caution to give way to O'Hare's conviction that the TBFs and F6Fs could operate throughout as fully integrated teams. The midnight to dawn window held (for now), but instead of being launched separately, the TBF and two F6Fs would immediately rendezvous and form up in a tight vee as the radar-equipped TBF guided the F6Fs to the bogey. Once the F6Fs had visual contact, the TBF would lift "up and out" and the F6Fs would attack.

With that concept in mind, O'Hare organized his "Black Panthers" into two night-fighting teams. Team 1 combined Hellcats piloted by O'Hare and VF-2 wingman, twenty-four-year-old Ensign Warren A. "Andy" Skon, with an Avenger flown by VT-6 CO Lieutenant Commander John L. Phillips Jr.

———

On November 26th, three days after *Independence*'s arrival at Funafuti in the Ellice Islands and the unloading of her aircraft, Stinky Harrison's VF-6 contingent was sent island-hopping north with vague instructions to rejoin TF 50. Their first stop was Nanumea, like Funafuti, a tranquil South Pacific atoll untouched by war's devastation. But if the pilots were lulled by the interlude of tropical serenity, the spell was broken when they reached their next destination.

The hard fighting on Tarawa's Betio Island was largely over by November 27th, but some Japanese were still holding out, hiding in caves or bunkers—waiting to shoot or be torched or blasted. By the time the mopping up eventually ended, only seventeen Japanese soldiers along with 129 Korean labor troops would be captured alive. The VF-6 pilots were supposed to sleep overnight in their cockpits on Betio's crater-pocked Hawkins Field (newly reopened for business and re-named to honor a fallen Marine officer), but the sound of gunfire soon drove them to the shelter of a tent in a Marine encampment. All night Vraciu and the others stayed flat on the deck, taking no chances with stray bullets.

The next morning, the fliers took a look around. Carnage was evident everywhere. The Marines warned them about booby-traps and told them not to touch anything. The assault troops, the fliers learned, had spent their first night ashore at Betio on a beachhead scarcely twenty feet wide. Many of the pillboxes and bunkers supposedly destroyed by ship guns or aerial bombs and strafing had remained intact and the enemy had used them to full advantage. The savage battle might well have been lost had individual ground-level courage not overcome unimaginable adversity.

Just before takeoff on the 28th, Harrison's fliers finally got their orders. They were to join carrier *Essex*, now operating south off Makin. It was not until they had touched down on *Essex* that Butch's Boys learned what had happened to their iconic leader.

It had been about 7:20 p.m. on November 26th, with Radford's TG 50.2 steaming south from Makin toward Tarawa, when John Phillips' TBF began to close in on the unsuspecting bogey. *Enterprise*'s FDO George Givens had supplied the original vector and then coached Phillips to put him just astern and slightly below a cluster of bogeys waiting twenty-five miles north of the task group.

Torpedo-equipped enemy aircraft were then attacking TG 50.2's perimeter. All ships save the carriers were cleared to open fire. Already, battleships *North Carolina*, *Indiana* (BB-58) and *Massachusetts* (BB-59), along with destroyer *Fletcher* (DD-445) were banging out five-inch projectiles armed with potent new Mark 32 proximity fuses. Meanwhile, beginning at 7:12 p.m., warnings rang out over the TBS circuit of torpedo wakes coursing through the formation.

Phillips' radar operator, twenty-five-year-old Lieutenant (junior grade) Hazen B. Rand (an MIT-educated electrical engineer attached to VT-6 as a radar instructor) finally picked up bogeys, distance three miles. Phillips was flying entirely on instruments by then, while Rand, sitting below in the radio compartment, kept his face close to the ASB-1's small green scope.

Rand eyed the bogey—a phosphor of light—as it wandered down from the top of the square screen. He called out the bogey's proximity to Phillips as the phosphor drifted into the scope's calibrated range circles:

"Two miles . . . mile and a half . . . a mile. . . ."

It was only then that Phillips looked up from his red-lit instrument gauges to scan the darkness ahead. Remarkably, he could see what he was looking for: the uneven blue flashes from an aircraft's exhaust stacks.

"I have them in sight, attacking," Phillips radioed *Enterprise* before adding throttle and charging his wing guns. Below, Rand had switched the scope to a larger scale.

"One thousand yards . . . eight hundred yards . . . six hundred. . . ."

Phillips could just make out the shadowy, but unmistakable silhouette—a Betty. He checked his altitude—1,200 feet. Then his speed and attitude—190 knots in level flight.

"Four hundred . . . Two. . . ."

Phillips squeezed his trigger, loosing two long red tracer streams. He held the trigger as the gap to the Betty's tail section narrowed. The TBF's fuselage and wings shivered from the recoil of the .50 caliber guns.

At fifty yards Phillips saw fires sprout from the Betty's left wing root. He stopped firing and pulled away, confident that dampeners installed on his engine exhaust ports would keep them from being detected. Next, Phillips leveled off to unmask his turret gunner, aviation ordnance man twenty-year-old Alvin B. Kernan. Kernan, although new to the turret assignment, was already a two-year veteran of VT-6's ordnance gang and had been selected to go into flight training after Big E's Pacific tour.

As Kernan swiveled the ball turret to starboard and fired down at the burning aircraft, the enemy gunners finally opened fire from tail, and side blisters. One enemy 7.7- millimeter incendiary round tore through the TBF's belly to ricochet in the radar compartment and graze Rand's left foot. But it was too late and too little—the Betty suddenly exploded in bright flame. Jettisoning its torpedo, the enemy plane crashed into the water where sections of its fuel-soaked wreckage would blaze for hours.

"Scratch one of the bastards," Phillips radioed triumphantly at 7:23 p.m.

Against a background of cheers and backslapping in CIC, Givens instructed Phillips (then at five hundred feet) to climb to two thousand feet and orbit. Phillips began to circle, but before he could climb he spotted the exhaust flames of two more Bettys at his altitude. Phillips selected one of the bombers and followed it through a slow right turn, all the while narrowing the distance and readying to fire.

Then all at once Phillips heard another voice on the circuit: "Turn on your lights. I'm going to start shooting." And moments later: "Phil this is Butch. I think I got me a Jap."

———

Two days before, Arthur Radford had approved the latest and boldest version of O'Hare's Black Panther tactics. Discarding the limitations of the midnight to dawn time window, a Black Panther team would instead be launched at sunset and immediately go bogey hunting. Its TBF and F6Fs would stay entirely clear of the task group, instead using the newly re-opened airstrip at Betio as a landing site when the mission concluded.

In no small part, the aggressive plan was borne of the past days' frustrations. There'd been distant shads aplenty and even the occasional Betty flying directly over a ship at masthead height. But Radford had been conservative about unleashing the Black Panthers—and probably for good reason. The Japanese aircraft seemed to be—and likely were—groping blindly. Opening fire or launching night fighters when the enemy planes were so close only risked revealing the task force's exact location. Not least, Radford had to be careful not to tip off his top secret eavesdropping. Better to take advantage whenever possible of timely maneuvering and opportune clouds and squalls.

O'Hare's two teams had been aloft early in the morning of November 24th, the day before Thanksgiving, hoping to intercept Japanese bombers bound for Tarawa, but they never came close. Then, shortly after 5:00 a.m. they had seen see a brilliant flash of light to the east and below the clouds. It turned out to be a submarine strike on *Liscome Bay* (CVE-56), an escort carrier attached to Turner's Makin amphibious force. With one pre-dawn torpedo, the Japanese had sunk a carrier and claimed the lives of more than six hundred sailors and airmen.

The sun was just about to go down when Skon, O'Hare, and then Phillips had been catapulted on the 26th. When O'Hare had emerged from the ready room with his flight gear he ran into United Press correspondent Charles P. Arnot. "Stocky Butch was pulling on his helmet over his close-cropped black hair," Arnot later wrote in a newspaper dispatch. "One of the pilots shouted, 'Go gettem, Butch.' O'Hare's reply was a grin. Then he dashed up a ladder to the flight deck."

The plan at launch was to have the three aircraft form up before setting off, but FDO Givens, hoping to splash nearby bogeys while there was still some daylight, first vectored O'Hare and Skon to the east. When Radford gruffly countermanded Givens's instructions, the FDO sheepishly reined in the F6Fs. By then, however, they had outpaced Phillips and the TBF was hard put to catch up.

The three had still not joined up when the sun set and twilight gave way to a black, moonless and overcast night. And soon there were so many bogeys lighting the CIC radar screens that the rendezvous became a secondary matter. Coached by Givens, the faster O'Hare and Skon hunted as a team to the north and northwest while the slower Phillips cut inside their turns, still trying to catch up.

"Can you join us on Phil?" O'Hare finally radioed Givens a few minutes after he and Skon noticed flaming wreckage—Phillips's first kill—several miles to the west.

"Affirmative," Givens replied and soon advised that Phillips was just slightly to port, four miles away—almost close enough to spot if Phillips showed a recognition light.

It was then that O'Hare had radioed Phillips who, though just about to bounce the Betty and anxious not to spook him, also didn't want to take friendly fire.

"Roger. Wilco. Out," Phillips snapped over the circuit and blinked his recognition light, all the while advancing on the Betty. The sudden light may have indeed spooked its pilots into an evasive turn, but by then Phillips was as close as he needed to be. A quick burst to the starboard wing root and cockpit torched the Betty and sent it to the water where it disintegrated and sank.

At 7:28 p.m., even as O'Hare and Skon closed—expecting at any moment to have the TBF in sight—Phillips called out his second kill.

"Which side do you want, Andy," O'Hare asked Skon.

The two were then in a gradual left turn, with Skon just below O'Hare and on the inside track. "I'll take port."

"Roger," O'Hare acknowledged—his last word.

Anticipating rendezvous, both O'Hare and Phillips switched on their dorsal white recognition signals.

"This is duck soup, Butch," a jubilant Phillips was exclaiming on the radio. "If you ride in on their slipstream and then just pick them off one at a time."

About then turret gunner Kernan detected a white light to port. He got ready to fire, but soon realized it was one of the approaching Hellcats, coming in high across the TBF's tail. The second Hellcat followed close behind.

But then Kernan also noticed a third aircraft—above and considerably behind the two friendlies. He alerted Phillips over the intercom.

"Butch," Phillips's voice came urgently over both radio and intercom. "There's a Jap joining up on you. I'm instructing Kernan to fire."

Moments before, Kernan had attached a new magazine to the turret gun. He opened up on the intruder with a long burst. From his vantage point at the starboard window of the TBF, Rand, now in some pain from his wounded foot, saw tracers stream down towards the starboard Hellcat.

With his ammunition expended, Kernan watched the intruder break away to port and disappear. Then the starboard Hellcat dropped off to port as well.

As yet Andy Skon had seen neither the TBF nor the intruder, but he had noticed a flash of tracers off to starboard and then the specter of O'Hare's Hellcat slicing down. Unsure if O'Hare had gone into a firing run or simply lost control, Skon first tried the radio but got no answer. Then Skon nosed down to follow, only to lose sight of O'Hare's recognition light. After dropping below three hundred feet, Skon finally pulled up to rejoin Phillips.

Phillips, meanwhile, was also trying to raise his team leader. "Butch, this is Phil. Over. Butch, this is Phil. Over." Still no response.

Moments later, Phillips relayed to *Enterprise's* CIC what a room full of officers and sailors had already surmised. "Butch may be down."

At 10:50 p.m., Radford broke radio silence to alert Tarawa of the exact position where O'Hare's plane had gone down and to request a rescue search after dawn. A search by VT-6 was also scheduled for the morning, but neither effort found a trace of Lieutenant Commander Edward Henry "Butch" O'Hare.

———

The Central Pacific task force that set sail from Pearl in late January 1944 had a new name, a new boss, many faults to address, many things still to prove—and many scores to settle.

Galvanic, which had wrapped up in December, had achieved its objectives but with grievous human loss and a host of operational flaws. Close air support at Tarawa had been poor and inefficient, complicated by breakdowns in ship-to-shore communications. Pilots were naïve enough to think they'd successfully completed their missions, while the Marines ashore knew otherwise. Task force defense had likewise been less than stellar—witness the damage to *Independence* and the sinking (with heavy losses) of *Liscome Bay*.

More problems ensued when Spruance sent six carriers under Baldy Pownall to neutralize enemy air resources in the Marshalls. Strikes at Kwajalein on December 4th had been poorly planned and executed with little damage to Japanese facilities, aircraft or ships. Then, to make matters worse, Pownall declined a second day of strikes—leaving many Bettys parked and unscathed on Roi Atoll's airfield. Retreating south and slowed by heavy weather, Pownall's carriers were exposed to more land-based night torpedo attacks. One aerial torpedo damaged carrier *Lexington*. Only skillful maneuvering saved the others. Afterwards, when *Yorktown's* CO Captain Joseph J. "Jocko" Clark went in secret to CincPac headquarters brandishing incriminating photographs of untouched enemy targets, Pownall's TF 50 command days were numbered.

Called into replace Pownall was Rear Admiral Marc Mitscher, then Commander Fleet Air West Coast. Mitscher, upon his arrival at Pearl, immediately relieved Pownall as Commander CarDiv 3. Next day the fast carriers became TF 58 (the counterpart to Halsey's TF 38), with Mitscher in charge (as senior carrier division commander) for the upcoming Marshall Islands campaign, operation Flintlock.

While Pacific aviators were particularly enthused to have Mitscher at the helm of the fast carriers, Mitscher bore some scars from his earlier Pacific War tour. He was remembered for captaining *Hornet* during the Doolittle Raid, but Mitscher's stature had suffered considerably at Midway. Misdirection of *Hornet's* strike force effectively left the carrier and most of her air group out of the battle equation. VT-8 had been all but massacred. *Hornet's* bombing and fighter squadrons never engaged the enemy but still lost precious aircraft and priceless pilots.

Part of the problem then had been Mitscher's reliance on BuAer cronies unfit to lead squadrons in combat. But another personal shortfall, then and since, was his stubborn underutilization of even the best staff resources. Mitscher often showed no interest in details, preferring instead concise verbal summaries from subordinates. Yet Mitscher was also prone to relying on personal instincts, sometimes shunning all advice.

———

Both the Central Pacific strategy and its TF 58 workhorses (twelve fast carriers, including new arrivals *Intrepid* [CV-11], *Langley* [CVL-27], and *Cabot* [CVL-28], in four CTGs) faced crucial tests in the Marshalls. If Japanese resistance proved as murderous as it had been at Tarawa or if the carrier task performed as unevenly, then the Central Pacific path might be subordinated to Douglas MacArthur's advance through New Guinea and into the Philippines.

Flintlock's overall objective was Kwajalein—at sixty-six miles long and eighteen miles wide, the largest atoll in the world. First on the agenda, in the north, was the capture of Roi and Namur by the 4th Marine Division. Assuming success at Roi-Namur, Kwajalein itself would thereafter be invaded by the 27th Army Division.

Neither operation called for a full frontal assault. Instead, initial landings were to be made on small islets where artillery could prepare the way for larger assaults. There would also be longer and more intensive softening up before D-Day. Accordingly, practice en route to Kwajalein was intense for TF 58's pilots and aircraft. Some new capabilities and operational procedures had been added, including the first use of aerial rockets and much more precise target selection.

Unknown to Flintlock's planners, however, Kwajalein's aerial defense capabilities were scarcely formidable. The last of Japan's best naval aviators had been expended at Rabaul and over the Gilberts. Anticipating the American invasions, most of the Marshall Island units had been evacuated to Palau. All that were left to defend the Marshalls were about 150 planes, most of them the Bettys responsible for the night torpedo attacks in November.

In the end, the Marshalls would be a mismatch for TF 58's formidable air armada. On January 29th, 1944, a day of ambitious aerial poundings of Roi, Kwajalein, Maloelap and Watje, most pilots came up empty. But for one fighter pilot flying a Target CAP over Roi, it proved an ideal time and place to start settling a personal score.

––––––

Seeing no planes airborne when they arrived over Roi's airfield at 10 a.m., *Intrepid* pilots Alex Vraciu and his wingman, Ensign Thomas Addison Hall, prepared to strafe a Japanese air transport sitting on the runway. They had begun their dive from seven thousand feet when Vraciu suddenly spotted a string of Bettys, new arrivals, flying low over the field.

Racing to bounce them, Vraciu got in position for a flat high-side run on the last plane in line. So anxious was Vraciu (he realized later) to snare a Betty that he began firing too soon. Still, he had a perfect shot. He barely touched the trigger and the Betty's starboard wing root burst into flame. Seconds later it crashed into the sea.

Looking ahead, Vraciu spotted another Betty flying at three hundred feet over the atoll lagoon. As Vraciu closed from astern, the Betty dropped even lower in an effort to escape. During the attack, Vraciu's Hellcat may have caught a round from the Betty's tail gunner, but his own .50 caliber burst exploded fuel and sent the bomber tumbling into the lagoon. Before the crash, Vraciu saw desperate crewmen trying to jump clear—they probably had no other choice.

Again looking ahead, Vraciu spotted two more Bettys in line. Pointing for Hall to go after the more distant Betty, Vraciu pursued the nearer one as it fled west, low on the water at maximum speed.

As he narrowed the distance on this tail chase, Vraciu worked to rein in his emotions. He needed to be more deliberate—less driven by adrenaline and his impulse for revenge. Vraciu meant to honor Butch by channeling his mentor's lessons. He had to be sure, for example, to stay clear of the twenty-millimeter tail stinger.

Once he overtook the Betty, Vraciu pulled up abeam, but out of range. The tail gunner was already firing. Vraciu executed what he'd practiced so often against friendly planes during routine hops in Hawaii: high-side full-deflection runs from either side, always on the move.

Vraciu's first run produced no visible effect. On the second run, he noticed that only one of his wing guns was firing. The Betty by now was barely above the water and Vraciu had all he could do to stay with the quarry, line up a shot and get his remaining gun to fire.

It was exasperating: with each pass Vraciu could get off just one or two rounds (on one pass, none), all the while dodging rounds from the Betty gunner.

Still, he was determined. He would do whatever it took—chasing his quarry to Eniwetok if need be. Over the course of another twenty-five miles, Vraciu figured he made six more firing passes until the Betty finally nosed down into the sea.

It was Vraciu's third kill of the day and the fifth of his short fighter pilot career. He was an ace, but more important was his vow, made after learning of Butch O'Hare's loss to a Betty. On an impulse, Vraciu had told Willie Callan, his wingman at the time: "I'm going to get ten of those bastards! Ten Bettys."

On the return flight to *Intrepid*, Vraciu savored the moment. He seemed well on his way.

19

THEY WILL BE KNOCKED DOWN

THE MASSIVE FIGHTER SWEEP AGAINST TRUK[1] ATOLL IN THE CAROLINE ISLANDS had all the earmarks of a Mitscher enterprise. The seventy-two Hellcats, launched from carriers positioned ninety miles northeast of Truk and approaching low off the water to avoid radar detection, were tasked with clearing the skies of enemy fighters in advance of a planned second day of bomb and torpedo strikes. It was, to be sure, a departure from Jumpin' Joe Clifton's "get them in there, get them out and get them home" escort tactics at Rabaul. It was instead a "pure fighter" mission—Hellcats as sharp, unencumbered spear tips.

Not that the prospects of taking on the "Gibraltar of the Pacific" were any less daunting. When Commander Phillip H. Torrey Jr., *Essex's* newly promoted Air Group 9 CO learned, well after TF 58's three CTGs (58.1's *Enterprise, Yorktown* and *Belleau Wood*; 58.2's *Essex, Intrepid* and *Cabot*; 58.3's *Bunker Hill, Cowpens* and *Monterey*) departed Majuro (TF 58's new advance base in the Marshalls), that the destination was Truk, his first instinct "was to jump overboard."

As CAG Torrey's VF-9 Hellcats reached the objective in the pre-dawn of February 16, they faced what Lieutenant John Sullivan described as a "black curtain of AA." "Right over the center of Truk all hell broke loose," was Lieutenant (junior grade) Marvin Franger's recollection. Lieutenant (junior grade) William Arthur, another VF-9 Hellcat pilot, "watched flak following just behind another plane in a sort of impersonal fascination." (It wasn't until later that Arthur realized that a trail of flak was likely following him as well.)

Japanese aircraft were also taking off to intercept—an estimated eighty at first, though more would join as the epic fight continued. For the most

---

1. pronounced "Trook"

part, neither the enemy aircraft nor their pilots were up to the challenge: waves of fearsome Hellcats flown by aggressive and thoroughly trained Navy carrier pilots. "Sometimes they just [kept] coming at us," VF-9 CO Lieutenant Commander Herbert N. Houck recalled, even though they must know "they will be knocked down."

––––––––

Just after sunrise that morning, Alex Vraciu and his wingman, Ensign Louis Gordon Little Jr. were at thirteen thousand feet, circling Truk's Moen Island airfield awaiting their turn to go in. For purposes of the sweep, a dozen VF-6 Hellcats were teamed with a dozen of *Enterprise's* VF-10 "Grim Reapers" led by Commander William R. "Killer" Kane.

Vraciu and Little were the last section positioned to dive in and blast parked aircraft. Before nosing over, however, Vraciu swiveled his head to peek over either shoulder—a simple precaution taught him by Butch O'Hare. What Vraciu saw immediately changed his intentions.

Three thousand feet above his Hellcat were Zekes diving in on the port quarter. Vraciu's tally-ho went unheeded by the planes below, but he knew if he and Little nosed over now, the Zekes would only follow. They had to stay and fight.

Vraciu and Little turned hard left to go head-to-head with the attackers' lead Zeke. The Japanese pilot was already shooting, but Vraciu squeezed a quick countering burst and the Zeke rolled over and dove for the water. As this lead Zeke evaded, however, another promptly latched onto Vraciu's tail.

To shake him off, Vraciu pulled into a steep direction-changing climb—a chandelle—using the Hellcat's superior power and strength to pull away in the vertical and then make a g-heavy roll onto the Zeke's six o'clock. It worked to perfection but as Vraciu lined up to shoot the stalled and spiraling Zeke, more enemy planes were ready to pounce from above. If Vraciu and Little were to survive, they somehow had to neutralize the Zekes' advantages in numbers and altitude.

Vraciu signaled his wingman to begin a weave—an ever-reliable way to give them mutual protection while they jockeyed for the upper hand. It was tough going. With so many attackers, the Japanese could pick their spots. Still, the enemy pilots were clearly frustrated by the tactic—and so sure of the outcome that they pressed the attack by coming down to the Hellcats' altitude. All at once, Vraciu's and Little's Hellcats had the advantage. They broke the weave and took on their tormentors.

Vraciu first turned the tables on an attacking Zeke whose pilot predictably dived to escape. The ploy might have saved him from an F4F—but not an F6F. Vraciu caught up and squeezed a burst that flamed the Zeke and then, without pause, he looked for another. The next Zeke pilot he bounced tried to dive away as well, but Vraciu just as easily reeled him in. Once on a prey's tail, Vraciu simply refused to let go until it was torched. Having scored two kills in a sky filled with opportunities, he had ambitions for a dozen more.

There was a lot of competition, but a relentless Vraciu went on to dispatch two more Japanese planes. The first of these, a Rufe (the Zeke's float plane cousin), went as quickly—and by the same means—as kills one and two. The fourth and final adversary, however, was flown by a nimble and pesky pilot who led Vraciu on a chase in and out of the clouds. Vraciu played the hide-and-seek game for a time but then broke away and climbed up-sun to wait. When the Zeke finally nosed into the clear and Vraciu raced in for a high-side deflection shot on its four o'clock, the Japanese pilot likely never saw him coming.

Aerial combat over Truk would rage for the balance of the day—a swirling, seemingly endless melee of aerial scuffles, dropping aircraft (most Japanese) and parachuting pilots (some Japanese were reported to have bailed still wearing pajamas) that reminded VF-5 skipper Lieutenant Commander Edward M. Owen of a "Hollywood war." In all, the Navy fighters would compile an impressive scorecard: claims of one hundred thirty airborne enemy planes and another seventy-four on the ground. VF-6 pilots claimed a dozen kills in addition to Vraciu's four. Eight VF-9 fliers claimed seventeen. VF-10's Killer Kane and his wingman bagged five planes in five minutes.

Vraciu was one of five pilots to chalk up a quadruple at Truk—another was VF-5's Bob Duncan, the first pilot credited with recording a Hellcat victory over the Zero (and now, with four confirmed Truk kills, an ace.) Vraciu, having reached nine confirmed kills, became the Navy's second leading fighter ace, trailing only VF-9's Lieutenant Hamilton "One Slug" McWhorter III with ten (two scored that same day in less than ten seconds of fighting).

American losses over Truk totaled seventeen aircraft (most to ground fire) and twenty-six crewmen. Two F6F casualties were *Intrepid* Hellcats flown by John Phillips and his wingman, Ensign John Ritchie Ogg—missing in action, apparently ambushed by Japanese fighters while directing strikes on Truk shipping.

After Butch O'Hare's death the previous November, Phillips had stepped up to Air Group 6 Commander. He had also been put in overall charge (with assistance from Gus Widhelm) of a program to equip each CV with a night-fighting "Bat Team". As the training progressed[2], however, the TBF-F6F tandem concept gave way to detachments of radar-equipped Corsairs and Hellcats.

One of the F4U detachments was assigned to *Intrepid*, but its presence didn't forestall what happened after darkness fell on the Truk raid's first day. A group of Kate torpedo bombers managed to elude a *Yorktown* night fighter to launch a torpedo straight and true into *Intrepid's* hull. The ship survived but, with damage to her rudder, she had to limp off (aided by a canvas sail jury-rigged to her forecastle) for repairs that would take several months.

———

The swift conquests of key objectives in the Marshalls (Roi-Namur, Kwajalein, Majuro and—coincident with the Truk raid—Eniwetok) served to accelerate the Pacific War timetable. Truk had weighed heavily on Ernest King's mind during joint Allied conferences in Cairo and Tehran where the Combined Chiefs of Staff (CCS) had approved Truk's seizure once the Marshalls were secured.

At the time, key Navy brass hoped somehow to be able to avoid a Truk invasion and now that seemed possible. Truk's defenses had proven hollow. During the second day of the raid, Navy bombers and torpedo planes faced virtually no opposition, enabling the sinking or beaching of an estimated 200,000 tons of Japanese shipping. Afterwards, the Japanese abandoned Truk's anchorage. Truk could be sealed off and left to "wither on the vine," as could Rabaul once MacArthur's forces secured surrounding islands. With Truk and Rabaul removed from the victory equation, King could turn his attention to the Marianas.

As early as January 1944 (with Truk and Rabaul not yet resolved), when he met with Nimitz and Halsey in San Francisco to share the Cairo-Tehran conference outcomes, King had stressed that the key to the entire Pacific lay in the Marianas. Capturing the Marianas was a means of closing off the Carolines (Truk), while their central location made them an ideal jumping-off point for advances west or northwest. Moreover, given the strategic importance of the Marianas to the Japanese, their fleet would have to come out and fight. When the U.S. fleet finished it off, the Pacific Ocean would belong to the Allies. The Japanese would be finished.

When King had first made these same arguments to the CCS at Cairo-

———

2. Alex Vraciu, Tom Hall and John Phillips were Bat Team members.

Tehran, his listeners had been puzzled. There was no mention of the Marianas in any of the American position papers. Not uncharacteristically, King had paid only passing attention to his planners' scribblings. He knew what he wanted.

The problem was that many of King's own subordinates disagreed with CominCh about the Marianas. To them, the island chain's harbors were unsuitable for anchorages and it was not located on the most direct route west. Moreover, they assumed its primary use would be as a base for long-range B-29 bombers. They were not particularly eager to expend Navy blood and treasure for the sole benefit of the Army Air Force.

To King however, the B-29 bases would merely be one of the outcomes from the Marianas' capture. The real objective was to cut off Japanese access to the Carolines and protect U.S. lines of communications to the Philippines. MacArthur could bluster all he wanted about winning the war via the New Guinea-Philippines track. In a scathing February letter to Nimitz, whom he thought insufficiently committed to conquest of the Marianas, King wrote: "I assume that sometime or other this thorn in the side of our communications to the western Pacific must be removed. In other words . . . we must take out time and forces to carry out the job."

"We have been sighted by the enemy," Marc Mitscher informed his airmen and sailors via *Yorktown's* intercom. "We will fight our way in."

After Truk, Mitscher's task force had not returned to Majuro—now developed into a massive mobile supply and refueling stop operated by the "pork chops" (supply personnel) of Service Squadron (ServRon) 10. Instead, in an unprecedented move, Mitscher was released by Spruance to mount independent offensive strikes against the Marianas' Saipan and Tinian, using two balanced task groups of three carriers each.

On February 22, *Essex, Yorktown, Belleau Wood, Bunker Hill, Monterey* and *Cowpens* launched strikes and supporting CAP that would destroy 168 Japanese aircraft (aloft and on the ground) at a cost of six of their own. Several Japanese supply ships were sunk in Saipan's Tanapang Harbor. Others that tried fleeing to open waters were handily dispatched by American submarines. Mitscher's carrier aircraft had landed a punch truly reminiscent of Japan's six-carrier strike on Pearl Harbor. They had also demonstrated a basic flaw in Japan's strategy of using island bases as "unsinkable carriers"—though indeed unsinkable, they were also unmovable and could always be found.

Even as Mitscher's fast carrier foray removed all doubt that the Marianas were wide open to invasion, the JCS equivocated on next moves. In late February and early March, Douglas MacArthur's forces had attacked the Admiralty Islands north of New Guinea. In the process they had captured Manus Island and its huge Seeadler Harbor anchorage—another major mobile fleet base for the westward push. Dispute as to who would control it (MacArthur or Nimitz) stalled JCS decision-making. It took a Nimitz trip to Washington, DC for two days of discussions with Roosevelt and the JCS to break the logjam.

Finally, on March 12, the JCS set the near-term course of Pacific War operations. While MacArthur completed isolation of Rabaul and continued his advance along New Guinea's northern coast, Nimitz would bypass Truk and seize the southern Marianas beginning June 15. With the Marianas campaign (code name Forager) on the timetable, King and Nimitz turned to related issues.

––––––

The end of major fighting in the Solomons had removed the need to distinguish between Central and South Pacific operations. Accordingly, on April 14, Central Pacific Forces officially became Fifth Fleet. But the downgrading of SoPac as a separate theater also meant that ComSoPac—William Halsey—had worked himself out of a job.

In the face of a potentially awkward leadership dilemma, King and Nimitz were ready with a novel solution. To accommodate the gathering pace and scale of Pacific War operations, Halsey would alternate fleet command with Spruance: When Spruance had the helm (as he would for Forager), it would be called Fifth Fleet; under Halsey it would be Third Fleet. The task designations would follow: Spruance's TF 58 would alternate with Halsey's TF 38.

"The team remains about the same, but the drivers change," was Nimitz's all-purpose explanation, and the quote held a good deal of truth. This tag team system enabled one fleet commander and his staff to plan the next big operation while the other team fought at sea. Looked at somewhat differently, however, the system also showcased two extraordinarily different command talents: Halsey, the impetuous, hard-driving aviator and Spruance, the brainy Gun Club strategist.

The only possible flaw in this arrangement was one of timing. Spruance had shown his mettle in the context of Midway; Halsey in the slugfest of Guadalcanal. Going forward, would Halsey (or Spruance) be in charge when a "Halsey" (or a "Spruance") was needed?

––––––

As Forager planning proceeded, King raised with Nimitz his renewed concerns about the threat of the Japanese fleet. Enemy warships had not been in battle for more than a year—plenty of time to rebuild, re-arm and train. Having abandoned Truk, Japan's fleet was presumably split between Southeast Asia and the Home Islands—but what were Japan's intentions for using it?

In early May, King believed a fleet action in the Marianas was unlikely. But then, after reviewing Spruance's plans for Fifth Fleet should Japan's fleet in fact intervene in the Marianas, King grew concerned. Both Spruance and Nimitz seemed to lack a specific plan, preferring instead to wait for the situation to develop.

Nimitz assured King that both TF 58 and Fifth Fleet's battle line were up to their respective tasks. But, in late May, when Nimitz passed word that much of the Japanese fleet had moved from Singapore south to Tawi Tawi, an anchorage between the Philippines and North Borneo, Kings' anxiety mounted. Nimitz reiterated that destruction of the Japanese fleet was always the prime objective. "Attempts by enemy fleet units to interfere with amphibious operations are both hoped for and provided against." Despite this, King felt Nimitz was courting trouble. In the end, however, King knew he couldn't fight CinCPac's war for him. Besides, he had other formidable matters on his mind: the Allies' forthcoming amphibious invasion of Northern Europe.

––––––

The Marianas are a chain of volcanic caps that poke from the surface of the Central Pacific just west of the Mariana Trench—at nearly seven miles, the deepest point in all the global oceans. The archipelago's fifteen islands—aligned roughly north-south along a westward-arcing crescent—are residue of the violent sideswiping of two continent-size tectonic plates. Eons after their formation, several of the biggest islands became pawns in the centuries-long struggle for Pacific conquest, colonization and exploitation.

In 1899 America seized Guam as a Spanish American War prize. After the war, an impoverished Spain offered to sell the rest of its interests in the Marianas, but America balked at the four-million-dollar price tag and the rights went instead to Germany. Following World War I, Japan displaced Germany and began aggressively exploiting two other islands, Saipan and Tinian—sizable, fertile and mountainous outcroppings within sight of each other across a narrow channel. All the while, Japan seethed at the U.S. presence just 150 miles to the south. Within two days of the attack on Pearl Harbor, Japanese troops based on Saipan stormed and captured Guam.

Unlike U.S. objectives in the Gilberts and Marshalls, Saipan, Tinian and Guam boasted considerable land mass and fairly sizable human populations. For the Japanese, the stakes in defending the Marianas were particularly high: with Japanese colonists outnumbering Chamorro natives roughly seven to one, what had begun as imperialistic "mandates" were now considered sovereign Japanese soil.

Operation Forager called for sequenced assaults on Saipan, Tinian and Guam. Securing Saipan came first because it had the Marianas' best airfield and sat a hundred miles closer to Japan than Guam. It was also considered the easiest to invade.

As was usual in these operations, a key to Forager's success was in having sufficient carrier air power to shield both the invasion fleet and the beachhead. The differences were ones of scale. Forager's invasion fleet consisted of more than 500 transports, supply ships and combatants; the ground assault forces numbered 127,000 Marines and GIs.

Although each of Forager's huge components—its amphibious armada, carrier striking arm and logistics—had a separate commander, each of these men in turn answered to Raymond Spruance. For the carriers, it was Marc Mitscher, whose January 1944 appointment as TF 58 senior carrier division commander had been made without Spruance's blessing.

Mitscher's performance in the Marshalls and at Truk had solidified (in some eyes, resurrected) his reputation. As far as Nimitz and King were concerned, Pete Mitscher was indispensible when it came to leading the Pacific war's fast carriers. Promoted to Vice Admiral (coincident with Spruance's promotion to full admiral), Mitscher was now Commander Fast Carrier Forces Pacific Fleet.

Mitscher would lead Forager's fast carrier component from a new flagship—carrier *Lexington*. Joining him for Forager would also be a new chief of staff, Captain Arleigh A. Burke. Mitscher had been given as little choice in Burke's assignment as had Spruance in his. Burke was no crony: displaying extraordinary daring and flair, he had commanded a destroyer squadron in the latter stages of the Solomons Campaign. During a November 1943 night engagement off Cape St. George at the tip of New Ireland, Destroyer Squadron (DesRon) 23 sank four Japanese de-

stroyers and damaged two more without a single American casualty.
Burke had earned a Navy Cross (and DesRon 23 a Presidential Unit Citation at war's end), but neither his battle achievements nor much else
about Burke impressed Mitscher. Burke's black shoe credentials (his assignment was part of a King mandate requiring aviation admirals to have
surface warfare chiefs of staff) and Mitscher's intractable style cast Burke
as a meddlesome outsider.

Ever since taking on the role at the end of March, Burke had smoldered
over his second-rate status. But, by early June, his persistence, displays of
shrewd common sense and visible efforts to learn (he flew tail gunner in
several combat missions) began to pay off. Burke had already allied himself with Gus Widhelm, Mitscher's new staff operations officer. Then on
June 5, just hours ahead of TF 58's departure from Majuro, a prospective
new confidante stepped aboard *Lexington*.

Jimmie Thach, now a full Commander, was to ride Lex solely as an observer. In March, at the end of his stateside tour, Thach had been tapped
by Vice Admiral John McCain (then slated to relieve Mitscher after Forager) to become McCain's operations officer. Although, as McCain's observer (McCain was aboard Spruance's flagship cruiser *Indianapolis*
[CA-35]), Thach required no official shipboard title, he found himself
listed as special assistant to Burke. While Thach performed special projects for Burke, his real value came through informal open-ended conversations that both eased Burke's carrier aviation learning curve and
sharpened his recommendations to Mitscher.

––––––––

Forager's TF 58 carriers were a "Murderer's Row" of nine CVs and seven
CVLs assigned to four separate CTGs. Altogether they embarked just over
nine hundred tail-hook aircraft, more than half of them Hellcats. The CTG
admirals—58.1's colorful, combative, part-Cherokee and newly-promoted
Rear Admiral "Jocko" Clark (new *Hornet* [CV-12], new *Yorktown*, *Belleau
Wood* and *Bataan* [CVL-29]); 58.2's "Monty" Montgomery (*Bunker Hill*,
new *Wasp* [CV-18], *Monterey* and *Cabot*); 58.3's stern and steady John W.
"Black Jack" Reeves (*Enterprise*, *Lexington*, *Princeton* and *San Jacinto* [CVL-
30]); and 58.4's courtly (and, it turned out, ailing) Tennessean William K.
"Keen" Harrill (*Essex*, *Langley* and *Cowpens*)—were longtime aviators who
knew their trade. Each was deeply seasoned in the intricacies of carrier-to-
carrier warfare—though to be sure, each set the fire in his belly with a different thermostat.

As they approached the Marianas from the east, the first job of the TF 58 admirals, ships, sailors and airmen was to take the Japanese by surprise. As much as the Americans were thoroughly practiced Pacific invaders, so were the Japanese thoroughly practiced (albeit less successful) defenders. The enemy was accustomed to dawn fighter sweeps before amphibious landings, so Mitscher's staff devised a different schedule. Instead of waiting to begin strikes on June 12, the schedule was advanced to 1 p.m. on the 11th.

Two hundred thirteen Hellcats, some carrying bombs, augmented by a handful of Avengers and Helldivers—"Beasts," as their pilots had taken to calling the new, powerful, but hard-to-tame Curtiss SB2C bombers—conducted the first strikes. Although aircraft from each CTG were allotted specific ground targets on the principal islands, by far the best hunting was found over Guam—the preserve for *Hornet, Yorktown* and *Belleau Wood.*

While strafing airfields and attending to the rescue of a downed flyer, *Hornet's* VF-2 pilots were bounced by an estimated thirty Guam-based Zekes. VF-2's skipper Commander William A. Dean Jr. emerged from the melee with four kills, which, combined with an earlier day's kill, made him the Ripper's first ace. Aggressively chasing a fast-climbing Zeke during one dogfight, Dean employed a powerful new capability in the F6F's Pratt and Whitney Double Wasp engine—a water-methanol fuel injection feature that added an instant 10 percent horsepower boost. Like any stimulant, this power surge had its limits: after five minutes the engine would begin to burn out. But this provided sufficient margin for Dean to corral and splash the Zeke.

Dean's was not the Hellcat's only feat of strength over Guam that first day. Sighting a lone Zeke north of the island, a division from *Belleau Wood's* VF-24 began a low-level water chase. While the Japanese pilot immediately dropped his auxiliary tank, three of the VF-24 pilots held on to theirs. Spotting the Zeke a three-mile head start—an insurmountable gap for an F4F in level flight—the Hellcats reached a sustained speed of 240 knots on an eight-mile pursuit that ultimately cornered and splashed their adversary. It was anecdotal proof that a Grumman could occasionally out-duel its erstwhile nemesis on the flats as well as the slopes.

———

June 11th would also prove to be memorable for the aerial combat debut of VF-15 CO Commander David "Dashing Dave" McCampbell. Although a deeply experienced aviator (two thousand hours' flight time, hundreds of them in Hellcats), it was just a month before that McCampbell first led pilots in combat, as part of a Marcus Island "warm up" raid. During a low-level strafing run, the fuselage of McCampbell's Hellcat had been shredded and its rudder controls severed. As he fought to steady the plane, McCampbell noticed smoke.

"Dave," a section leader warned him. "Your belly tank's on fire."

"Thanks, Bert," McCampbell acknowledged. He jettisoned his tank, but noticing smoke from his tail section and hydraulics as well, also donned his oxygen mask. During the flight, McCampbell's wingman had been lost to ground fire, and he literally had to wrestle his plane to an emergency landing on *Essex*. After McCampbell snared a wire, deck personnel looked over his Hellcat, tore out a few replacement parts and shoved the wreck overboard. Despite that first horrific combat experience, however, McCampbell never doubted his cockpit skills. From his training as a collegiate diver, McCampbell also never felt disoriented or out of control in the air.

On the afternoon of June 11, during the second wave of strikes against Tinian, McCampbell spotted a lone Zeke dropping out of cloud cover. Although, as a CAG, McCampbell's primary job was to orchestrate rather than partake of the action, he was never one to hesitate. McCampbell added power, closed range and, after some jockeying and three separate bursts, sent the Zeke down like a smoke-propelled spear. It was one more victory claim among scores more by dozens of other pilots—but it was also the beginning of a remarkable run. "I knew I could shoot him down and I did," McCampbell later described it to a journalist. "That's all there was to it."

––––––

June 11th's harvest—claims of eighty-six air-to-air victories and thirty-three planes destroyed on the ground—was, as always, not without costs and casualties. Eleven F6Fs were lost to ground and aerial gunfire and with them three aviators. But the devastating impact to the enemy was soon apparent. The next day, TF 58 aerial kill claims dwindled to twenty-two, half of them claimed by *Hornet* Hellcats. Although three more American aircraft and six fliers were lost to ground fire early on the 13th, TF 58's accomplishments seemed indisputable. Afforded four days to dominate the Marianas' skies before June 15's D-Day, task force aviators had needed only two.

Flush with success, Spruance and Mitscher decided to spread the air supremacy blanket. Intercepted radio intelligence revealed that the Japanese were staging aircraft from Kyushu into the Bonin and Volcano islands, especially Iwo Jima and Chichi Jima. Two CTGs—"Jocko" Clark's 58.2 and "Keen" Harrill's 58.4— were dispatched north for strikes on June 16 and 17.

While neither Clark nor Harrill were eager to leave the main action, Clark, courtesy of some ego-massaging by Mitscher, saw the roundtrip foray across the fringes of a typhoon into higher latitudes (and back) as a challenge. Harrill, on the other hand, was none too enthused. Though he was four years junior to Harrill, Clark forced a showdown, threatening to "do it myself" if Harrill didn't join him. Harrill finally agreed and the two task groups steamed north, bonded by a competitive—and to Harrill, humbling—"joint command" arrangement. They made an odd couple, indeed: Mitscher's most- and least-aggressive carrier admirals.

All this time, snoopers had been probing the carrier formations—proof the Japanese knew TF 58's composition and movements with considerable precision. Fully six shads were found and splashed on June 13, including one by CAG McCampbell (his second aerial kill). Then news arrived from American submarines lurking off Tawi Tawi: the Japanese fleet had upped anchor and sailed east. As submarines stalked their progress and task force air searches were expanded, Spruance and Mitscher assessed their situation. They would have three, perhaps four days before the Japanese fleet threatened. A message was dispatched to Clark and Harrill: limit the Bonin strikes to one day (June 16), then speed south to be available for the main event.

———

On June 14, Alex Vraciu led a division of VF-16 Hellcats on a bombing escort mission near Farallon de Medinilla, a tiny coral crag forty-five miles north of Saipan. The assignment was to hit any Japanese capabilities that might threaten the amphibious landings on Saipan, but, after three straight days of sweeps and strikes, there was little to see and nothing to destroy. The SBDs would likely end up just jettisoning their bombs. But, if the dive-bomber crews were frustrated, the Hellcat pilots were even more so. To the Hellcat pilots' thinking, the Marianas now seemed devoid of opportunities.

———

When *Intrepid* was damaged off Truk in February, it marked the second time Alex Vraciu had been aboard a carrier when it was torpedoed. Then, after the carrier reached Pearl on February 24, he learned that his unit— Air Group 6—was slated to rotate home.

That the air group was being relieved after little more than six months' combat duty was just another sign of how dramatically the Pacific War tide had turned. While virtually all group personnel were ecstatic about the news, Vraciu wasn't. With no pressing stateside obligations, a vow of revenge to keep and his aerial kills near the top of the Navy's aviation leader board, Vraciu wanted to stay close to the action.

As luck would have it (at least in this instance), while Vraciu was ashore pleading his case to AirPac brass, he ran into Mark Bright, a VF-16 veteran aviator. Bright had seen action with VF-5 during the Guadalcanal campaign and, like Vraciu, was a fighter ace. But Vraciu had known him first as a fellow student and intramural basketball competitor at DePauw. Bright, a minister's son, was kicked out of school after being caught sneaking a coed into her sorority house to circumvent curfew. The banishment had prompted Bright to enlist in the Navy and he had reached flight training ahead of Vraciu.

"Heck, come join us," Bright suggested when he learned of Vraciu's plight. It turned out there actually was a squadron opening. With AirPac approval, Vraciu boarded Lex before it sortied in support of MacArthur's Hollandia invasion.

It was not until April 29, during another raid against Truk, that Vraciu scored his first victories as a VF-16 "Airedale"—two Zeros that upped his score to eleven. On a second hop that day, however, Vraciu's Hellcat was hit by ground fire which shattered portions of his canopy and disabled his landing gear.

It became Vraciu's second water landing. The first, a month before, had been dicey. Vraciu was overshot twice by the rescue destroyer before being hoisted aboard. Fortunately, this splashdown went better. But, after being picked up by destroyer *Ingersoll* (DD-652), undergoing a painful procedure to extract a Plexiglas sliver from his eye and spending a night in rough seas aboard the small tin can, Vraciu was ready to return to sturdier and more familiar surroundings. He persuaded the *Ingersoll's* skipper to signal Gus Widhelm on Lex: "Get me off this dang roller coaster or I'll vote for MacArthur, so help me!"

Vraciu knew Widhelm well—he could always be found kibitzing with the pilots in the ready rooms and was always looking to scare up wagering opportunities. And the message was a lark—MacArthur, widely disliked in Fifth Fleet circles, was rumored to be running against Roosevelt in 1944. Still, its flippancy gave Vraciu some second thoughts and anxious moments until he was retrieved by Lex via breeches buoy the next day.

Widhelm was waiting for Vraciu when he got aboard the carrier and immediately took him up to meet Pete Mitscher in Flag Plot. "Admiral," Widhelm said, "this is Alex Vraciu—Grumman's Best Customer."

———

By the time of the June 14 escort mission, Vraciu had reason to wonder if the Truk Zeros were the last he would ever see of the enemy. But then, as if to toy with his frustrations, Vraciu happened to spot a speck high above the bomber formation—a reconnaissance Betty.

"Got one up there," Vraciu blandly alerted the flight leader.

"Go get him," the leader replied—all that Vraciu needed to hear. He dropped his belly tank, went to full power and climbed with his division. All were anxious to bag the Betty, so it became a race.

The Betty was at eighteen thousand feet, so to stay hidden, Vraciu kept his approach steep. Above him, the mottled green and grey bomber cruised along serenely, its crew apparently clueless to what was coming. By the time Vraciu's Hellcat was spotted and the Betty nosed down to gain speed and escape, it was too late. Vraciu had all the altitude he needed. Following the bomber down and centering its wing root in his gun sight's reticle, Vraciu squeezed a short burst that torched the Betty and sent it spiraling out of control.

"Vraciu!" a pilot left behind in the chase shouted over the circuit for all to hear. "You Son of a Bitch!"

———

When Saburo Sakai first learned of the American invasion of Saipan, it seemed one more in a litany of Japan's wartime reverses. Not only was his country no longer on the offensive, its Pacific empire was crumbling.

For months, Sakai and Omuro Air Base's other instructors had been trying to build fighter pilots from the raw human materials thrust on them. It was hopeless. The facilities were too meager, the demand for combat pilots too great and the students' ineptitude too overwhelming. At one time these students could never have dreamed of getting close to a fighter aircraft. Now the instructors were somehow supposed to prepare them for battle.

Despite the futility, everything about the effort was urgent. Flight instructors were admonished to forget the fine points—just concentrate on the basics: flying and shooting. Sakai could only watch in dismay as the planes flown by the students staggered along the runway and lurched into the air. It was like watching a sky filled with inebriates. Again and again, students collided in midair or crashed—sometimes killing their instructors in the process. Meanwhile, Sakai's own skills, already compromised by diminished vision, eroded further.

Some days, between trying to make headway with his students and digesting the latest news from the war, Sakai was on the verge of tears. But even in April 1944, when he finally got released from Omuro and transferred to the Yokosuka Air Wing, Sakai took little solace or pride in what once would have been a coveted assignment. Before the war, the Yokosuka Air Wing, an Imperial Guard unit charged with protecting Tokyo's air approaches, was a prestigious outfit. Now Yokosuka was just another demoralized unit with inferior aircraft and worse pilots.

When Sakai's duties took him to nearby Tokyo, he noticed appalling changes in people's dress, demeanor and behavior. Despite hints of summer, people were no longer turned out in bright colors. They moved along, heads mostly down, through dreary, lifeless streets. Though the "Warship March" still blared from street speakers, its cadence didn't seem to generate much enthusiasm. People who once strode proudly to its beat had lost too many fathers, husbands, sons and brothers under its sway.

The city stores were now short of commodities and rationing was in force for many items. Instead of bustling about, arms filled with packages, people stood listlessly in long queues, sometimes for things as simple as bowls of hot broth.

The war, once so remote, had at last reached Japan's doorstep. Toward mid-June word leaked out that a flight of massive new American bombers, apparently flying from China, had bombed a city in northern Kyushu. The particular raid did little damage, but that was beside the point. The more distressing aspect was that Japanese fighters had been unable to stop the big bombers. If one city could be hit from the air with impunity, others would surely follow—victims to even larger bomber formations, to more and bigger bombs.

———

But perhaps worst was the news from Saipan. There was fear that Iwo Jima, just 650 miles south of Yokosuka, would be next—and soon. As poorly defended as Iwo Jima was, an invasion could scarcely be withstood. Moreover, with a foothold at Iwo Jima, the enemy could easily imperil all of Japan.

Responding to the threat, the high command immediately sent troops and weapons to bolster the island's defenses. As part of the push, Yokosuka Wing was ordered to establish Iwo Jima's air defense.

As it was, the Wing could muster only thirty flyable Zeros. The planes to be used were old models and the pilots available to fly them were mostly lacking in training and combat experience. Even so, when Sakai reported to the wing commander's office on the day before deployment, he was expecting to hear Iwo Jima was no place for one-eyed fighter pilots. Instead, the commander all but pleaded for Sakai to join the deployment. Given Japan's wartime fortunes, anyone with combat experience was no longer a liability.

The next morning—June 16—Sakai flew one of thirty Zeros bound for Iwo Jima. Taking off from Yokosuka, the planes turned south, only to be forced back by thick overcast and torrential rains. Sakai and the other veterans in the flight could have probably made it, but the fledglings, along with their aircraft, would have gotten hopelessly lost.

The pilots tried to reach Iwo Jima over the next two days but were forced back each time. It was agonizing: while rain and wind lashed Japan, the weather over Iwo Jima and Saipan was said to be perfect. The pilots could only retreat to their barracks where radio reports told of furious and relentless aerial battles.

———

Daylight on June 19 indeed revealed beautiful flying weather over the Marianas—bright and warm with a few clouds and unlimited visibility. The same weather held one hundred miles northwest of Guam, where Mitscher had arrayed TF 58 north to south across a front twenty-five miles wide and twelve to fifteen miles deep. CTG 58.3 with flagship *Lexington* was in the middle. A dozen miles north and south were Clark's CTG 58.1 and Montgomery's 58.2. Twelve miles west of Clark was Harrill's 58.4; fifteen miles west of Reeve were the battleships and cruisers of Vice Admiral Willis A. "Ching" Lee's TG 58.7. Because of a prevailing nine to twelve knot easterly wind, the American carriers would have to turn east and crank up speed to launch. During the day, some TF 58 ships would close to within twenty-five miles of Guam.

There were dual possibilities about what was just about to unfold. Days before, assessing the possible course of events from his post at Pearl, Vice Admiral Jack Towers, now elevated to be Nimitz' deputy, raised the distinctly plausible prospect that the Japanese might proceed to a point out of range from TF 58 strikes, using the Marianas as a back-and-forth shuttle point as they hammered the carriers. This notion argued for lunging west to seek out the Japanese fleet, launching peremptory air strikes and, afterwards, mopping up the remnants with Lee's fast battle line.

But Raymond Spruance had another—and prevailing—perspective. Relying on submarine reports for intelligence on Japanese intentions, Spruance learned, on the evening of June 15, that, while the main portion of the Japanese fleet had cleared the Philippine Islands' San Bernardino Strait to enter the Philippine Sea, another powerful battleship contingent was advancing separately several hundred miles to the south. To Spruance, the victor at Midway, it had all the earmarks of a classic Japanese "pincer." Best for now, Spruance decided, to keep his carriers closer at hand to Saipan and the critical—and still heavily contested—amphibious invasion.

Spruance's decision, while it upset Mitscher, mortified the likes of subordinates like Burke and Widhelm—and observers like McCain and Thach. Why not go west? If they didn't, they would be locked in to a disadvantage throughout—always, because of prevailing winds, having to turn east (away from the enemy) while the enemy could always advance east.

But Spruance, it turned out, had his own countering clincher. Heading west now would invite a night surface battle, a specialty of the Japanese. However, when Mitscher asked Willis Lee about his readiness for such a contingency, Lee's response (as foreshadowed by Ernest King's concern) was emphatic: "Do not—repeat not—believe we should seek night engagement."

———

"Hey Rube!" The recall order, flashed at 10:00 a.m. on June 19, went out to Hellcats dueling dozens of Japanese aircraft over Guam's Orete airfield. Earlier that morning, a *Belleau Woods* Hellcat division dispatched to Guam had encountered airborne carrier-type Zekes—proof that enemy aircraft were being staged into the Marianas via the Carolines as well as in the Bonins. More Hellcats flew in to help and aerial battles had flared through the morning. Pilots claimed thirty Japanese fighters and five bombers, but they also reported many more still taking off. However, with task force radars picking up bogeys orbiting at high altitude a hundred miles west—a sign of an imminent attack—neutralizing Guam would have to wait.

Beginning at 10:04 a.m., one hundred forty additional TF 58 fighters were scrambled to join the sixty CAP already aloft. Simultaneously, task force Avengers, Helldivers and SBDs not out on search were ordered to clear the area, freeing up flight decks for fighter operations.

At fifty-five miles out, two divisions of VF-15 Hellcats were the lead skirmishers to confront a sixty-plane strong formation of enemy Zeke fighter-bombers and Jill torpedo-bombers, altitude eighteen thousand feet. The first tally-ho sounded at 10:35 a.m. as "Fabulous Fifteen" Hellcats sliced in from twenty-four thousand feet. Before reinforcements arrived, they shot twenty enemy aircraft out of a Pacific sky uncharacteristically scribbled with contrails.

Ultimately, fifty-four Hellcats from as many as eight other squadrons joined the aerial scrum as it edged eastward to within twenty miles of TF 58. During twenty-five minutes of furious action, an estimated forty-two Japanese aircraft were destroyed in exchange for the loss of three Hellcats and their pilots. A few Zekes and Jills made it into the fringes of the task force. One bomb-equipped Zeke scored a hit on *South Dakota*, punching a hole in her deck and killing twenty-three and wounding twenty-seven.

During one skirmish, a Zeke latched onto the tail of a VF-15 Hellcat piloted by Lieutenant (junior grade) George F. Carr. Carr, a Floridian who had once volunteered with Britain's RAF, made good his escape using lessons learned from the Akutan Zero. Too smart to try to turn with his opponent, Carr instead pushed his stick forward and poured on the coal. Diving headlong, Carr reached nearly 500 miles per hour, easily outdistancing the Zeke before abruptly banking right. True to spec, the Zeke's ailerons froze and the Japanese pilot lost his victim. In other duels that morning, Carr would claim five Japanese aircraft.

At 11:07 a.m., *Lexington's* radar got first sight of the next incoming raid—what proved to be over a hundred Zekes, Judys and Jills. The welcoming party—VF-15 Hellcats led by CAG David McCampbell—reached them at 11:40 a.m., forty miles out from the task force. McCampbell left one division to stave off the top-cover Zekes while he took the rest down to tend to the Judys.

In a series of high-side runs, even with his guns jamming repeatedly, McCampbell—arguably the best aerial marksman in the U.S. Navy—shot down five aircraft, while other VF-15 pilots claimed a combined total of thirteen more. When their portion of the battle ended, its residue was a line of splashes where the Japanese planes had fallen. Despite dreadful losses, Japanese remnants closed ranks and soldiered on. Minutes later, however, they flew into an ambush of more than forty TF 58 Hellcats—half from VF-16.

VF-16 CO Commander Paul D. Buie led three Lex divisions on a vector supplied by FDO Joe Eggert: a heading of 250 degrees and an altitude of twenty-five thousand feet. Buie's Hellcat boasted a new engine. Pushing into high blower and climbing, Buie left several of pilots in his wake— bound, it turned out, for a sector where the fighting was mostly done.

One of the reluctant stragglers was Buie's wingman Lieutenant (junior grade) William C. B. Birkholm, whose own engine was gushing oil. A cowling leak smeared Birkholm's windscreen before the engine seized entirely, forcing him into a water landing (and twelve perilous hours adrift). Others included Alex Vraciu and his wingman, twenty-one-year-old Ensign Homer Brockmeyer. Brockmeyer kept pointing toward his section leader's wings, making Vraciu think the wingman might have spotted bogeys. If so, protocol was to turn over the lead, but when Vraciu tried repeatedly, Brockmeyer emphatically shook his head.

Meanwhile, Vraciu had other problems. His supercharger was stuck in low blower and his engine was misting oil onto the windscreen. Without high blower, his ceiling was limited to 20,000 feet.

A few days before Vraciu and some other Airedales had been suckered into a thousand-dollar bet with Gus Widhelm that there wouldn't be a battle with the Japanese fleet off the Marianas. They should have suspected Widhelm of having the inside scoop. Now, having lost his share (125 dollars) of the bet, it looked like Vraciu was going to miss the action, too.

———————

Vraciu, Brockmeyer and five other stragglers returned and circled the task force. For the moment disconsolate, but still hoping to get into the fight, Vraciu requested another vector from Eggert. Eggert surprised Vraciu by pointing him to bogeys bearing 265 degrees, seventy-five miles out. Vraciu and the stragglers set off again.

Something about the Eggert's voice suggested a fat target might be waiting, so when Vraciu tallyho-d a trio of bandits twenty-five miles out, he was sure there had to be more. He kept looking—intently "spot gazing"—until he detected, lower, off to port and closing fast, a large mass of Japanese aircraft. There had to be at least fifty of them and, strangely, they looked to be without escort overhead. Even on low blower, Vraciu's Hellcat was perfectly positioned for a high-side run. Vraciu waggled his wings to get the others' attention—so near now to the TF 58 outer screen's flak, there was no time to waste.

During his first run, Vraciu got cut off by another Hellcat. "Plenty of cookies on the plate for everyone," he reminded himself as he aborted his run to streak below the formation.

After radioing Joe Eggert that the bogeys were a mix of Judys, Jills and Zeros, Vraciu pulled up and over to single out a Judy on the perimeter. When he closed in and triggered a burst, the Judy erupted in fire and headed down, trailing a plume of black smoke.

Even as this first Judy dropped, Vraciu stalked new targets—two more Judys flying in loose formation. His windshield by now was so smeared with oil that Vraciu had to work in even closer for a good shot. Still, with short bursts, he dispatched both Judys in a matter of seconds. As he pulled out, the sky around Vraciu was a riot of contrails, tracers, smoke and aircraft debris. Almost like murderous cowhands, the Hellcats were trying to corral the Judys to keep them from scattering. Just now they were all edging into range of ships' guns.

Against the brown and black of exploding antiaircraft rounds, Vraciu picked out another Judy dropping from formation. Vraciu was soon on it, pouring tracers into the wing root. Flames instantly sprouted and the Judy twisted out of control—either its control cables were severed or its pilot was dead.

By now, Vraciu had drifted into the flak, but he ignored it to go after three Judys just nosing into bombing runs. Catching up easily with the closest, Vraciu had scarcely squeezed the trigger before the Judy burst into flames and plummeted.

A mere touch also got the second of the three—an explosion so spectacular and close that Vraciu had to yank his stick wildly to get out of the way. He'd never seen anything blow up like that.

The last Judy was now too far below to catch, so Vraciu got on the circuit. "Splash number six," he radioed exuberantly, but then warned: "There's one more ahead and he's diving on a BB."

He'd barely added, "I don't think he'll make it," before the Judy hit the AA curtain and was destroyed by a direct hit.

Vraciu would learn later that the whole sequence had lasted less than eight minutes. During that time, the armorers told him, his guns had expended fewer than four hundred rounds. Vraciu also found out why Brockmeyer had been pointing at his plane so insistently. The telltale Sto-Wing "pins" were showing—Vraciu's wings were not fully locked.

———

Two additional Japanese raids were staged against TF 58 in the afternoon, and while neither developed as fully as the first two, each met more or less the same fate.

Raid three proved to be the smallest and least capable. At about 1 p.m., eight *Hornet* VF-2 CAP Hellcats took on a meandering flight of fifteen bandits about fifty miles northwest of CTG 58.4, claiming nine kills for no American losses. Twenty minutes later a few Zeke fighter-bombers reached the formation. One Zeke dropped a bomb well wide of *Essex*, but it was quickly cornered and splashed by a pair of *Langley* Hellcats. In all, sixteen kills were claimed for the loss of one American Corsair night fighter—whose pilot was retrieved that same afternoon.

Enemy planes of the fourth and final raid—about eighty in all—were pummeled in three separate engagements. One group of eighteen planes that had turned back west after failing to find TF 58 was intercepted by a *Lexington* search team of two Hellcats and a TBF. Joined by a search team from an adjacent sector, the Americans ended up claiming six kills.

The balance of the raid—two separate formations—set course east for Guam's Orote field. The smaller group—about fifteen in all—made glide-bombing attacks on *Wasp* and *Bunker Hill*, then in the midst of recovering aircraft. There were several near misses but no hits, and ships' gunners splashed five bandits.

When the rest of the Raid three planes—about fifty Vals, Zekes and Kates low on fuel—reached Orote, there were forty-one Hellcats off four separate carriers waiting in ambush. Several crafty Hellcat pilots managed to skulk into the Orote field landing pattern. Then, like disguised wolves in a herd of sheep, they shot down Japanese aircraft two and three at a clip.

Essex's Dave McCampbell also showed up over Orote, leading two VF-15 divisions into the confused last moments of the mid-afternoon fight. McCampbell, who had begun the day with two confirmed kills and racked up five more during the morning's second raid, splashed two more to up his combined total to nine.

———

Pete Mitscher knew all along his CAP aircraft were mauling the Japanese, but it wasn't until about 2:30 p.m. that he directed his CTG commanders to keep him updated on the tally. As of 3 p.m., with the fighting still in full swing, the shoot-down count exceeded two hundred. Ever mindful of his bigger objective, Mitscher ordered out searches whenever the shooting eased up.

Mitscher wanted badly to find and pursue the Japanese fleet. Shooting down enemy planes was great, but sinking their bases was the real point of this. Both Mitscher and Spruance had been at Midway and this new battle had elements of a reprise (though with roles reversed): the choice of trying to finish off a foe on the ropes or protect embattled real estate (Midway then, Saipan now).

In the end, Spruance gave some ground in the dispute over priorities by signaling Mitscher at 4:30 p.m.: "Desire to attack enemy tomorrow if we know his position with sufficient accuracy." Mitscher could take three CTGs plus Lee's battleships in pursuit of the Japanese, provided he left behind one CTG to cover Saipan and Guam. That choice was easy: Keen Harrill's 58.4—a way for Mitscher to shed his least-esteemed admiral.

The last aerial engagement of the day came at 7 p.m., a claim of a "probable" by a VF-51 Hellcat thirty miles out. Minutes later, the last light of a long and eventful day was gone. By 8 p.m., three CTGs preceded by Lee's battle line—ninety combatants in all—turned west to overhaul a Japanese fleet that had not yet been seen by task force searchers.

Meanwhile, the pilots that gathered to tally, gab, grieve and brag in their respective ready rooms knew that they had accomplished something special. Not only combating the largest and most intense aerial assaults on carriers ever—but handily repulsing them all. It was unprecedented and it had been achieved in what was the Pacific War's fifth and (unknown to the fliers) final carrier-to-carrier battle.

For individual pilots, success was measured not just in quadruplets (by ten fighter pilots from eight separate squadrons), but in quintuplets (by three, including VF-15 CO Commander Charles W. Brewer who was killed that day), sextuplets (Vraciu and Ripper Ensign Wilbur W. "Spider" Webb), and even a septuplet (McCampbell). Many must have sensed that the numbers being bandied about—preliminary reports showed 365 aerial kills and fifteen strafing destructions—were more a product of the day's unbridled exuberance then detached objectivity. An "inflation factor" of 30 to 50 percent was common for these big aerial battles. If so, a figure near 250 might be more like it. Still, what counted was air supremacy and no one could dispute that—least of all the Japanese.

There were any number of superlatives for the day, but VF-16's Lieutenant (junior grade) Zeigel "Ziggy" Neff, a Missouri farm boy who had flown two hops and claimed four kills (his total for the war) perhaps put it best—and certainly most memorably.

"It was," he told VF-16's intelligence officer during a routine debriefing, "just like an old-time turkey shoot."

MISSIONS BEYOND DARKNESS

SEVEN TBMs, FIFTEEN SBDs AND ELEVEN F6Fs, LEXINGTON'S PORTION OF A 216-plane strike force, began taking off at 4:30 p.m. on June 20. The aircraft had been ready for hours, the pilots, too: some decked out with shoulder holsters, backpacks and life jackets, the rest with gear close at hand. Their chart boards were filled with the necessary code, weather and navigation data—all the information needed except for the Japanese fleet's position, course and speed.

At 4:10 p.m., when the launch order finally showed on the ready room Teletype screens, that last piece fell in place. It was not welcome news—but there was worse to come.

Learning that the Japanese position was 230 miles west, VF-16's Lieutenant James Alvin "Sy" Seybert Jr., twenty-six, penciled a dot beyond the outer margin of his chart circle and audibly gasped: "I've got to fly out to here?" Others whistled or groaned. Most were visibly sobered: Covering the distance, surviving the fight, bucking the headwind coming back and trapping a wire after dark. Already, Lex was turned into the wind for launch—opening, not closing, the distance to the Japanese fleet.

Dutifully, the birdmen grabbed their gear and trooped up to *Lexington's* flight deck. On the way they caught snatches of Arleigh Burke's TBS announcement: "All task group commanders from Commander Task Group 58. . . . There are two, possibly three groups of enemy ships. . . . The primary objective is the carriers."

They hardly needed reminding: "GET THE CARRIERS" had been chalked in block letters on dozens of TF 58 ready room blackboards.

Throughout that morning, as TF 58 had continued its westward chase after the Japanese carriers, search teams (usually Avenger and Hellcat trios) had more luck finding Japanese aircraft than ships. *Hornet* pilots claimed five splashes, a novice aviator from *Wasp* shot down a scout float plane about two hundred fifty miles out and Air Group 10's Killer Kane (who had missed June 19's fight due to a crash injury and whose skull was still bandaged above a shiner) shot down two more. This was proof that the Japanese were searching as well, but none of the teams returned with any surface ship sightings.

Everyone was tense and anxious. Knowing that the stern chase was draining his ships' fuel bunkers, Mitscher requested that oilers proceed west as soon as possible. Though he likely didn't need any reminding about his paramount obligation, Mitscher nonetheless heard about it from his boss. Spruance reassured Mitscher of his commitment to the day's effort, but also, however diplomatically, reminded him of the constraints: "If no contact with enemy fleet results, consider it indication fleet is withdrawing and further pursuit after today will be unprofitable. If you concur, retire tonight toward Saipan."

———

VF-16's twenty-seven-year-old Lieutenant Henry Marzey Kosciusko piloted the first F6F off Lex's deck. As he lifted off, swerved to starboard and tucked in his wheels, Kosciusko's twenty-two-year-old wingman, Ensign William John Seyfferle, was already well into his deck run. Lieutenant (junior grade) Arthur Payne "Whitey" Whiteway and Lieutenant (junior grade) John Wilson Bartol, both twenty-three—the remainder of Kosciusko's division—soon followed.

Sy Seybert led the next division aloft, but two of his birds unexpectedly scratched—one with an oil leak, the other a dead radio— leaving only the Hellcat flown by second section leader Ensign Edward George "Ted" Wendorf, twenty-two, to join him.

Alex Vraciu's division, itself short one plane, rounded out Lex's fighter contingent. Ensign "Brock" Brockmeyer was airborne first, followed by Vraciu and then Lieutenant (junior grade) James Howard Arquette, twenty-three.

Usually eager for a fight, today Vraciu felt stale and uneasy, almost as if he'd been dragooned. It didn't help that after splashing six Japanese planes yesterday, he'd been simultaneously "congratulated" and "confined to quarters" after CO Pail Buie touched down. Buie had returned empty-handed and thought Vraciu had willfully disobeyed by not following him.

The misunderstanding was quickly cleared up by Joe Eggert, but it still left a bad taste.

———

The seven TBMs launched next. Lieutenant (junior grade) Clyde LeRoy "Tom" Bronn, twenty-two, went first, followed by Lieutenant (junior grade) Warren Ernest "Mac" McLellan, twenty-two, Lieutenant Kent Manning Cushman, twenty-five, Lieutenant (junior grade) Clinton Vance Swanson, twenty-five and Lieutenant (junior grade) William "Bill" Linn. Almost at once, Linn experienced engine problems. With just enough time to jettison bombs, Linn landed on a nearby CVL before his engine seized.

Linn's troubles delayed the launch for fifty seconds; finally, though, twenty-eight-year-old Lieutenant (junior grade) Harry Charles "Buzz" Thomas got the checkered flag, as did twenty-six-year-old Lieutenant Norman Anderson Sterrie, flying Lex's seventh and last Avenger. The way was cleared for VB-16.

———

As June 20 lengthened into afternoon, Raymond Spruance—as anxious as anyone for TF 58 fliers to have a go at the Japanese carriers—relented a bit on his earlier deadline. "Would like to continue pursuit of enemy to northwestward tonight," he informed Mitscher, "if this afternoon's operations give any indication it will be profitable." Spruance also asked about fuel status, something that was very much on Mitscher's mind too. His destroyers would be running dry by dawn on June 21, he told Spruance, but they could top off from carriers if the chase were to continue.

Meanwhile, Mitscher transmitted an all-hands message to task force sailors and airmen. "Indication our birdmen have sighted something big." It was intended as a morale-booster, but it was also a bit disingenuous and certainly premature. Nothing had been found yet.

———

VB-16's CO Lieutenant Commander Ralph Weymouth, a Guadalcanal veteran and, at twenty-seven, second oldest among the flight's pilots, was overall leader for the Lex's late afternoon strike. *Lexington's* VB-16 and *Enterprise's* VB-10, led by Lieutenant Commander James D. "Jig Dog" Ramage ("Rampage without the P"), another twenty-seven-year-old, were the last fleet carrier squadrons flying SBDs. Weymouth's eighteen-plane contingent (three divisions with three to a section) took off nearly as nimbly as the fighters, but once airborne the SBDs—the "Slow But Deadlies"—would be the formation's laggards.

Weymouth's third division leader, twenty-seven-year-old Lieutenant Donald Kirkpatrick Jr., had been shot up eighteen times in forty-one previous missions, enough to make any pilot superstitious. Yet despite being assigned aircraft number thirteen, Kirkpatrick merely took it in stride. "Here we go again!" Kirkpatrick had shrugged to his radioman-gunner, Aviation Ordnanceman Second Class Richard LeRoy Bentley. "Here we go again," echoed Bentley.

Bentley, at nineteen, was the flight's youngest crewmen (the oldest, another VB-16 radioman-gunner, was forty-three). The flight's youngest pilot and VB-16's newest addition was twenty-year-old Ensign Eugene Vincent Conklin in Kirkpatrick's division. Despite his youth, Conklin showed a "feel for the stick." But Conklin also fancied himself impervious to death—a concern for Weymouth and Kirkpatrick, not to mention his radioman-gunner twenty-three-year-old Aviation Ordnanceman Third Class John Williams Sample.

———

At 1:45 p.m., four teams of two TBFs and one F6F each had launched from *Enterprise* and fanned out to the northwest to search adjacent ten-degree sectors. At 3:28 p.m., VT-10's Lieutenant Robert S. Nelson, the lead TBF pilot in the more northerly of the middle sections, happened to notice a ripple on the surface off to port. Afternoon squalls made visibility difficult, but Lieutenant (junior grade) Edward Laster, a TBM pilot covering the sector adjacent to the south, spotted the same thing at about the same time. Approaching from opposite sides of a large rain cloud, both beheld what no American aviator had seen for nearly two years (and what many in the current crop of aviators had never seen at all): a Japanese carrier task force.

Nelson was the first to break radio silence to transmit a position report. Just to be sure, he repeated it twice. The fix he gave was just slightly south of the enemy's actual location. Of more consequence, the fix had the Japanese fleet sixty miles closer (one degree of longitude) to TF 58 than they actually were. At 4 p.m., Nelson's radio-gunner transmitted a Morse code version of the position sighting, this time correcting the longitudinal error. Ed Laster's Morse code report also corrected the longitude, but Nelson's initial, unwitting error was to create some confusion and angst.

As Laster's search team turned and sped home, all the while working their radios to be sure the message got through, Nelson's team went in for a closer look. Before finally high-tailing back at 4:10 p.m., Nelson saw the formation's carrier turn, leaving behind it a huge curving wake. While inbound to *Enterprise*, his team got confirmation that their reports had been received: westbound air groups passing in resolute succession high overhead. Hearing radio chatter reporting them as bogeys, Hellcat pilot Lieutenant Edward G. "Ned" Colgan spoke up for the team.

"Negative bogeys!" Colgan assured them. "This is two turkeys and an F6!"

———

Before the *Essex* pilots' sighting reports reached Lex's Flag Pot, Gus Widhelm had been thinking of ways to extricate himself from his latest wager. Having scored on the thousand-dollar bet about the fleet engagement, Widhelm had doubled down—betting two squadron COs that the Japanese carriers would indeed be found.

Grasping the sighting reports that secured his stakes, Widhelm had leaned over the plotting table to work out the math—the intercept heading and the all-important matter of round-trip distance and time.

"Expect to launch everything we have," Mitscher signaled just before 4 p.m. (and receipt of Nelson's updated position report). "We will probably have to recover at night."

"We can make it," Widhelm said when he finally looked up. "But it's going to be tight."

Whenever Mitscher spoke, those around him were accustomed to listening closely because his projection was soft, sometimes barely discernible. It was no different now, but neither was there sign of hesitation. "Launch 'em."

———

To conserve fuel, planes immediately turned west after launch and formed up by running rendezvous on the outbound course—290 degrees, slightly north of west. They also flew as low as they could as long as they dared, keeping fuel mixtures lean and manifold pressures low. When they eventually climbed, they climbed slowly—making the outbound leg a long uphill journey. To cut wind resistance, cockpit canopies stayed closed. For the SBD and TBM pilots (most of whom carried bombs, not torpedoes), balancing fuel loads was just as important as conservation. No one wanted to attack with "asymmetrical" wings.

About twenty minutes into the flight, Weymouth and other flight leaders began receiving position updates and it was bad news for fuel consumption: the Japanese were seventy miles further west than first reported, fully 300 miles from the point of launch. Many pilots did quick re-calculations (heading, wind drift, indicated speed, likely enemy movement) on their fuel situations. Things would be tight for fighters (who carved fuel-sucking S turns so as not to overtake their flocks) and TBMs; it didn't look at all good for the SBDs and especially the SB2Cs. Twenty-four-year-old Lieutenant Cook "Cookie" Cleland, one of Weymouth's section leaders, had already sent one plane back because of leaking fuel. Meanwhile, the notoriously faulty carburetor in Cleland's old SBD was guzzling gas at an alarming rate. Cleland kept mum lest Weymouth order him back as well.

In Flag Plot, Mitscher debated with Burke, Thach, Widhelm and others on his staff the wisdom of sending other deck loads. They were now being prepared, not only on the carriers engaged, but also on Harrell's 58.4 "stay-behinds": *Essex, Langley* and *Princeton.*

Mitscher had not watched the launch. He knew the four hundred men aloft faced landings after dark and most were not night-qualified. Arleigh Burke was already checking plans for illuminating the task force for homing pilots.

Mitscher mulled it over. There would be heavy losses in the first strike and extending recovery further into the night would only compound the casualties. "Hold that second strike," he said finally. "There's no telling how many we'll lose from this flight. We've got to have something left to hit them with tomorrow."

Outbound, strike pilots flooded the circuits with premature sightings—phantom ship formations which turned out to be small clouds low on the water. Some even mistook their top cover for bogeys. The first real sighting came nearly two hours into the mission—a large oil slick, a bronze-colored trail that soon led to a formation of Japanese destroyers and tankers.

It was 6:35 p.m. when circuits again crackled with do-or-die chatter. Pilots from another formation were veering off to attack. "Look at this oil slick!" shouted one. Another: "Haven't got time to look around!" And a third: "Is this the force to attack? My gas is half-gone."

Those planes, mostly SB2Cs, were heading in, much to the disdain of VB-10's Ramage who, like Weymouth, kept his flock in the hunt for the "Charlie Victors." "Unknown flight leader, what are you trying to do," Ramage broke in on the guard circuit, "sink their Merchant Marine?"

Weymouth wasn't so ready to mock. Sometimes the obsession with hitting big-ticket combatants (not only among the aviators but the Gun Clubbers and submariners as well) came at the expense of passing up other targets, oilers included, that were just as vital to the Japanese. Besides, it was possible that the Lex and Big E aircraft might not find the Japanese carriers at all—or too late to do anything about it. At least these guys were on the attack.

Still, Weymouth pressed on. Ten minutes later his persistence finally paid off. As the flight dipped under the overhang of a huge anvil-topped cumulous cloud, a pilot spotted what they were looking for. "Looks like we found the whole Goddamn Jap navy!"

———

There were three groups of Japanese ships—more than the scouting reports indicated—each centered on huge vessels most had seen before only in photos: Japanese fleet aircraft carriers.

One group with three carriers was just ahead, a second carrier group lay to the north and a third group, uncounted and unidentified, lay even further to the west. Ralph Weymouth, who had last seen an enemy carrier two years before in the Eastern Solomons, considered his options. The sky over the carrier group to the north was already crowded with attackers—planes from *Enterprise* and *Hornet*—while the group to the west was just too far. He decided to unleash his TBMs and SBDs on the ships immediately below.

At first the coast looked clear. TBM pilot Norm Sterrie heard someone shout: "No enemy planes in the air over the target!" But no sooner did he hear that than eight Zeros swooped in from nowhere. One was already behind and below Warren McLellan's TBM, peppering its belly.

All McLellan saw was a spurt of tracers close to his canopy. Then he felt a jolt from below and his cockpit filled with smoke. He tried pulling up sharply to get clear of whatever it was that had hit him, but it was no use. The cockpit was on fire and he had to get out. As McLellan reached for his microphone to warn radioman Aviation Radioman Second Class Selbie Greenhalgh and gunner Aviation Machinist Mate Second Class John Seaman Hutchinson to bail out, flames scorched his wrist and the handset fell out of reach into the fire. Unable to wait any longer, McLellan bailed out, hoping Greenhalgh and Hutchinson had the alertness and instincts to follow.

As soon as Sterrie's gunner, twenty-six-year-old Aviation Machinist

Mate First Class Jack William Webb, saw McLellan jump, he got on the intercom to tell his pilot. "Who is it?" Sterrie asked frantically, but Webb was already too busy to reply. With the same bandit now full in his gun sight, Webb gave it two bursts and got ready to take on others. Nearby, Buzz Thomas's gunner smoked a second Japanese fighter and Kent Cushman's a third. Between them, Tom Bronn's TBM crewmen—gunner twenty-three-year-old Aviation Radioman Second Class Paul Linson on the .50 caliber turret gun and twenty-two-year-old Aviation Ordnanceman First Class Michael Aloysius Banazak on the .30 caliber belly stinger—shook four Zeros from his tail.

It was good work, but where were their fighters?

———

When Weymouth's bombers dipped below the towering cumulous, the Lex's fighters—split into top and middle cover—were still close by. But Weymouth's maneuver caught them off guard. They lost contact and several were distracted by a tally-ho of two distant Zekes.

Even as these decoys vanished into a cloud, a second group of Zekes was striking the TBMs and SBDs from below and a third was crowding the escorts' flanks. Alex Vraciu had seen McLellan and his crew bail, but then he and Brockmeyer were virtually surrounded by bandits—and forced to fight for their lives.

Vraciu and Brockmeyer scissored to fend off the attacks, but they were simply outnumbered. Briefly coming abeam of Brockmeyer, Vraciu saw his wingman's Hellcat being peppered from astern and thought he heard Brockmeyer say "I've been hit." Vraciu rolled hard right, taking out the attacking Zeke with two deflection bursts, but Brockmeyer's Hellcat was by then smoking and spiraling seaward.

Vraciu dove, hoping to mark Brockmeyer's splash, only to have two Zekes climb on his tail. Pulling up to shake these two, he snap-rolled to slow down, only to find his guns lined up on a third Zeke. Firing at close range, Vraciu scored hits and saw this Zeke fall away. All at once he found himself alone—no Zekes, but no SBDs or TBMs either. The Japanese fighters had dashed ahead in pursuit of the bombers.

———

It was just past 7 p.m. as Weymouth's SBDs, after skirting the north end of the largest cloud formation, jockeyed into attack position. Three had taken hits from Zekes but all were still airworthy. Soon their crews were more concerned with flak than bandits.

In the gathering dusk, the decks of the Japanese ships below were ablaze with antiaircraft muzzle flashes. Above, a "roof" of explosive bursts—in green, yellow, black, blue, white, pink and purple—seemed impermeable. At least the flak kept the Zekes at bay.

Flak concussions buffeted Ralph Weymouth's plane as the SBDs turned to approach from the west. Weymouth had his target (what was probably carrier *Hiyo*). Two years before in the Eastern Solomons, Weymouth had another Japanese carrier (most likely *Ryūjō*) dead in his sights, only to miss. This looked twice the size and Weymouth was determined to score this time.

Weymouth looked around for Sterrie's TBMs. For the moment he couldn't see them, but fully expected that Sterrie would hold them wide to make room for the SBDs' dives. Weymouth signaled—a fisted right hand up, a waggle of his wings to execute. His sections (and, in well-drilled sequence, his other divisions) broke their vees to cross above Weymouth and edge into right echelons.

Weymouth took a last look: The northbound carriers were now turning west—a maneuver that in time would cancel the crosswind and drift effects of the easterly breeze. But, as big as the ships were, they couldn't spin on their heels. They were still sitting ducks—a dive-bomber's dream.

Weymouth pushed over at ten thousand five hundred feet into a seventy-degree incline and got busy lining up his sight pipper on a point of impact midway down the axis of the carrier's flight deck. His altimeter spun off nine thousand more feet—thirty seconds from sun into twilight. There was no time now to savor the performance gifts bestowed by Douglas designers on SBD veterans like Weymouth. Still, they were undeniable: unwavering stability as the bomber accelerated and simple controls obedient to a deft touch.

At fifteen hundred feet Weymouth finally pressed his bomb release: a red "B" engraved button on his control stick. Below and behind him a trapeze-like "displacing fork" pulled the half-ton bomb from its belly shackles and threw it forward, clear of the propeller.

It was a thousand feet more before Weymouth reversed stick. In the process of bottoming out, he and his gunner pulled six to eight gs—a force that turned a 160-pound man into twelve hundred pounds of flattened, blind, bloodless and useless flesh. When consciousness and shadowy sight finally returned to Weymouth, the nose of his SBD was hanging just above the horizon. He quickly added power and pulled in flaps. In the back seat, twenty-one-year-old Aviation Radioman First Class William Arthur McElhiney groggily confirmed a hit: black smoke from the deck just aft of the flattop's superstructure.

Meanwhile, the other SBDs were dropping bombs in intervals so compressed that it was impossible to tell which bomb was whose. Soon, stacked-up planes fouled the sight line to *Hiyo*. Several pilots skidded to get a better view while others shifted aim to the carrier ahead (most likely *Junyō*.) In the stampede, some pilots dispensed with dive brakes and zoomed past planes ahead of them in queue. Gene Conklin's "feel for the stick" took him so near to the drink before bomb release and pullout that his gunner, John Sample, was certain "the kid" at the controls had been killed.

Gunners in other SBD back seats (privy to the same sensations and fears as the pilots though "just along for the ride") struggled to compensate for their helplessness. Most sat facing aft (in effect, on their backs), but at least one perched sideways, watching with the thought that if the pilot's cockpit splintered, he might still somehow wrestle the plane under control. Some bargained with their maker, an inchoate universe or themselves: *If you get through this—you won't, but if you do—you're going to be the best little boy in the world!*

Still others sought distraction in the brilliant panoply of flak bursts or simply sat back to await oblivion.

———

Norm Sterrie's seven Avengers, now free of the enemy CAP assault, had indeed stood aside for Weymouth's SBDs. But even as they got into position for their bomb runs, four torpedo-equipped *Belleau Wood* Avengers that had accompanied the Lex aircraft on the outbound leg were already testing the meat grinder. VT-24 Division leader Lieutenant George "Brownie" Brown and his wingman approached carrier *Hiyo*'s port bow and quarter, while Brown's other two TBMs completed the "torpecker sandwich" by bracketing her starboard bow and quarter.

Brown's division had broached three rings of crossfire from Japanese destroyers, cruisers and battleships. Brown's Avenger took hits and caught on fire, but while his two crewmen bailed, Brown stayed put. Just four hundred feet off the deck, the four TBMs launched torpedoes. While you never knew quite what to expect from the troublesome torpedoes (the reason so few Avengers carried them this day), they were at least barreling in simultaneously from all quadrants.

———

Sterrie's seven glide-bombing TBMs went in next to finish the work of Weymouth's SBDs and Brown's four torpeckers. The Grumman pilots opened their bomb-bay doors at seven thousand feet and released their five hundred pounders (four to a plane) at three thousand feet. As with Brown's division, Sterrie's Avengers made fat targets for shipboard gunners, but they compensated with speed—as high as 320 knots, pressing terminal velocity.

Norm Sterrie went in first, followed by Clint Swanson and then Tom Bronn. As Kent Cushman made his approach, his bomb bay's starboard door unexpectedly crumpled. The two portside bombs dropped clear, but the starboard bombs clipped metal on their way out. Buzz Thomas was last to go in. By now the area was so thick with smoke that Thomas couldn't even see Cushman ahead. For a moment he thought he was hit by shipboard fire, but it turned out to be cockpit panels sheared off by the wind. Thomas wasn't wearing goggles and specks of cinder and dirt hit his eyes. Still, he was sure that two bombs had exploded just forward of the carrier's fantail.

As they fled the scene, virtually all the pilots were convinced they'd scored either direct hits or near misses. The objective truth could be resolved by gun camera footage and crosschecked debriefings. The question now was whether they'd ever get back to tell the story.

———

There were two ways to get to the Lex flight's rendezvous point. One was to skirt the commotion, the other to go straight through it. Most took the direct route, either because they were already in it or because it seemed to offer the best chance of saving fuel and joining up for the trip home.

Ralph Weymouth and his wingman took the direct route and almost at once he regretted it. Shells of every caliber were being thrown at them. His gunner, McElhiney, tried to fight back by spraying tracers across the deck of a destroyer, but intense and accurate return fire sent him ducking behind cockpit armor.

VB-16 pilot twenty-four-year-old Lieutenant Thomas Earl "Dupe" Dupree, tried to join with Weymouth, only to think better of it when he saw a solid wall of fire directly ahead. Instead he circled southeast just outside the range of a Japanese cruiser only to find an enemy CAP formation waiting to ambush the "round-abouts." When one Zeke dove on Dupree's starboard wing, he turned to confront it only to find his guns were jammed. Dupree frantically recharged them and squeezed again—

still jammed. He was a goner, but the Japanese pilot apparently had taste for other game: he zoomed over Dupree's head without firing a shot.

Dupree banked back east in hopes of catching up with two distant Avengers. These turned out to be VT-16's Norm Sterrie and Clint Swanson who, just fifty feet above the water, were about to bisect the crossfire of two Japanese destroyers. Dupree caught up with them on the other side of this enfilade only to join them in taking broadsides from a cruiser.

About now, young Gene Conklin was also skimming the waves, hoping to stay concealed in the dusk. But down so low, he also had to dodge waterspouts thrown up by battleship gun salvos. When he and another VB-16 pilot slid in behind Weymouth's vee, cruiser and destroyer gunfire seemed to have all five of them bracketed. One shell fragment punctured Conklin's canopy and bounced off his helmet.

"I'm hit but I don't think I'm hurt!" Conklin radioed his gunner John Sample. Sample looked over his shoulder apprehensively with thoughts about taking the stick if need be.

———

On the far side of the flak gauntlet, aircraft joined up as much out of chance as choice. Remarkably, *Belleau Wood* Avenger pilots Lieutenants (junior grade) Benjamin Tate and Warren R. Omark met up with their division leader's bullet-riddled plane. When Brown held up his right arm, Tate could see it was bloodstained. Brown look stunned, like a football player who had been hit in the head. Tate talked to him on the radio but the return transmission was unintelligible. The two pilots tried to keep Brown with them. Both Omark and Tate turned on their lights in the gloom, but Brown didn't follow suit. Either his lighting system was shot or Brown was indeed as shocked and senseless as he looked.

Meanwhile, VB-10's Lieutenant Don "Hound Dog" Nelson managed to join up with another VB-10 SBD. The two *Enterprise* pilots briefly fell in with a formation of Lex SBDs. But as Nelson checked his gas, he realized he couldn't—or shouldn't—keep up with them. Against the fourteen-knot headwind, he was running at 2,100 rpm just to hold his place—too much juice. Then Nelson spotted another, slower formation off to starboard. They turned out to be VB-10 planes, so Nelson and his companion broke away to join them.

After failing to find any Group 16 TBMs or SBDs, VF-16's Whiteway, Kosciusko, Bartol, Arquette and Seyfferle turned for home. Whiteway was uncertain about the return course, so when he spotted a flight of SB2Cs ahead, he suggested to the others that they follow. But then, realizing the fuel-guzzling Beasts might not make it that far, they decided to overtake them and press on. Their getting home first would clear flight decks for the slower stragglers. They climbed to brighter air at seven thousand feet and set speed at 170 knots. Arquette figured they'd reach TF 58 about 8:30 p.m.

————

VT-16 Mac McLellan's free fall carried him below the horizon where it was difficult to distinguish sky from sea. Still, McLellan pulled his ripcord with room to spare and, by the time he hit the water, he'd also undone his chute buckles and inflated one side of his Mae West.

McLellan landed in six-foot swells and quickly squirmed free of his parachute harness. He worked to unhook the raft pack still attached to the chute harness and the survival pack strapped over his shoulders. It took McLellan precious seconds to free the backpack and by then, the parachute canopy was filled with water and sinking. McLellan fumbled to release the raft pack but the flooded canopy was pulling him down. He had to let the chute and life raft go.

Clutching his survival pack, McLellan now only had his Mae West for buoyancy. More important, he'd lost his best chance at survival—the bright yellow raft that search planes could easily spot. Fighting to hold his composure, McLellan pulled the lanyard to inflate the other side of the Mae West.

Riding the wave crests, McLellan was front row to quite a show. First, he saw one carrier that had taken a hit forward of its island and then a second carrier already afire and listing. Then a cruiser swept by, its bow and starboard side so close he could discern the color of its sailors' uniforms, all in khaki except one man in white. Next—thankfully further out—two battleships cut the cruiser's wake.

Finally, in the last of the light, McLellan saw a flight of Zekes circling the burning carrier. Trailing thick, black smoke from its stacks, the carrier continued downwind, leaving the planes without a nest. Now three hundred miles from his own nest, McLellan was left to wonder: Just how many other pilots and crewmen would share his fate this night?

————

It was late—nearing 9 p.m.—and dark. On the first night of a new moon, there was no illumination except for the dim red back light of the cockpit gauges.

Don Nelson's SBD fuel readings indicated that three of four fuel tanks were dry—and the final one wouldn't last much longer. Ten minutes before, the pilots (those with working receivers, anyway) heard a welcome transmission from the task force: "Land at nearest base. Land at nearest base..." Still, Nelson and his gunner would need luck to make it.

Already planes were dropping out—the radio circuits were full of last transmissions. One pilot told his gunner to prepare for a water landing. A Hellcat pilot told his wingman he'd been hit in one tank and was going down; the wingman replied he'd ditch with him. Nelson watched one group of lights, a whole division of planes, drift lower and lower until the lights extinguished. VB-10's formation was hanging in there, but it was ragged. Every few minutes another pilot would come on the circuit, calling a wingman, calling his carrier, announcing he was going in. Each time silence followed.

———

Radar operators in CICs throughout TF 58 began seeing contacts on their screens at about 8:15 p.m. Most were to the west, but a few were to the north and south. Fifteen minutes later, carriers reversed course to the east and cranked up speed to twenty knots. In the roughly four hours since launch, the task force had traveled ninety miles.

As early as the day before, Arleigh Burke, Jimmie Thach and Gus Widhelm had discussed the possibility of a full-scale night recovery. Now the word went out to prepare to illuminate the task force: Carriers were to turn on their running lights, masthead truck lights and deck-edge lights; also, each task group flagship was to point its biggest search light vertically as a beacon.

Then, at 8:30 p.m., CTG 58.1's Jocko Clark jumped the gun. Hearing the panic in the returning aviators' chatter, he ordered all his carriers to immediately turn on their brightest beams. He also ordered cruisers to start firing star shells. Soon, unprompted, screen destroyers began aiming their searchlights at the carriers. Realizing that Clark's formation was already lit like a carnival, Mitscher gave word for the other groups to follow suit: "Turn on the lights."

———

Art Whiteway was fighting the effects of vertigo when he, Bartol and Arquette saw lights flashing. They edged south to approach the lights—what turned out to be lightning. They continued on—now running low on fuel—temporarily blocked by a blanket of clouds. Then, realizing they'd probably passed the task force, Whiteway, with Bartol and Arquette on either wing, turned northeast. Suddenly a star shell flashed nearby, blinding Whiteway and bringing on another wave of dizziness. When he finally got his bearings he was only two hundred or so feet above the water. Bartol and Arquette were nowhere in sight.

Now his fuel situation was critical—maybe five more minutes' worth. Whiteway considered ditching, but as he descended and unbuckled his parachute harness, he could see, even in the darkness, that the water was rough—swells at least ten feet high. "Good God," he said aloud. "Give me a break."

———

When he finally saw lights, Alex Vraciu's first unsettling thought was that he must be approaching Yap—a Japanese-held island south of the Marianas. If so, it validated all the bomber pilots' snide remarks about fighter jocks not being able to navigate. But then he started to hear voices over the radio circuit: "Land at nearest base. Land at nearest base." Maybe he'd been on the right track all along.

Vraciu had flown most of the return leg without company. After escaping the Zekes that had cornered Brockmeyer and him over the Japanese fleet, Vraciu had headed for the rendezvous point and briefly joined up with a TBF from another carrier. Vraciu was anxious to climb in hopes of picking up the task group's homing signal. But the torpedo bomber was shot up and low on fuel; its pilot wasn't able to join Vraciu. Circling below were seven SB2Cs. The radio traffic Vraciu copied suggested all were short of fuel and readying to ditch. Vraciu gave a final salute as the TBF left to join them.

Climbing to eight thousand feet, Vraciu soon picked up the homing signal. Though he had more than enough fuel to make it back, the circuit was filled with more discouraging chatter from pilots who didn't. Some transmissions were business-like, others plaintive or even panicky. Each in its way was mournful. For a time, as he cruised in the darkness, determined to follow the homing signal and keep his emotions under wraps, Vraciu turned off the voice receiver.

———

Despite the open invitation to land on any carrier deck, Vraciu was anxious to reach *Lexington*—and his own sack. And, as he got closer, he found precisely what he was looking for: the distinctive broad stack of *Enterprise*. That meant Lex was right next door.

Her landing circle was crowded, so Vraciu initially held back, waiting for things to thin out. A veteran of Bat Team training, he wasn't particularly concerned about night landing and he still had plenty of fuel—let those with less get aboard first. But when he finally let down for his approach, *Lexington* had suspended recovery—likely a deck crash.

Giving up on the hoped-for comforts of home base, Vraciu shifted to *Enterprise's* landing circle and touched down on the first pass. As he taxied up the deck, though, the plane behind him plowed into the barrier. As a result, the anxious flight deck crewman who jumped on the Hellcat's wing urged Vraciu to get below fast. "Some from your bombing squadron are aboard."

Among the VB-16 pilots and crewmen resting up in VB-10's ready room was Cook Cleland. After landing on Big E and taxiing forward to the bow, crewmen surveyed the busted-up SBD and prepared to heave it over the side. Only when Cleland reached for his sidearm did they relent.

———

Rough water or not, Art Whiteway was running out of options. He lifted the Hellcat's nose for another look around—nothing. He then lowered it and braced for the inevitable. At least he could tell that the waves had moderated.

Then Whiteway detected a searchlight. It turned out to be a destroyer, but five miles further on he saw another. Closing on this searchlight, Whiteway saw red truck lights blink below his wing and a carrier's deck-edge lights flash on. A Helldiver was already in its landing circle; Whiteway got behind it, followed it around and, after it landed, he got into the groove and landed too. He was aboard *Cabot*.

———

Don Nelson's first glimmer of hope came when he picked up *Enterprise's* homing beacon signal—it meant he had about seventy-five miles to go. Then Nelson saw—or imagined he saw—the arc of a star shell. He thought maybe it was lightning, but then he saw others. Definitely star shells. It was 9:20 p.m. The planes in his group were approaching the outer screen. Then, a bit further on, searchlights: some vertical, others horizontal (pointers to the carriers). Some of the verticals were blunted by low clouds but the rest stood tall. In the darkness, broken until now only by the navigation lights of other planes, the searchlights were a spectacular welcome.

———

Mac McLellan still had his Very pistol and when things seemed to have settled down he used it to shoot off a red flare. If Greenhalgh or Hutchinson were nearby they might see it. The flare lit up the patch of ocean, a reminder of how alone he was. After two minutes, McLellan fired a round from his .38 pistol and ten seconds later another. He turned slowly in the water—watching and listening, but seeing nothing, hearing nothing.

Even though it wasn't waterproof, his watch ticked on, and as time crept by McLellan occasionally felt muffled underwater concussions. He reasoned they might be the implosion of watertight compartments in the ships his group had sunk. He tried floating on his back, but the concussions hurt his ears.

Eventually McLellan had nothing else but his thoughts to keep him occupied. He tried to keep these positive—things he should do once the sun was up. But then a thought as dark as the night intruded: he had no girlfriend, no wife, no children and no legacy.

The thought stayed with McLellan all that night, sometimes weighing him down in despair, sometimes buoying him with anger and determination. Once he considered putting his pistol to his head and getting it over with. But he shook that off.

––––––

Don Nelson realized his troubles weren't over. All around him were the lights of arriving aircraft—a traffic jam of red and green and white and yellow. All the aircraft seemed to converge at once, all starved for gas and desperate to land. Though the base circuit had told them to land on any carrier with a clear deck, Nelson knew all the landing circles would fill quickly and many pilots would be desperate enough to crowd others aside.

Nelson also saw lights below him, but they were confusing. Every ship's foremast displayed red truck lights, with no way of telling whether they were carriers. Nelson's fuel gauges showed dry. His best bet was to find a carrier with a clear deck and no other aircraft in its landing circle. Once Nelson lowered wheels and flaps and went full power, his remaining fuel would go fast.

Then he heard what he was praying for: a carrier saying it had a clear deck and no waiting. They'd signal their position with two blinks of their largest searchlight, and there it was, off to Nelson's left.

Nelson got in the groove. Ahead of him he could see the carrier's deck-edge lights and the LSO's fluorescent light wands. But now they spelled out bad news: aloft, crossing and uncrossing. A wave-off. Nelson considered landing anyway, but instead gunned his engine and circled for another approach only to get another wave-off, this time because of a fouled deck.

Nelson pulled up his wheels and flaps, gained a little attitude and throttled back as much as he dared. He was incredibly tired. He doubted there was enough fuel for another pass—even if he spotted a carrier ready to take him now. Nelson saw lights further ahead. He kept going, kept gaining on the lights. Sure enough, it was another carrier, a big one.

Nelson went by its port side and looked down. The LSO was giving him a wheels-down land signal. When Nelson circled and got in the groove, he could see the deck was clear. The LSO was signaling high and fast, so Nelson dropped his nose and took off some throttle. When he got the cut, Nelson dropped the nose a bit more. The SBD's wheels touched and bounced and the tail hook grabbed a wire. It was a solid, blessed, welcoming yank—almost like a hug.

Of the two hundred and more planes that had launched that afternoon, roughly one hundred forty made carrier landings that night—though often not at their home base. For example, of the twenty-one aircraft trapped by *Lexington*, only nine (including Ralph Weymouth's, Don Kirkpatrick's and Gene Conklin's SBDs; Kent Cushman's and Norm Sterrie's TBMs; and Sy Seybert's F6F) were her own. Among the unexpected guests was the TBM flown by VT-24's Warren Omark, courtesy of a Corsair night-fighter pilot who used radar to intercept Omark and guide him to an open deck.

At one point during Lex's long, white-knuckle night, two Beasts from *Hornet* touched down, the latter of them shot up and flown by a wounded pilot. The aircraft hurtled two woven-steel barriers, pierced a third and plowed into the Helldiver just ahead of it—killing its tail gunner and tossing debris that killed a ship's company sailor. (It was this crash that prevented Alex Vraciu from landing aboard Lex.)

Lex had perhaps the worst of the night's flight deck calamities, but there were numerous other small ones that as surely fouled decks and clogged landing circles. All who eventually caught a wire—like VF-16's Bill Seyferle[1] (aboard *Hornet*), John Bartol (aboard *Wasp*), Jim Arquette and Hank Kosciusko (both aboard unknown carriers), and VT-16's Clint Swanson (aboard *Princeton*)—were simply grateful to find a solid deck under wings and wheels.

---

1. Bill Seyfferle would be killed in a flight accident on June 21 as he flew back to *Lexington*.

When flight deck recovery operations finally shut down, there were still 172 pilots and crew unaccounted for. Many men who might well still be alive were strewn across a vast swath of ocean. Before dawn, about ninety fortunate ones were rescued by task force destroyers and even cruisers. Among the wet but lucky: VT-16's Tom Bronn aboard *Reno* (CL-96) with his crew, and Buzz Thomas aboard *Gatling* (DD-671) with his crew; VB-16's Dupe Dupree aboard *Terry* (DD-513) with his gunner; VF-16's Ted Wendorf aboard *C.K. Bronson* (DD-668); and VT-24's Ben Tate aboard *Knapp* (DD-653) with his crew.

At dawn, air searches would be dispatched in hopes of finding still more missing fliers. For the time being, the survivors, many of them unable to sleep, hung out in the ready rooms, trading wide-eyed chatter, quaffing paper cups of water or orange juice (usually laced with "medicinal brandy") and trying to explain what they'd done, seen, heard, and felt to awestruck squadron intelligence officers (IOs).

"Well," as VB-16's Donald Kirkpatrick, a veteran of both Midway and the Santa Cruz Islands, described it to his squadron's IO, "I've been jumped worse by Zekes, and there have been missions when I've had to be on the ball more, and I've landed with less gas, but I've never had all that trouble together until now. It was the hop supreme."

———

June 21, 1944

Mac McLellan, still soaking wet, stood on *Lexington's* catwalk, being unhitched from a breeches buoy. The ship's loudspeaker was calling him, requesting he go up immediately to the flag bridge. The day was such a blur that McLellan's mind had trouble keeping up with the pace of things. But this was no dream.

———

When McLellan first heard engines that morning, he had checked his watch: 7:30 a.m. The first planes he saw were high-flying Helldivers with Hellcat escorts—no chance he'd be seen. Low-flying Hellcats came next, then Avengers and with them a shower of life rafts. McLellan finally reached one, inflated it and heaved himself in. The exertion made him vomit, but he pulled the raft's sail over his head and drifted off to sleep.

Sleep, interrupted by more vomiting, ended at 4:00 p.m. with the noise of a flight of Hellcats trailed by four float planes. One settled near McLellan's raft and its pilot leaned out, grinning. "How about it? Want a lift?"

McLellan managed to croak, "You're the best sight I've seen since I've been living!"

The float plane flew McLellan to a cruiser. He learned en route that dozens of scout planes were out—sent by Mitscher—and that he'd been spotted close to a huge oil slick. As important, he found out Greenhalgh and Hutchinson had been picked up, too.

McLellan was onboard the cruiser briefly—it seemed only long enough to get a pair of dry socks and shoes—before he was strapped into a breeches buoy and swung over to a destroyer. The destroyer, it turned out, had also been sent by Mitscher to fetch him. By the time McLellan was ushered before Mitscher's small, rumpled presence on *Lexington*'s flag bridge, he hardly knew how to begin speaking his thanks through lips and a tongue that were just then beginning to feel like normal.

There was no need. Mitscher quietly shook his hand, welcomed McLellan back and asked him what he'd seen. McLellan told Mitscher—the two carriers, one with a fiery deck and a fifteen degree list, the cruiser passing close by, the two battleships further out, and the homeless Japanese aircraft. Mitscher smiled and nodded: "I think we got two carriers last night."

As it turned out, TF 58's bold aerial strike into darkness on June 20 claimed only one Japanese carrier— Hiyo. Two others—Zuikaku and Chiyoda—were hit but survived. But this was only one measure of the achievement. Japan's loss of Hiyo compounded the loss of Shokaku and Taiho to submarine torpedoes on June 19.

A final count for the two days of epic aerial battles would show that Japan's Mobile Fleet had lost 92 percent of its carrier aircraft and 72 percent of its float planes. Combined with the loss of fifty Guam-based aircraft, the two-day total climbed to nearly five hundred aircraft—and, along with them, nearly as many skilled flyers.

By contrast, TF 58's June 19 and 20 toll amounted to no ships and forty-two aircraft. The June 20 "mission beyond darkness," meanwhile, had cost the lives of sixteen pilots and forty-two crewmen.

———

June 23, 1944

Pete Mitscher wished it to be "personal" rather than "official"—not a publicity shot but a memento. For purposes of the photograph, Mitscher and Alex Vraciu stood shaking hands atop the starboard wing of Vraciu's Hellcat. Mitscher wore his usual khakis and his idiosyncratic lobsterman's hat, Vraciu his flight gear. Prominently displayed between them, arrayed in five rows just below the Hellcat's canopy, are nineteen "Rising Sun" decals, emblematic of Vraciu's aerial victory count—which at the time made him the U.S. Navy's leading fighter ace.

Intended or not, the photo reflects the connections among generations of naval aviators whose service, exploits, sacrifice and legacies had led to this moment— a once-gutted seagoing navy transformed into a powerful aviation-centric navy; a momentous victory against a once-dominant foe not yet complete but certain to be.

Mitscher, then fifty-seven (but looking older), of course, represented Naval Aviation's origins—military pioneers such as William Moffett and John Tower and industry pioneers such as Red Mike Grumman and Jimmy Collins. Vraciu, meanwhile, stood for the present and—at twenty-five and looking younger— the future.

Missing from the frame (but in the minds of both) were men of the generation between. Men such as Jimmie Thach and Jimmy Flatley (who were still serving and shaping naval aviation's future) and John Waldron and Butch O'Hare—who had both paid the ultimate sacrifice.

Within months, visibly exhausted after his grueling command tours in the Pacific War, Mitscher would be leaving for duty in Washington, D.C. (He would die at age sixty while commanding the U.S. Navy's Atlantic Fleet.)

Vraciu would be returning Stateside even sooner than Mitscher—for home leave and for a 'victory lap' celebrating his exploits during what became widely known as the 'Marianas Turkey Shoot.' Back in the States, Vraciu would be lavishly feted, particularly at a parade and award ceremony in his hometown of East Chicago, Indiana.

While at home, Vraciu would find, woo, win and marry Kathryn Horn, a girl he'd known since childhood but who had blossomed into an incredible beauty while her bridegroom was away at college, in flight training and overseas. Their wartime marriage, however, did not curb Vraciu's impulse to return to Pacific War combat. After a honeymoon in New York, and Navy efforts to coax him into a publicity tour like that endured by his mentor Butch O'Hare, Vraciu wangled assignment to duty with VF-20 aboard Enterprise.

On a December 14, 1944 mission (just his second since returning to the Pacific) over Luzon in the Philippines, Vraciu's Hellcat was shot down by ground fire. Parachuting safely, Vraciu was rescued by Philippine guerillas. Evading Japanese captivity over the next month, Vraciu eventually led a guerilla contingent that met up with U.S. Army forces invading Luzon. His Philippines ex-

ploits, however, spelled an end to his aerial combat ambitions. His knowledge of Philippine guerilla operations meant the Navy could not afford to risk having Vraciu fall into enemy hands.

Vraciu ended the Pacific War as the U.S. Navy's fourth-ranking fighter ace (he is now its highest-ranking surviving ace.) The overall leading ace was David McCampbell—a Medal of Honor recipient with a final combat total of thirty-four aerial kills, many of them in the closing days of the war. Vraciu, a recipient of the Navy Cross, has been nominated for the Medal of Honor.

In April 1957, as a Navy jet squadron CO, Vraciu again put his singular aerial combat skills on display. With his squadron (VF-51) competing in the U.S. Navy's annual Air Weapons Meet in El Centro, California, Vraciu won the trophy for High Individual Air-to-Air Competition—a precursor of the "Top Gun" laurels later made famous in an eponymous Hollywood movie. Now retired from the Navy (where he rose to the rank of Commander) and a widower (Kathryn died in 2003), Alex Vraciu resides in Northern California. Though now slower of gate, his eyes, intellect and reflexes remain in good order. An inveterate fighter pilot, Vraciu is still wont to practice his skills. As he drives a highway off-ramp, Alex Vraciu will on occasion get on the six o'clock of the car ahead of him to line up a low- or no-deflection shot.

July 5, 1944

On June 20, when the Yokosuka Air Group pilots had made their fifth attempt to reach Iwo Jima, the weather conditions were still miserable. But, with inexperienced pilots sticking close to the lead Zeros, they somehow made it through the storm front to land on an airfield in the center of the island.

Saburo Sakai's thirty-plane detachment had arrived during a fighting lull that continued for three more days. They knew by then that the Japanese fleet had been shattered off Saipan and that most of its carrier pilots had perished. It was decided that while the fighters remained behind for defense, the Bettys would foray at night to attack American warships off Saipan.

It was sickening to see those flights take off and then to wait for the few stragglers that managed to return. Their crews told of American fighters coming after them in total darkness and the merciless, seemingly unerring antiaircraft fire from the American ships.

The American carriers returned to Iwo Jima on June 24 and eighty Zeros were scrambled to confront them. It was the first battle in which any of their pilots had battled the new Grummans—the Hellcats. Sakai was amazed with their speed, power and agility. He also realized what a disadvantage his reduced vision was: it left half his field of vision blank and hindered his distance perception.

The one advantage Sakai possessed was his reservoir of experience. He sensed that many of the American pilot's skills weren't up to the quality of their formidable fighters. During the battle, Sakai claimed two kills, but he also ended up encircled by a dozen or more Hellcats. Just escaping took all his skill and strength and, in the process, he pushed his aircraft beyond the maximum of its capabilities. When Sakai touched down, he was thronged by the other fliers—he had escaped with his Zero totally unscathed. But the day's results soon brought them all back to painful reality. Forty Zeros—nearly half Iwo's fighter strength—had been shot down.

On three successive days, July 2 through 4, the Hellcats returned, this time accompanied by wave after wave of Avengers, which bombed the field while the Hellcats occupied the Zeros. When it was all over on the third day, the airfield was in shambles and there were only nine Zeros and eight single-engine torpedo planes still operable.

The next day, July 5, these seventeen planes, Sakai's among them, were dispatched with orders to find the American carriers at all costs. They were to stick together throughout, shielding the torpedo planes so that that they could deliver their payloads. It was, they realized, nothing less than a suicide mission.

Angered as he was at the futility of the mission—as if some foolish spirituality could overcome their meager numbers and inferior aircraft—Saburo Sakai set off intending to obey orders. Still fifty miles short of their target, however, the formation was swarmed by dozens of Hellcats. The Japanese pilots adhered to their orders, but in the process most of their fighters and torpedo planes were shot down.

Somehow Sakai and his two wingmen managed to escape and press on, only to run into horrible weather—clouds and squalls that made it impossible to do anything but fight to stay aloft. In the end, with darkness overtaking them, Sakai made a decision—to turn back. When he and his wingmen finally touched down, Sakai assumed he had returned in disgrace. To his surprise and relief, another fighter had also returned, as had one of the torpedo bombers. The surviving members of the Wing were overjoyed to see these pilots still alive. Don't worry, they comforted them, you have lived to help us fight on another day.

Iwo Jima lay prostrate in July 1944 with no Japanese aircraft, no ships and few soldiers to defend it. Saburo Sakai and other aviation personnel were organized into an "Iwo Marine Company" and fully expected to die on the desolate, volcanic island. The Americans, however, next turned their attention to the Philippines, delaying the Iwo Jima invasion until February, 1945, by which time the island was a formidable bastion. In the interim, Sakai and the other surviving Yokosuka Air Group personnel were evacuated from the island.

After returning to Japan, Sakai was promoted to ensign and became a test pilot. He took part in the development of two new aircraft, one designed to battle the Hellcat, the other to take on the B-29 bombers. With enough of these aircraft, Sakai imagined, Japan might at least stem the American tide. The problem was that development and production were ultimately insufficient. In the end, Japan's aviation resources—its youngest pilots and its inferior aircraft—were channeled to suicide warfare: the Kamikaze Special Attack units.

In January 1945, Sakai was assigned to the Matsuyama Wing, commanded by none other than Captain Minoru Genda. In February, despite anticipating that he would surely die before the war ended, he married his cousin Hatsuyo. In April, the Matsuyama Wing transferred to Southern Kyushu, there to contest the invasion of Okinawa. Unequipped with radar, their field was systematically demolished by Corsairs and Hellcats, now equipped as fighter-bombers. Those pilots who got aloft—many of them Japan's highest-scoring aces—were shot down one after another.

In June, Sakai was transferred once more, this time to Nagoya to test an even newer and more formidable fighter aircraft. He and Hatsuyo were there when they learned of the final hammer blows to Japan—the Soviet invasion of Manchuria, the bombings of Hiroshima and Nagasaki, and the Emperor's surrender broadcast.

After Japan's surrender, Saburo Sakai was expelled from the Japanese navy without hope of a pension. Occupation rules forbade his taking control of an aircraft or obtaining a public position. He resorted to years of manual labor and primitive living conditions during which Hatsuyo died from illness.

Finally Sakai scraped together enough money to open a small printing business. Even after sanctions against Sakai were lifted, he refused any offers to join Japan's reconstituted defense forces. Saburo Sakai, the Imperial Japanese Navy's fourth-ranking ace and Japan's second-leading fighter pilot to survive the war, died on September 22, 2000 at age eighty-four.

———

July 17, 1944

When Admiral Ernest King arrived on Saipan, his first conspicuous act was to assure Raymond Spruance that, no matter what others might say, Spruance had done exactly the correct thing. King's gesture was meant to reassure Spruance of his continued faith in him and to quiet the criticism—especially from the naval aviation community—about his decisions off the Marianas in June.

As far as most carrier commanders were concerned, Spruance, in not striking earlier and more boldly, had missed "the chance of the century." They were certain it would prolong the war for months.

Indeed, the Pacific War did continue—on land, sea and in the air—for more than a year, though for circumstances infinitely more complex than the failure to completely vanquish the balance of Japan's essentially plane-less and pilot-less aircraft carriers.

The Marianas were, as the two sides envisaged, a key to the Pacific War— but not the only key. The Japanese fleet would sortie two more times. The first, in October 1944 to oppose the invasion of Leyte, would be almost entirely without air cover—an insurmountable disadvantage. The second sortie, in July 1945, would be to contest the invasion of Okinawa. It was little more than a suicidal gesture—as was the Empire's much more prolonged and effective resort to aerial Kamikaze warfare.

In each of these confrontations (and in subsequent offensive strikes against Japan's Home Islands) American carrier-borne aircraft would play a vital role. But no battle or aerial confrontation would be vaguely reminiscent of the five epic carrier battles that began in May 1942 with Coral Sea, continued at Midway, Eastern Solomons and Santa Cruz—and ended, in June 1944, with Philippine Sea.

———

August 15, 1945

The axe fell on the day after Japan's surrender announcement. The planning for it, which had begun several weeks before the dropping of the atomic bomb on Hiroshima, centered on three questions. What military business would Grumman have after Japan's surrender? Which plants and people would the company need to fulfill that business? And how could it build up peacetime business?

Production of the Hellcats, executives figured, would end altogether. Production of the twin-engine Tigercat (the night-fighter) and the F8F Bearcat (successor to the Hellcat) would continue, but at a diminished pace. Grumman's immediate manpower needs were estimated to be about 5,400—a precipitous drop from an already somewhat reduced workforce of about 20,500 men and women.

To prepare for employee cuts, plant foremen were asked to prepare lists of employees in descending order of proficiency. With these lists in hand, Roy Grumman and Jake Swirbul devised a scheme intended to eliminate, at least on the day of reckoning itself, the trauma of selectively dismissing people.

Shortly after the plants opened on August 15, public address systems announced that all Grumman operations were suspended immediately and that all employees should go home, taking their personal tools and possessions with them. Grumman would be out of business for the time it took to evaluate the Navy's production needs. When employment needs were decided, those being called back would be notified by telegram.

It was dramatic and, to many, arbitrary and heartless. Feelings of joy about the end of the war mingled with uncertainty and outright dejection—this at a time when the similar cutbacks were cutting wide swaths across the landscape of American industry.

The total shutdown, announced on Thursday, extended through the weekend. The Grumman callback started the following Monday, August 19, 1945. By the end of the week, production was underway again, though at a much-reduced rate.

In all, about thirty thousand Grumman-designed aircraft were produced (either directly by Grumman or by General Motor's Eastern Aviation) for Allied use during World War II. The company's crowning achievement was the design and production of just over twelve thousand F6F Hellcats. During approximately two years of combat in the Pacific, F6F pilots were credited with destroying about 5,300 Japanese aircraft in aerial combat—in the process producing a remarkable overall "kill-loss" ratio of nineteen to one.

Although Hellcats would continue in military use well into the 1950s, their final Pacific War appearance occurred on September 2, 1945, the day of Japan's formal surrender ceremony. General Douglas MacArthur, who presided over the ceremonies aboard battleship Missouri *(BB-63), had scarcely finished announcing "These proceedings are closed," when hundreds of carrier-based F6F Hellcats, part of a 450 plane-strong Operation Air Show, flew over Tokyo Bay.*

CHAPTER 1

1 "there were nearly seven thousand Grumman employees…": The primary sources for this chapter's facts and data about Grumman Aircraft Engineering are from: "The Embattled Farmers"; *The Grumman Story*; and "Pioneers on the Runway: Raising Grumman."

4 "including Long Island industry neighbors such as Republic, Chance Vought and Pratt and Whitney": *Hellcat*, 21

4 "Already the previous summer, these worrisome contingencies fully in mind, Swirbul, the firm's production head, had taken a bomber-ferry to England.": "Wings for the Navy"

11 "a torpedo bomber aircraft dubbed the TBF": Navy aircraft designations are a combination of letters and numbers indicating aircraft type, model sequence and manufacturer. In the case of "TBF," the T stands for Torpedo and the B for Bomber (it was a combined Torpedo-Bomber type aircraft). There is no model number in this instance the aircraft was still pre-production. Grumman's manufacturer designation happened to be the letter F because another firm (Great Lakes Aeronautical Corporation) had already preempted the letter G. See the Glossary for information on the specific designations for this and other Navy and Army (both American and Japanese) aircraft designations, familiar names and code names.

CHAPTER 2

12 "At 9:50 a.m.": Throughout this book I use the more familiar notations for time of day (as well as day of month and year.) Much of the book's action also occurs across the International Date Line, a challenge to date- and timekeepers. To make matters potentially worse, American and Japanese forces used different conventions when it came to specifying time zones. Accordingly, I have, for the sake of readers, though with as much accuracy as possible, simplified these matters. If inadvertent errors result, they are hopefully small, few, and don't detract from the focus on flesh-and-blood people and compelling events. The primary sources for the time and event sequences used in this chapter are *The Big E*, *Day of Infamy*, *The First Team*, and *Long Day's Journey Into War*.

12 "It was this flight of eighteen VT-6 Devastators": The V in these designations for naval aviation squadrons indicates "heaver-than-air" (at the time, and for years after, the U.S. Navy flew "lighter-than-air" craft). Similar to aircraft designations, the T stands for Torpedo Squadron; the B for Bombing Squadron; the F for Fighting Squadron; and the S for Scouting Squadron. In everyday usage, squadrons were identified by the combination of their function and squadron number: as examples, Torpedo Six, Bombing Six, and Fighting Six. Finally, this early in the war, a common squadron number indicated assignment to the same multi-function air group, in this case Carrier Air Group Six. In a final piece of logic that was soon to fall apart, carrier and squadron (and air group) number matched the hull number of the carrier to which they were attached.

13 "Sandwiched between Hebel and Allen in the Wildcats' right echelon formation": An echelon formation is a military flight formation where aircraft are arranged diagonally, either to the right or left. The usage is from the French word *échelle*, meaning ladder.

14 "…it would snuff the lives …of roughly a third the men who dared venture from aircraft carrier decks …": *Retribution*, 105

17 "In the words of Ford Island's commanding officer Captain James H. Shoemaker, 'all hell broke loose.'": *At Dawn We Slept*, 570

17 "'My God,' Fritz Hebel screamed to the tower as he banked his Wildcat north through heavy gunfire intent on reaching distant Wheeler Field. "What's happened?'": *The First Team*, 21

18 "…Menges, the very first U.S. Navy fighter pilot to die in the Pacific War,": Ibid.,, 19

18 "We got you, you little yellow sons of bitches.": *Long Day's Journey into War*, 568

20 "…most of the day's thousands of casualties": The combined killed, missing and died of wounds toll (military and civilian) would reach 2403; the wounded survivor toll settled at 1178. *At Dawn We Slept*, 539

CHAPTER 3

23 "When Jimmy Collins received Jake Swirbul's call…": Collins's account is based in part on an article ("Return to Earth") he wrote for the February 9, 1935 issue of the *Saturday Evening Post*. In his article, Collins neither specifies the name of the executive placing the call nor the firm in question. However, given other sources (chiefly, *The Grumman Story*), the firm is undoubtedly Grumman. Moreover, the purpose and tenor of the conversation strongly infer that it was Jake Swirbul.

23 "They were also among just four selected for specialized training…": *Test Pilot*, 2

24 "Now to make matters worse…": Jimmy Collins is also the grandfather of author (*Built to Last: Successful Habits of Visionary Companies*) and Stanford academic Jim Collins.

24 "Though there was some comfort in Swirbul's upbeat assertion that the ship was production, not experimental 'Return to Earth,'": 8. Other sources (*The Grumman Story*, 77) point to it being the XF2F. While still experimental, the craft was by then in a configuration close to the version finally accepted—following its own testing—by the U.S. Navy.)

25 "Regretfully, the time had finally come when he "would rather eat than fly.": *Test Pilot*, 176

25 "The Navy then had scout and observation planes, products of Chance Vought.": (The company, a 1922 startup, was named for its founder Chance M. Vought, chief engineer for Wright Aircraft, Wilbur and Orville Wright's commercial aviation venture.)

26 "The key to the float's weight reduction was something called monocoque construction.": (The word's derivation is from the Greek for single [*mono*] and French for shell [*coque*].)

29 "Bill McAvoy, the NACA pilot…": In his *Saturday Evening Post* article, Collins doesn't explicitly name Grumman as the manufacturer that had retained him for the dive demonstrations. Collins indicates he was given the tour by "Bill…their chief test pilot." Collins also writes: "I learned that a pilot had been up there and had gone over the whole stress analysis with them and had recommended only one little change in the ship, which had been made. I learned that he had expressed willingness to dive the ship after that, but that he had to because another job he had contracted to do some time previously was coming up at the same time this one was." The assumption here is that in both cases this was Bill McAvoy. Without naming Grumman in the article, Collins also describes Bill as the firm's chief test pilot. NACA's Bill McAvoy, although not on Grumman's payroll, was then the company's primary test pilot.

30 "The vee-gee, Collins learned, etched a pattern on a small piece of smoked glass as the plane was flown.": "Return to Earth," 9

31 "When either built up enough wind resistance offset its own weight…": (More precisely, terminal velocity is reached when the frictional resistance of the medium enveloping the falling body equals the force of gravity.)

34 "The skies over Farmingdale were as blue as indigo and as clear as a mountain stream.": "Return to Earth," 52

35 "Boy, I thought you were never going to pull that out.": Ibid., 54

35 "even true Immelmanns…": Named for its purported inventor, WWI German Ace Max Immelmann, the maneuver begins in fast level flight with the pilot pulling the aircraft into a steep climb and half loop. At apex of the loop, the pilot then rolls the aircraft upright, thereby gaining altitude on an opposite heading.

CHAPTER 4

38 "During his senior year he reached the rank of Cadet Lieutenant Commander, then the highest cadet ranking possible.": *History of United States Naval Operations in World War II, Volume I*, 51

38 "During King's time Annapolis was a neglected institution…": *Master of Sea Power*, 8-9 (When King first entered the Naval Academy, students were known as cadets. They later became midshipmen.)

38 "'Temper? Don't fool with nitroglycerin,' the Academy's Lucky Bag warned about King when he graduated 4th in his class 1901.": "Stormy Man, Stormy Weather"

40 "…he was flag officer for a sub division before assuming command of the entire base.": (It was King who devised the U.S. Navy's submariner twin dolphin insignia, through he never earned the right to wear them himself.)

40 "Indeed, his greatest plaudits came in response to catastrophe": King earned a Distinguished Service Medal (DSM) for the salvage of the submarine *S-51* and another, in 1929, for the salvage of *S-4*.)

40 "…a demonstration flight over New York Harbor conducted by none other than Wilbur Wright…": *The Fast Carriers*, 1

41 "In the years ahead Towers would bemoan it as the one great mistake of his career.": *Master of Sea Power*, 364

43 "The Boeing men became unglued, howling that Thach was showing off and demanding another go.": *Thach Weave*, 18

44 "Because James, a footballer, was called Jim or Jimmie during his Academy years…": (John Thach entered the academy in the fall after of 1923, James's graduation year.)

44 "…was promptly labeled 'little Jimmie.'": *Thach Weave*, 5. Some sources (for example, *Fateful Rendezvous, Shattered Sword, The First Team, The First Team and the Guadalcanal Campaign*) spell Thach's nickname Jimmy while others (*Clash of the Carriers, Thach Weave*) spell it Jimmie. Jimmie is used here because it is the spelling used in *Thach Weave*, Steve Ewing's biography of Thach.

44 "Since graduating in June 1927…" *Thach Weave*, 6

44 "Soon afterwards, he joined Fighting Squadron 1 (VF-1B) stationed at San Diego's North Island NAS, poor relation to the Army Air Corp's more spacious (and more generously paved) Rockwell Field.": *Thach Weave*, 9

46 "Too bad, because it would have been a scoop for Arch.": *Test Pilot*, 174

46 "Arch was Archer Winsten": (Winsten's career with the *Post* stretched for more than fifty years, most of them spent reviewing films. He died in 1997.)

47 "In 1935 Patterson even helped conceive *Terry and the Pirates*, a comic strip featuring the exploits of aviators and adventurers in the Far East.": "The Press: Escape Artist." (Patterson also conceived the names for comic strips such as *Dick Tracy* and *Orphan Annie*, usually by a "thoughtful thumbing" through the telephone book.)

47 "He took a long swig and listened to his motor again. It had smoothed right out.": *Test Pilot*, 44

48 "I guess it must have been tough, because He cracked her up. He piled into that last ridge outside of Bellefonte.": *Test Pilot*, 117

48 "I'll let you know how I make out.": "Terminal Velocity Flying Story"

48 "Thursday's edition of the *Daily News* also includes a 'Flying Stories' article…": "Terminal Velocity Flying Story"

49 "Here's to Jimmy Collins," Shock would toast every night at dinner. "The average life of the aviator is forty hours.": *Test Pilot*, 58

49 "The next thing the ground observers realized….": *The Grumman Story*, 85

49 "Schwendler and the others raced to the grounds of nearby Pinelawn Cemetery.": (The following year, the U.S. Government purchased 175 Pinelawn acres for the establishment of a national memorial. Burials for World War I veterans began at Long Island National Cemetery in March 1937. Over the next eight years, Long Island National Memorial saw over 10,000 interments of veterans from both that war and from World War II.)

CHAPTER 5

51 "twenty-one-year-old Saburo Sakai…": Japanese conventions regarding persons' names are to place the surname first followed by the given name (e.g. Sakai Saburo). Western conventions with regard to names (i.e. given name followed by surname) are used here and elsewhere in the book.

52 "Do not forget that you are the son of a Samurai. Tears are not for you.": *Samurai!* 14.

53 "By the end of the decade, enlisted aviators would comprise more than ninety per cent of the roughly 3,500 active IJN pilots.'" *The First Team*, 454-455.

54 "…owing to his own experience, he assured her, no son of his would ever attend a military academy.": *Fateful Rendezvous*, 43.

56 "…he also understood that only the best naval pilots—most with a minimum of eight years' experience—were ever rotated to carrier duty.": *The Fast Carriers*, 4.

56 " ..later identified by Allied forces with the code designation Claude.": (The code name system for Japanese aircraft originated with U.S. forces in the Southwest Pacific in 1942 when Army intelligence officer Captain Frank T. McCoy headed a team assigned to identify and classify Japanese aircraft. Captain McCoy, a native of Tennessee, initially assigned down-home names such as Claude, Jake, Nate, Rufe, and (most memorably) Zeke to Japanese aircraft. Seventy-five code names were as-

signed during the first month and soon these names were in wide use throughout the entire Pacific. In 1944, a joint Army-Navy Air Technical Center in Washington took over responsibility for assigning the names. The code names were then allotted according to the following system: male first names for fighters and reconnaissance seaplanes; female first names for bombers, attack bombers, dive-bombers, reconnaissance aircraft and flying boats; names beginning with letter T for transports; tree names for trainers; and bird names for gliders. For purposes of these pages, Japanese aircraft will generally be denoted first by their more formal designation and thereafter by their shorter U.S. code names.)

58   "Bowing to the inevitable, the XF4F-1 had been scrapped and the long, intense process of designing, prototyping, testing and refining the XF4F-2 had begun.": *The Grumman Story*, 92.

60   "But it was all but certain that he'd somehow learned of EJ's turncoat role...": (The account of EJ O'Hare's involvement in the prosecution of Al Capone finally came to light in a 1947 *Collier's* article. As E.J. Wilson, one of the Treasury officials instrumental in gathering [and deciphering] accounting ledger information that underpinned Capone's conviction, admitted in the article, "On the inside of the gang I had one of the best undercover men I have ever known: Eddie O'Hare." *Fateful Rendezvous*, 31).

61   "His daily report on November 28 noted: 'Refresher period after long lay-off.'": *Fateful Rendezvous*, 87.

62   "Initially organized in 1921 as Combat Squadron Three.": Ibid., 91.

64   "They were the new Mitsubishi Zero fighters—Zero-sens.": (This was apparently the A6M Type 0 Carrier Fighter, which took its informal name Zero from its IJN type designation, in turn derived from the last digit of the Imperial year 2600 [1940] when it first entered service. Most Japanese pilots called it the Zero-sen—its adversaries either Zero or Zeke. The official A6M designation signified the sixth IJN model [6] of a carrier-based fighter [A] manufactured by Mitsubishi. The A6M's precursor was the A5M, which had just entered China combat service in early 1937 when the IJN first started looking for a new generation carrier-based fighter aircraft with high speed, climb rate, endurance and maneuverability.)

CHAPTER 6

66   "...a blistering V max ranging somewhere between 322 and 380 mph...": *The First Team*, 480.

66   "Sid Harvey died of a heart attack while en route to Great Britain to observe the air war.": *Thach Weave*, 32.

67   "Their Brewster F2A-2 Buffaloes—a heavier model than the F2A-1 predecessor—had always been prone to landing-gear failures. *Fateful Rendezvous*, 95.

67   "...the small rental house in nearby Coronado...": "Butch O'Hare and the Thach Weave," 50.

67   "He normally used a pile of about thirty matchsticks...": *Thach Weave*, 36.

67   "This was when fighter aircraft were most vulnerable to surprise attack.": *The First Team*, 480.

68   "Madalyn reminded him that he had to fly the next morning.": "Butch O'Hare and the Thach Weave," 50.

69   "In combat the wingman's job was elemental: stick with his leader and protect his tail.": *First Team*, 480

71   "I'll even wager you a little bet that he'll get on your tail the first time and stay there.": "Butch O'Hare and the Thach Weave," 49.

71   "...two-thirds predicted a forthcoming conflict with Japan.": *Fighter Pilot*, 32.

72   "CPTP enabled college students like Vraciu to earn their private pilot licenses.": (Before war's end, CPTP and its successor the War Training Service (WTS) trained nearly a half million people to fly.)

72   "It's the aircraft carrier that will spearhead the action in the next war.": *Master of Sea Power*, 363.

73   "...answers 'from Captain Jack Towers...and not from Admiral Towers, who is taking orders from too many line admirals.'": "Sailors Aloft."

73   "A 3,500-man naval aviator cadre at year's beginning was slated to grow to 6,000 by year's end. U.S. Navy aviator ranks were projected to eventually swell to 16,000."" (Data on naval aviation growth is from "Sailors Aloft").

75   "...they received an unexpected visit from Vice Admiral Eikichi Katagiri, the Naval Air Force Commander in China.": *Samurai*, 46.

75   "Thach called it the 'beam defense position.'": *Thach Weave*, 37.

77   " Did it give the 'Japanese' Wildcats any problems?": "Butch O'Hare and the Thach Weave," 51.

78   "The normal fuel capacity for a Zero-sen was 182 gallons.": *Samurai*, 48.

79   "… heritage that earned the tall, rugged Waldron some ridicule": (as the. class "Redskin" and a "seago-ing cowpuncher") throughout his Naval Academy years. *A Dawn Like Thunder*, 14.

79   "After his 1924 graduation…" In the same year as Ernest J. King, but evidently in a different class.

80   "…lugging a torpedo, they could scarcely break 100 knots.": *Shattered Sword*, 207.

81   "… the after ball turret was even power driven to increase response speed and torque.": *The Grumman Story*, 124.

CHAPTER 7

85   "…a small electronic device needed to control the variable pitch of the Wildcat propeller.": *Thach Weave*, 46

87   "… counting down the 'bombing days' until Christmas…": *Fateful Rendezvous*, 109

87   "The setup seemed perfect," he confided to his diary, 'for those of us who did not have a complete picture of the strategical situation.'": *The First Team*, 43.

88   "A New Year's "sans celebration, sans hangover": (in the words of VF-3 aviator Onia B. "Burt" Stanley) … *Fateful Rendezvous*, 111.

89   "Sakai had managed to shoot down…": Sakai's account claimed that this was the Flying Fortress piloted by Army Air Corps Captain Collin P. Kelly, the first B-17 to be shot down during the Pacific War. On December 10, 1941, Kelly's B-17, flying from Clark Field, scored a bombing hit on a Japanese cruiser. On the return flight, the bomber was attacked by Zeros, including one flown by Saburo Sakai. Kelly stayed at the controls while surviving crew members bailed out. Kelly's co-pilot survived but Kelly did not. Early reports mistakenly claimed that Kelly had crashed his plane into the smokestack of an IJN battleship, thereby becoming the war's first suicide pilot. Other erroneous reports had Kelly receiving the Medal of Honor; it was instead a posthumous Distinguished Service Cross. *Samurai*, 53-56; "Valor: Colin Kelly."

CHAPTER 8

94   "…that the three planes had merged.": *Thach Weave*, 52.

94   "You put him right into my lap.": *The First Team*, 92.

94   "Information—radar sighting, bearing and time—were passed by phone for plotting on a large polar chart.": *Guadalcanal: The Carrier Battles*, 152.

96   "… kicked upstairs to vice admiral …": *Fateful Rendezvous*, 115.

102 " "Thach in 13, Sellstrom take 2, O'Hare in 15, Dufilho, 4.": Ibid., 125.

104 ".two three-plane 'vees' and an echeloned pair…": Ibid., 103.

106 "…a long-time China veteran with more than 3,000 hours flight experience. *The Rising Sun*, 156.

106 "In fact it was Fuchida's radioman who had tapped out the momentous radio message: *Tora, Tora, Tora* (Tiger, Tiger, Tiger).": *The First Team and the Guadalcanal Campaign*, 386-387.

106 "…unleashed its might against just one coastal gun emplacement, one cargo ship, two enemy planes and two dusty, otherwise deserted air fields." *Midway, The Battle that Doomed Japan*, 61.

108 "… a make-do assemblage of tender *Langley*, two cruisers and two oilers." *History of the United States Naval Operations in World War II, Volume III*, 193.

109 "All but sixteen of *Langley's* ship's company and air crew passengers, nearly 500 men in all, were pulled safely aboard of *Edsall* and *Whipple*.": However, hundreds of survivors were soon lost in the March 1 sinking of *Pecos* (AO-6) and the disappearance of *Edsall*.

CHAPTER 9

110 "Even before the action in the Coral Sea began…": The primary source for this chapter's information about King's career and his early wartime dealings with Nimitz is *Master of Sea Power*

116 "Only if conditions were bad he felt relieved.": *Midway: The Battle That Doomed Japan*, 91

117 "Ito quietly nodded his assent.": Ibid., 86

117 "… Sherman's after action report credited him with five.": (Available American and Japanese postwar

records indicate that O'Hare actually shot down four Bettys during the engagement. Three crashed near the task force. A fourth ditched during the return flight. Two other Bettys, while seriously damaged during O'Hare's firing runs, survived the mission and successfully flew back to Rabaul.) *Fateful Rendezvous*, 140

118 "Something that would go upstairs faster.": *Fateful Rendezvous*, 155

118 "Grumman design Number 50 was being built as the XF6F-1.": *Hellcat*, 5.

CHAPTER 10

122 "...as they started their torpedo runs on the Japanese carrier.": The primary sources for the event sequences, times and battle data used in this chapter are *History of United States Naval Operations in World War II, Volume IV: Coral Sea, Midway and Submarine Actions*' and *The First Team: Pacific Naval Air Combat from pearl Harbor to Midway.*

135 "(He would mandate, among other things, that each flattop be equipped with an admiral and its own separate screen of cruisers and destroyers.)": *The Fast Carriers*

136 "... was short, wiry and energetic...": *The Big E*, 91

137 "He ordered Nimitz 'to employ strong attrition tactics and not—repeat—not allow our forces to accept such decisive actions as would be likely to incur heavy losses in our carriers and cruisers.'": *Master of Sea Power*, 202.

CHAPTER 11

138 "Fuchida found his legs still unsteady...": The primary sources for the times and event sequences in this and the next chapter include: *A Dawn like Thunder; Carrier Combat; Incredible Victory; Midway: The Battle that Doomed Japan; Miracle at Midway; Shattered Sword; The Big E; The First Team: Pacific Naval Air Combat from Pearl Harbor to Midway; The Reminiscences of John S. Thach;* and *The Rising Sun.* Additional sources include contemporaneous coverage in the *New York Times* and *Time* and *The Saturday Evening Post* article "Never a Battle like Midway." The times used for both American and Japanese forces are local Midway time (Greenwich + 12).

153 "Deciding they must be Lindsey's TBDs...": In May 1988, as part of a Naval Symposium on Midway convened in Pensacola, Jim Gray stated that he knew all along that he was following VT-8, not VT-6. His belated account, made forty-six years after the event, is at variance with all the primary and secondary resources I have reviewed about this particular aspect of the battle.

CHAPTER 12

162 "very puny things to be sending against big Japanese carriers, battleships and cruisers.": "'Never a Dull Moment' at Midway, Reporter Watching Battle Found"

163 "You don't want to go back there, sir." *Dawn like Thunder*, 145

163 "You're the only one so far," he said. Ibid., 145

164 "'This is Gray,'" he radioed at 10 a.m.'": *The First Team*, 344

168 "Shipboard antiaircraft fire and *Akagi*'s maneuvering ...": *Shattered Sword*'s co-author Jonathan Parshall disputes this account of events by Fuchida. Had VT-3 aircraft gotten close enough to *Akagi* to launch torpedoes they doubtless would have. Parshall's and Tully's analysis holds instead that VT-3 pilots were actually targeting carrier *Soryu*, diverting to *Hiryu* when they realized it was closer. (Manuscript review by Jonathan Parshall)

168 "At 10:24 a.m., eyes and anticipation turned back to *Akagi*'s flight deck ...": Akagi flight records indicate it was a CAP aircraft, not a strike aircraft. (Manuscript review by Jonathan Parshall)

169 "A near-miss close astern ...": Fuchida's account claimed two direct hits: one at the after rim of the amidships elevator, a second on the ship's port side. Fuchida also asserts that strike aircraft positioned wingtip-to-wingtip on the flight deck were fully ablaze. Subsequent analysis by Parshall, Tully and others holds that most if not all *Akagi* strike aircraft were still being readied below decks. (Manuscript review by Jonathan Parshall)

174 "Fred Mears was on *Hornet*'s flight deck when the last of Air Group 8's returning SBDs touched down at 12:09...": Mears' *Carrier Combat* account points to a 12:35 p.m. return time. I have opted for the time sequence contained in Lundstrom's *The First Team.*

179 "…he couldn't help catching some of their enthusiasm.": *Carrier Combat*, 59.

CHAPTER 13

183 "…Navy pilots either checked into the Moana Hotel or the Royal Hawaiian.": (The main source for this and subsequent accounts of Frederick Mears' experiences are from his posthumous memoir, *Carrier Combat*)

185 "After all, three Zero kills had been claimed for each Wildcat loss…": (A factor not considered at the time was that pilot aerial kill claims are inexact—and usually overstated by both sides.)

188 "…two days leading up to the invasion, the invasion itself and then, if possible, the withdrawal of the transports.": *The First Team and the Guadalcanal Campaign*, 18.

191 "…McCain was one mad little admiral.": Ibid., 28.

191 "A child who knows not its own mother is not so smart.": Ibid., 30.

191 "Well, I'm convinced the airplane is here to stay, but I'm not so sure about the pilot.": *Carrier Combat*, 97.

192 "All bedding was stacked on deck in the middle of sleeping compartments, loose items were secured and flammables were stowed in steel lockers and cabinets.": *The First Team and the Guadalcanal Campaign*, 33.

193 "…seventeen Guadalcanal-bound Zero-sens.": Ibid., 48.

194 "…put gun switches and sight lamps on. Let's go get 'em boys.": Ibid., 48.

198 "an aircraft from carrier *Wasp*'s VS-71": *The First Team and the Guadalcanal Campaign*,

CHAPTER 14

201 "'Admiral, you've got to see this'… 'It isn't good.'": *Master of Sea Power*, 221

202 "It was these casualties that weighed on Frank Jack Fletcher's mind when, at about 5:00 a.m. on August 9…": (The primary sources for the times and event sequences in this chapter include: *The Big E*; *Carrier Combat*; *The First Team and the Guadalcanal Campaign*; *Guadalcanal: The Carrier Battles*; *History of United States Naval Operations in World War II: Volume V, The Struggle for Guadalcanal, August 1942 – February 1943*; and *Master of Sea Power*.)

202 "Request cover for attack on enemy surface force this area.": *The First Team and the Guadalcanal Campaign*, 83

205 "The nation seemed drunk on false victories.": *Samurai!* 170-71

208 "… Radioman Third Class Delmer D. Wiley survived the ordeal.": (Wiley spent fifteen days on a raft until he washed up on an island northeast of Buka, and far behind Japanese lines. It was another eight months before he made his way to Guadalcanal, by then in American hands. *The First Team and the Guadalcanal Campaign*, 121)

209 "…They're dive bombers.": Ibid., 129

215 "… Weasel Weissenborn and Fred Mears approached *Enterprise*'s landing circle.": (The primary source for Mears' account is *Carrier Combat*.)

CHAPTER 15

218 "On September 3, 1942…": The primary sources for the times and event sequences in this chapter include: *The Big E*; *Carrier Combat*; *Carrier Strike*; *A Dawn Like Thunder*; *The First Team and the Guadalcanal Campaign*; *Guadalcanal: The Carrier Battles*; *History of United States Naval Operations in World War II: Volume V, The Struggle for Guadalcanal, August 1942 – February 1943*; *Master of Sea Power*; and *Samurai!*.

221 "These have got us," *Guadalcanal: The Carrier Battles*, 262

222 "But circling close by were their sanctuaries: cruiser *Juneau* (CL-52) and destroyers *Farenholt* (DD-491), *Lansdowne* (DD-486), *Laffey* (DD-459) and *Lardner* (DD-487).": Ibid., 227

225 "On June 26, 1942, three weeks after Midway and two weeks before the Akutan discovery, Grumman test pilot Robert L. Hall had taken the XF6F-1 up for a 25-minute test.": *Hellcat*, 6

232 " … emergency production teams working virtually nonstop had assembled twenty-four additional Wildcats from spare parts inventories.": *The Grumman Story*, 148.

CHAPTER 16

233 "At 7:14 a.m. on October 26…": The primary sources for the times and event sequences in this chapter include: *The Big E; Carrier Combat; Carrier Strike; A Dawn Like Thunder; The First Team and the Guadalcanal Campaign; Guadalcanal: The Carrier Battles;* and *History of United States Naval Operations in World War II: Volume V, The Struggle for Guadalcanal, August 1942 – February 1943*

233 "I had to begin throwing punches": *The First Team and the Guadalcanal Campaign*, 337

235 "With his engine and cockpit on fire, Collett stepped onto his right wing and jumped, never to be seen again.": (Turret gunner Aviation Machinist First Class Stephen Nadison Jr. was also killed. The third crewman, Aviation Radioman First Class Thomas C. Nelson, Jr., parachuted safely but became a POW.)

241 "We must use everything we have to the limit.": *The First Team and the Guadalcanal Campaign*, 409

241 "Look for bogeys diving on port bow.": Ibid. 413

246 "Let's line abreast. Keep sharp lookout. If you see anything, start weaving…Cliff, stay on line abreast and keep your eyes open.": Ibid. 437

246 "the greatest contribution to air combat traits that has been made to date.": Ibid. 438.

249 "There were Japs on all sides of me. All I had to do was swing the barrel in a circle.": *Carrier Combat*, 150.

249 "They are all dead. You and I, Saburo…We are the only ones still alive.": *Samurai!*, 188.

CHAPTER 17

253 "Kenneth A. Jernstedt, a former Marine aviator working for Republic Aviation, was one of many test pilots who swapped rides with industry counterparts.": *Hellcat*, 23.

254 "These men were the professional—and spiritual—descendents of Jimmy Collins.": Grumman was at least one wartime aviation manufacturer who employed women as production test pilots, beginning in spring 1942. A production test pilot was the first to fly each new airplane as it left the production line; each production aircraft went through an average of two to three such flights, each flight lasting from fifteen to twenty minutes. During the war Grumman employed at least three women as production test pilots; one of them, Cecile "Teddy" Kenyon, the wife of a Grumman engineer, logged a thousand hours flying F4Fs, TBFs, and F6Fs during the war. *The Grumman Story*, 148-150.

254 "To these workers, the fortunes of the planes and the men who flew them mattered as much or more than production figures.": If a climate of cooperation flourished for most manufacturers, there were still some business settings where selfless cooperation never dared show its face. One of the grossest examples turned out to be Brewster Aviation. Early in 1943, Agnes E. Meyer, a *Washington Post* journalist (and wife of its publisher) who made her reputation by exposing war industry waste and profligacy, reported the results of an in-depth investigation into operations at Brewster's Long Island City and Johnsville, Pennsylvania plants. In a front-page expose, Meyer reported that she never expected to see in America "such a picture of managerial chaos, such a complete breakdown of worker morale as these factories presented." Among other things, Meyer's investigation brought to light a plant union leader who, in her estimation, had connived with a succession of inefficient managers to bring aircraft production to a virtual standstill. So enmeshed was the union man in his ego and venality that he bragged to Meyer: "If I had brothers at the front who needed the ten or twelve [Brewster] planes we sacrificed in our last strike, I'd let them die if necessary to preserve our union rights." It was during her extensive interviews of Brewster employees that Meyer's attention was called to strikingly contrasting conditions elsewhere. "The workers," Meyer wrote in a follow-up article, "said repeatedly and sadly: 'Oh, you ought to see Grumman. There's where we'd really like to work.")

258 "We have quite a few pilots and a third of our planes and they really are good ones this time.": *Fateful Rendezvous*, 186.

260 "On May 14, Lieutenant Douglas Henderson was killed during a strafing run into what was called Massacre Valley.": *Fateful Rendezvous*, 188.

262 "The notion got the endorsement…": That June, however, the reorientation of Pacific strategy from the Southwest to the Central Pacific got the endorsement of the high-level Joint Strategic Survey Committee. *The Fast Carriers*, 51.

263 "hitting a splinter with a bolt of lightning.": *Fateful Rendezvous*, 198

265 "You look good out there, honey.": *The Fast Carriers*, 78.

266 "On June 26, 1943, Lieutenant Fed Mears took off in his Avenger from North Island on a routine training flight.": *A Dawn Like Thunder*, 440

268 "…a bottle of Old Crow to the first air group pilot to shoot down a Japanese plane.": *Hellcat*, 32. The first Japanese aircraft to be downed by Hellcat pilots was not a Zero but instead a Kawanishi H8K flying boat—code name Emily—shot down on September 1, 1943. Another Emily was shot down on September 3, and a third on September 8. *Hellcat*, 32.

CHAPTER 18

273 "On November 18, 1943…": The primary sources for the times and event sequences in this chapter include: *The Big E; The Fast Carriers; Fatal Rendezvous; Hellcat;* and *History of United States Naval Operations in World War II: Volume VII, Aleutians, Gilberts and Marshalls, June 1942 – April 1944*

374 "TF-50, Galvanic's umbrella organization, consisted of four CTGs with a combined total of eleven fast carriers.": *The Fast Carriers*, 110–112.

275 "According to Carrier Division Commander Rear Admiral Arthur W. Radford, the sector idea made the CTGs 'little more than sitting ducks.'": *Fateful Rendezvous*, 242.

277 "Clifton's philosophy was: "Get them in there, get them out and get them home—no dogfighting.": *The Fast Carriers*, 98.

278 "A glorious victory," an elated Ted Sherman scribbled in his war diary as TF-38 high-tailed it south, "a second Pearl Harbor in reverse.": Ibid., 99.

278 "…as later described in his memoirs, at changing "the name of Rabaul to Rubble.": Ibid., 100.

278 "Man your guns and shoot those bastards out of the sky!": Ibid., 100.

286 "One of the pilots shouted, 'Go gettem, Butch.' O'Hare's reply was a grin. Then he dashed up a ladder to the flight deck.": *Fateful Rendezvous*, 267.

288 "Butch may be down.": Controversy continues as to whether O'Hare was the victim of "friendly fire" or of fire from the encroaching Betty. For this account, I rely on the analysis and conclusions of Steve Ewing and John B. Lundstrom in *Fateful Rendezvous*.

CHAPTER 19

292 The primary sources for the times and event sequences in this chapter include: *The Big E; Clash of the Carriers, The Fast Carriers; Hellcat* and *History of United States Naval Operations in World War II: Volume VIII, New Guinea and the Marianas, March 1944 – August 1944*

293 "When Commander Phil Torrey, Essex's Air Group 9 CO learned that their objective would be Truk, his first instinct "was to jump overboard.": This and subsequent quotes from Air Group personnel are from *The Fast Carriers*, 137-138.

294 "…that reminded VF-5 skipper Lieutenant Commander Edward M. Owen of a 'Hollywood war.'": *Hellcat*, 57.

294 "American losses over Truk totaled seventeen aircraft (most to ground fire) and twenty-six crewmen.": *The Fast Carriers*, 139.

294 "But two F6F casualties were *Intrepid* Hellcats flown by John Phillips and his wingman, Ensign John Ritchie Ogg, missing in action after evidently being ambushed by Japanese fighters while directing strikes against Truk shipping.": *Fateful Rendezvous*, 297.

296 "There was no mention of the Marianas in any of the American position papers.": *Master of Sea Power*, 336.

296 "I assume that sometime or other this thorn in the side of our communications to the western Pacific must be removed. In other words,…we must take out time and forces to carry out the job…": Ibid., 440.

297 "The team remains about the same, but the drivers change.": *New Guinea and the Marianas*, 161.

298 "Attempts by enemy fleet units to interfere with amphibious operations are both hoped for and provided against…": Ibid., 446.

298 "Some suspected that Amelia Earhart crashed near Saipan during her 1937 around-the-world flight and that she and her navigator were captured by the Japanese and eventually shot as spies.Five CVEs were assigned to Forager itself.

299 "Stationed in the Marianas at the time of Forager was none other than Vice Admiral Chuichi Nagumo, the victor at Pearl Harbor, the vanquished Japanese leader at Midway—now demoted to command of a small area fleet comprising patrol craft, barges, and some ground troops. Despite being headquar-

tered at Saipan and nominally in overall command, Nagumo would not interfere with the island's defense. Near the conclusion of the battle for Saipan, Nagumo would end his life with a pistol shot.": *New Guinea and the Marianas*, 167, 337.

301 "…a water-methanol fuel injection feature that added an instant ten per cent horsepower boost.": *Clash of the Carriers*, 60-61.

302 "Thanks, Bert,": Bert was Lt. Bert Dwayne Morris, better known as Wayne Morris, a movie star in the 1930s and 1940s. Morris became a Pacific War ace, with seven planes to his credit. Morris was also David McCampbell's nephew, having married a daughter of McCampbell's sister Frances. "4-F Hero, 109.

CHAPTER 20

314 The primary sources for the times and event sequences in this chapter include: *The Big E; Carrier Warfare in the Pacific: An Oral History Collection; Clash of the Carriers; The Fast Carriers; Hellcat; History of United States Naval Operations in World War II: Volume VIII, New Guinea and the Marianas; March 1944 – August 1944; Mission Beyond Darkness*; interviews with Warren McLellan, Alex Vraciu, and Arthur Whiteway.

314 "'I've got to fly out to here?'" *Mission Beyond Darkness*, 16.

314 "All task group commanders from Commander Task Group 58…There are two, possibly three groups of enemy ships…The primary objective is the carriers.": Ibid., 17.

315 "It didn't help that after splashing six Japanese planes yesterday he'd been simultaneously 'congratulated' and 'confined to quarters' after CO Pail Buie touched down.": Interview with Alex Vraciu.

318 "'Negative bogeys!' Colgan assured them. 'This is two turkeys and an F6!'": *The Big E*, 402.

319 "'Hold that second strike,' he said finally. 'There's no telling how many we'll lose from this flight. We've got to have something left to hit them with tomorrow.'": *Mission Beyond Darkness*, 23.

319 "'Look at this oil slick!' shouted one. Another: 'Haven't got time to look around!' And a third: 'Is this the force to attack? My gas is half-gone.'" Ibid., 28–29.

320 "'Looks like we found the whole Goddamn Jap navy!'": Ibid., 29. All McLellan saw was a spurt of tracers close to his canopy. Interview with Warren McLellan.

332 "It was the hop supreme.": *Mission Beyond Darkness*, 106.

338 "When Admiral Ernest King arrived on Saipan, his first act was to tell Raymond Spruance that, no matter what anyone else might say, Spruance had done exactly the correct thing.": *The Fast Carriers*, 206.

'Canal	Guadalcanal
AA	Antiaircraft fire
AAF	Army Air Force
ABDA	American-British-Dutch-Australian Command
ACTG	U.S. Navy Advance Carrier Tactical Group
AG	Air Group
Aileron	Hinged component on the trailing edge of a wing that controls aircraft roll
AMM	Aviation Machinist Mate (U.S. Navy enlisted rating)
Amphtrac	Amphibious tractor
Angels	Altitude
Anzac	Australia-New Zealand Force
AO	Fleet Oiler
ASB-1	Short-range radar designed to find surface targets
Ass End Charlie	The last aircraft in an aerial formation (usually flown by the most junior and least experienced pilot)
ATG	Air Task Group
Bat team	Crew assigned to carrier-based night-fighter aircraft
Battle II	A U.S. Navy ship's secondary control and command center
Betty	Mitsubishi G4M2 land-based bomber
BuAer	U.S. Navy's Bureau of Aeronautics
Buster	Top sustained air speed
CA	Heavy cruiser
CAG	Carrier Air Group/Commander Air Group
CarDiv	Carrier Division
Cactus	Code name for Guadalcanal
CAG	Commander Air Group
CAP	Combat air patrol
CCS	Combined Chiefs of Staff
CIC	Combat Information Center
CinCPac	Commander in Chief, Pacific Fleet
CinCPOA	Commander in Chief, Pacific Ocean Areas
CL	Light cruiser
Claude	Allied code name for Mitsubishi Type 96 fighter plane
CO	Commanding officer
ComAirBasFor	Commander, Aircraft, Base Force

ComAirBatFor	Commander, Aircraft, Battle Force
ComAirPac	Commander, Air Forces, Pacific Fleet
ComAirSoPac	Commander, Aircraft, South Pacific
ComCarPac	Commander Carriers Pacific
CominCH	Commander in Chief, U.S. Fleet
ComSoPac	Commander South Pacific
CA	Heavy cruiser
CL	Light cruiser
CTG	Carrier Task Group
CPTP	Civilian Pilot Training Program
CTF	Carrier Task Force
CV	Fleet aircraft carrier
CVE	Escort aircraft carrier
CVL	Light aircraft carrier
Dauntless	Douglass SBD dive bomber aircraft
DD	Destroyer
DesRon	Destroyer Squadron
Devastator	Douglass TBD torpedo aircraft
DRT	Dead Reckoning Tracer radar
FATU	Fleet Air Tactical Unit
FDO	Fighter Director (Direction) Officer
Fish	Torpedoes, also Torpedo bomber aircraft
Flattop	Aircraft carrier
Fleet up	Be promoted
Flintlock	Code name for the Marshall Islands campaign
Fly one	The forward launch point on an aircraft carrier flight deck
Forager	Code name for the Mariana Islands campaign
Galvanic	Code name for the Gilbert Islands campaign
Goldfish bowl	After turret in the Grumman TBF
GQ	General Quarters
Hawks	Bomber aircraft
High blower	Higher stage setting of two-stage aircraft engine supercharger
IJN	Imperial Japanese Navy
Inter-coolers	Engine components to cool air flow between supercharger compression stages
JCS	Joint Chiefs of Staff
Jill	Nakajima B6N Tenzan torpedo-bomber

350

Kate Nakajima B5N2 Type 97 carrier attack plane

Lamplighter Japanese night-flying aircraft using flares to illuminate ground or seagoing targets

Low blower Lower stage setting of two-stage aircraft engine supercharger

Mavis Kawanishi H6K reconnaissance seaplane

NACA National Advisory Committee for Aeronautics (predecessor to NASA)

NAP Naval Aviation Pilot

NAS Naval Air Station

NATC Naval Air Training Center

Nell Mitsubishi G3M Type 96 land-based attack aircraft

PBY Curtis PBY patrol seaplane

Pensacola Admiral Flag rank naval officer who qualified for aviation in mid-career

Pestilence Code-name for operation to occupy the Santa Cruz Islands

Point Option Anticipated position of carrier group when carrier aircraft return from a mission

Pork Chops U.S. Navy supply personnel

PPI Position Plan Indicator radar

RAF Royal Air Force

Rufe Nakajima A6M2-N Navy Type 2 float plane

SK Long-range aerial search radar

SBD Douglass Scout Bomber aircraft

ServRon Service Squadron

shad Reconnaissance (shadowing) aircraft

SM Height-finding radar system used for tracking low-level aircraft

Supercharger Air compressor that forces air into engine cylinders at higher altitudes, to increase engine power and efficiency

TBD Douglass TBD Devastator torpedo bomber

TBF Grumman TBF Avenger torpedo bomber

TBS Talk Between Ships radio circuit

TF Task Force

Torpecker Torpedo plane

Trade School United States Naval Academy (USNA)

USNA United States Naval Academy

V max Aircraft's highest rated speed

Val Aichi D3A1 Type 99 carrier bomber

Vee Aerial formation with three (or more) aircraft aligned (when looked at from above or below) as an inverted V:

```
     ^
   ^   ^
```

Vee-of-vees Aerial formation where aircraft fly in multiple three-plane groups (elements or sections):

```
       ^
     ^   ^
  ^           ^
 ^ ^         ^ ^
```

VF U.S. Navy fighter squadron

VP U.S. Navy patrol squadron

VT U.S. Navy torpedo squadron

Watchtower Code name for operation to capture Guadalcanal and Tulagi in the Solomon Islands

Wildcat Grumman F4F fighter aircraft

XO Executive Officer

Zed Baker Aircraft homing device

Zeke (Zero) Allied code name for Mitsubishi A6M2 Type O carrier fighter, Model 21

Name	Squadron (s)	Confirmed Kills	Status[2]
ENS[3] John P. Adams	VF-42, 3	2.0	
NAP[4] Clayton Allard	VF-2, 6	—[5]	KIFAD[6]
LTJG[7] John P. "Johnny" Altemus	VF-5, 6	1.0	
LTJG James Howard Arquette	VF-16	—	
LTJG William Arthur	VF-9	—	
ENS John B. Bain	VF-2, 42, 3	2.0	
ENS John D. Baker	VF-42	—	KIA/MIA[8]
AOM[9]1C[10] Michael Aloysius Banazak	VT-16 Crew	—	
Doyle C. "Ted" Barnes	VF-6	3.0	KIA/MIA
LTJG John Wilson Bartol	VF-16	2.0	
ENS Edgar R. "Red Dog" Bassett	VF-42,3	2.0	KIA/MIA
AOM 2C[11] Richard LeRoy Bentley	VB-16 Crew	—	
LTJG William C. B. Birkholm	VF-16	—	
Jack Booth	VC-18 Crew	—	KIFAD
ENS C. E. "Charlie" Brannon	VT-8	—	KIA/MIA
NAP Charles E. Brewer	VF-5, 6	3.0	
CDR[12] Charles W. Brewer	VF-15 CO	6.0	KIA/MIA
LT Mark K. Bright	VF-5,16	9.0	KIA/MIA
ENS Homer W. Brockmeyer	VF-16	—	KIA/MIA
LTJG Clyde LeRoy "Tom" Bronn	VT-16	—	
LT George "Brownie" Brown	VT-24	—	KIA/MIA
CDR Paul D. Buie	VF-16 CO	—	
LT[13] Richard S. Bull Jr.	VF-2	—	KIA/MIA
ENS Robert J. Bye	VT-3	—	
CDR Howard H. Caldwell	AG[14]-12 CO	—	
ENS Allie Willis "Willie" Callan Jr.	VF-6	—	
LTJG George F. Carr	VF-15	11.5	KIFAF[15]
NAP Tom F. Cheek	VF-2,6,3	1.0	
LTJG Howard F. Clark	VF-3, 2	0.5	KIA/MIA
LT Cook "Cookie" Cleland	VB-16	—	
CDR Joseph C. "Jumpin' Joe" Clifton	VF-12 CO	—	
LCDR[16] Thaddeus T. Coleman Jr.	VF-6	10.0	
LT Edward G. "Ned" Colgan	VF-10	1.0[17]	
LCDR John A. Collett	VT-10 CO	—	KIA/MIA

---

1. Primary sources for information on pilot squadron affiliations, Japanese aircraft shot down and status (Killed, KIA, MIA, POW) are *Fateful Rendezvous, The First Team, The First Team and the Guadalcanal Campaign,* and *Hellcat.*This listing is limited to the principal Grumman aircraft pilot and air crew personnel mentioned in the book
2. Status while serving in the U.S. Navy
3. Ensign
4. Naval Aviation Pilot
5. None or unable to determine
6. Killed in flight accident during the war
7. Lieutenant (junior grade)
8. Killed in Action or Missing in Action during World War II
9. Aviation Ordnanceman
10. First Class
11. Second Class
12. Commander
13. Lieutenant
14. Air Group
15. Killed in flight accident following World War II
16. Lieutenant Commander

Name	Squadron (s)	Confirmed Kills	Status
ENS Eugene Vincent Conklin	VB-16	—	
LCDR Frank T. Corbin	VF-6	—	
NAP Harry L. Corl	VT-3	—	KIA/MIA
LT Howard W. Crews	VF-5	2.0	
LTJG Richard G. Crommelin	VF-42, 3	3.5	KIFAD
LT Kent Manning Cushman	VT-16	—	
Joe Daniels	VC-18 Crew	—	KIFAD
ENS James G. Daniels III	VF-6	—	
CDR William A. Dean Jr.	VF-2 CO	11.0	
Warren Deitsch	VT-3 Crew	—	
LTJG Robert A.M. "Ram" Dibb	VF-3	7.0	KIFAD
LTJG Robert "Andy" Divine	VT-8	—	
LT Marion W. "Duff" Dufilho	V-3, 2, 5	—	KIA/MIA
ENS Robert W. Duncan	VF-5	7.0	
LT Thomas Earl Dupree	VB-16	—	
ENS Bert Earnest	VT-8	—	
ENS Robert C. Evans	VF-3	—	
LCDR Charles R. Fenton	VF-42 CO	—	
RM[18]3C[19] Harry Ferrier	VT-8 Crew	—	
LT Langdon Fieberling	VT-8	—	KIA/MIA
LCDR James H."Jimmy" Flatley Jr.	VF-2, 42 XO, 10 CO	4.0	
ENS David R. Flynn	VF-6	—	
LTJG Marvin Franger	VF-9	—	
LTJG John R. Franklin	VF-72	—	KIA/MIA
LTJG Victor M. Gadrow	VF-3	—	KIFAD
CDR Richard K. Gaines	AG 10 CO	—	
LTJG Thomas J. Gallagher Jr.	VF-72	—	
ENS George "Tex" Gay	VT-8, 11	—	
LT Noel A.M. Gayler	VF-3, 2	5.0	
ENS O. J. "Ozzie" Gaynier	VT-8	—	KIA/MIA
ARM[20]3C Murray Glasser	VT-10	—	POW[21]
LT James S. Gray Jr.	VF-6 CO	6.0	
LTJG Richard Gray	VF-8	2.0	
ARM2C Selbie Greenhalgh	VT-16 Crew	—	
LTJG Walter A. Haas	VF-42, 3	4.833	
ENS Thomas Addison Hall	VF-6	—	KIFAD
LT Richard E. "Chick" Harmer	VF-5 X0	3.0	
LT Leroy E. "Tex" Harris	VF-10	9.25	
LCDR Harry W. "Stinky" Harrison Jr.	VF-6 CO	—	
ENS Leon W. Haynes	VF-3, 2	1.5	
LTJG Francis Frederick Hebel	VF-6, VC-21	—	
LT Douglas Henderson	VF-3	—	KIA/MIA
ENS Gayle L. Hermann	VF-6	—	
LT Edward W. "Red" Hessel	VF-72	3.333	
George Hicks	VT-8 Crew	—	
ENS George R. Hill	VF-8	—	KIA/MIA

17. Incomplete information
18. Radioman
19. Third Class
20. Aviation Radioman
21. Prisoner of War

Name	Squadron (s)	Confirmed Kills	Status
LT Melvin C. "Boogie" Hoffman	VF-5	3.0[22]	
ENS George A. Hopper Jr.	VF-2, 42, 3	—	KIA/MIA
LCDR Herbert N. Houck	VF-9 CO	—	
AMM[23]2C John Seaman Hutchinson	VT-16 Crew	—	
LTJG Donald A. "Stinky" Innis	VF-5	—	KIFAD
LTJG Minuard F. Jennings	VF-8	—	KIFAF
LT Hayden M. Jensen	VF-5	7.0	
Charles M. Jett	VT-3	—	
LTJG Douglas M. Johnson	VF-6	1.0	
LT William R. "Killer" Kane	VF-10 XO, AG-10 CAG	6.0	KIFAF
LTJG John C. Kelley	VF-6	—	
ENS C. Markland Kelly Jr.	VF-8	—	KIA/MIA
LT Donald Kirkpatrick Jr.	VB-16	—	
ENS John M. Kleinman	VF-5	3.0	KIFAD
LT Henry Marzey Kosciusko	VF-16	—	
ENS Henry T. "Hank" Landry	VF-6	—	
LT Harold "Swede" Larsen	VT-8 CO	—	
LTJG Edward Laster	VT-10	—	
ENS William H. "Hank" Leder	VF-10	2.25	KIFAD
LTJG Rolla S. Lemmon	VF-3	4.5	KIA/MIA
LTJG John A. Leppla	VS-2, VF-10	5.0	KIA/MIA
ENS Victor A. Lewis	VT-8	—	KIA/MIA
LTJG William "Bill" Linn	VT-16	—	
ARM2C Paul Linson	VT-16	—	
ENS Louis Gordon Little Jr.	VF-16	1.0[24]	
Richard L. "Dix" Loesch	VF-6, 5	1.0	
LCDR Donald A. Lovelace	VF-3 XO	0.5	KIFAD
LTJG Brainard T. Macomber	VF-42,3	1.0	
ENS John Magda	VF-8	4.0	
Jay Darrell Manning	VT-8 Crew	—	KIA/MIA
ENS Newton H. Mason	VF-3, 2	—	KIA/MIA
CDR David "Dashing Dave" McCampbell	VF-15, CAG[25]-15	34	
CDR Clarence Wade McClusky	VF-6	—	
LT Vincent F. McCormack	VF-42	1.833	
LTJG E. Scott McCuskey	VF-42,3	13.5	
LTJG John B. "Jughead" McDonald Jr.	VF-5	2.0	
ARM1C William Arthur McElhiney	VB-16	—	
ENS John E. McInerny	VF-8	—	
LTJG Warren Ernest "Mac" McLellan	VT-16	—	
LT Hamilton "One Slug" McWhorter III	VF-9	12	
ENS Albert E. Mead	VF-10	—	POW
LTJG Frederick "Fred" Mears III	VT-8, 3	—	KIFAD
LTJG Sy E. Mendenhall	VF-6	—	

---

18. Radioman
19. Air Group
20. Aviation Radioman
21. Prisoner of War
22. Information from other sources
23. Aviation Machinist Mate
24. Incomplete information
25. Commander Air Group

Name	Squadron (s)	Confirmed Kills	Status
ENS Herbert H. Menges	VF-6	—	
LCDR Samuel G. "Pat" Mitchell	VF-8	—	
LT Bert Dwayne Morris	VF-15	7.0	
LT John N. Myers	VT-3	—	
AM[26]1C Stephen Nadison Jr.	VT-10	—	KIA/MIA
LTJG Zeigel "Ziggy" Neff	VF-16	4.0	
LT Robert S. Nelson	VT-10	—	
ARM3C Thomas C. Nelson Jr.	VT-10	—	
ENS John Ritchie Ogg	VF-6	—	KIA/MIA
LCDR Edward H. "Butch" O'Hare	VF-3,6, CAG-6	7.0	KIA/MIA
ACRM[27] I.H. Olson	VT-3 Crew	—	POW
LTJG Warren R. Omark	VT-24	—	
LCDR Edward M. Owen	VF-5 CO	—	
LCDR Oscar Pederson	VF-42 CO	—	
ENS Dale W. Peterson	VF-3, 2	1.5	
LT Claude R. Phillips	VF-72	2.0	
LCDR John L. Phillips Jr.	VT-6 CO, CAG-6	2.0[28]	KIA/MIA
LT Albert D. Pollock Jr.	VF-10	2.0	KIFAF
ENS Robert L. Price	VF-5	—	KIA/MIA
LCDR James D. Ramage	VB-16 CO	—	
LCDR Paul H. Ramsey	VF-2 CO	3.0	
LTJG Hazen B. Rand	VT-6 Crew	—	
ENS John N. Reed	VT-10	—	KIA/MIA
LTJG Francis R. "Cash" Register	VF-6, 5, 3, VC-21	6.0	KIA/MIA
LTJG Russell L. Reiserer	VT-10	9.25	
LTJG Clark F. Rinehart	VF-2	—	KIA/MIA
ENS Melvin C. Roach	VF-6	—	KIA/MIA
LT Stanley Ruehlow	VF-8	2.0	
LTJG Harold E. Rutherford	VF-6	—	KIFAD
AOM3C John Williams Sample	VB-16 Crew	—	
LCDR Henry G. "Mike" Sanchez	VF-72 CO	—	
ENS Edward "Doc" Sellstrom Jr.	VF-3, 2	4.5	KIFAD
LT James Alvin "Sy" Seybert Jr.	VF-16	1.0	
ENS William John Seyfferle	VF-16	—	KIFAD
ENS Daniel C. Sheedy	VF-3	1.0	
ENS Warren A. "Andy" Skon	VF-2	7.0	
LT James J. "Pug" Southerland II	VF-5	5.0	KIFAF
LTJG Onia B. "Burt" Stanley	VF-3	0.5	
ENS Carlton B. Starkes	VF-5	2.5	
LT Norman Anderson Sterrie	VT-16	—	
LT John Sullivan	VF-9	—	
NAP Howell M. "Muscles" Sumrall	VF-6	1.5	
LTJG Clinton Vance Swanson	VT-16	—	
LT Charles A. "Tabby" Tabberer	VF-5	—	KIA/MIA
ENS Johnny A. Talbot	VF-8	—	
ENS Humphrey L. Tallman	VF-8	—	
LTJG Benjamin Tate	VT-24	—	
CDR Johns S. "Jimmie" Thach	VF-3 CO	6.0	

26. Aviation Machinist
27. Aviation Chief Radioman
28. Incomplete information

Name	Squadron (s)	Confirmed Kills	Status
LTJG Harry Charles "Buzz" Thomas	VT-16	—	
LT MacDonald Thompson	VT-10	—	
CDR Phillip H. Torrey Jr.	AG-9 CO	—	
LT Stanley W. "Swede" Vejtasa	VF-10	8.25	
LT Albert O. "Scoop" Vorse Jr.	VF-6	11.5	
LTJG Alexander "Alex" Vraciu	VF-3,16	19.0	
AMM1C Jack William Webb	VT-16 Crew	—	
ENS Wilbur W. "Spider" Webb	VF-2	6.0	
LTJG D.E. "Weasel" Weissenborn	VT-3	—	
ENS Edward George "Ted" Wendorf	VF-16	—	
LCDR Ralph Weymouth	VS-3,VB-16 CO	—	
LTJG Arthur Payne "Whitey" Whiteway	VF-16	—	
CDR William J. "Gus" Widhelm	VS-8 CO	—	KIFAF
RM3C Delmer D. Wiley	VT-3 Crew	—	
ENS Roland R. Witte	VF-10	3.25	
NAP Darrel D. Woodside	VT-8	—	KIA/MIA
ENS George L. Wrenn	VF-72	5.25	

BIBLIOGRAPHY

Books

Boomhower, Ray E. *Fighter Pilot: The World War II Career of Alex Vraciu*. Indiana Historical Society Press, 2010.

Bryan, J. and Philip Reed, *Mission Beyond Darkness*. New York: Duell, Sloan and Pearce, 1945.

Buell, Thomas B., *Master of Sea Power: A Biography of Fleet Admiral Ernest J. King*. Boston: Little Brown, 1980.

Collins, Jimmy, *Test Pilot*. New York: The Sun Dial Press, 1935.

Ewing, Steve, *Thach Weave: The Life of Jimmie Thach*, Annapolis, MD: Naval Institute Press, 2004.

Ewing, Steve and John B. Lundstrom, *Fateful Rendezvous: The Life of Butch O'Hare*, Annapolis, MD: Naval Institute Press, 2004.

Fuchida, Mitsuo and Masatake Okumiya, *Midway: The Battle That Doomed Japan, The Japanese Navy's Story*, Annapolis, MD: Naval Institute Press, 1992.

Groom, Winston, *1942: The Year That Tried Men's Souls*, New York: Atlantic Monthly Press, 2005.

Halsey, William F. and J. Bryan III, *Admiral Halsey's Story*, New York: McGraw-Hill, 1947.

Hammel, Eric, *Guadalcanal: The Carrier Battles*, New York: Crown, 1987.

Hastings, Max, *Retribution*, New York: Vintage Books, 2009.

Lord, Walter, *Day of Infamy*, New York: Henry Holt and Company, 1957.

_____, *Incredible Victory*, Harper & Row, 1967.

Lundstrom, John B., *The First Team and the Guadalcanal Campaign: Naval Fighter Combat from August to November 1942*, Annapolis, MD: Naval Institute Press, 1994.

_____, *The First Team: Pacific Naval Air Combat from Pearl Harbor to Midway*, Annapolis, MD: Naval Institute Press, 1984.

Mears, Lieutenant Frederick, *Carrier Combat*, Garden City, New York: Doubleday, Doran and Co., Inc., 1944.

Meyers, Agnes E., *Out of these Roots*, Boston: Little Brown and Company, 1953.

Morison, Samuel Eliot, *History of United States Naval Operations in World War II, Volume III, The Rising Sun in the Pacific, 1931- April 1942*, Boston: Little Brown and Company, 1948.

_____, *History of United States Naval Operations in World War II, Volume IV, Coral Sea, Midway and Submarine Actions, May 1942-August 1942*, Chicago: University of Illinois Press, 2001.

_____, *History of United States Naval Operations in World War II, Volume V, The Struggle for Guadalcanal, August 1942 – February 1943*, Boston: Little Brown and Company, 1948.

_____, *History of United States Naval Operations in World War II, Volume VII, Aleutians, Gilberts and Marshalls, June 1942 – April 1944*. Boston: Little Brown and Company, 1948.

_____, *History of United States Naval Operations in World War II, Volume VIII, New Guinea and the Marianas, March 1944-August 1944*. Boston: Little Brown and Company, 1975.

Mrazek, Robert J., *A Dawn Like Thunder: The True Story of Torpedo Squadron Eight*. New York: Back Bay Books, 2009.

Parshall, Jonathan and Anthony Tunnell, *Shattered Sword: The Untold Story of the Battle of Midway*. Dulles, VA: Potomac Books, Inc. 2007.

Prang, Gordon W., Donald M. Goldstein, and Katherine V. Dillon, *At Dawn We Slept: The Untold Story of Pearl Harbor*. New York: Penguin Books, 1982.

Reynolds, Clark G., *The Fast Carriers: The Forging of an Air Navy*. McGraw-Hill, 1968.

Sakai, Saburo with Martin Caidin and Fred Saito, *Samurai!: The Personal Story of Japan's Greatest Living Fighter Pilot*. New York: Ballantine Books, 1957.

Sakaida, Henry, *Winged Samurai*, Mesa, AZ: Champlin Fighter Museum Press, 1985.

Spector, Ronald H., *Eagle Against the Sun: The American War with Japan*. New York: Vintage Books, 1985.

Stafford, Edward P., *The Big E: The Story of the USS* Enterprise. Annapolis, MD: Bluejacket Books, 2002.

Thruelson, Richard, *The Grumman Story*. New York: Praeger Publishers, 1976.

Tillman, Barrett, *Clash of the Carriers: The True Story of the Marianas Turkey Shoot of World War II.* New York: NAL Caliber, 2006.

_____, *Hellcat: The F6F in World War II.* Annapolis, MD: Naval Institute Press, 1979.

Toland, John, *But Not in Shame: The Six Months after Pearl Harbor.* New York: Random House, 1961.

_____, *The Rising Sun: The Decline and Fall of the Japanese Empire, 1936-1945.* New York: The Modern Library, 1987.

Weintraub, Stanley, *Long Day's Journey Into War: December 7, 1941.* New York: Truman Talley Books (Dutton), 1991.

Wooldridge, E.T. (ed.), *Carrier Warfare in the Pacific: An Oral History Collection.* Washington: Smithsonian Institution, 1993.

Magazine and Newspaper Articles

"4-F Hero" by David G. Wittels, *Saturday Evening Post*, April 14, 1945.

"Aided by Perception and Luck" by Norman Friedman, *Naval History*, October 2010.

"Air Group Six," *Aviation News*, October 1949.

"Archer Winsten, 92, Movie Reviewer at The Post, Dies" by Robert McG. Thomas Jr., *New York Times*, February 23, 1997.

"Dagger Thrust at Marcus," *Time*, September 13, 1943.

"Escape Artist," *Time*, January 13, 1947.

"Greatest Sea-Air Battle" by Hanson W. Baldwin, *New York Times Magazine,* April 1950.

"Hellcat 40467" by Richard M. Hill, *AAHS* (American Aero Historians Society) *Journal*, Fall 1972.

"How O'Hare Downed 5 Jap Planes in One Day" by John Field, *Life* (April 13, 1942), 12-18.

"'I wasn't going to be captured'" by Bob Tutt, *Houston Chronicle*, August 6, 1994.

"King's Way," *Time*, June 15, 1942.

"Missouri Endgame" by Alan P. Rems, *Naval History*, August 2010, 32–40.

"Never a Battle Like Midway" by J. Bryan, III, *The Saturday Evening Post,* March 26, 1949, 24-74.

"'Never a Dull Moment' at Midway, Reporter Watching Battle Found" by Foster Hailey, *The New York Times*, June 22, 1942.

"One Year of War," *Time*, December 7, 1942.

"Return to Earth: Diving Ten Thousand Feet Straight Down" by Jim Collins, *The Saturday Evening Post,* February 9, 1935, 8 – 54.

"Ruin in Two Phases," *Time*, July 3, 1944.

"Sailors Aloft" *Time*, June 23, 1941.

"Stormy Man, Stormy Weather," *Time*, June 2, 1941.

"Terminal Velocity Flying Story, March 1935 Chapter 108" by Jay Maeder, *New York Daily News*, June 9, 2000.

"The Admirals," *Time*, December 6, 1943.

"The Embattled Farmers," *Time*, September 11, 1944, 79–88.

"The First Carrier Raids" by Clarke Van Vleet, *The Hook*, Volume 6, Number 4, Winter 1978.

"The Red Rain of Battle: The Story of Fighter Squadron 3" by Lt. Commander John S. Thach, U.S.N., *Collier's,* December 5, December 12, 1942.

"Valor at Midway Casual Kind" by Foster Hailey, *The New York Times*, June 23, 1942.

"Victory at Sea" by David M. Kennedy, *The Atlantic Monthly,* May, 1999.

"We Rode the Covered Wagon" by Jackson R. Tate, RADM USN, *United States Naval Institute Proceedings*, October 1978, 65.

"Wings for the Navy," *Time*, May 18, 1942.

Official Documents

Air Group 16 Action Report Dog Plus Four Day (June 20, 1944).

Commander Carrier Air Group 6 Action Report, 30 November 1943.

FIRST REPORT TO THE SECRETARY OF THE NAVY Covering our Peacetime Navy and our Wartime Navy and including combat operations up to 1 March 1944. ADMIRAL ERNEST J. KING, Commander in

Chief, United States Fleet, and Chief of Naval Operations.

Flight Log Book, Alexander Vraciu (selected pages).

ROSTER OF OFFICERS (NAVPERS 353), UNITED STATES PACIFIC FLEET AIR FORCE, FIGHTING SQUADRON SIX, February 1, 1944.

Oral History

Clanin, Douglas E., Alex Vraciu Oral History Interview, Danville, California, June 14–15, 1990.

Marcello, Ronald E. Oral History Project - Alex Vraciu. University of North Texas, 1994.

Thach, Admiral John S. U.S. Navy (Retired) *Reminiscences of Admiral John S. Thach,* Naval Institute Press, 1977.

Interviews

A series of phone and in-person interviews with Alex Vraciu between April and November 2010.

A series of phone interviews with Warren McLellan in 2007.

A series of phone interviews with Arthur Whiteway in 2007.

Online Articles and Documents

New book salutes EC pilot's high-flying feats, by Bob Kostanczuk, Post Tribune, April 11, 2010 (http://www.post-trib.com/lifestyles/2148175,vvv.article, retrieved April 23, 2010).

Pilots shot down by friendly fire remembered, The Honolulu Advertiser, (http://the.honoluluadvertiser.com/specials/pearlharbor60/chapter2.html, retrieved April 8, 2010).

"Pioneers on the Runway: Raising Grumman." by Drew Fetherston, LI History.com (http://www.grumanpark.org/runway1.htm, retrieved April 8, 2010).

"Valor: Colin Kelly" by John L. Frisbee, airforce-magazine.com (http://www.airforce-magazine.com/MagazineArchive/Pages/1994/June%201994/0694valor.aspx , retrieved July 26, 2010).

ACKNOWLEDGMENTS

My unflagging ambition is to tell compelling human stories against the backdrop of transformative history. I embarked (as before) with the near certainty that many of the people I would have wished to interview would not be accessible—a reality made all the more certain by both the gap in time and by the "occupational attrition" of Navy aviators both in combat and peace.

I was uncommonly fortunate in locating, meeting and talking extensively with Alex Vraciu, a celebrated wartime Pacific War combat ace whose first-person accounts proved indispensible this book. Alex, going strong into his 90s, is an exemplar of the youthful energy, incredible skill and practical patriotism that characterize the dozens of naval aviators depicted in these pages.

I was also most fortunate in having access to six individuals (five author-historians and an aviation curator) whose works, professions and collective knowledge represent standards of excellence for this slice of history. Their willingness to review and critique portions of the manuscript helped bolster my confidence about getting the stories essentially right. (Any residue of error, however, rests with me, not them!)

They are (alphabetically):

Ray Boomhower: Ray's excellent *Fighter Pilot: The World War II Career of Alex Vraciu* was a touch point for my many conversations with Alex. Along the way, Ray gave me the benefit of his own research, including two extensive oral history interviews with Alex. Ray was also most helpful in providing ready access to photographs that might otherwise have been difficult to find.

Eric Boehm is Curator, Aviation and Aircraft Restoration at the New York City-based *Intrepid* Sea, Air, & Space Museum. Among the foundations of Eric's interest in carrier aviation is a father who served during World War II as a turret gunner in a Grumman Avenger.

John B. Lundstrom: John's two "First Team" books about U.S. Naval Aviation and Naval Aviators in the opening rounds of the Pacific War (*The First Team* and *The First Team and the Guadalcanal Campaign*) are as close as any admiring historian can get to the "source code" of that time and place. John's meticulous recounting of the period from the Pacific War's beginning to the conclusion of the Battle for Guadalcanal is indispensible if you hope to get the story straight, in proper sequence and in realistic perspective. His biography of Butch O'Hare (*Fateful Rendezvous*, co-authored with Steve Ewing) is similarly essential to understanding the life of this Pacific War hero.

Bob Mrazek's *A Dawn like Thunder* is a particularly evocative account of the pilots and crews of VT-8 during Midway and Guadalcanal. Bob's account made me aware of *Carrier Combat*—a poignant memoir by VT-8 veteran Fred Mears.

Jonathan Parshall and co-author Anthony Tully's book *Shattered Sword* has brought new perspective and fresh understanding to Japanese strategy and tactics during the decisive Battle of Midway. Their exhaustive research and path-breaking conclusions challenge a number of time-honored assumptions about the "hows" and "whys" of the IJN at Midway. *Shattered Sword* provided an important counterpoint to other traditional, well-worn accounts.

Barrett Tillman (a prolific writer and font of knowledge on U.S. Navy aviators and aircraft) has written *Clash of Carriers*, a fine, fast-paced account of the actions building up to and culminating in the "Marianas Turkey Shoot". His book *Hellcat: The F6F in World War II* is an essential source for F6F back stories and data. Barrett is ever-willing and reliable—as he was with this book—in offering his well-grounded perspective.

If Alex, Ray, Eric, John, Bob, Jon and Barrett represent a "First Team" when it comes to the researching, writing and flight testing of *Pacific Air*, several others offered important help at key junctures. A partial list of these individuals include Butch O'Hare niece Athalia Howell, Jeffrey W. Dale from the office of Jim Collins (the grandson of daredevil pilot Jimmy Collins) and the front desk staff of the National Archives photographic section.

Final appreciation goes to individuals who in different but crucial ways are instrumental in bringing this book to market: My persevering agent Jim McCarthy of Dystel & Goderich; my Da Capo editor Robert Pigeon and his associate Jonathan Crowe (both models of unflagging support and composure); Da Capo Publicity VP Lissa Warren for her sure-handed advocacy on behalf of my books; and my wife Mary whose encouragement and forbearance during these projects makes it all possible.